Psychology Revivals

Developing Narrative Structure

Effective narration, the telling of stories or recounting of personal experiences, is an art requiring skills that appear crucial for children's language development and literacy acquisition. *Developing Narrative Structure*, originally published in 1991, served an important purpose because it pulled together the widely scattered literature in the field, exploring the ways in which oral narrative structure develops in children and how it may be facilitated. It presented new empirical studies of the time, on genres of narrative, the role narrative structure plays in emergent literacy, the relationship between narrative language and autobiographical memory, and ways in which teachers and parents facilitate or hinder children's narrative development. The empirical research presented here draws from diverse groups, including Hispanic, African-American, and Anglo-American children from rural and urban America and Canada. Today it can be read in its historical context.

Developing Narrative Structure

Edited by

Allyssa McCabe and Carole Peterson

Routledge
Taylor & Francis Group
LONDON AND NEW YORK

First published in 1991
by Lawrence Erlbaum Associates, Inc.

This edition first published in 2026 by Routledge
4 Park Square, Milton Park, Abingdon, Oxon, OX14 4RN

and by Routledge
605 Third Avenue, New York, NY 10158

Routledge is an imprint of the Taylor & Francis Group, an informa business

A Library of Congress record exists under ISBN: 9780805804751

ISBN: 978-1-041-37760-3 (hbk)
ISBN: 978-1-042-00968-8 (ebk)
ISBN: 978-1-041-37763-4 (pbk)

Book DOI 10.4324/9781042009688

DEVELOPING NARRATIVE STRUCTURE

Edited by

Allyssa McCabe
Harvard University
and
Tufts University

Carole Peterson
Memorial University,
St. John's, Newfoundland

LEA
LAWRENCE ERLBAUM ASSOCIATES, PUBLISHERS
1991 Hillsdale, New Jersey Hove and London

Lawrence Erlbaum Associates, Inc., Publishers
365 Broadway
Hillsdale, New Jersey 07642

Library of Congress Cataloging in Publication Data

Developing narrative structure / edited by Allyssa McCabe and Carole Peterson
p. cm.
Includes bibliographical references and index.
ISBN 0-8058-0475-7 (case).—ISBN 0-8058-0476-5 (paper)
1. Discourse analysis, Narrative. 2. Children—Language.
I. McCabe, Allyssa. II. Peterson, Carole.
P302.7.D48 1990
401'.41—dc20 90-3677
CIP

Printed in the United States of America
10 9 8 7 6 5 4 3 2 1

Contents

Contributors

Earl Capron
Department of Psychology
Southeastern Louisiana University
Hammond, LA 70402

David K. Dickinson
Department of Education
Clark University
Worcester, MA 01610

James Paul Gee
Department of Linguistics
University of Southern California
Los Angeles, CA 90089

Deborah Hicks
Department of Educational Development
College of Education
University of Delaware
Newark, DE 19716

Judith A. Hudson
Department of Psychology
Rutgers, the State University of New Jersey
Tillett Hall, Kilmer Campus
New Brunswick, NJ 08903

Allyssa McCabe
Harvard Graduate School of Education
Cambridge, MA 02138
and
Eliot-Pearson Department of Child Study
Tufts University
Medford, MA 02155

Sarah Michaels
The Literacies Institute
Education Development Center
55 Chapel Street
Newton, MA 02160

Carole Peterson
Department of Psychology
Memorial University of Newfoundland
St. John's, Newfoundland A1B 3X9

Lauren R. Shapiro
Department of Psychology
Rutgers, the State University of New Jersey
Tillett Hall, Kilmer Campus
New Brunswick, NJ 08903

Elizabeth Sulzby
School of Education
University of Michigan
610 East University
Ann Arbor, MI 48109

Liliano Barro Zecker
School of Education
University of Michigan
610 East University
Ann Arbor, MI 48109

Preface: Structure as a Way of Understanding

Allyssa McCabe
Harvard University and Tufts University

Narrative is a word of ancient origin and recent popularity. It derives from the Latin word, *gnarus,* which means "knowing," a telling history. It now is used to refer to a variety of language games: some with factual, some with fictional reference, some decontextualized activities, some that occur in the context of playing with toys. Most are oral exchanges but some are written performances. In fact, some chapters in this volume are directed to sorting out and systematically relating these many genres of narratives.

Narrative may be defined narrowly despite these genre differences; Labov (1972) defined a minimal narrative as two temporally ordered clauses in the past tense, and narrative in general as "one method of recapitulating past experience by matching a verbal sequence of clauses to the sequence of events which (it is inferred) actually occurred" (pp. 359–360). The working definition of narrative circulated among the authors in the present volume was less strict: the oral sequencing of temporally successive events, real or imaginary. As a result of the research reported in this volume, even this may be too restrictive a definition (see Gee, this volume).

Narratives are typically given in the past tense. Some, however, are delivered in the present tense or even potentially in the future tense. These latter forms might best be thought of as marked cases of narrative, relatively unusual, providing comment on what is narrated by virtue of departing from our expectations otherwise. As Ursula Le-Guin (1989) pointed out: "Narrative does not normally use the present tense except for special effect or out of affectation. It locates itself in the past (whether the real or an imagined, fictional past) in order to allow itself forward movement. . . . The present tense, which some writers of narrative fiction currently employ because it is supposed to make the telling 'more actual,' actually distances the story. . . . The present tense takes the story out of time" (p. 38).

Narrative is a vital human activity. Through narrative we present ourselves as heros, victims, wise guys, nice guys. Through narrative we find ourselves in the process of presenting ourselves and our experiences. "We are the stories we tell" (Martin, January 8, 1989).

Through narrative we bridge separations from loved ones, filling them in on experiences we have had in their absence. Might not our knowledge of the personal narratives of someone we know be a measure of our intimacy with that person?

Through narrative we warn others of lessons we have learned from our own experience or the experience of others. There are morals to some personal narratives of ordinary people as well as to well-established cultural myths. Perhaps it is not too farfetched to say that gossip can save lives as well ruin them.

Through narrative we remember personal experiences, we translate knowing into telling (see Hudson & Shapiro, chap. 3 in this volume). A chapter in the present volume is devoted to assessing how young adults' memories of early childhood experiences fare assessed as narratives. What exactly is the relationship between narrative language and memory encoded in that language?

If there are no narratives of an experience, it might be said not to have really existed in some sense. LeGuin (1989) brought to our attention Des Pres's series of quotes from survivors of the Nazi death camps, quotes that collectively emphasize this point: "[In Treblinka] the dead were being unearthed and burned [by work squads], and soon the work squads too would go up in smoke. If that had come to pass, Treblinka would never have existed. The aim of the revolt was to ensure the memory of that place, and we know the story of Treblinka because forty survived" (Des Pres, cited in LeGuin, 1989, p. 27).

"I found it most difficult to stay alive, but I had to live, to give the world the story" (Glastein, from Treblinka).

Of the vital importance of narratives, Dell Hymes (1982) wrote:

> In the serious and scheduled occasions when [American Indian] children were the specific audience for the telling of myths or when children were simply present when myths or other narratives were being told, not only were samples of language being presented, but over and over again, at every level, an *implicit organization of experience into set, satisfying*

> *patterns* [emphasis mine] was being conveyed and internalized. . . . Again and again, instead of a chaos of events, experience was organized into sometimes subtle patterns. . . . [A particular story] takes only a few minutes to tell or read, but its apparent bareness, if skimmed as prose, belies an underlying process of arousal and satisfying of formal expectations of some complexity. (pp. 121–122)

Again, LeGuin (1989) collected a nice quote relevant to this point from Liam Hudson: "The thinking we do without thinking about it [i.e., during sleep] consists in the translation of our experience to narrative, irrespective of whether our experience fits the narrative form or not . . . Asleep and awake it is just the same: we are telling ourselves stories all the time . . . *tidier stories than the evidence warrants*" (emphasis mine, p. 40).

The cohesiveness of narratives, the way in which clauses within narratives are explicitly connected to each other, reflects the way in which the narrator connects the events being narrated and is a well-documented phenomenon. Chapter 1 in this volume reviews that documentation of the connections of experience.

Because of their human importance, narratives have been of interest to scholars almost from the beginning of scholarship. We even have the traditional quote from Aristotle on this point, a quote that marks the beginning of the articulation of narrative structure. According to Aristotle (1920), a narrative consists of the following: "A beginning [of a narrative] is that which is not itself necessarily after anything else, and which has naturally something else after it; an end, that which is naturally after something else, either as its necessary or usual consequent, and with nothing else after it; and a middle, that which is by nature after one thing and has also another after it" (p. 40).

Ever since Aristotle, narrative has been the subject of scrutiny by scholars of English, French—the literature of many languages—as well as scholars of religion, history, anthropology, sociology, psychoanalysis, and, relatively recently, psychology and education. Research on narrative is scattered through hundreds of books and journals in all these disciplines. It seems advisable for all disciplines to at least be superficially familiar with work on narrative by the other disciplines, although it is a daunting prospect even to attempt a survey of the major work on narrative in the social sciences alone. It was a major goal of the present volume to review such extensive past research, consequently the introductions to many chapters are longer than is typical.

The extent of work on narrative necessitates collaboration, and such was an impetus for such an edited volume. In inviting people to contribute to this volume, we were very much aware of what we saw as a need for the collaboration of statistical treatments of a number of subjects along with the detailed ethnographic analysis of relatively few subjects in a mutual attempt to satisfyingly understand a phenomenon as complex as developing narrative structure. Nonetheless, it is important to recognize that unfortunately these two methods are sometimes seen as antagonistic.

In a similar way, with research on language development in general, structural, linguistic analysis has often been seen as anathema to any sort of functional, empirical analysis (Bohannon & Warren-Leubecker, 1989). Thus it may seem strange to see chapters devoted to further articulating the structure of children's narratives alongside others devoted to studying the way in which adults enhance the development of children's narratives. This is not a case of lions accidently being allowed to lie down with lambs (I do not wish to name the fictive lions here). Rather, reconciliation of structural and empirical analyses of developing narratives was a deliberate goal of this volume and the reason for its title, which is a pun. Narratives develop in certain ways; narratives are developed in certain ways.

There are scholars who articulate a structure of narrative that they believe to be universal. Levi-Strauss was one (see Leach, 1970); he believed, roughly, that all narratives from all cultures could be characterized in terms of the structural opposition of nature and culture. Similarly, some individuals (e.g., Mandler, Scribner, Cole, & DeForest, 1980) argue that all good stories articulate a protagonist's goals, their formation, the protagonist's efforts to achieve them, and the outcomes of such efforts.

Other scholars (e.g., Cazden, Michaels, & Tabors, 1985; Chafe, 1980; Gee, 1985, 1986; Heath, 1982, 1986; Hinds, 1984; Hymes, 1980, 1982; Kintsch & Green, 1978; Michaels, chap. 8 in this volume; Schieffelin & Eisenberg, 1984; Scollon & Scollon, 1981; Tannen, 1984; Tedlock, 1978; Watson, 1975; Watson-Gegeo & Boggs, 1977) have documented ways in which native Americans, African-Americans, Africans, Hawaiians, and other groups, tell narratives with structures rather different from those of our white middle-class American culture.

All this concern for cultural convergence or divergence in narrative structures has sometimes seemed pertinent to the question of just what those structures are. However, many scholars in both camps feel that narrative structures are structures of mind or memory, whether inherited or encultured. Structures recapitulate stories, which recapitulate events. Peterson and McCabe (1983, pp. 9–13) took issue with this interpretation, arguing that structures are linguistic representations rather than structures of memory. I believe we can go further than that.

Just as narratives may be considered as a primary means by which humans make sense of their experience (Gee, 1985; Hymes, 1982), the articulation of narrative structure is a primary means of making sense of narratives. In other words, a narrative structure represents our understanding of a narrative.

To reify narrative structures as memories or as something in the narratives themselves is tempting, but it is also, I believe, to deny the efforts of the structurers, which are sometimes quite marvelous. To articulate some aspect of the structure of a narrative is sometimes to make explicit what ordinary listeners do when they nod knowingly or say something like, "I get your point." Such articulation has proven very useful. But some structurers have done even more. They have made sense of narratives that strike most listeners of their culture as baffling, odd, unintelligible. These structurers might be said to have cast off the deafening earphones of their culture to hear and understand the radically different ways other cultures make sense of experience (e.g., Gee, 1985; Hymes, 1982; Michaels, 1981; Watson-Gegeo & Boggs, 1977). They have represented such understanding by means of structural analyses.

To acknowledge that structural description is invented is not to say that it is not true, in some sense of that complicated word. That is, the more widely used a method for analyzing narrative structure, the more that structure presumably reflects an element of many narratives that strikes many listeners or readers. Nonetheless, Peterson and McCabe (1983) pointed out that there were many ways of analyzing narratives; as this volume reflects, there are now even more ways available. Some ways of analyzing narrative structure are widely known, yet there are very good ways of analyzing narrative structure that are virtually unknown within, let alone outside, the discipline of their authors. In other words, our picture of narrative structure is continually being trued up by new types of analyses as well as extensions of older analyses to populations of different ages or cultures.

In view of what is known about the cultural diversity of narrative structure, it is perhaps not surprising that there is individual diversity in narrative structure. Among modern creative writers, the ability to invent novel narrative structures is recognized, valued, even demanded of writers hoping to achieve such status as Gertrude Stein, William Faulkner, James Joyce, and Donald Barthelme. Ordinary readers sometimes have been left behind, many preferring fiction (such as detective novels) that conforms to familiar structures. In other words, our familiar personal ways of understanding occasionally founder when confronted with truly novel narrative structure. It becomes the task of literary critics and teachers to articulate the structure of such novel fiction so that it makes sense to many. Added to such deliberate individual diversity of the authors of published narratives is the less deliberate individual diversity of children, a topic of concern to a number of contributors to this volume. It would be surprising, indeed, if all this diversity could be handled by a few structural analyses.

It is likely, then, that our picture of narrative structure is in need of further trueing up; that is, I am certain there are many aspects of narrative structure we have yet to appreciate. In this respect, McCabe and Peterson (1984) found that when ordinary white adults (not scholars of narrative) judged the quality of white children's narratives, their judgments of these narratives were not explained by the structural sophistication of those narratives according to story grammar, Labov's (1972) analysis, or Deese's dependency analysis (see Peterson & McCabe, 1983, chap. 8, pp. 109–142 for description of latter). Rather, the narratives judged best by naive listeners were those that were deemed good by at least two of the three systems for analyzing narrative structure to which they were submitted for analysis. Existing ways of understanding narratives may founder when confronted by truly novel narratives; our goal should always be the understanding of narrative rather than the glorification of a particular way of understanding narrative—a particular type of analysis—if the latter is at the expense of the former.

The fact that readers have continually rejected published narratives with a structure radically different from those they are used to and the fact that teachers have been known to reject the narratives of children from cultures other than their own (Michaels, 1981) has led some researchers (e.g., Gee, 1985) to conclude that we should not judge some people to be better storytellers than others. I sympathesize with the need to ask people to suspend judgments, especially of narratives from different cultures. People should be encouraged to engage in a little more understanding, a little more structural analysis, before coming to a conclusion about the quality of some narratives. But, as Labov (1972) pointed out, evaluation of events is a key component of narratives. Similarly, evaluation of narratives is something that members of every culture engage in, so far as I know. There are always individuals who are singled out as exceptional storytellers. To ask us to suspend such aesthetic judgment is to paralyze the process of understanding narratives. You cannot truly judge a narrative you do not understand, nor truly understand a narrative you do not judge. Understanding often amounts to appreciation.

In view of the importance of narrative, my next comment may come as a surprise: Narrative is a word in danger of being overused these days. It has been used to denote problem-solving conversation of any sort, including negotiations at the dinner table involving the promise of dessert if a child will eat her peas (Ochs, Smith, & Taylor, 1988). Bus and van IJzendoorn (1988, p. 1264) defined narration as "all maternal explanations, questions, and comments about the meaning of objects, stories, and illustrations; narration also included interpretations of content through other means, such as naming and *pointing out*" (emphasis mine). Informal conversations reveal that some use narrative interchangeably with discourse. We need to question whether such usage advances our understanding of narrative; of course there are fuzzy boundaries to the definition of narrative, as well as to the definition of anything else.

Perhaps it might be easier to say what narrative is not rather than what it is. It is not exposition, reports, science. As LeGuin (1989) so nicely put it,

> Even of an entity relatively so immense and biologically so complex as a gene, the little packet of instructions that tells us what to be, there is no story to be told; because the gene, barring accident, is immortal. All you can say of it is that it is, and it is, and it is. No beginning, no end. All middle. . . . [In contrast to science,] narrative is a stratagem of mortality. (p. 39)

In sum, narration is fundamentally a collaborative activity. So should be the study of narrative. Parents and teachers do or should collaborate with children in extending their ability to make verbal sense of their experience, as several chapters suggest. Structuralists and functionalists should recognize the sense in which their activities are complementary, as should statistical researchers and ethnomethodologists. Such are the points we hope to make with this volume.

ACKNOWLEDGMENTS

Helpful comments on various chapters in the present volume were received from the following individuals: Elliot Mishler, Cathy Riessman, Jane Attanucci, Catherine Snow, Michael Bamberg, Irma Rosenfield, Ellen Rintell, Susan Bell, Paul Abraham, Diane Beals, Jeanne DeTemple, Kimberley Elkins, Christine Herot, Julie Hirschler, Diane Lund, Masahiko Minami, Joy Moreton, Sara Schley, Kathleen Steubing. We very much appreciate your thoughtful contributions.

REFERENCES

Aristotle. (1920). *On the art of poetry* (I. Bywater, trans.). Oxford: Oxford University Press, 1920.

Bohannon, J. N., & Warren-Leubecker, A. (1989). Theoretical approaches to language acquisition. In J. Berko Gleason (Ed.), *The development of language* (2nd ed.). Columbus, OH: Merrill.

Bus, A. G., & van IJzendoorn, M. H. (1988). Mother-child interactions, attachment, and emergent literacy: A cross-sectional study. *Child Development, 59,* 1262–1272.

Cazden, C. B., Michaels, S., & Tabors, P. (1985). Spontaneous repairs in sharing time narratives: The intersection of metalinguistic awareness, speech event, and narrative style. In S. W. Freedman (Ed.), *The acquisition of written language.* Norwood, NJ: Ablex.

Chafe, W. C. (Ed.). (1980). *The pear stories: Cognitive, cultural, and linguistic aspects of narrative production.* Norwood, NJ: Ablex.

Gee, J. P. (1985). The narrativization of experience in the oral style. *Journal of Education, 167,* 9–35.

Gee, J. P. (1986). Units in the production of narrative discourse. *Discourse Processes, 9,* 391–422.

Heath, S. B. (1982). What no bedtime story means: Narrative skills at home and at school. *Language in Society, 11,* 49–76.

Heath, S. B. (1986). Taking a cross-cultural look at narratives. *Topics in Language Disorders, 7,* 84–94.

Hinds, J. (1984). Topic maintenance in Japanese narratives and Japanese conversational interaction. *Discourse Processes, 7,* 465–482.

Hymes, D. (1982). Narrative form as a "grammar" of experience: Native Americans and a glimpse of English. *Journal of Education, 2,* 121–142.

Hymes, D. (1980). Partical, pause, and pattern in American Indian narrative verse. *American Indian Culture and Research Journal, 4,* 7–51.

Kintsch, W., & Greene, E. (1978). The role of culture-specific schemata in the comprehension and recall of stories. *Discourse Processes, 1,* 1–13.

Labov, W. (1972). *Language in the inner city.* Philadelphia, PA: University of Pennsylvania Press.

Leach, E. (1970). *Claude Levi-Strauss.* New York: Penguin.

LeGuin, U. K. (1989). *Dancing at the edge of the world.* New York: Grove Press.

Mandler, J., Scribner, S., Cole, M., & DeForest, M. (1980). Cross-cultural invariance in story recall. *Child Development, 51,* 19–26.

Martin, W. (1989, January 8). We are the stories we tell. *New York Times Book Review.*

McCabe, A., & Peterson, C. (1984). What makes a good story? *Journal of Psycholinguistic Research, 13,* 457–480.

Michaels, S. (1981). "Sharing time": Children's narrative styles and differential access to literacy. *Language in Society, 10,* 423–442.

Ochs, E., Smith, R., & Taylor, C. (1988, October). *Putting problems on the table: Dinner and literacy.* Paper presented at the annual Boston University Conference on Language Development.

Peterson, C., & McCabe, A. (1983). *Developmental psycholinguistics: Three ways of looking at a child's narrative.* New York: Plenum.

Schieffelin, B. B., & Eisenberg, A. R. (1984). Cultural variation in children's conversations. In R. L. Schiefelbusch & J. Pickar (Eds.), *The acquisition of communicative competence* (pp. 378–420). Baltimore, MD: University Park Press.

Scollon, R., & Scollon, S.B.K. (1981). *Narrative, literacy, and face in interethnic communication.* Norwood, NJ: Ablex.

Tannen, D. (Ed.). (1984). *Coherence in spoken and written discourse.* Norwood, NJ: Ablex.

Tedlock, D. (1978). *Finding the center: Narrative poetry of the Zuni Indian.* Lincoln: University of Nebraska Press.

Watson, K. A. (1975). Transferable communicative routines: Strategies and group identity in two speech events. *Language in Society, 4,* 53–72.

Watson-Gegeo, K. A., & Boggs, S. T. (1977). From verbal play to talk story: The role of routines in speech events among Hawaiian children. In S. Ervin-Tripp & C. Mitchell-Kernan (Eds.), *Child discourse* (pp. 67–90). New York: Academic Press.

Memory and Myth: A Perspective on Narrative

James Paul Gee
Department of Linguistics
University of Southern California

The chapters in this volume represent a state of the art overview of narrative development. As such they take a variety of perspectives, ranging from psycholinguistics to sociolinguistics and several places in between. What I intend to do in this chapter is to offer a single perspective on the nature of narrative. Whereas the chapters in this volume by no means all accept this perspective in full, they all speak to it in important ways.

The way I proceed is, I believe, typical of a linguist. Linguists seek to characterize the fundamental nature of human language, what differentiates it from other sign systems. Here I ask about the fundamental nature of narrative: What are the *unmarked* (normative, typical, basic) features of narrative? I believe that an answer to this question has important implications for how we evaluate the study of narrative in the past, especially in psychology, and how we propose to study narrative in the future. It also has important social and political implications in regard to the view of narrative that mainstream institutions (like schools and the discipline of psychology) have tended to take as normal.

One way to understand the fundamental nature of narrative is to first consider the nature of human memory. Unfortunately, like much else, our understanding of human memory has been privatized by contemporary cognitive psychology. Memory is treated like a picture hidden away in the closet of the mind. Like pictures, our memories can fade, and even disappear altogether, but they cannot radically change. Memory is a personal affair, an image fixed by the camera of the mind, with little or nothing to do with the people with whom we associate or the institutions to which we belong. I believe this asocial view of memory must be questioned if we are to fully appreciate the development, structure, and function of narrative.

To begin to develop an alternative view, consider a matter that at first sight seems quite unconnected to our present concern: the Moslem view of the Crusades, a set of events that "happened" between the end of the 11th and the end of the 13th centuries.[1] Medieval Moslem historians did not use the words *Crusade* and *Crusader*. As far as they were concerned there was no such event as the Crusades taking place. Unlike medieval European Christians, they did not have the sense of witnessing an epic struggle between Islam and Christendom for the control of the Holy Land. Rather, Moslem historians spoke of the Crusaders either as the Infidels or as the Franks, and viewed the attacks launched by them in Syria, Egypt, and Mesopotamia as being in no way fundamentally different from the former wars waged between Islam and the Infidels: in Syria itself, in the course of the 10th century and before, in Andalus throughout the Spanish Reconquista, and in Sicily against the Normans.

However, in the period since 1945, Arabic writing on the Crusades has changed considerably. Contemporary Moslem historians have come to see a parallelism between the period of the Crusades and the last 100 years. In both cases the Islamic Middle East was attacked by European forces that managed to impose their control on a large part of the region. The Crusades have come to be seen as the primary phase of European colonization, the beginnings of a long-term movement—including the Bonaparte expedition, the British conquest of Egypt, and the Mandate system in the Levant—and culminating in the foundation of the state of Israel. The Crusaders, who established an independent state in Palestine, are seen, then, as proto-Zionists.

So here we see that the "actual events" that constituted the Crusades are placed in two quite different narrative contexts in Moslem historiography, and within these different narrative frameworks, the actual events are remembered quite differently. We see too how future events radically change the perspective taken on past events. I see no way in which either account can be said to be privileged or more authentic.

Did the Crusades happen? There is no such event apart from a narrative about it, and that narrative can change radically depending on the wider set of narratives within which we choose to embed it. For

---

[1]My main source for this example is Connerton (1989, pp. 15–16). Connerton's work has significantly informed the view I take of personal and social memory in this chapter.

Moslem historians the Crusades only come to exist when future events suggest a narrative in which Crusaders are the historical ancestors of characters who come later in the story (Napoleon, the British, Zionists, etc). Thus, any event is contingent on a narrative, and any single narrative is contingent on a wider set of narratives (a narrative context within which it is embedded). And where does this wider narrative context come from? It can only come from one's history, traditions, socialization, and the narratives groups of people share with and repeat to one another. To look at an event outside of a narrative, or a narrative outside of a wider narrative context, or a narrative context outside the social traditions, history, and practices of a group of people is both misleading and pointless.

I argue that personal memory works in just the same way. Personal memories that are *unrehearsed* disappear, but to rehearse them means to retell them in a narrative fashion. This retold narrative will, like historical ones, be shaped by the larger narrative context of the person's everchanging past, present, and future (see McCabe, Capron, & Peterson, chap. 4 in this vol.). It will also be shaped by the narratives others tell in the social groups to which the person belongs. And these too are everchanging (and here the distinction between historical and personal narratives becomes blurred). Moslems' historical memory of the Crusades is not fixed; nor is my personal memory of episodes in my life. Both exist and have meaning, but only in relation to a changing historical and social context.

Histography is a form of social memory. Modern psychology would have us believe that there is a great divide between personal memory on the one hand (stored in our heads) and social memory on the other (stored in histography, myths, public ceremonies, and the habitual routines in which members of a society engage). Social memory is held to be largely irrelevant to personal memory, and thus, rarely mentioned in cognitive psychology. I would argue, however, that we leave social memory out at the peril of losing the whole enterprise of understanding the mind.

We can see the social nature of memory and narrative particularly clearly in the case of so-called premodern societies, with their rich traditions of ritual-traditional language and myth. In the case of these societies, we are much less tempted to try to understand the personal apart from the social. The question is, should we be tempted to do so in the case of modern societies, and why are we so tempted?

In premodern societies mythic stories constituted a socially shared "reservoir of meanings and structures of thought" (Connerton, 1989, pp. 56–57), from which people could draw to create new meanings that resembled, echoed, cohered with older ones. The symbolic content of myth is not exhausted in any single formal arrangement, but rather offers many potential arrangements, each of which count as solutions in the system.

To see this, consider the following two stories from the Old Testament.[2] The first is the famous Abraham and Isaac story, the other is a somewhat less well known variant of the Abraham and Isaac story, the story of Jephthah and his daughter:

Abraham and Isaac. Genesis 22.1–19

1. After these things God tested Abraham, and said to him, "Abraham!" And he said, "Here am I."
2. He said, "Take your son, your only son Isaac, whom you love, and go to the land of Mori'ah, and offer him there as a burnt offering upon one of the mountains of which I shall tell you."
3. So Abraham rose early in the morning, saddled his ass, and took two of his young men with him, and his son Isaac; and he cut the wood for the burnt offering, and arose and went to the place of which God had told him.
4. On the third day Abraham lifted up his eyes and saw the place afar off.
5. Then Abraham said to his young men, "Stay here with the ass; I and the lad will go yonder and worship, and come again to you."
6. And Abraham took the wood of the burnt offering, and laid it on Isaac his son; and he took in his hand the fire and the knife. So they went both of them together.
7. And Isaac said to his father Abraham, "My father!" And he said, "Here am I, my son." He said, "Behold, the fire and the wood, but where is the lamb for burnt offering?"
8. Abraham said, "God will provide himself the lamb for a burnt offering, my son." So they went both of them together.
9. When they came to the place of which God had told him, Abraham built an altar there, and laid the wood in order, and bound Isaac his son, and laid him on the altar, upon the wood.
10. Then Abraham put forth his hand, and took the knife to slay his son.
11. But the angel of the Lord called to him from heaven, and said, "Abraham, Abraham!" And he said, "Here I am."
12. He said, "Do not lay your hand on the lad or do anything to him; for now I know that you fear God, seeing you have not withheld your son, your only son from me."
13. And Abraham lifted up his eyes and looked, and behold, behind

[2]The following translations are from *The New Oxford Annotated Bible* (Oxford, England: Oxford University Press, 1973).

him was a ram, caught in a thicket by his horns; and Abraham went and took the ram, and offered it up as a burnt offering instead of his son.

14. So Abraham called the name of that place the Lord will provide; as it is said to this day, "On the mount of the Lord it shall be provided."
15. And the angel of the Lord called to Abraham a second time from heaven,
16. and said, "By myself I have sworn, says the Lord, because you have done this, and have not withheld your son, your only son.
17. I will indeed bless you, and I will multiply your descendants as the stars of heaven and as the sand which is on the seashore. And your descendants shall possess the gate of their enemies,
18. and by your descendants shall all the nations of the earth bless themselves, because you have obeyed my voice."
19. So Abraham returned to his young men, and they arose and went together to Beersheba; and Abraham dwelt at Beersheba.

Jephthah and his daughter. Judges 12.29–40

29. Then the Spirit of the Lord came upon Jephthah, and he passed through Gilead and Manas'seh, and passed on to Mizpah of Gilead, and from Mizpah of Gilead he passed on the Ammonites.
30. And Jephthah made a vow to the Lord, and said, "If thou wilt give the Ammonites into my hand,
31. then whoever comes forth from the doors of my house to meet me, when I return victorious from the Ammonites, shall be the Lord's, and I will offer him up for a burnt offering."
32. So Jephthah crossed over to the Ammonites to fight against them; and the Lord gave them into his hand.
33. And he smote them from Aro'er to the neighborhood of Minnith, twenty cities, and as far as Abel-keramim, with a very great slaughter. So the Ammonites were subdued before the people of Israel.
34. The Jephthah came to his home at Mizpah; and behold, his daughter came out to meet him with timbrels and with dances; she was his only child; beside her he had neither son nor daughter.
35. And when he saw her, he rent his clothes, and said, "Alas, my daughter! you have brought me very low, and you have become the cause of great trouble for me; for I have opened my mouth to the Lord, and I cannot take back my vow."
36. And she said to him, "My father, if you have opened your mouth to the Lord, do to me according to what has gone forth from your mouth, now that the Lord has avenged you on your enemies, on the Ammonites."
37. And she said to her father, "Let this thing be done for me; let me alone two months, that I may go and wander on the mountains, and bewail my virginity, I and my companions."

38. And he said, "Go." And he sent her away for two months: and she departed, she and her companions, and bewailed her virginity upon the mountains.
39. And at the end of two months, she returned to her father, who did with her according to his vow which he had made. She had never known a man. And it became a custom in Israel
40. that the daughters of Israel went year by year to lament the daughter of Jephthah the Gileadite four days in the year.

The Jephthah story is a mirror-image reversal of the Abraham story, a different arrangement of the same materials.[3] I have diagrammed the two stories in such a way as to bring out their mirror-image qualities. This essentially involves reading the Jephthah story forward and the Abraham story backward (that is, the last event in the Abraham story corresponds to the first of the Jephthah story, the second-to-last in the Abraham story to the second of the Jephthah story, and so on).

Jephthah (read forward)	Abraham (read backward)
1.	
Man gives his word to God (vows)	God gives his word to Man (promises)
that God will have a dead sacrifice (sacrifice turns out = his daughter)	that Man will have many live descendants
if (in future) God gives Man	because (in past) Man gave God
a gift (= God allowed killing of foreigners)	a gift (= Man is willing to kill kin/son)
but only daughter replaces animal	but animal replaces only son
thus Man loses only child by actually killing foreigners	thus Man gains many relatives by potentially killing only child
2.	
Jephthah does slay foreigners	Abraham starts to slay son
3.	
A child "happens" to come out; Jephthah's only child replaces an animal	A ram "happens" to be there; the animal replaces Abraham's only child

[3]The approach I take to biblical texts is best exemplified in the work of Edmund Leach (1969, 1976) and Leach and Aycock (1983). I believe it was a paper by Leach that years ago called my attention to these texts, but I can no longer recover the source.

4.	
Father tells child that she is the offering	Child asks father where the offering is
Child tells father to provide the offering he has promised	Father assures child that God will provide the offering He wishes
5.	
Daughter goes up the mountain with companions, apart from father	Father and son go up the mountain together, leave companions behind
6.	
Father honors vow (of the past) to kill only child (daughter)	God commands (future) father to kill only child (son)

Although I cannot give a detailed analysis of these two stories here, it is clear that there are a central set of problems behind both. One of these is surely the nature of one's duties and responsibilities to kin, to fellow humans who are not kin, and to God, and how these are to be balanced. In addition, there is the problem of how one adjudicates two conflicting moral imperatives. The Israelites faced conflict between their taboo against killing others and their moral need to keep their social identity, through not integrating with other groups and through warfare to establish their society within the framework of its historical narratives. In this regard it is interesting that Jephthah, who is only half Jewish, kills foreigners, thus valuing kin (his fellow Israelites) above nonkin and establishing Israel, but having his own line die out (presumably because he killed human beings). Abraham by not valuing even kin above God has many descendants.

There is much more that could be said about these stories. But it is clear that, whereas they are narratives, the actual temporal and causal ordering of events is much less important to them than the way in which certain elements (themes), like God, Man, kin, nonkin, giving of words, sacrifice, and so forth, are related to and fall into a satisfying pattern vis-à-vis each other. We can think of them as puzzles in which the same pieces are fit together in different ways, but in both cases give a coherent picture (Levi-Strauss, 1963, 1964–1971, 1966, 1979). There are other possible arrangements. The meaning of each story resides not just in that story alone, but in the other actual and possible arrangements. The problems that these two stories deal with are addressed, not by each story as a single, isolated entity, but rather by combining and juxtaposing the two stories and other variants (of course, the New Testament story of Christ's death and resurrection is a variant of the same story). The set of variants are never closed, thus the meaning of any story, like the previous historical narratives, is saturated with the present and awaits the future as well. Thus, the meaning of the story is rooted in history and the social group, not just in the personal mind.

Mythic stories like those previously mentioned do not sit well with our current sense of narrative. They use temporal and causal order to embed themes and events whose juxtaposition and relationships in an imaginary space is much more important than that order itself. They always take on their meaning in relationship to other stories, some of which are in a tradition rooted in history, and some of which are merely potential, rooted in the present exigencies and alternative futures of specific social groups. Meaning seeps, so to speak, out of the head and into history and society. And they are prototypical in the sense that the society sees them as events and ways of being that can and ought to be reenacted in the present.

Of course, at this point, one could simply deny the relevance of premodern societies and myth to our understanding of the modern human mind and narrativizing. This issue, in fact, brings us square up against a paradox. When we look at modern society, only some people look modern. A number of investigators have pointed out that many non-mainstream people in our modern society tell narratives that, in many respects, still deeply resemble the premodern practices already discussed (Abrahams, 1964; Finnegan, 1988; Gee, 1985; Heath, 1983; Hymes, 1981; Jackson, 1974; Labov, 1972a; Nichols, 1989; Rosenberg, 1970; Scollon & Scollon, 1981; Smitherman, 1977; Stahl, 1989; Taussig, 1987). We usually assume this is because these people are less influenced by the institutions of modernity (like the school) and, thus, that their behavior is untypical, in linguists' terms, *marked,* as against the typical, unmarked narrative practices of more school-focused, mainstream people. I want to suggest that the situation is, in fact, just the reverse: The practices of these nonmainstream people reflect the fundamental, normal, unmarked nature of human narrative, and it is the practices of the mainstream group that need to be explained, in the sense that they deviate from what we would expect.

Consider briefly a story (which I name "Cakes") told by a 7-year-old Black child (whom I call "Leona").[4] I reprint the story in terms of its *lines and stanzas.* In other work (Gee, 1985, 1986, 1989a, 1989b; see

[4]This story was collected as part of research project at Harvard Graduate School of Education directed by Courtney Cazden and Sarah Michaels. I am indebted to Sarah Michaels for calling my attention to the story.

also Chafe, 1980; Hymes, 1981; Scollon & Scollon, 1981; Tedlock, 1977), I argue that all speech is produced in terms of *lines* (often a clause long) and *stanzas* (a small group of lines with one perspective and a narrow topic). Here I do not detail how, psycholinguistically, lines and stanzas are found in a text (but see Gee, 1986). Although all speech is produced in lines and stanzas, different cultures and social groups organize language within stanzas in different and culturally distinctive ways.

CAKES

Frame
Stanza
1. Today
2. it's Friday the 13th
3. an' it's bad luck day
4. an' my grandmother's birthday is on bad luck day

Part 1: Making cakes
Stanza 2
5. an' my mother's bakin a cake
6. an' I went up my grandmother's house while my mother's bakin' a cake
7. an' my mother was bakin' a cheese cake
8. my grandmother was bakin a whipped cream cup cakes

Stanza 3
9. an' we bof went over my mother's house
10. an' then my grandmother had made a chocolate cake
11. an' then we went over my aunt's house
12. an' she had make a cake

Stanza 4
13. an' everybody had made a cake for nana
14. so we came out with six cakes

Part 2: Grandmother eats cakes
Stanza 5
15. last night
16. my grandmother snuck out
17. an' she ate all the cake
18. an' we hadda make more

Stanza 6
(she knew we was makin' cakes)
19. an' we was sleepin'
20. an' she went in the room
21. an' gobbled em up
22. an' we hadda bake a whole bunch more

Stanza 7
23. she said mmmm
24. she had all chocolate on her face, cream, strawberries
25. she said mmmm
26. that was good

Stanza 8
27. an' then an' then all came out
28. an' my grandmother had ate all of it
29. she said "what's this cheese cake doin' here"—she didn't like cheese cakes
30. an' she told everybody that she didn't like cheese cakes

Stanza 9
31. an' we kept makin' cakes
32. an' she kept eatin' 'em
33. an' we finally got tired of makin' cakes
34. an' so we all ate 'em

Part 3: Grandmother goes outside the home
Non-narrative section (35–41)

Stanza 10
35. an' now
36. today's my grandmother's birthday
37. an' a lot o'people's makin' a cake again
38. but my grandmother is goin t'get her own cake at her bakery
39. an' she's gonna come out with a cake
40. that we didn't make
41. cause she likes chocolate cream

Stanza 11
42. an' I went t'the bakery with her
43. an' my grandmother ate cup cakes
44. an' an' she finally got sick on today
45. an' she was growling like a dog cause she ate so many cakes

Frame
Stanza 12
46. an' I finally told her that it was
47. it was Friday the thirteenth bad luck day

The style of the language of the text is fairly obvious and recognizably part of a Black cultural tradition (Abrahams, 1964, 1970, 1976; Baugh, 1983; Finnegan, 1970; Kochman, 1972, 1981; Smitherman, 1977; Stucky, 1987). The child uses language in a poetic, rather than a prosaic way; she tries to involve the audience, rather than just to inform them (Nichols, 1989). She uses a good deal of syntactic parallelism, repetition, and sound devices (phonological sequences, intonation, and rate changes) to set up rhythmic and poetic patterning within and across her stanzas. For example, stanzas 2 and 3 have the sort of structuring shown in the following diagram:

Stanza 2

1.		my mother's	bakin a cake
2.	my grandmother's	my mother's	bakin a cake
3.		my mother	bakin a X cake
4.	my grandmother was		bakin a X cake

Stanza 3

1.	we		went over my X's house
2.		Y had made a cake	
3.	we		went over my Z's house
4.		Z had made a cake	

Stanza 6 repeats line by line, with different language, the content of stanza 5; stanza 8 is just a "different take" on the same episode enacted by stanza 7. Stanza 4 is a two-line summary of all of part 1, whereas stanza 9 is a four-line summary of all of part 2. Clearly the narrator here is not primarily interested in making rapid and linear progress to "the point." Rather, she is interested in creating a pattern out of language, within and across her stanzas, much like a painting or a poem, a pattern that will generate meaning through the sets of relationships and contrasts that it sets up, like the multiple relationships and contrasts, points of contact and stress, in a painting or a poem (Frank, 1963).

And what might that meaning be? Of course, there are always multiple plausible and nonplausible interpretations of a text. But if we follow the clues or guides the child has placed in the organization of her text, and are sensitive to the child's culture, we can offer a reading that accepts the invitations of her text. The nonnarrative "evaluative" (Labov, 1972b) section in stanza 10 suggests that there is something significant in the fact that the grandmother is going to get a cake at the bakery and thus "come out with a cake that we [the family] didn't make." And, indeed, the story as a whole places a great deal of emphasis on the production of cakes within the family, a production that does not cease even when the grandmother keeps eating them. The grandmother, the matriarch and repository of the culture's norms, is behaving like a child, sneaking out and eating the cakes and rudely announcing that she does not like cheese cake even though the cake has been made by her relatives for her birthday. The story, in fact, contains a humorous paradox about cakes: the grandmother eats innumerable (normal-sized) cakes at home, made by her relatives, and never gets sick. Then she goes outside the home, buys little cakes (cup cakes) at the bakery, and, not only does she get sick, she "growls like a dog," that is, loses her human status and turns into an animal. Why?

I would argue the following: The grandmother is learning, and the child narrator is enacting, a lesson about signs or symbols. A birthday cake is a material object, but it is also an immaterial sign or symbol of kinship, when made within the family—a celebration of birth and family membership. The cake at the bakery looks the same, but it is a duplicitous symbol—it is not actually a sign of kinship, rather it is a commodity that nonkin have made to sell, not to celebrate the birth of someone they care about. To mistake the baker's cake as a true symbol of birth and kin is to think, mistakenly, that signs have meaning outside the contexts that give them meaning (Birch, 1989; Hodge & Kress, 1988; Stahl, 1989). In the context of the family, the cake means kinship and celebration; in the context of the bakery and market society, it signals exchange and commodities. The grandmother, in her greed, overvalues the material base of the sign (its cakehood) and misses its meaning, undervaluing the network of kin that gives meaning to the cakes. This is particularly dangerous when we consider that the grandmother is a senior representative of the family and culture. Her penalty is to momentarily lose her human status, that is, the status of a giver and taker of symbolic meaning—she becomes an animal, merely an eater. We may remember Levi-Strauss's claim that to many cultures, the material world is not only "good to eat," but "good to think with" (Levi-Strauss, 1966, p. 9).

And now, of course, I must face the inevitable question: Could this 7-year-old really have meant this? I would argue that this question seems so compelling to us because we have a less adequate theory of signs than this child. We think meaning is a matter of privatized intentions locked in people's heads that are indicative of their individual intelligence or skill. But once we deny this view of meaning, the questions lose most of their force; in fact, they become somewhat odd. This little girl has inherited, by her apprenticeship in the discourses of her community, ways of making sense of experience that, in fact, have a long and rich history going back thousands of years. This enculturation/apprenticeship has given her certain forms of language, ranging from devices at the word and clause level through the stanza level to the story level as a whole, that are intimately connected to forms of life. These forms of language are not merely structural, rather they encapsulate and carry through time and space meanings shared by and lived out in a variety of (creative) ways by the social group.[5]

It is easy to see the narrative performance of this child as a fresh and creative incarnation of an ongoing tradition. It is also clear that a

---

[5]The notions of discourse and forms of life are taken up in more detail in Gee (1989c).

focus on linear chronological development would be a grave disservice to this narrative, its teller, and her cultural ways of understanding the world. It is easy too to see how this child's current and future memory of her grandmother and her birthday is shaped (and will be reshaped) by its narrativization, a narrativization that, in turn, is itself shaped and reshaped by her personal history and the social practices, narratives, and history of her social group(s). Thus, it is easy to see the relationships between this narrative and the workings of premodern societies and systems of myth (which is not to say they are the same in every regard, of course).

So, then, what do we make of the reportive, linear, chronologically based narratives that mainstream children (according to much literature, e.g., Heath, 1983; Hicks, chap. 2 in this vol.; Michaels, 1981; Wolf, 1985), tend to tell, and that have so often been related to "essayist," school-based ways of making sense? These narratives are often contrasted with narratives like Leona's in terms of the contrast between a report and a story, where the latter is seen as emplotted and the former as not emplotted. However, I have tried to suggest that a report, to the extent that it is a narrative, would be meaningless apart from a surrounding narrative context, connections to social memory, and the resources of a system of themes that can create (what counts in a given group as) a coherent (satisfying) pattern. The report-story contrast, and that between (so-called) mainstream and nonmainstream children, needs, I believe, to be retheorized.

It is certainly true that much of our psycholinguistically based research on narrative tends to encourage reportive narratives by giving subjects linear, chronologically based stimulus materials in which the subjects have little interest and on which they have no particular perspective. Rarely do such materials have anything to do with the subjects' social group memberships or personal histories. Much that happens in school is disappointingly analogous. If, as I argue here, narrative is fundamentally a perspective that human beings take on the way in which certain themes fall into a satisfying pattern, a perspective stemming from their social identity and the resources their social group(s) make available to them, then such materials are, of course, encouraging "marked" behavior. We are not studying normative behavior when we study such materials (though there may, of course, be quite good reasons for studying nonnormative behavior).

However, I believe that the now common view that there is a fundamental difference (of genre, for instance) between narratives like Leona's and the narratives mainstream children tell is mistaken, provided we get real narratives from mainstream children, which is not always all that easy given what schools do to them and psychologists try to get from them. This is not, of course, to say that there are no differences. To see the similarities and differences, briefly consider a story by a 12-year-old upper-middle-class girl (who I call "Sandy"), a girl who is quite successful in school. I call Sandy's story, "The Kid."[6] I reprint it in its lines and stanzas:

THE KID

Part 1: First Day

Stanza 1
well see, we have this park near our house
and it really stinks
but me and my friend Sarah were over there
and we were playin on the swings

Stanza 2
and this other kid
we call "tin head cans," or whatever
because he goes around through garbage and stuff and picks up cans
and brings em to the store to get the money

Stanza 3
and so we're playin
and he starts callin us names
and so we call him names back
and then he starts talkin about our mothers

Stanza 4
so I take a rock and I threw it at him
it missed him
I made sure it missed him
it just banged on the slide

Stanza 5
and then he started throwing rocks at us
and now he was throwin rocks
and he was spittin and everything else
he wouldn't dare have hit us with it though

Stanza 6
and my mother was going down the street, okay?
and she saw him spittin at us
so my mother was trying to go over to his house
but she couldn't find 'im

Stanza 7
and instead she went to Jeremy and Erica's house

[6]This story was collected as part of a research project at Project Zero, Harvard Graduate School of Education, directed by Dennie Wolf. I am indebted to Dennie Wolf for sharing the story with me.

they're brats
they do everything he does
except they get buckets and they dump'em on people, and stuff like that

Stanza 8
and so then him and my mother went over there
and she went up to where he was sittin
and I was telling my mother that he was up to the tree
and I told him that my mother was coming

Stanza 9
and my mother came up
and she goes: "what's your name?"
and he goes: "I'm not gonna tell you,
you're not my mother"

Stanza 10
and my mother started calling him names and stuff like that
and then it turns out that he has this problem
like cause he's got some disease or somethin
and he doesn't quite know how to make friends, or anything like that

Part 2: Second Day

Stanza 11
and one day we went over there, another day
he starts swingin chains around, okay?
and he whips Sarah with a chain
and whipped me with a padlock that was on the chain

Stanza 12
and I didn't do anything,
but I grabbed him, okay?
and I go: "you hit me again
and you're gonna be in so much trouble you're not gonna believe it"

Stanza 13
so instead he starts swinging a swing
he wasn't on it
he just started swinging it
he swung it into me

Stanza 14
I go up to him
and I kicked him so hard he was like ahhhhhh
and he fell after I kicked him
I kicked him in both of his shins so it really hurt
and he'd get big bruises on his shins

Stanza 15
and the mark I had from the padlock was about a lump
it was about like that
and the mark went—oohhhh

and it was all black and blue
and you should see the shape of the padlock

Stanza 16
and then, let's see, Sarah's mother starts talkin to him
not to Jay—we finally found out his name was Jay
and started talkin to his mother
and the mother said: "I'll be glad to pay any hospital bills and anything like that"

Stanza 17
and Sarah goes: "all I want him to do is apologize"
and he goes, like this: "I did apologize"
and Sarah, yeah, like, "oh you wanna be my friend,
after you whipped me with a chain?"

Stanza 18
he whipped her in the n—
he whipped once in her leg
and once in her arm
and once on her stomach

Stanza 19
and then I go like this
after he yells at her like: "I'm sorry, I'm sorry"
and I go like this: "oh yeah that's a great way to make friends
whip people with chains and say 'hi I wanna be your friend'
that's dumb"

Part 3: Third Day

Stanza 20
and so then the next day we went over there
he was up in the tree
and he has a bunch of rocks and a bucket of sand up there, kay?
and he started throwin sand at us

Stanza 21
And Debbie Moraine got sand thrown at her
she goes up in the tree
she took the bucket of sand
and dumped it over his head

Stanza 22
and he went home screamin and cryin
he's thirteen
and he went home screamin and cryin
and told his mother

Stanza 23
and everybody ran
cause they didn't want to get in trouble

Stanza 24
and then he doesn't cause any trouble anymore
cept when people start with him

[big pause]

Stanza 25
he's dumb
you threaten his life and he laughs
he's got some problem

As I have mentioned, a lot has been written about the differences between the sorts of narratives many lower socioeconomic Black children tell and those many mainstream children tell (Cazden, 1988; Gee, 1989a; Heath, 1983; Michaels, 1981; Nichols, 1989). Elsewhere (Gee, 1989a) I have argued that Sandy relies more on linear and chronological development in her narrative than Leona (in comparison to Leona's later 12-year-old narratives) and that Leona's narratives are more "performed" (e.g., in terms of Wolfson's [1982] "performed narrative" features) and rely more than Sandy's on poetic devices of repetition and parallelism and rate and intonation changes. But here I want to point to the deeper commonalities between the two girl's narratives.

Sandy, just as Leona, creates a pattern out of contrasting themes drawn from her social background. To see this, consider the following diagram of the basic structure of Sandy's text:

BEGINNING (PART 1):			
CHILDREN FIGHTING leads to	MOTHER INTERVENES	leads to	FAILED RESOLUTION
MIDDLE (PART 2):			
CHILDREN FIGHTING leads to	MOTHER INTERVENES	leads to	FAILED RESOLUTION
END (PART 3):			
CHILDREN FIGHTING leads to	0 [ZERO]	leads to	REAL RESOLUTION

Sandy creates a structure that could go on forever (children fighting → mother intervenes → failed resolution → children fighting, etc.). By part 3 of the story we expect once again to get an intervention attempt on the part of a parent, but our expectation is frustrated. This is a perfect device for closure (Smith, 1968), and leads us to see the fact that the children settle the conflict by themselves, without parental intervention, as significant. Sandy's structure is quite sequential. It is the fact that part 2 follows part 1 with an identical structure that sets up the expectations for part 3, and these can then be frustrated, both as a device for closure and meaning. Furthermore, the three parts have an almost syllogistic structure: The 0 in part 3 (absence of parent) is to the parental intervention of parts 1 and 2 as the successful resolution of part 3 is to the failed ones of parts 1 and 2. We can almost deduce a successful resolution for part 3 from the absence of parental intervention. In fact, in part 3 the misbehaving boy runs home to his mother, the exact inverse of the other mothers coming out to the children in parts 1 and 2.

Both girls' stories are organized thematically around contrasts or oppositions juxtaposed throughout the texts. Sandy's story involves at least the following set of oppositions: park (outside) versus home (inside); the kid (outsider) versus the girls (insiders); the kid (outsider) versus the mothers (insiders); the girls and kid (youthful peers) versus the parents (the adult world); violence (lack of socialization) versus parental intervention (socialization). These oppositions can perhaps be summed up as an opposition between inside (belonging) and outside (not belonging), with the girls playing a somewhat ambivalent role as outsiders vis-à-vis the kid as a threat to their social world, but insiders with him as youthful peers with rules of their own opposed to the adult world. At one level the story seems to be about the way in which conflict is settled in the world outside the home, a world that does not always respect the norms of the girls' middle-class socializing institutions of home and school. In the first two scenes, parents try unsuccessfully to resolve the conflict (through words), whereas in the final scene, where they are absent, the conflict is resolved by the action of the children themselves, though the kid does run home to his mother (to be socialized?). One in fact senses here the anxiety of the middle class over the success of their children in a world whose norms of competition they by and large accept and control through their access to quality schools and supportive home environments, but whose actual workings they cannot guarantee. There is also a certain paradox or contradiction in Sandy's story. The story involves three episodes of violence from the kid reacted to by the girls. Debbie's response in the third scene is successful in resolving the conflict, but the narrator has responded just as aggressively in the first two scenes with no such results. Why is Debbie successful where the narrator is not? There is a displacement of the violence from the narrator, who acts, to another, whose act is successful, much as in a dream where we might displace the achievement of a result we desire but cannot accept to someone else. Violence is not accepted as a resolution to conflicts by the middle class, but at the same time they cannot fully control what competition in the outside world demands for success.

Of course, I do not insist on any of this; rather, I insist that the previous oppositions, the absence of the parental figure in the final scene, and the displacement of the successful violence are elements that any acceptable analysis will probably have to make reference to in order to make sense of the story and the storyteller's social world. The juxtaposition of the previous oppositions, of the presence versus the absence of parents, of the acts of the narrator versus the acts of others, are elements that must be simultaneously related and held together as a spatial unit throughout the text. The deeper, nonliteral meaning of this text—as I would argue for any text—is largely spatial in form, the actual sequence of events being secondary in importance at this level except as they serve to set up contrasts like presence versus absence (Levi-Strauss, 1963; Scholes, 1974, 1982). Thus, at a deeper level, Sandy's narrative works, just like Leona's (and the biblical stories given earlier), in terms of satisfying patterns of themes that are ultimately drawn from a system of sense making that resides in her social group.

I have tried to suggest a larger framework within which to view narrative, and have suggested what I take the fundamental or unmarked nature of narrative to be. This sociohistorical approach to knowing and talking is not the perspective of mainstream psycholinguistics, though there is a growing body of work on sociocognitive approaches to the human mind (Hickman, 1987; Lave, 1988; Rogoff & Lave, 1984; Scribner & Cole, 1981; Vygotsky, 1987; Wertsch, 1985a, 1985b). The chapters in this volume, although they stand in various relations to the sort of approach to narrative I have sketched, all speak in important ways to certain aspects.

McCabe, Capron, and Peterson (chap. 4 in this vol.) deal with the issue with which I started: the relationship between memory and narrative. Following Adler, they argue that out of the almost infinite number of experiences available, individuals unconsciously select to remember only those things that are consistent with their current framework. If memories were unchanging pictures in the mind, reflecting the cognitive state of the individual when she took the picture, we would expect that adults would report memories from early in life in quite different terms than they do those from later in life. But they do no such thing. Rather, memories are rehearsed and reshaped continuously through narrativization, and are thus saturated with one's present and future.

Peterson and McCabe (chap. 1 in this vol.) point to a fascinating paradox. They show that children's use of connectives (*so, because, but, then, and then,* and *and*) reflect the macrostructure of narratives, for example, whether a sentence conveys on-the-line events or tributary off-the-line information. Yet earlier research has found that although narratives are bristling with connectives, connectives are not essential for semantic deciphering of the story. This paradox is resolvable, I believe, only if we see that the fundamental function of narrative in human life is not to report a chronological sequence of events, but to signal a perspective on events and create a satisfying pattern of themes one has drawn from one's various social traditions. Semantically deciphering a narrative is only a superficial and relatively trivial task of a listener in the case of real narratives. The listener's main job is to recognize and respond to a perspective (attitude, values, beliefs) and a pattern within the context of its larger narrative, historical, and social setting. We know little about how connectives—or any linguistic feature for that matter—function in regard to this wider perspective.

Hudson and Shapiro (chap. 3 in this vol.) are concerned with the relationship between knowledge ("in the head") and the telling of that knowledge, studying the ways in which narrative production draws on many kinds of knowledge (e.g., event knowledge, memory of specific events, social interactional knowledge, and structural knowledge of different narrative genres, linguistic knowledge about tense and connectives, and knowledge about the listener's needs). They look at several genres of narrative (scripts,[7] personal narratives, and fictional stories) across various age groups, showing how the topic and the sorts of knowledge the child has, as well as the genre the child is trying to produce, interact with, and affect the structure of the narrative told. In particular, children tell more fully structured personal narratives about event types whose scripts are rather variable (e.g., going on trip) versus those event types that are rather routinized (e.g., going to the doctor), whereas their fictional stories are more fully structured in just the reverse cases. Presumably, this is because routinized scripts supply a problem for children to organize their narrative around, whereas personal narratives come out of children's own social activity and larger narrative context, which can perhaps get co-opted by too rigid a script. What we need to know, however, is how children form personal narratives out of their own larger narrative context, which is after all how they constitute a "life history" for themselves. We also need to know how this narrativization process affects their knowing (scripts, memories, beliefs, values, etc), in addition to the crucial information

[7]In my view, scripts are not a genre of narrative.

Hudson and Shapiro supply us on how knowledge shapes narrative structure.

Deborah Hicks (chap. 2 in this vol.) also studies the development of different narrative genres (newscasts, on-line narration, stories), but in this case in children from different socioeconomic backgrounds. She appeals to Bruner's idea that genre is both a means by which humans structure events in the real and fictional worlds and structure their ways of recounting such events. Hicks gets at some of the differences between lower socioeconomic Black children and mainstream children that I argue need to be retheorized. She argues that mainstream children interpret both on-line and story-telling tasks as tasks providing a temporally connected account of events, whereas lower socioeconomic children appear to interpret narrative tasks far more freely. If one accepts my suggestion that all true narrativization involves the signaling of perspective and the spatial patterning of contrasts and themes, then an important question arises: Why have mainstream practices so effaced the spatial and poetic workings of narrative, at least at a superficial (but not unimportant) level? Much of the work on modernity, commodification (turning everything into a product for sale), and modern multinational capitalism speaks to this issue (e.g., Connor, 1989; Harvey, 1989), a body of work that needs to be eventually related to our work on narrative.

McCabe and Peterson (chap. 6 in this vol.), focus not on larger social group differences, but on social differences within middle-class homes, an important focus if we are to break down simplistic reifications of social groups. They demonstrate that the structure of children's personal narratives reflects their habitual interactions with their parents. For example, children develop the ability to orient their listener in narratives in anticipation of parental questions that were experienced during the telling of previous narratives. Thus, they argue that narrative structure develops as a response to others. I would argue that all social groups inculcate in their children narratives that orient their listeners, because the function of narrative is to form a perspective on experience, a perspective formed out of traditions one partly shares with, and wants to reconstitute/share/communicate to a listener. But not all groups inculcate the sorts of superficial expressions of orientation and narrative structure that mainstream institutions like schools value. And, indeed, McCabe and Peterson also show that some middle-class parents are better than others at facilitating the use of language in a decontextualized way that appears to relate to later school success.

Both Dickinson (chap. 7 in this vol.) and Michaels (chap. 8 in this vol.) study the relationship between narrative development and schools. Dickinson assumes that discourse development arises from opportunities for supportive interactions with adults and, to a lesser extent, peers. He then studies the ways in which the content and structure of teacher-child talk is affected by organizational features of classrooms such as the nature of the activities engaged in by children and teachers and the number of participants. He shows that in school activities where management concerns dominate, talk is mostly restricted to the present and there are limited opportunities for the development of extended discourse. At the same time, Dickinson found that school activities of any sort did not encourage any great deal of extended narrativization, which is indeed a paradox if narrative plays the central role in human sense making for which I have argued.

Michaels helps partially resolve this paradox, arguing that much of what goes on in urban, public school settings relates to the dismantling or breaking down of narrative performance and artistry—in favor of alternative forms of meaning making deemed more scientific, rigorous, reliable, intelligent, or important. Furthermore, from the early grades on, the narrative discourse that is tolerated is often shaped by teachers and instructional activities into a simplified, homogenized form. Michaels, looking at both oral sharing time stories and writing conferences, argues that across a range of classrooms and grade levels, teachers tend to interpret and evaluate student discourse against a narrowly defined literate standard. Teachers are looking for a certain kind of narrative account, with literatelike characteristics, closer to simple descriptive prose. She argues, in the case of writing, that it is not particular classroom methodologies, but rather the *writing system* ("the activities, norms, rights and obligations for speaking and acting, including uses of technology") in the classroom that determines what students take into their texts and what perspectives on discourse, knowledge, and voice they take along with the text.

A perspective on discourse, knowledge, and voice is always socially formed and is largely a matter of what counts to a particular group as a satisfying solution to real human problems. To the extent that schools undervalue the narratives of children from certain groups they undervalue their memories, their histories, and their traditions. To the extent that they undervalue narrative in general they undervalue human memory, history, and tradition.

ACKNOWLEDGMENTS

I am greatly indebted to Courtney Cazden, James Collins, Deborah Hicks, Sarah Michaels, Dennie Wolf, and James Wertsch for discussion of and perspectives on narrative that have been very helpful, although none of them would necessarily accept all I have to say here. My remarks here have also been inspired, sometimes with and sometimes against the grain, by the chapters in this volume, though I do not at each juncture indicate which point in which chapter I am reacting to, with, or against.

REFERENCES

Abrahams, R. D. (1964). *Deep down in the jungle: Negro narrative folklore from the streets of Philadelphia.* Hatboro, PA.: Folklore Associates.

Abrahams, R. D. (1970). *Positively black.* Englewood Cliffs, NJ: Prentice-Hall.

Abrahams, R. D. (1976). *Talking Black.* Rowley, MA: Newburg House.

Baugh, J. (1983). *Black street speech: Its history, structure and survival.* Austin, TX: University of Texas Press.

Birch, D. (1989). *Language, literature and critical practice: Ways of analyzing texts.* London: Routledge & Kegan Paul.

Cazden, C. (1988). *Classroom discourse: The language of teaching and learning.* Portsmouth, NH: Heinemann.

Chafe, W. L. (1980). The deployment of consciousness in the production of a narrative. In W. L. Chafe, (Ed.), *The pear stories; Cognitive, cultural, and linguistic aspects of narrative production* (pp. 9–50). Norwood, NJ: Ablex.

Connerton, P. (1989). *How societies remember.* Cambridge: Cambridge University Press.

Connor, S. (1989). *Postmodern culture: An introduction to theories of the contemporary.* Oxford: Basil Blackwell.

Finnegan, R. (1970). *Oral literature in Africa.* Oxford, England: Clarendon Press.

Finnegan, R. (1988). *Literacy and orality.* Oxford, England: Basil Blackwell.

Frank, J. (1963). Spatial form in modern literature. In J. Frank, *The widening gyre: Crisis and mastery in modern literature* (pp. 3–62).

Gee, J. P. (1985). The narrativization of experience in the oral style. *Journal of Education, 167,* 9–35.

Gee, J. P. (1986). Units in the production of narrative discourse. *Discourse Processes, 9,* 391–422.

Gee, J. P. (1989a). Commonalities and differences in narrative construction. *Discourse Processes, 12,* 287–307.

Gee, J. P. (1989b). "Literariness", formalism, and sense making: The line and stanza structure of human thought. *Journal of Education, 171,* 61–74.

Harvey, D. (1989). *The condition of postmodernity.* Oxford, England: Basil Blackwell.

Heath, S. B. (1983). *Ways with words: Language, life, and work in communities and classrooms.* Cambridge: Cambridge University Press.

Hickman, M. (Ed.) (1987). *Social and functional approaches to language and thought.* Orlando, FL: Academic Press.

Hodge, R., & Kress, G. (1988). *Social semiotics.* Ithaca, NY: Cornell University Press.

Hymes, D. (1981). *"In vain I tried to tell you": Essays in Native American ethnopoetics.* Philadelphia: University of Pennsylvania Press.

Jackson, B. (1974). *"Get your ass in the water and swim like me": Narrative poetry from Black oral tradition.* Cambridge, MA: Harvard University Press.

Kochman, T. (Ed.) (1972). *Rappin' and stylin' out: Communication in urban Black America.* Urbana: University of Illinois Press.

Kochman, T. (1981). *Black and white styles in conflict.* Chicago: University of Chicago Press.

Labov, W. (1972a). *Language in the inner city.* Philadelphia: University of Pennsylvania Press.

Labov, W. (1972b). The transformation of experience in narrative syntax. In W. Labov, *Language in the inner city* (pp. 354–396). Philadelphia: University of Pennsylvania Press.

Lave, J. (1988) *Cognition in practice.* Cambridge: Cambridge University Press.

Leach, E. (1969) *"Genesis as myth" and other essays.* London: Jonathan Cape.

Leach, E. (1976). *Culture and communication: The logic by which symbols are connected.* Cambridge: Cambridge University Press.

Leach, E. & Aycock, D. A. (1983). *Structuralist interpretations of biblical myth.* Cambridge: Cambridge University Press.

Levi-Strauss, C. (1963). *Structural anthropology.* New York: Basic Books.

Levi-Strauss, C. (1966). *The savage mind.* Chicago: University of Chicago Press.

Levi-Strauss, C. (1964–1971). *Mythologiques: 4 Volumes.* Paris: Plon.

Levi-Strauss, C. (1979). *Myth and meaning.* New York: Schocken Books.

Michaels, S. (1981). "Sharing time:" Children's narrative styles and differential access to literacy. *Language in Society, 10,* 423–42.

Nichols, P. C. (1989). Storytelling in Carolina: Continuities and contrasts. *Anthropology and Education Quarterly, 20,* 232–245.

Rogoff, B., & Lave, J. (1984). (Eds.). *Everyday cognition: Its development in social context.* Cambridge, MA: Harvard University Press.

Rosenberg, B. A. (1970). *The art of the American folk preacher.* New York: Oxford University Press.

Scholes, R. (1974). *Structuralism in literature: An introduction.* New Haven, CT & London: Yale University Press.

Scholes, R. (1982). *Semiotics and interpretation.* New Haven, CT: Yale University Press.

Scollon, R., & Scollon, S.B.K. (1981). *Narrative, literacy, and face in interethnic communication.* Norwood, NJ: Ablex.

Scribner, S., & Cole, M. (1981). *The psychology of literacy.* Cambridge, MA: Harvard University Press.

Smith, B. H. (1968). *Poetic closure: A study of how poems end.* Chicago & London: University of Chicago Press.

Smitherman, G. (1977). *Talkin and testifyin: The language of Black America.* Boston: Houghton Mifflin.

Stahl, S. D. (1989) *Literary folkloristics and the personal narrative.* Bloomington: Indiana University Press.

Stucky, S. (1987). *Slave culture: Nationalist theory and the foundations of black America.* Oxford, England: Oxford University Press.

Taussig, M. (1987). *Shamanism, colonialism, and the wild man: A study in terror and healing.* Chicago: University of Chicago Press.

Tedlock, D. (1977). Toward an oral poetics. *New Literary History, 8,* 507–19

Vygotsky, L. S. (1987). *The collected works of L. S. Vygotsky, Volume 1: Problems of general psychology. Including the volume Thinking and Speech* (R. W. Rieber & A. S. Carton, Eds.). New York: Plenum.

Wertsch, J. V. (1985a). (Ed.). *Culture, communication, and cognition: Vygotskian perspectives.* Cambridge: Cambridge University Press.

Wertsch, J. V. (1985b). *Vygotsky and the social formation of mind.* Cambridge, MA: Harvard University Press.

Wolf, D. (1985). Ways of telling: Text repertoires in elementary school children. *Journal of Education, 168,* 71–87.

Wolfson, N. (1982). *CHP: The conversational historical present in American English narrative.* Dordrecht: Foris.

PART I:

SOME WAYS IN WHICH NARRATIVE DEVELOPS

CHAPTER 1

Linking Children's Connective Use and Narrative Macrostructure

Carole Peterson
Memorial University of Newfoundland

Allyssa McCabe
Harvard University and Tufts University

A major transition in the study of language has been from an exclusive focus on the individual sentence to an analysis of larger units of text. Narratives in particular have been the object of much study, for a number of reasons. The telling of stories, both those that are fictional and those that recount past personal experience, seems to play a major role in interpersonal interaction in all societies that have been studied. It is as natural to talk about "what happened to me yesterday," or "last week," or "once on the way to . . ." as it is to discuss the here-and-now. Narratives have also been frequently studied because they are typically monologues that have a recognizable beginning and end and thus are relatively easy units to identify; they are also familiar to people of all ages, excepting only infants and toddlers. Even children as young as 2 years of age at times talk about their past adventures in their conversations with parents (Eisenberg, 1985; Miller & Sperry, 1988; Sachs, 1983), and 3- to 5-year-olds include narratives in their conversations with peers (Umiker-Sebeok, 1979).

Grimes (1975, 1978) summarized studies of narratives in over 100 languages and 25 countries, and highlighted three recurrent themes that seem to characterize narratives: (a) *content,* including structure (what here is termed *macrostructure*); (b) *cohesion,* or how the things one is currently saying relate back to what has gone before, that is, relationships between sentences; and (c) *staging,* or how the speaker controls the perspective from which parts of the story are presented. This chapter focuses on the first two properties of narratives, macrostructure and cohesion, and argues that the use of one particular marker of cohesion (namely intersentential connectives) is systematically related to the macrostructure of a narrative.

Macrostructure

What exactly is a narrative? Although definitions differ in detail, all agree on central properties. Most importantly, a narrative must include a recounting of events that follow each other in time (de Beaugrande, 1980; Grimes, 1975, 1978; Labov, 1972; Labov & Waletzky, 1967; Longacre, 1983; Peterson & McCabe, 1983; Polanyi, 1985; Prince, 1982). Although some consider a narrative (albeit a minimal one) to be any recounting of two temporally sequenced events (e.g., Labov, 1972; Labov & Waletzky, 1967; Peterson & McCabe, 1983), others include an additional property: According to Polanyi (1985, p. 33), a story must be structured conventionally—it must include not only *main line event clauses,* but also contextualizing *state clauses.* Main line event clauses have been frequently described as the backbone or "bare bones" of a narrative and describe what happened, whereas contextualizing clauses include identification of participants, setting, explanation, evaluation, and collateral information. Longacre (1983) stated that a narrative "involves a distinction between on-the-line or backbone material and supportive, explanatory, tributary or what-have-you material in the balance of the discourse" (p. 99). Such a distinction between on-the-line and tributary information is so important that many languages mark the two components with different syntax, affixes or special particles, verb tenses, or word order (Longacre, 1983). Both the specifics of what type of nonevent information is important as well as the specifics of how narratives are structurally organized differ among researchers.

Cohesion

In a narrative there are multiple clauses. Cohesion describes the linguistic relationships between those clauses, that is, how the surface linguistic elements of a text are linked to each other in order to create a cohesive whole. Halliday and Hasan (1976) perhaps made the most extensive analysis of cohesive devices in language. As an example, they saw the use of pronouns as cohesive in that any use of *she* points backward in text and refers to a person who has been specified before. Thus, the pronoun explicitly links the relevant clauses by referring to the same entity. Likewise, use of ellipsis (omitting what goes without saying), substitution of a generic element such as *one* for another that was previously specified, use of intersentential connectives, and making lexical choices that either repeat previous words or use related vocabulary items are all cohesive devices that explicitly relate one clause with previous clauses. In effect, they tie the discourse together linguistically. Recently, there has been burgeoning interest in children's developing mastery of all of these cohesive devices (e.g., Dore, 1985; Gopnik, 1986; Hedberg, 1984; Hedberg & Stoel-Gammon, 1984; Johnson & Johnson, 1985; Klecab-Aker & Lopez, 1985; McCutchen & Perfetti, 1982; Pellegrini, 1982, 1984; Pratt & MacKenzie-Keating, 1985; Romaine, 1985; Zammuner, 1986).

Intersentential connectives are particularly interesting cohesive devices for students of narrative. Such connectives explicitly state that two clauses are related by means of temporal sequence, cause-effect relationship, antithesis, mere continuity, and so on. But connectives are not necessary for cohesion to be inferred in narratives. According to Grice's (1975) *Maxim of Orderliness,* two sequentially stated event clauses are assumed by the listener to be an accurate reflection of the order of occurrence of those events, that is, the act of stating or describing one event before the other is automatically assumed to mean that the event mentioned first actually occurred first. Furthermore, speakers almost always state sequential events in their correct chronological order unless they are explicitly tagged as violating this expectation. This is true even for young preschool-aged children (Brown, 1975; Brown & Murphy, 1975; Nelson, 1978, 1986; Peterson & McCabe, 1983). Many clauses in a narrative are devoted to recapitulating the sequence of what happened, consequently it is unnecessary for intersentential temporal links to be present for the narrative to be understood. The temporal relationships between the events are accurately inferred by listeners on the basis of the order in which the events are stated. Thus, it is surprising that narratives are texts that characteristically make heavy use of connectives to mark intersentential links, including simple temporal sequence. Narratives have been found to have a particularly high density of connectives in comparison to other types of texts; for example, connectives are substantially more common in narratives than in conversation (Laubitz, 1988; Peterson & McCabe, 1988; Sulzby & Barro Zecker, chap. 5. in this vol.) or in explanations (Laubitz, 1988). Although connectives are often unnecessary for the listener to comprehend the narrative, they nonetheless seem to be obligatory in the production of well-formed narratives; a narrative without them sounds anomalous (Peterson & McCabe, 1988).

In this chapter, we summarize our prior research and extend it with new analyses to make the following points: sentential connectives in narratives are used to facilitate semantic coherence only some of the time; they also serve pragmatic functions and mark narrative macrostructure.

DESCRIPTION OF DATA CORPUS

The data we present from our own work comes from a large corpus of elicited personal narratives, told by 96 children ranging in age from 3;6 to 9;6 years. There were eight boys and eight girls in each of six yearly age groups, with mean ages of 4;1, 5;0, 6;0, 7;0, 8;0 and 9;0. The children came from a predominantly working-class small town in Ohio and were all Caucasian. They were taken individually to a small room in their school or preschool and given an art project to do. While doing it, prompts about personal experiences were sandwiched into the conversation followed by questions such as "Have you ever been to the doctor? You have? Tell me about it." The prompts were about pet adventures, visits to the doctor and hospital, accidents, parties, vacations, and so on. While narrating, children were encouraged to continue with such nondirective statements as "uh-huh," "yeah?," or repeating verbatim their last utterance. (For details of the procedure, see Peterson & McCabe, 1983). Each child produced a minimum of three narratives about personal experience (average number of narratives: 11½), with a total corpus of 1124. Because the experimenters carefully restricted their follow-up comments to echoes of the child and nonspecific encouragement, use of connectives within them can be seen as reflexive of children's spontaneous production capabilities.

CONNECTIVES AS MARKERS OF SEMANTIC COHERENCE

Connectives that Frequently Occur in Narratives

The defining property of a narrative is a recapitulation of temporally sequenced events, thus one would expect narratives to make use of explicitly temporal markers like *then.* In addition, causal relationships between clauses are commonly present, partly because so many narratives describe goal-oriented behavior. Consequently, the connectives *because* and *so* are common. Adversative (*but*) and coordinating (*and*) connectives are also present because of the aforementioned presence of contextual information and evaluation. These connectives are the focus of our study.

Much research has centered on the logical semantic properties of these connectives and when children come to understand these meanings and express them in spontaneous speech by means of the appropriate connective (see Bloom, Lahey, Hood, Lifter, & Feiss, 1980; Clancy, Jacobsen, & Silva, 1976; Eisenberg, 1980; French & Nelson, 1985; Hood, Lahey, Lifter, & Bloom, 1978). By the time children have reached 3;6 years, they use all of the previously mentioned connectives productively, albeit not always accurately. The following semantic relationships are those typically described for the connectives under consideration. (The following examples are from our corpus; prototypical connectives are used for illustration.)

- Coordinating relationships, involving the simple co-occurrence of two independent events and/or states, e.g., *Pam and Barbara was fighting* and *Daddy was at work.*
- Temporal relationships, involving the sequential ordering of events in time, e.g., *It was so hot I kept on changing and changing my pillow* and then *next morning we had to go back.*
- Enabling relationships, when one event establishes the necessary preconditions for another event to occur but does not actually cause the second event, e.g., *Somebody went straight by them on the road* and *they crashed.*
- Causal relationships, in which the first event causes the second to occur, e.g., *She wanted to hurt him so she hit him.*
- Antithetical relationships, involving contrast such as opposition or negation between two clauses, or exception. (Others have labeled these relationships adversative.), e.g., *My little sister's cute* but *my big sister is awful and ugly.*

Children's Use of these Connectives and the Semantic Relationships They Express

Then

Young children commonly use *then;* it is the most frequent connective after *and* in both narration (Gopnik, 1986) and here-and-now talk (Bloom et al., 1980). In the narratives analyzed here, fully one in four connectives used by 4-year-olds involved *then* (many were combined with *and* to form *and then*); this decreased to one in eight for 8- and 9-year-olds. Although the connective *then* can be used for nontemporal purposes (e.g., inferentially in *if then* constructions, see Scott, 1984), its use by young children during narration is mostly confined to temporal succession (Gopnik, 1986). In our corpus, fully 90% of its uses encoded temporal sequence of some type. The remaining 10% of occurrences connected clauses that had no temporal sequence of any sort between them but only a coordinate relationship. Such noncanonical use of *then* could be seen as errors. We return to a discussion of these so-called errors later. Returning to the 90% of *then* occurrences that involve temporal sequence, such connected events may have no other relationship between them than chronological order, or they may have additional relationships such as enablement or causality. In our data, over half of *then* occurrences reflected simple temporal sequence, with the other instances distributed equally between clauses with enabling and causal relationships.

Because and So

Causal connectives are frequently used by children; in our data, *because* and *so* each comprise about 10% of all connectives used. The types of causality found between causally connected clauses have also been studied. For children, psychological causality predominates; the most frequent relationship is between an intention and its motivated behavior, and the intention can be either explicitly stated or implicit and easily inferred (McCabe & Peterson, 1985a). When physical causality is present between clauses, children prefer to use the noncausal connective *and* rather than an explicitly causal connective. Interesting differences in what kinds of causality are preferentially encoded by *because* versus *so* have been found, with *so* used almost exclusively for psychological causality and *because* used for both psychological and physical causality (McCabe & Peterson, 1985a). As well, there are differences in the use of these connectives by adults versus children, with adults using both connectives to encode physical causality more than children. In addition, there were distributional differences in the frequencies of various types of psychological causality between adults and children (McCabe & Peterson, 1988).

Some researchers, beginning with Piaget (1930/1972), have been struck by children's misuse of causal connectives and have concluded, as a result of such mistaken language, that children were cognitively immature. But there are at least two problems with this interpretation. First, almost none of the errors children make are the type predicted by Piaget (McCabe & Peterson, 1985a). In fact, a number of investigators have found that children are more competent at understanding causality than Piaget supposed (Bullock & Gelman, 1979; Green, 1977; Kun, 1978), and that task variables greatly influence the sort of confused connective use noted by Piaget (Peterson & McCabe, 1985). In addition, adults "misuse" these causal connectives with the same frequency as children and in similar ways (McCabe & Peterson, 1988). Two common noncanonical uses are enabling relationships and instances of inferred causality, where the causal relationship between two clauses is not explicitly stated but easily inferable. Such links have been termed *weak causal* or *precausal* by others (Hood et al., 1978). For purposes of the present analysis, these have been included under the category of *semantic uses* in our tables. However, there are some uses of *because* and *so* that are still unexplained by a semantic analysis. Many of these so-called semantic mistakes are actually uses of these connectives for pragmatic purposes, something that happens about a quarter of the time children use these connectives.

But

The connective *but* prototypically encodes adversative or antithetical relationships between two clauses, including semantic opposition or direct contrast between clauses, violation of expectation, qualification of the first clause, and so on (see Carlson, 1983; Kail & Weissenborn, 1984; McClure & Geva, 1983; Peterson, 1986; Zammuner, 1986). It appears with reasonable frequency in children's narratives (Peterson, 1986), moreso in those of children between 3;6 and 6;6 (15% of all connectives in our data) than in those of 7- to 9-year-olds (7% of all connectives). Four- and 5-year-olds are more likely to misuse *but,* whereas older children are more likely to use *but* in appropriate antithetical situations, and they also use it when more sophisticated forms of antithesis are involved (Peterson, 1986; Zammuner, 1986).

Again, as in the semantic analyses of other connectives, there are many instances in which this connective is used noncanonically, but they are not clear-cut errors either. This noncanonical use of *but* ranges from 28% of all instances of use in the 4- and 5-year-olds to about 18% of instances in all of the older age groups. Again, we turn to nonsemantic sorts of analyses to understand the functioning of this connective.

And

Research on the form of *and* coordinations in children's language is reviewed by Peterson and McCabe (1987a). Children are fond of linking their narrative clauses by means of an intersentential *and* (Beaman, 1984; Gopnik, 1986; McCutchen & Perfetti, 1982; Peterson & McCabe, 1987a, 1987b, 1988). The connective *and* can have any semantic function; it can be used to express virtually any link between virtually any elements, although it seldom expresses adversative relationships (Peterson, 1986).

To illustrate the versatility of the connective *and,* consider the following two narratives produced by a 9-year-old girl and a 9-year-old boy respectively (E is the experimenter, G indicates Girl, and B indicates Boy):

Narrative 1

E: Have you ever been to a doctor?

G: Yeah, I couldn't breathe.

E: Tell me about it. What happened?

G: Why one morning I woke up and I came out and my Dad was getting ready for work. It was 4 o'clock in the morning and he was getting dressed for work and my mom was making him cereal and I think it was cream of wheat and I told Mom I was sick and I couldn't breathe and she asked me what was the matter and I told her and then I told her I wanted my Daddy so he came out and brought me to the hospital. Brought me in a car and my Mom followed me behind and after they got me to the hospital they made sure I was alright and everything and then my Dad went to work and my Mom went back home to do the housework.

Narrative 2

E: Have you ever spilled anything?

B: That's what happened last year. I looked right at it and I got it.

E: Oh, really? Tell me about it.

B: See, I was painting and the glue couldn't come out so I got mad at it and I threw the bottle and I went to pick it up and I looked into it and I tried to squirt it and I got it right in the face. My teacher asked me what happened and I told her that the glue had got me in the face and she laughed at me and I said "That ain't funny. What if you got it in your face?" and she said "I'd cry" but I said "I'm not a bawlbaby." I got mad too.

In the previous narratives, 82% and 65% respectively of the sentences are connected by *and.* In the first narrative, 36% of the *and*-links are temporal, 50% coordinating, and 14% causal, whereas in the second narrative, 9% are temporal, 18% are coordinating, 55% are causal, and 18% are enabling relationships. A straightforward definition of the semantic function of *and* seems impossible, and it is typically seen as having little if any semantic content (e.g., Beaman, 1984; McCutchen & Perfetti, 1982).

The literature is contradictory about whether or not *and* becomes replaced by more semantically specific connectives as children get older. Some investigators have tracked the emergence of more sophisticated forms of connective and have suggested that with age, connective variety in any discourse increases while dependence on *and* decreases (Jisa, 1987; Laubitz, 1988; Martin, 1983; Scott, 1984). Others have similarly suggested that connective usage in children's narratives changes from an early dependence on temporal relationships between events to more causally linked chains of events, and this shift is reflected in a relative decrease of the connectives *and, then,* and *and then* while there is a simultaneous increase in *so, and so, and so then* and other causal connectors (Kernan, 1977; McCutchen & Perfetti, 1982).

In our own work, we assessed the use of 2,660 instances of *and* used alone, without a second connective to alter its interpretation (Peterson & McCabe, 1987b), and we found no age differences in the types of relationships obtaining between clauses that were connected by *and.* That is, the 9-year-olds were using this connective in the same way as the 4-year-olds: A simple temporal relationship between the connected sentences was present about a third of the time, followed by enabling, causal, and coordinating relationships, which were each present about a fifth of the time. About 10% of the relationships involved antithesis. Inconsistencies with the data of other investigators could be because both Jisa (1987) and Laubitz (1988) studied children who would all have fallen into our youngest age group (or possibly youngest two); thus, the changes they track could well be disguised by placing these children into one age category, as we did. On the other hand, Kernan (1977) and Scott (1984) included older children. Although our age range is wide, encompassing 6 years, there could well be changes in the use of *and* outside this range.

Although there is debate about whether or not there are changes in the semantic relationships encoded by *and,* there is little debate about its function to mark continuity (Cieri, 1985; Gopnik, 1986; Jisa, 1987; Peterson & McCabe, 1987b). It has even been described as an all-purpose discourse glue (McNeill, 1987; Peterson & McCabe, 1988). According to Cieri (1985), the use of *and* indicates continuity even in cases where this might not otherwise be apparent, that is, its use imposes continuity and thus helps make a narrative not only cohesive but coherent.

CONNECTIVES AS MARKERS OF PRAGMATIC FUNCTION

As we have said, a strictly semantic analysis of connective use could leave one with the impression that children have much room for improving the match of connective form with meaning, at least for those connectives that encode rather specific meanings (i.e., connectives other than *and*). However, there is increasing evidence that connectives are plurifunctional morphemes, capable of serving not only semantic but also pragmatic roles (Eisenberg, 1980; Gallagher & Craig, 1987; Jisa, 1984–1985, 1987; Peterson, 1986; Scott, 1984; van Dijk, 1979, 1981). Van Dijk (1979) contrasted these two functions of connectives in the following way: "Whereas semantic connectives express relations between denoted facts, pragmatic connectives express relations between speech acts" (p. 447). It has been suggested that most, if not all, connectives can be used pragmatically as well as semantically (van Dijk, 1979, 1981).

Most investigations of pragmatic use of connectives have focused on dialogue and the ways in which individuals can link their turns at talk with those of their conversational partners, particularly by using the connectives *but* and *and* (Eisenberg, 1980; Gallagher & Craig, 1987; Jisa, 1984–1985; Scott, 1984; van Dijk, 1979, 1981). For example, connectives at the initiation of a turn at talk can indicate protest or objection to what the other speaker has just said, denial of expectation across speakers, surprise, addition to the other speaker's assertion, or simply a bid for a turn at talking. Others have described the use of *and* as a conversational placeholder or stalling tactic, indicating that the speaker is not finished and does not wish to relinquish the floor even though the next sentence is not yet planned (Jisa, 1984–1985; NcNeill, 1987).

Of particular interest to us is the way in which connectives can be used pragmatically within one speaker's turn at talk, rather than as between-speaker links. Polanyi (1985) suggested that when adults begin narrating, they often begin a story with an abstract statement that is immediately followed by the first event of the timeline. However, the retelling of this first event is often interrupted in midstream by the speaker's citation of some relevant background material or orienting context. Narrators then regularly resume the interrupted timeline with the connective *so*. Use of this connective for a return to a main topic from some kind of digression has also been found by others for both adults (e.g., Auchlin, 1981 cited in Jisa, 1987; Reichman, 1985) and children (Jisa, 1987; Peterson & McCabe, in press). The connective *but* has also been found to function at times in the same way for children, to mark resumption of a previous topic (Jisa, 1987; Peterson, 1986). Narrators use connectives at transition points when they are departing from the timeline of their narratives to insert other relevant information, specifically *so, but,* and occasionally *because* (Jisa, 1987; Peterson, 1986; Peterson & McCabe, in press).

Other pragmatic functions within the context of conversational narration have been noted as well. During narration, the narrator must hold the floor; standard conversational turn-taking does not apply and interruptions by the listener are generally confined to indications of interest, encouragement to continue, questions of clarification, or prompts for specific important information that has been left out. All these are relevant to the ongoing narrative and are not attempts to take over the conversation. In view of the fact that listeners usually yield the floor to narrators, it would smooth conversational interactions were narrators to signal listeners when a narrative begins, as well as when it ends; in fact, even young narrators do this to some extent. Some connectives have been found to function at these junctures as narrative delimiters. Peterson (1986) found that some preschool-aged children are particularly fond of using the connective *but* as a narrative initiator. When her own 4-year-old suddenly announced "But . . .", it was a reliable indicator that a narrative was about to follow. Although at times older children also use *but* this way, this use decreased with age. Other connectives are used by children at the initiation of a narrative, including *so* (Jisa, 1987; Peterson & McCabe, in press), *because* (Peterson & McCabe, in press), and *well* (Jisa, 1987). Connectives do not function in a parallel way at the closing of a narrative for children; they are seldom present in English (except for an occasional use of *so;* see Peterson & McCabe, in press), although both "*alors*" ("so") and "*et puis*" ("and then") occasionally precede the standard French marker for narrative closing, "*voilà*" (Jisa, 1987).

We have noted one other pragmatic function for connectives (Peterson, 1986; Peterson & McCabe, in press). The standard form of the narrative timeline is a succession of chronological events. If this expected linear sequence is violated in some way, such as by the speaker giving two events in the wrong order, recycling back to a previous point in the timeline, or backing up and repeating the just-stated clause, narrators commonly mark this violation by means of an inserted connective such as *but, so,* or even *because.* Some examples of pragmatic use of connectives by our child narrators follow (E is the experimenter, and C denotes the child):

- Beginnings, to initiate the narrative as a whole (or a subepisode of it).

  Example 6 E: *I bet you see the sun come up in the morning.*
  C: But *I saw the zoo.*

  Example 7 E: *Do you have any brothers or sisters?*
  C: *No. Yeah but I got some friends that do. I got Tracy, Carolyn and Phillip and Chippy.*
  E: *Oh.*
  C: 'Cause *Connie's mother's back home from the hospital . . .*

- Departure from the timeline in order to insert tributary material such as orientation or evaluation. This category includes departures to insert attention-getters. In other work (Peterson, 1986; Peterson & McCabe, in press), departures from the timeline were not differentiated from returns to the timeline (see next category). However, for purposes of the analyses presented later, such differentiation is useful. (Classification of utterances in terms of timeline event or nontimeline categories is provided. For detailed discussion and examples of these categories, see Peterson & McCabe, 1983.)

Example 8 *And then I fell down* but *you know what?* (timeline event, *but* attention-getter)

Example 9 *I asked him (the doctor) a lot of questions. He goes, "Why, you're nosy." I go " 'You are.' "* 'Cause *I never had him before, you know.* (three timeline events, *'cause* orientation)

- Return to the timeline after a departure to insert tributary material.

Example 10 *Know what we did?* So *the car went down the hill. . .* (attention-getter, *so* timeline event)

Example 11 *David was there and my uncle Pete,* and then *I said, "Pete . . ."* (orientation, *and then* timeline event)

- Chronology violation, as a signal that the sequential order of events that listeners expect is violated.

Example 12 *We went to Florida* but *first we went to Texas.*

Example 13 *I was just sitting there, I didn't say a word.* So *I didn't say nothing.*

- Endings, signaling the termination of the narrated events by means of stepping back and evaluating the narrative as a whole, or other means of returning the focus of discourse to the present.

Example 14 *(Narrative about a car accident and how many people died.) . . .* So *they dead right now too.*

Our semantic analysis of the connectives *then, because, so,* and *but* left one with the impression that children were often using these connectives noncanonically. Let us return to these so-called semantic errors. How many are in fact instances of the sorts of pragmatic uses just described? These data are shown in Table 1.1 (Note that *and* is deleted because of its lack of semantic content.)

Children between 3;6 and 9;6 use connectives both semantically and pragmatically. Most of the so-called errors in connective use according to a strict semantic analysis are instead systematic uses for pragmatic purposes. Children frequently use both *so* and *but* pragmatically; on the other hand, both *then* and *because* are seldom used this way. The only developmental difference noted in our data was for the

TABLE 1.1
Instances of Connective Use That Are Semantic, Pragmatic, or Errors

	Semantic	*Pragmatic*	*Errors*
Then	615 (93%)	26 (4%)	18 (3%)
Because	358 (90%)	36 (9%)	4 (1%)
So	241 (67%)	111 (31%)	8 (2%)
But	297 (73%)	91 (22%)	19 (5%)

Note. And is deleted here because it has no semantic content, strictly speaking.

connective *but.* The 4- and 5-year-olds were using *but* far more for pragmatic purposes, particularly for narrative initiations, than children at all older ages. These younger children were also committing many errors when using *but;* they do not yet have full mastery of this connective (Peterson, 1986). Table 1.1 summarizes the instances of use that were neither canonical semantic uses nor pragmatic uses, and the error rate is quite low.

In summary, a good understanding of how children use causal, temporal, and adversative connectives in their narratives requires not only an assessment of their semantic functions but of their pragmatic functions as well. Children use connectives as plurifunctional morphemes from a very young age. The next section closely scrutinizes the coordinating conjunction *and,* as well as the temporal, causal, and adversative connectives, for a third type of usage: marking narrative macrostructure. Note that although semantic and pragmatic analyses of connectives were mutually exclusive, the following analysis is orthogonal to both of those; that is, a connective could be used either semantically or pragmatically or classified as an "error," but in any case it could also function as a marker of narrative macrostructure.

CONNECTIVES AS MARKERS OF NARRATIVE MACROSTRUCTURE

Recall that the most basic requirement of a narrative is a chronological recapitulation of the successive events that comprise the reported personal experience (the eventline or timeline of a narrative) but that most narratives also contain various elaborations. Although there are a number of different versions of narrative analysis available (see Peterson & McCabe, 1983), the focus here is on one that has stimulated much thinking in the field of personal narratives, namely, Labov's (1972) high point analysis.

In Labov's description of narrative structure, the following elements occur (note that not all must be present in all narratives):

The *abstract* functions as a brief summary of the narrative as a whole or of its main point. In essence, it briefly informs the listener of what is to come. The occurrence of an abstract within an ongoing dialogue can also function as a speech act seeking permission to narrate (Romaine, 1985).

Orientation is the part of the narrative that provides contextual embedding for the listener. Here the speaker digresses from the events of the narrative in order to inform the listener of who the participants were, where and when the events occurred, to describe character and motivation, and so on. These are placed preponderantly at the beginning of a narrative but they can and do occur at any point.

The *complicating action* is the only obligatory component of a narrative. This consists of the chronologically described events that occurred prior to the climax or highpoint of the narrative. Recall that Labov's minimal definition of a narrative includes only two sequentially ordered events; these are complicating actions and they must be present for a narrative to be defined as such.

Evaluation is the provision of emotional information about the narrative. Labov saw narratives as consisting of two important functions, *reference* (what happened) and *evaluation*. The latter lets the listener know why the narrative was told, what its point is, what the narrator thought about the events, and so on. Evaluation can be incorporated into any narrative clause, of course, by means of phonological stress or other type of emphasis or highly colored vocabulary (see Peterson & McCabe, 1983). Nonetheless, it tends to regularly occur in independent clauses at the crisis or high point event of a narrative. Here the narrator pauses from event recapitulation in order to suspend the action, create tension and suspense, convey emotional significance, check on attentiveness of the listener, and so on. A number of researchers who do not necessarily agree with the other structural properties of narratives concur that evaluation (or communicating the "point" of a narrative) is crucial (Brewer, 1985; Longacre, 1983; Polanyi, 1985; Reichman, 1985; Romaine, 1985).

Resolution is the recapitulation of events that occur after the evaluative high point of the narrative. Such later events resolve the high point action in some sense, "clearing the stage or capping off the experience" (Peterson & McCabe, 1983, p. 31).

Codas are formalized endings of the narrative. Labov suggested that they return the focus of the conversation to the present, perhaps by showing relevance of the narrated events to the present situation. Others (Peterson & McCabe, 1983) have defined codas more broadly, seeing them as any sort of formal ending including "the end" or "that's all."

Although Labov's description of narrative structure was developed for adolescent and adult narrative productions, it has been applied to children's narratives as well (e.g., Kemper, 1984; Kernan, 1977; Umiker-Sebeok, 1979). The most extensive analysis of child narrative structures in terms of Labov's system to date, however, was done by ourselves (Peterson & McCabe, 1983). We traced the developmental acquisition of the classic pattern of Labovian structure in our 3½- to 9½-year-old subjects' three longest narratives (288 narratives in all) and found that although even our youngest children at times could approximate this pattern, it did not become predominant until children were 6 years of age. (See McCabe & Peterson, chap. 6 in this vol.) In addition, we described a number of alternative patterns of structure found in children's productions; these are detailed and illustrated in Peterson and McCabe (1983).

A narrative that was produced by a 7-year-old boy illustrating Labov's classic structure for personal narratives is the following (from Peterson & McCabe, 1983, pp. 233–234):

Narrative 3

E: Have you ever ridden it (his sister's horse Little Man)?

B: Yeah, just once.

E: Once?

B: Yeah, just once.

E: What happened?

B: We rode down around the pasture and *we* then *Little Man stopped* and then *I saw a rattlesnake. His tail was rattling. He was probably SCARED of it.*

E: And then what happened?

B: We rode right back and *he SQUASHED it with his hoof.*

E: Did he?

B: Yep. He squashed the snake with his hoof. It was real fast.

E: Oh. He squashed the snake with his hoof huh?

B: Yep. It was real quick. Then *we went back to the barn. He didn't want to step on any more snakes or his hoof would get all bloody and everything.*

In this narrative, the child details the events leading up to the high point event (seeing the rattlesnake) by means of three complicating actions, all connected by *and* or *and then.* The child then departs from the timeline in order to provide orientation about the snake's behavior and evaluation about someone being scared (although one is not sure if it was the horse or the snake). Note that there is no connective at the point of departure from the timeline nor between the orientation and evaluation. The narrator then returns to the timeline for a resolution event after an insertion of "And then what happened?" by the adult, and no connective could be expected here because the adult provided one. The child provides a second resolution (squashing the snake), connecting the two resolution clauses with *and.* After a repetition of one of these resolution events the child departs from the timeline again to add more evaluation about speed (no connective used), repeats this evaluation and then returns to the timeline with *then* to describe the resolution timeline event of going to the barn. Finally, the child leaves the timeline for the last time (using no connective) to talk about what the horse was probably feeling.

In the previous narrative, the narrator weaves a story that alternates between timeline events and off-the-line ancillary information that either orients the listener or provides evaluation. An important question is whether or not connectives are systematically used differently depending on the function of the narrative clauses they are connecting. Next, we compare the sorts of connections found between clauses that are both on the timeline versus between clauses that are both off the timeline. We also assess whether these two situations are different from the way that connectives are used when connecting a timeline event with an off-line event (i.e., a departure from the timeline), or an off-line event with a timeline event (i.e., a return to the timeline).

The narratives of our most productive and sophisticated narrators, the 9-year-olds, were analyzed in terms of how connective use interacted with type of juncture. In this analysis we included only contiguous child utterances with no intervening adult utterance. The oldest children were selected because younger ones were far more likely to take short turns at talk, with the adult inserting encouraging comments or back-channel responses or repeating for clarity what the child just said. In contrast, 9-year-olds were more likely to have long, uninterrupted stretches of narrative talk. Each narrative clause was classified in terms of the six units described by Labov. (See Peterson & McCabe, 1983, for extensive discussion and illustration of this classification.) Both abstracts and codas were rare, thus data on how they are connected with preceding and succeeding clauses is not presented and these junctures are not further analyzed. In addition, both complicating actions and resolutions are similar timeline events; because the only difference between them is whether they fall before or after the high point of the narrative, they are combined into timeline events in our analyses.

Each juncture between two clauses was classified as having no connective, connected by *and,* or connected by some other connective. In the present table, occurrences of *and then* and *and so* are summed with those occurrences of *and* in which it occurs alone. Our findings for the 9-year-olds are presented in Table 1.2.

Whether or not two clauses are linked by a connective is to some degree determined by whether those events are on or off the timeline. We look first at pairs of clauses that are homogeneous, that is, they involve no change of state from the first clause to the second. If one compares the pattern of connective use between two timeline events versus two off-the-line clauses, *and* is common in the former but less so in the latter. The majority of off-the-line clauses are merely juxtaposed, with no connective at all. A chi-square was calculated on the different patterns of use (no connective, *and,* or different connective) in these two situations (junctures between timeline clauses versus junctures between off-the-line clauses, regardless of whether they are orientation or evaluation), and the association was significant, $\chi^2(2, N = 16) = 116.59, p < .001$.[1]

Next, we analyzed pairs of clauses that involved changes of state between the first and second clause, that is, where one clause was on the timeline and the other clause was not. Comparing departures from the timeline with returns to the timeline, children use connectives differently in these two situations [$\chi^2(2, N = 16) = 35.74, p < .001$]. They are more likely to use simple juxtaposition when linking timeline events with off-the-line clauses (i.e., departures); in contrast, when returning to the timeline children are likely to use the connector *and*. Inspecting Table 1.2, it is apparent that evaluation and orientation are not equivalent off-the-line entities. When departing from the timeline, simple juxtaposition is most likely when the child departs to insert evaluation. On the other hand, returns to the timeline from orientation are more likely to elicit the connector *and* than are returns from the insertion of evaluation.

The differential use of juxtaposition found extends work done by Jisa (1987). When analyzing the narratives of 4- and 5-year-old French children that were produced during sessions of "show-and-tell," she commented that the children were likely to mark transitions between story events and teacher-directed or off-story comments by means of simple juxtaposition of the two clauses rather than linkage by *and*.

Chi-squares were calculated for comparisons between connective use and type of juncture with respect to orientation and evaluation separately. Comparing departures from the timeline to insert orientation with returns from orienting, a significantly different pattern of linkage was found, $\chi^2(2, N = 16) = 19.68, p < .001$. Although children equivalently use *and* and juxtaposition when they depart from the timeline to provide orientation, they are much more likely to use *and* when they return from orientation to the timeline. Comparing departures from the timeline to insert evaluation with returns from such comments, a significantly different pattern was again found, $\chi^2(2, N = 16) = 13.87, p < .001$. Children are most likely to rely on simple juxtaposition when departing from the timeline, but when returning they are more likely to use a connective of some kind.

Table 1.2 does not differentiate between various connectives; how-

---

[1]Note that although chi-square analysis assumes independent observation, and that assumption was violated here (the same subjects produced more than one memory), no other statistical analysis was more appropriate. Such statistical analysis as we did is congruent with inspection of the data. Furthermore, no subject contributed disproportionately to this pattern. This disclaimer holds throughout this chapter.

TABLE 1.2
Relationship Between Type of Juncture and Connective Use Between Narrative Clauses

	And	*No Connective*	*Other Connective*
Timeline + timeline	708 (62%)	300 (26%)	126 (11%)
Offline + offline	153 (35%)	239 (55%)	46 (10%)
Total departures	145 (38%)	198 (52%)	40 (10%)
For orientation	92 (42%)	100 (46%)	25 (12%)
For evaluation	53 (32%)	98 (59%)	15 (9%)
Total returns	230 (55%)	130 (31%)	60 (14%)
From orientation	179 (60%)	82 (28%)	35 (12%)
From evaluation	51 (41%)	48 (39%)	25 (20%)

ever, there are different patterns of use among them. In Table 1.3, for each connective, we have calculated the percentage of its usage for all types of links between timeline and off-line events.

In narratives of 9-year-olds, most occurrences of *then* (either alone or with *and*) link timeline events. The connectives *so* (again, by itself or combined with *and*), as well as the simple connector *and* are also found over half the time between two events. On the other hand, *because* mostly participates in junctures in which the second clause is off-the-line information and it makes no difference whether the first clause is off the timeline or on it (i.e., whether the connection is between two off-line comments or is a departure from the timeline). *Well* and *see* are more likely to mark returns to the timeline, and *but* seems to be used almost equivalently everywhere. In short, for the

TABLE 1.3
For Each Connective, the Percentage of its Uses that Link Different Types of Narrative Clauses

	Timeline + Timeline	*Offline + Offline*	*Departures from Timeline*	*Returns to Timeline*
Then	36 (78%)	0 (0%)	6 (13%)	4 (9%)
And Then	57 (61%)	11 (12%)	8 (8%)	18 (19%)
And	640 (57%)	141 (13%)	136 (12%)	205 (18%)
And So	11 (55%)	1 (5%)	1 (5%)	7 (35%)
So	58 (54%)	15 (14%)	10 (9%)	25 (23%)
But	21 (33%)	16 (25%)	9 (14%)	17 (27%)
Because	5 (16%)	11 (34%)	12 (38%)	4 (12%)
Well, See	3 (15%)	4 (20%)	3 (15%)	10 (50%)

Note. Connectives used for narrative openings are not tabulated here because these are found at the initiation of a child's turn at talk and do not connect two narrative clauses, as do the uses tabulated here.

most part children are using connectives differently at the various types of narrative junctures, and further, the connective that is chosen is related to the type of juncture being filled.

CONCLUSIONS

The crucial and definitional component of narrative is the reiteration of sequential events. The application of Grice's (1975) *Maxim of Orderliness* to any series of events told by a speaker to a listener results in the listener assuming the chronological order of those events. It is unnecessary for temporal relationship to be marked, or even for connectives to be used much at all unless some specialized semantic relationship such as causality is present. Nevertheless, narratives have a very high density of these theoretically unnecessary connective links, and the highest linkage of all is between events on the timeline where they are completely superfluous. Fully three-quarters of these clauses are linked by connectives, mostly by *and.*

Recall that a major distinction found in narrative clauses is between on-the-line event clauses and off-the-line tributary clauses and this distinction is so fundamental that some languages mark it by means of special affixes, particles, or word order (Longacre, 1983). In English, adults use different sentence syntax to differentiate these two (Labov, 1972). Our 9-year-old narrators were also differentially marking these two types of narrative components. Clearly there was no completely reliable signal based on connective usage; however, there were tendencies of use that were remarkably consistent. The connective *and* in particular seems to play a major role in demarcating whether or not any particular sentence conveys on-the-line events or tributary, off-the-line information. It is more likely to be present if the clause it introduces is a timeline event, or, in other words, *and* seems to be a signal that the following is probably an event belonging to the timeline. On the other hand, the lack of any sort of connective is most likely if the second clause is off the timeline, and it matters little whether or not the preceding clause was similarly an off-the-line comment or a timeline event.

In view of the regularity and complexity of the usage of connectives by young children, it would seem that connectives serve some crucial role as catalysts for comprehending extended discourse. In earlier work (McCabe & Peterson, 1985b), we explored the role of connectives in aiding narrative comprehensibility. We selected a sample of children's narratives and altered them in three ways. Although the clauses remained intact, the interclausal connectives were changed. In one experimental condition, all connectives were deleted. In a second condition, all junctures were filled by *and.* In a third condition, the connective that encoded the most specific semantic relationship existing between each two neighboring clauses was provided. Thus, causal relationships were encoded by *so* or *because,* temporal ones by *then,* antithetical ones by *but,* and simple coordinate relationships by *and.* The three versions of these child narratives were recorded and then played to college students who rated them on comprehensibility. To our surprise, presence or absence of connectives made no difference to narrative comprehensibility, nor did the specific identity of the connectives matter. Although narratives are typically bristling with connectives, they do not seem to register in understanding a story.

Furthermore, various researchers have noted the ubiquitousness of *and* in narration; McCutcheon and Perfetti (1982) and Beaman (1984) both concluded that such ubiquity meant children were not really using it systematically; that is, they dismissed *and* as a filler. Thus, even though connectives are used with great regularity in narrative, such nonsemantic usage, at least regarding the marking of narrative macrostructure, is not apparent even to those who have expended great effort studying connectives in narratives. Why such regularity of usage goes unappreciated even by close listeners and readers remains a puzzle regarding the use of connectives in narratives.

To conclude, connective use interfaces with the macrostructure of a narrative. Children produce conversational narratives as a multilevel event, with both comments that are chronological recapitulations of "what happened," and tributary comments that are directed to the listener to aid comprehension, monitor interest, and so on. Children use connectives to move between these two levels of discourse and to indicate where they are. Thus, a full understanding of a child's use of connectives requires an understanding of semantic usage, pragmatic usage, and of the macrostructure of the units linked by connectives.

SUMMARY

The study of narrative has focused on three themes: (a) narrative macrostructure, (b) cohesion between sentences, and (c) staging of perspective. This chapter focuses on the first two; specifically, we investigated one type of cohesion, intersentential connectives, and ways in which use of this cohesive device reflects narrative macrostructure.

Over 1,100 personal narratives told by 96 children between 3;6 and 9;6 constituted the data corpus. Connectives that occurred with regularity in these narratives were selected for investigation, including *so, because, but, then,* and *and.* The semantic relationships between clauses conjoined by each of these connectives was assessed, and although most uses of specific connectives were appropriately matched to their canonical meanings, a number of uses were not. The occurrence of some connectives in particular locations within a narrative could only be understood if one assessed pragmatic as well as semantic usage.

Pragmatically, connectives could mark narrative initiations and terminations within the ongoing conversation, chronological misordering of event recapitulation, and transitions between description of specific chronologically ordered events and listener-directed comments that served as embellishments. The connectives *so* and *but* in particular are frequently used at these pragmatic intersections, whereas *because* and *then* rarely are.

The connective *and* is also used pragmatically but serves a different role. It is likely to occur between successive events that lie on the timeline, and is relatively infrequent between listener-directed tributary comments such as background orientation or evaluation. More specifically, its use is a signal that the clause to come probably encodes an event within the chronological sequence of events that constitute the backbone or timeline of the narrative, and the absence of any connective indicates that the clause to come probably encodes tributary information. Thus, children use connectives in systematic ways to mark the macrostructure of narratives.

ACKNOWLEDGMENTS

We thank Michael Bruce-Lockhart for the development and use of the NARRAN software package. Further information about NARRAN or its availability can be obtained from Carole Peterson, Psychology Department, Memorial University of Newfoundland, St. John's, Newfoundland, Canada A1B 3X9. This research was supported by Natural Sciences and Engineering Research Council grant AO513 to Carole Peterson.

REFERENCES

Beaman, K. (1984). Coordination and subordination revisited: Syntactic complexity in spoken and written narrative discourse. In D. Tannen (Ed.), *Coherence in spoken and written discourse* (pp. 45–80). Norwood, NJ: Ablex.

Bloom, L., Lahey, M., Hood, L., Lifter, K., & Fiess, K. (1980). Complex sentences: Acquisition of syntactic connectives and the semantic relations they encode. *Journal of Child Language, 7,* 235–261.

Brewer, W. (1985). The story schema: Universal and culture-specific properties. In D. Olson, N. Torrance, & A. Hildyard (Eds.), *Literacy, language and learning.* Cambridge, Eng.: Cambridge University Press.

Brown, A. L. (1975). Recognition, reconstruction, and recall of narrative sequences by preoperational children. *Child Development, 46,* 156–166.

Brown, A. L., & Murphy, M. D. (1975). Reconstruction of arbitrary logical sequences by preschool children. *Journal of Experimental Child Psychology, 20,* 307–326.

Bullock, M., & Gelman, R. (1979). Preschool children's assumptions about cause and effect: Temporal ordering. *Child Development, 50,* 89–96.

Carlson, L. (1983). *Dialogue games.* Dordrecht, Netherlands: Reidel.

Cieri, C. (1985). AND and the English narrative: A story of continuity. *Penn Review of Linguistics, 9,* 116.

Clancy, P., Jacobsen, T., & Silva, M. (1976). The acquisition of conjunction: A cross-linguistic study. *Papers & Reports on Child Language Development, 12,* 71–80.

de Beaugrande, R. (1980). *Text, discourse, and process: Toward a multidisciplinary science of texts.* Norwood, NJ: Ablex.

Dore, J. (1985). Children's conversations. In T. A. van Dijk (Ed.), *Handbook of discourse analysis, Vol. 3: Discourse and dialogue* (pp. 47–65). London: Academic Press.

Eisenberg, A. R. (1980). A syntactic, semantic, and pragmatic analysis of conjunction. *Papers & Reports on Child Language Development, 19,* 70–78.

Eisenberg, A. R. (1985). Learning to describe past experiences in conversation. *Discourse Processes, 8,* 177–204.

French, L., & Nelson, K. (1985). *Young children's knowledge of relational terms: Some ifs, ors, and buts.* New York: Springer-Verlag.

Gallagher, T., & Craig, H. (1987). An investigation of pragmatic connectives within preschool peer interactions. *Journal of Pragmatics, 11,* 27–37.

Gopnik, M. (1986). The development of connexity in young children. In J. S. Petöfi (Ed.), *Text connectedness from a psychological point of view.* Hamburg, Germany: Helmut Buske Verlag, 64–95.

Green, S. (1977). Causal attribution of emotion in kindergarten children. *Developmental Psychology, 13,* 533–534.

Grice, H. P. (1975). Logic and conversation. In P. Cole & J. L. Morgan (Eds.), *Syntax and semantics, Vol. 3: Speech acts.* New York: Academic Press, 41–58.

Grimes, J. (1975). *The thread of discourse.* The Hague: Mouton.

Grimes, J. (1978). Narrative studies in oral texts. In W. U. Dressler (Ed.), *Current trends in textlinguistics.* Berlin: Walter de Gruyter, 123–132.

Halliday, M. A. K., & Hasan, R. (1976). *Cohesion in English.* New York: Longman.

Hedberg, N. L. (1984). Development of narrative abilities in preschool children: A cross-sectional study. In D. S. Rood (Ed.), *1983 MidAmerica linguis-*

tics conference papers. Boulder, CO: Department of Linguistics, University of Colorado, 165–173.

Hedberg, N. L., & Stoel-Gammon, C. (1984). The development of procedures for analyzing cohesion. In D. S. Rood (Ed.), *1983 MidAmerica linguistics conference papers* (174–180). Boulder, CO: Department of Linguistics, University of Colorado.

Hood, L., Lahey, M., Lifter, K., & Bloom, L. (1978). Observational, descriptive methodology in studying child language: Preliminary results on the development of complex sentences. In G. P. Sackett (Ed.), *Observing behavior, Vol. 1: Theory and application in mental retardation* (pp. 239–263). Baltimore: University Park Press.

Jisa, H. (1984–1985). French preschoolers' use of *et pis* ('and then'). *First Language, 5,* 169–184.

Jisa, H. (1987). Sentence connectors in French children's monologue performance. *Journal of Pragmatics, 11,* 607–621.

Johnson, B. E., & Johnson, D. D. (1985). Elementary students' comprehension of anaphora in well-formed stories. *Journal of Educational Research, 78,* 221–223.

Kail, M., & Weissenborn, J. (1984). A developmental cross-linguistic study in adversative connectives: French 'mais' and German 'aber/sondern.' *Journal of Child Language, 11,* 143–158.

Kemper, S. (1984). The development of narrative skills: Explanations and entertainments. In S. Kuczaj (Ed.), *Discourse development.* New York: Springer-Verlag, 101–124.

Kernan, K. T. (1977). Semantic and expressive elaboration in children's narratives. In S. Ervin-Tripp & C. Mitchell-Kernan (Eds.), *Child discourse.* New York: Academic Press, 91–102.

Klecab-Aker, J. S., & Lopez, B. (1985). A comparison of T-units and cohesive ties used by first and third grade children. *Language and Speech, 28,* 307–315.

Kun, A. (1978). Evidence for preschoolers' understanding of causal direction in extended causal sequences. *Child Development, 49,* 218–222.

Labov, W. (1972). *Language in the inner city.* Philadelphia: University of Pennsylvania Press.

Labov, W., & Waletzky, J. (1967). Narrative analysis: Oral versions of personal experience. In J. Helm (Ed.), *Essays on the verbal and visual arts* (pp. 12–44). Seattle: University of Washington Press.

Laubitz, A. (1988). *Coordinate and subordinate conjunctions in children's texts.* Unpublished doctoral dissertation, McGill University, Montreal.

Longacre, R. (1983). Vertical threads of cohesion in discourse. In F. Neubauer (Ed.), *Coherence in natural language texts* (pp. 99–113). Philadelphia: John Benjamin.

Martin, J. R. (1983). The development of register. In J. Fine & R. Freedle (Ed.), *Developmental issues in discourse* (1–39). Norwood, NJ: Ablex.

McCabe, A., & Peterson, C. (1985a). A naturalistic study of the production of causal connectives by children. *Journal of Child Language, 12,* 145–159.

McCabe, A., & Peterson, C. (1985b, August). *The function of sentential connectives in discourse.* Paper presented at the meetings of the American Psychological Association, Los Angeles.

McCabe, A., & Peterson, C. (1988). A comparison of adults' versus children's spontaneous use of *because* and *so. Journal of Genetic Psychology, 149,* 257–268.

McClure, E., & Geva, E. (1983). The development of the cohesive use of adversative conjunctions in discourse. *Discourse Processes, 6,* 411–432.

McCutchen, D., & Perfetti, C. (1982). Coherence and connectedness in the development of discourse production. *Text, 2,* 113–139.

NcNeill, D. (1987). *Psycholinguistics: A new approach.* New York: Harper & Row.

Miller, P. J., & Sperry, L. L. (1988). Early talk about the past: The origins of conversational stories of personal experience. *Journal of Child Language, 15,* 293–315.

Nelson, K. (1978). How young children represent knowledge of their world in and out of language: A preliminary report. In R. Siegler (Ed.), *Children's thinking what develops?* (pp. 255–273). Hillsdale, NJ: Lawrence Erlbaum Associates.

Nelson, K. (1986). *Event knowledge: Structure and function in development.* Hillsdale, NJ: Lawrence Erlbaum Associates.

Pellegrini, A. D. (1982). The construction of cohesive text by preschoolers in two play contexts. *Discourse Processes, 5,* 101–108.

Pellegrini, A. D. (1984). The effect of dramatic play on children's generation of cohesive text. *Discourse Processes, 7,* 57–67.

Peterson, C. (1986). Semantic and pragmatic uses of *but. Journal of Child Language, 13,* 583–590.

Peterson, C., & McCabe, A. (1983). *Developmental psycholinguistics: Three ways of looking at a child's narrative.* New York: Plenum.

Peterson, C., & McCabe, A. (1985). Understanding "because": How important is the task? *Journal of Psycholinguistic Research, 14,* 199–218.

Peterson, C., & McCabe, A. (1987a). The structure of *and* coordinations in children's narratives. *Journal of Psycholinguistic Research, 16,* 467–490.

Peterson, C., & McCabe, A. (1987b). The connective *and:* Do older children use it less as they learn other connectives? *Journal of Child Language, 14,* 375–381.

Peterson, C., & McCabe, A. (1988). The connective *and* as discourse glue. *First Language, 8,* 19–28.

Peterson, C., & McCabe, A. (in press). On the threshold of the storyrealm: Semantic versus pragmatic use of connectives in narratives. *Merrill Palmer Quarterly.*

Piaget, J. (1972). *The child's conception of physical causality.* Totowa, NJ: Littlefield, Adams. (Original work published 1930).

Polanyi, L. (1985). *Telling the American story.* Norwood, NJ: Ablex.

Pratt, M. W., & MacKenzie-Keating, S. (1985). Organizing stories: Effects of development and task difficulty on referential cohesion in narrative. *Developmental Psychology, 21,* 350–356.

Prince, G. (1982). *Narratology: The form and functioning of narrative.* Berlin: Moutin.

Reichman, R. (1985). *Getting computers to talk like you and me: Discourse context, focus and semantics (An ATN Model).* Cambridge, MA: MIT Press.

Romaine, S. (1985). Grammar and style in children's narratives. *Linguistics, 23,* 83–104.

Sachs, J. (1983). Talking about the there and then: The emergence of displaced reference in parent-child discourse. In K. E. Nelson (Ed.), *Children's language.* (Vol. 4, pp. 1–28). New York: Gardner Press.

Scott, C. (1984). Adverbial connectivity in conversations of children 6-12. *Journal of Child Language, 11,* 423–452.

Umiker-Sebeok, D. J. (1979). Preschool children's intraconversational narratives. *Journal of Child Language, 6,* 91–109.

van Dijk, T. A. (1979). Pragmatic connectives. *Journal of Pragmatics, 3,* 447–456.

van Dijk, T. A. (1981). *Studies in the pragmatics of discourse.* New York: Mouton.

Zammuner, V. L. (1986). Children's coherence in discourse: A review. In J. S. Petöfi (Ed.), *Text connectedness from a psychological point of view* (pp. 24–63). Hamburg, Germany: Helmut Buske Verlag.

CHAPTER 2

Kinds of Narrative: Genre Skills Among First Graders From Two Communities

Deborah Hicks
Department of Educational Development
University of Delaware

INTRODUCTION

A salient type of discourse in children's preschool language learning environment is *narrative* discourse, the linguistic means through which speakers represent both real-life and fictional events. Not surprisingly, narrative is also the link to many classroom activities, such as fictional story telling, sharing time episodes, and running commentaries or explanations. And yet, narrative is not simply one kind of discourse, but a family of discourses in which speakers make references to series of events and actions. Narrative texts may range in kind from ongoing descriptions of everyday activities ("I'm gonna add some water to this soup.") to lengthy fictional accounts ("Sam Spade walked in the door, took the telephone off its hook, and sat down.").

The ability to produce narrative renditions of events occurring in both real and fictional contexts is a skill that emerges as early as 2 years of age (McCabe & Peterson, chap. 6 in this vol.). The kinds of narrative skills that are refined during the early years of schooling, however, are of particular interest for several reasons. First, the range of social interactions that children experience is greatly expanded during the primary school years, calling for the use of more widely differentiated forms of discourse. Moreover, children experience cognitive development during the 5- to 7-year age range that is unique, consistent with their expanding social worlds (White, 1970; White & Siegel, 1984). Finally, during the early years of schooling, children make the important transition to the use of second-order symbol systems: writing, drawing, and dramatic enactment (Gardner, 1982; Vygotsky, 1978). Thus, language development in the primary school years is intimately linked to children's rapidly expanding social and representational worlds.

In this chapter, I examine first-grade children's abilities to produce a range of kinds of narratives, or narrative genres. The analyses in this chapter are drawn from a study in which children from two communities were shown a shortened version of the film, *The Red Balloon,* and were asked to narrate the film's events in three ways. The chapter has three sections. In the first section, I propose a theoretical framework in which narrative development is viewed as the development of a repertoire of narrative genre skills. To arrive at this theory, I explore multiple perspectives on genre and multiple perspectives on children's narrative development. In a second section, I present a case study of narrative texts produced by a low-income African-American first grader and by a middle-income white first grader. Through qualitative textual analyses, I explore differences in the children's interpretations of the narrative tasks. Finally, in a concluding section, I turn to the issue of cultural differences in children's narrative genre skills. I suggest that narrative development as a universal phenomenon is manifested in multiple ways, reflecting the differing social worlds in which children are participants.

GENRE SKILLS AS SOCIAL KNOWLEDGE

The term *genre* is used intuitively to refer to different ways of representing events, whether the medium of expression be written text, film, or art. One can easily imagine a conversation in which a certain film is depicted as representative of *film noir* (*Breathless*) or new wave cinema (*Jules and Jim*), or in which a particular novel is described as being a detective genre (*The Thin Man*) or a piece of fantasy (*The Hobbit*). In addition to its more casual usage, genre has occupied a central place in literary theory. In classical genre theory, from the time of the Renaissance and extending into the 18th century, genre was used to refer to literary kinds, such as ode, tragedy, satire, comedy, and elegy (Wellek & Warren, 1949). In contemporary theory, however, the defining characteristic of genre is the notion of change, in that literary kinds undergo continual renewal with the addition of each new piece of literature (Fowler, 1982).

Aside from occupying a key position in literary theory over the course of several centuries, genre has been examined more recently as both a cognitive and social/semiotic phenomenon. First, in his work on different "modes" of thought—narrative and nonnarrative—Bruner (1986) explored the possibility that genre may be a means through which speakers both cognitively and linguistically structure events in real-life and fictional contexts. Thus, for Bruner, genre is not simply an important facet of literary interpretation; it is an essential component of the way in which individuals represent events.

> If we ask then about the nature and role of *psychological* genre—the reader's conception of what kind of story or text he is encountering or "recreating"—we are in fact asking not only a morphological question about the actual text, but also a question about the interpretative processes that are loosed by the text in the reader's mind. (p. 7)

In contrast to this view of genre as a cognitive phenomenon, Bakhtin (1986) presented a theory of genre as a social phenomenon. Bakhtin extended genre to characterize any discourse, be it a casual conversation or a lengthy written text. Central to his theory of genre is the belief that what he terms *secondary* genres—novels, dramas, scientific texts—are derived from *primary* genres that arise in everyday contexts. Thus, for Bakhtin, genre is an essential component of meaning, of how two speakers construct a mutually intelligible discourse. As an example, in a discussion of a new computer software package, speakers arrive at shared meaning in part through their knowledge of "how one talks about computers" (see Sperber & Wilson, 1986). Thus, genre becomes a key component of the shared construction of meaning rather than simply a means of categorizing texts.

> We speak only in definite speech genres, that is, all our utterances have definite and relatively stable forms of constructions of the whole. . . . If speech genres did not exist and we had not mastered them, if we had to originate them during the speech process and construct each utterance at will for the first time, speech communication would be almost impossible. (p. 78–79)

Genre can therefore be examined from a variety of theoretical perspectives: literary, cognitive, and social/semiotic. In the present study, I focus on the sociolinguistic origins of genre knowledge. In particular, I adopt the perspective that speakers' abilities to enter into conversation, narrate past and present events, and engage in story telling and word play are linked to their repertoires of social knowledge. As children move within ever-widening circles of social interaction, they develop multiple ways of representing their knowledge through language. The development of a repertoire of narrative skills can thus be viewed as a dimension of children's increasingly sophisticated use of language in a variety of social contexts.

NARRATIVE DEVELOPMENT AND GENRE SKILLS

Research on language development in the preschool years suggests that narrative skills arise within the rich environment of children's interactions with peers and family members. The cognitive and linguistic ability to represent a series of events can be linked among young children to activities that are experienced on a regular basis. Children develop repertoires of knowledge about routine events in their lives: eating, playing, sleeping, grocery shopping. This event knowledge then becomes the basis for the linguistic representation of past and present events (Gerhardt, 1988; Nelson, 1978, 1986; Nelson & Gruendel, 1981). Thus, the cognitive ability to represent events has its origin in children's interaction with their social world (McNamee, 1979; Vygotsky, 1962, 1973; White & Siegel, 1984).

Children's repertoire of event knowledge is not, however, unidimensional, limited to one and only one means of representing events. As children move among a range of social settings in their primary language learning environments, they experience different ways of representing knowledge through narrative. The research on narrative development has in fact documented a range of narrative skills among preschool children. Through conversations about past and present events, children develop what Stoel-Gammon and Scliar-Cabral (1977) termed the *reportative function,* or the ability to make reference to personally experienced events (Eisenberg, 1985; Engel, 1986; Fivush & Fromhoff, 1988; Fivush, Gray, & Fromhoff, 1987; Miller & Sperry, 1988; Ninio, 1988; Peterson & McCabe, 1983). Young children also develop the ability to talk about fictional events through their involvement with fantasy play (Applebee, 1978; Hicks & Wolf, 1988; Rubin & Wolf, 1979; Sutton-Smith, Botvin, & Mahoney, 1976). Thus, children bring to their primary school classrooms a repertoire of narrative skills acquired through social interactions in a range of contexts (Hudson & Shapiro, chap. 3 in this vol.; Preece, 1987).

Even though all children share the common experience of representing their knowledge through narrative discourse, there are also sociocultural differences in what Heath (1982, 1983) termed "ways of telling." Children from predominately white middle-income communities are likely to experience narrative as factual accounts of personally experienced events and as fictional stories read from storybooks (Heath, 1982, 1983; Scollon & Scollon, 1981; Snow, 1983; Wells, 1985). Children from some African-American communities are more likely to experience narrative as personal accounts told in the midst of lively conversation (Heath, 1982, 1983). Finally, children from both Hawaiian and Athabaskan communities are likely to experience narrative as a performance in which the text is jointly constructed by speaker and audience (Scollon & Scollon, 1980, 1984; Watson-Gegeo & Boggs, 1977). Thus, there is considerable variation among communities in the kinds of narrative texts that children experience in their primary language learning environments, and bring as background knowledge to their first-grade (or kindergarten) classrooms.

In summary, narrative development can be viewed as multifaceted. All children develop repertoires of event knowledge based on their participation in a range of social settings. Also, children from diverse sociocultural communities experience narrative discourse in different forms because they are participants in differing kinds of social settings. When viewed from a sociolinguistic perspective, the development of narrative skills, or the ability to talk about series of events, cannot be distinguished from the development of genre skills, or the ability to adapt to specific occasions of language use. In the research study described later, I explore the narrative genre skills of first graders from two communities. Through textual analyses of their differing "ways of telling," I hope to shed light on the range of narrative skills that children from both communities bring to their primary school classrooms.

DATA COLLECTION AND ANALYSIS

The narratives that are the basis for the present analysis were collected at two separate elementary schools. The first was a private elementary school in the vicinity of Cambridge, Massachusetts. Children in this school were for the most part members of middle-income families in which one or both parents worked in professional job settings. The second was a public elementary school in the vicinity of Wilmington, Delaware. Children in this school were largely members of working-class or low-income families, although the school also drew on a housing development of mostly middle-income families.

Fifty-eight children from the private elementary school (20 first graders) and 12 children from the public elementary school (all first graders) performed three narrative tasks. In the present analysis, I examine in detail the oral narratives produced by one first grader from each of the two schools. These two children were chosen as highly skilled speakers who produced complete (in terms of plot structure) and engaging texts for all three narrative tasks. Through detailed textual analyses, I demonstrate that both children bring a sophisticated repertoire of narrative skills to the tasks. I also suggest that the two children interpret the tasks in subtly different ways. I discuss these interpretative differences in light of the theoretical approach presented earlier in this chapter.

The data collection in the private elementary school formed part of a larger research project examining primary school children's narrative skills. The project was based on Heath's (1982, 1983) ethnographic research on language learning in three communities. The project was designed to examine the abilities of children in grades K–2 to perform language tasks that draw on a range of narrative genre skills (Hicks, 1988, 1990a, 1990b). The second research project represents an attempt to extend this research to members of a different community setting. In this second school setting (already noted), I identified children from low-income families through their participation in the school's free lunch program. Although it was not my original intent to base this second study on issues of ethnicity, I found that the majority of children participating in the free lunch program were members of African-American communities. The research on language development in the preschool years suggests that African-American and white children may be exposed to different ways of representing events through narrative. Consequently, I decided to focus this second study specifically on low-income African-American first graders.

Children in both research settings were given identical narrative tasks. Children were shown a shortened (14-minute) version of the silent film, *The Red Balloon,* and were asked to perform three tasks: (a) provide a simultaneous *eventcast* (sportscast) as they rewatched a 3-minute segment from the film, (b) provide a factual *news report* of the events in the film, and (c) tell the film's events as a *story.* As a facilitation of their understanding of the tasks, children were provided with an opening script for each task. These opening scripts are shown in the appendix. For the story-telling task, children were also given as a prop a "storybook," having one large picture from the film on its front cover (a closeup of the main character—a young boy—putting the balloon's string in his mouth) but only blank white pages inside.

The film shown for the two projects is a classic children's film, in which the very few words spoken are in French (the boy calls to the balloon on several occasions). For the purposes of the study, the film was edited, so that a number of subplots were excluded. This edited version of the film consisted of the basic sequence of events shown in Table 2.1.

In the analysis of narrative texts, the way in which one determines the boundaries of individual utterances (or lines) constitutes an important methodological decision. Various criteria have been adopted for delineating utterances in studies of children's narratives: clausal (predicate) structure (Berman & Slobin, 1986); intonation and breathing boundaries (Scollon & Scollon, 1981); "idea units," or tonal groups corresponding to speakers' cognitive chunking of words (Chafe, 1980); and, with very young children in particular, episodes of talk about events (Miller & Sperry, 1988). In this study, I base my analyses of texts on a delineation of what Gee (1986) referred to as *lines* and *stanzas* (see also Hymes, 1981, 1982). Lines are individual utterances within the narrative, most often simple clauses (at least in the case of children's narratives), that terminate in a rising or falling pitch glide. Stanzas are groupings of lines, determined in part from common topics or themes and in part from structural, lexical, and intonational parallelism found between contiguous lines. An analysis based on lines and stanzas enables one to address sociocultural differences in how children thematically and structurally organize their narrative tellings. In other words, it is not simply the relations existing between utterances that are of importance in the analysis of narrative texts. Rather, it is the organization of sets of utterances, or what Hymes (1982) referred to as the "grammar of experience."

The delineation of lines and stanzas within texts is not a linguistic "given" in that there is no one defining set of characteristics on which

TABLE 2.1
Sequence of Events in *The Red Balloon*

1.	A boy finds a red balloon tied to a lamppost.
2.	He takes a bus on his way home, and the balloon follows the bus.
3.	After leaving the bus, a gang of boys tries to take the balloon from him.
4.	The following day, the boy goes to church with an elderly woman (grandmother?), and the balloon follows.
5.	The boy and the balloon are taken out of church by a guard.
6.	The boy goes inside a bakery and leaves his balloon outside.
7.	The gang of boys steals his balloon.
8.	The boy recaptures his balloon from the gang, and the gang of boys chases the boy and the balloon.
9.	The gang of boys surrounds the boy and pops the balloon.
10.	A large number of balloons come down to the boy and carry him into the sky.

to base an analysis. Some elements of language can easily be determined on the basis of a simple constitutive feature, as in the case of the *-ing* ending that marks progressive aspect. In text analyses, however, the analysis is based on constellations of linguistic features that lend evidence for a particular structural analysis. In the text analyses that follow, I draw on patterns of grammatical, lexical, and prosodic similarity as I attempt to determine how lines are grouped within texts. In fact, the determination of groupings of lines within the four texts examined is a central part of my analysis. I would like to end this discussion of analytic methods by stressing that the analyses in this chapter are interpretative in nature. That is to say, although in each instance I provide support for my particular textual analyses, the possibility exists that other equally plausible analyses exist for each of the narratives in question. This does not, in my view, undermine the analyses presented. In fact, anthropologists and cultural critics have recently begun to call into question the existence of empirical "facts," suggesting that multiple interpretations form part of what Rosaldo (1989) termed the "remaking of social analysis" (see also Clifford, 1988, for a discussion of similar issues).

THE NARRATIVE SKILLS OF A LOW-INCOME BLACK FIRST GRADER

A textual examination of the three narratives produced by a low-income African-American first grader, Cynthia, reveals a range of sophisticated narrative skills. Rather than simply listing the events from the film in a sequential manner, Cynthia manipulates temporal sequence as she creates individual texts. The three texts produced by Cynthia are distinct both in terms of the amount of information provided and in terms of how the information is presented. Interestingly, her news-reporting and event-casting narratives are highly evaluated texts, through the use of expressive intonation and references to characters' internal states. Her story text (or that produced for the story-telling task) is more a summary of events. As I point out later in this section, this particular approach to the narrative tasks differs substantially from that of Jessica, a middle-income white first grader. Cynthia's news-reporting narrative is outlined below.

The transcription symbols used in the excerpts from children's narrative texts are derived from the CHILDES coding system for child language analysis (see MacWhinney & Snow, 1985). The following key to these symbols may facilitate the reading of narrative texts in this chapter:

#	pause
# #	long pause
/	retracing
/ /	retracing with correction
!	phonological stress
^	rising intonation
-	falling intonation
^-	rising-falling (sing-song) intonation
<>	marking of text (often to indicate overlap)

Cynthia:

Stanza 1
well # when they was to the end
he had all^ these balloons
he was flying up in the sky
and no! boys couldn't reach him

Stanza 2
and so what I^ see happen
he / he // him and his mama # they went to the church
and # so # he went out
and he went

Stanza 3
and all this noise # all this racket came
and this man [the church guard] came out there trying to get 'im
and the man said xxxx

Deborah:
the man what?

Cynthia:
the man just stood like this [she demonstrates the stance of the guard at the church—very stern and stiff]
and they just let the boy go

Stanza 4
and then come all^ these boys chasin 'im
at first the / the boys started # 'cause they^ wanted that red balloon
the boy wanted it first
that little boy he had his mom # he wanted it first

Stanza 5
so he / so he went on a bus
he let it go
and it was following him
whereever he was going

Stanza 6
so that boy got off

and just grabbed the balloon(s)
and he had all^ them balloons up in the sky
and that was the end

As I noted in an earlier discussion of methods of analysis, I focus my textual analyses on an examination of the *stanza* structure within individual texts. In Cynthia's news-reporting text, stanzas appear to be groupings of four lines, each ending with evaluative commentary, with a rephrasing of information presented in a previous line, or with both evaluation and repetition. If one considers Cynthia's use of lexical and phrasal repetition to be a type of evaluation, a commonly occurring pattern of (a) narrative events, followed by (b) evaluation, emerges in her text.

In stanza 1, Cynthia presents a summary of the events seen in the film. This first stanza is a complete narrative in itself, in that the climactic final events from the film are recounted. Through the use of a temporal adverbial phrase ("when they was to the end"), Cynthia orients the listener to the temporal locus of events. Then, through the use of two stressed intensifiers (*all, no*!), she produces a highly evaluated account of the final events occurring in the film. Thus, in her opening stanza, Cynthia provides what might be termed an *abstract* (Labov, 1972), in which she swiftly summarizes the most climactic events in the film.

In the first line of stanza 2, Cynthia reorients the listener by calling on some phrasing introduced by the experimenter. Recall that the experimenter (myself) provided an opening script for each task in order to facilitate children's transition between tasks. In the opening script for the news-reporting task, I used the phrasing "the first thing that I saw happen" in an effort to elicit a factual report as opposed to a more highly evaluated story (see appendix). This phrasing is utilized by Cynthia in stanza 2 as a means of shifting to sequentially earlier events in the film ("and so what I^ see happen . . ."). She provides an account of the church scene in the film, in which the main character is taken to church by an elderly woman. As is the case with additional stanzas in her text, in line 4 Cynthia repeats information from the third line of the stanza:

and # so # he went out
and he went

Given that the following line contains a shift in thematic topic ("and all this noise . . ."), I have interpreted line 4 as the final line in stanza 2.

In the grouping of lines that I have designated as stanza 3, Cynthia relates the events centered on the young boy being taken from church by a guard (the balloon has entered the church, creating havoc inside). I interrupted Cynthia midstream to ask for a clarification, consequently it is difficult to determine the precise boundaries of this stanza. Given the assumption that stanzas are often organized around one central thematic subject (Gee, 1986), I have interpreted Cynthia's thematic shift to the gang of boys ("and then come all^ these boys . . ."), marked linguistically by use of the indefinite form *these,* as the beginning of stanza 4. Given this grouping of lines, the final line in stanza 3 ("and they just let the boy go") functions as a summary of the events taking place in the church.

Stanza 4 as a whole seems to be mostly evaluative in nature. Cynthia describes the internal motivations underlying the gang's attempts to steal the balloon ("at first the / the boys started # 'cause they wanted that red balloon") as well as the motivations behind the main character's attempts to protect his balloon from the gang ("the boy wanted it first"). In the final line of stanza 4, she provides elaboration on the referent of *the boy* as she also repeats information related in the previous line:

> the boy wanted it first
> that little boy he had his mom # he wanted it first

In my view, stanza 4 represents a sophisticated narrative move, in which the narrator steps aside from a sequential rendition of "what happened" in order to provide evaluative detail on the underlying motivations of characters. This account of character motivations in stanza 4 underscores the conflict that permeates the entire text.

The grouping of lines that I have interpreted as stanza 5 marks a temporal shift in the action. The scene described by Cynthia in stanza 5, in which the boy gets on a bus with his balloon, actually occurs near the beginning of the film, long before the events occurring at the church. As was the case with stanza 4, however, stanza 5 appears to be largely evaluative in nature. Here, Cynthia relates an important dimension of the relationship between the young boy and the balloon: the fact that the balloon followed the boy under its own volition. Through the use of a postposed adverbial phrase, Cynthia underscores this unique friendship:

> and it [the balloon] was following him everywhere
> whereever he was going

It may well be the case that, although sequentially noncontiguous with stanza 4, stanza 5 is thematically contiguous with Cynthia's emphasis on the nature of the boy's relationship with the balloon. In stanza 4, Cynthia stresses the conflict that arises when both the gang of boys and the young boy want the balloon. In stanza 5, she reminds the listener that, in fact, the balloon follows the young boy even when he rides a bus. Thus, in stanzas 4 and 5, both a conflict and also its partial resolution are established.

Finally, in stanza 6 Cynthia juxtaposes events from the previous stanza (the balloon following the bus) with information drawn from the final scenes of the film. Returning to a theme established in stanza 1, she relates how the boy is carried away by balloons. Instead of focusing her conclusion on the popping of the balloon by the gang of boys, Cynthia focuses her conclusion on the resolution of the conflict between the boy and the gang of boys. At the end of her text, the young boy gets not only his balloon (the red balloon) but also additional balloons. Interestingly, the resolution narrated in stanza 6 is symmetrical with the summary presented in stanza 1. Thus, considered as a whole, Cynthia's response to the news-reporting task is a complex manipulation of temporal sequence that results in a symmetrical and highly evaluated rendition of events in the film.

In her response to the story-telling task, Cynthia provides a shorter summary of the events occurring in the film. In what I have represented as two stanzas, she provides detail on the events occurring at the beginning of the film, in which the boy gets the balloon from a lamppost, then swiftly moves to the final events in the film. Interestingly, this story-telling summary of events more closely resembles a newscast of events than her response to the news-reporting task. Here, only extremely important events are narrated. However, it is probably the case that Cynthia interpreted the story-telling task as one of telling *about* the book. Before I was able to finish my opening script for the story-telling task, Cynthia began a narration centered on the storybook prop she was holding. Because of the importance of this spontaneous narration for an interpretation of her text, I have included my opening script along with Cynthia's response. The following is Cynthia's story-telling narrative:

Deborah:
ok # this is Cynthia and Deborah
and we're gonna be great^ storytellers . . .

Cynthia:
about this book
when it gets to the end

this boy's gonna have # all these balloons
and it's gonna fly him up

Deborah:
right!

Cynthia:
I think I'll do this

Deborah:
ok # so let me start off being the storyteller
and then Cynthia is gonna take over
The Red Balloon
once upon a time there was a little boy who lived in France
one day # on his way to the busstop # he found a big # beautiful # red balloon
he wanted the balloon to be his friend
and here's Cynthia # storyteller

Cynthia:
Stanza 1
he climbed up
and got the red balloon
and he put it in his mouth

Stanza 2
so when it was to the end
he flied^ up # in the sky with all^ these balloons
and # the end

Clearly, Cynthia's response to the story-telling task is based on the fact that she is describing the fictional contents of the book she is holding in addition to narrating the sequential events from the film. In stanza 1 (or, stanza 2, if one interprets her initial narration as the first part of her story text), she provides detail on the opening scene from the film. This may well be a response to my opening script, in which I emphasize this initial scene. In stanza 2 (stanza 3?), Cynthia orients the listener to a change in temporal locus through her use of a temporal adverbial phrase ("so when it was to the end"). As was the case with her earlier spontaneous narration ("about this book . . ."), she centers her story on the final scene from the film. Given the task at hand, which is one of narrating a story while holding a book, her response is both engaging and appropriate. Rather than providing the listener with a detailed listing of events, she assumes the perspective of providing a report about the book as she summarizes the essential plotline of the film.

The final narrative text to be examined in this section is the one produced by Cynthia for the event-casting, or on-line, narration task.

Recall that for this task children were presented with a 3-minute segment from the film, after having already seen the film in its entirety, and were asked to provide an ongoing "sportscast" of the film (see appendix). Most of the children performed this task with a good deal of enthusiasm, and Cynthia was no exception. Her on-line narration of the 3-minute clip from the film was lengthy and engaging. In the text to come, I have presented the narrative as a whole, without attempting to segment this text into stanzas. I have chosen to omit a stanza analysis for the on-line narratives produced by both Cynthia and Jessica, because these simultaneous, film-driven narrations do not readily lend themselves to an analysis based on groupings of lines. Cynthia's on-line narrative suggests that many lines in her text represent a linguistic *description* of events. I have numbered individual lines so that I can refer to these line numbers in my discussion of the text.

Cynthia:

1. I see that red balloon
2. they took! it
3. and they ran
4. and then the boy's # he # the boy's looking all / looking all over for it
5. and what he's eatin is a hot dog
6. and them boys is running up to take // they is going // they uhm / they got the red balloon
7. and they is running
8. and one has gone to the end
9. he's gonna get all them balloons
10. he's gonna be flyin # up on the // up in the sky
11. and the boys cannot catch 'im
12. and what they gonna do # he gonna find them boys
13. he gonna see the red^ balloon [with rhythmic, almost musical intonation]
14. and gonna // the boys gonna pull it
15. and he's gonna pull
16. and them boys run after^ him
17. and they're gonna // and the boy / the boy gonna run

Deborah:
can you say what you see happening here?

Cynthia:
what's happening here?

Deborah:
yeah

Cynthia:

18. I see the boy's! walkin
19. and he's puttin his head up in the sky
20. and he's looking for it
21. and they was tryin to shoot the balloon
22. and they fightin
23. and they're / and they're pullin the balloon
24. and he said # "come here balloon # balloon"
25. he's sayin that

do you want me to say everything that I see? [to Deborah]

Deborah:

yeah # I want you to say everything that you see happening

Cynthia:

26. they're fighting
27. and he / and he got the thing
28. then finally he! got the / got the hand caught
29. he got the hand caught
30. and he // 'cause he's tryin to push the door open
31. and he's / and he's lookin in there
32. and he's gonna uhm # get the boy
33. he's gonna try to // he gonna // he's gonna uhm // the balloon^ # it's coming down
34. and he's gonna pull
35. and the boys pullin
36. they pull and pull and pull
37. and it [long pause] and they fell down
38. and he got it
39. the boys gonna climb down
40. and they're gonna try to get the red balloon
41. and # he's running away from him
42. the boy is running
43. and they just running
44. and that dog is standin in the way
45. and # there's gonna be a lady walkin up there
46. and they're gonna uh / they're gonna move
47. and the balloon is shakin and shakin to the wall
48. and there's that lady now
49. and then that lady's walkin
50. an' he just went out
51. an' he's running
52. see they wanted to uh / they want to uhm # get the red balloon
53. you see # and them lights was shinin>
54. and he // and they gonna hide

Deborah:

I think we'll stop here [we have come to the end of the three-minute segment of the film]

Cynthia begins the on-line narration task with an utterance that clearly indicates she is describing ongoing events in the film ("I see that red balloon"). In lines 1–8, she provides a description of the first events shown in the 3-minute film clip, the scene in which the gang of boys steals the balloon outside a bakery shop. In line 9, however, she begins to project forward in the film to the final scene in which the young boy gets a large number of balloons and flies away with them. Lines 9–17 all represent a narration of events occurring long after the bakery scene. Cynthia's use of the verb form *gonna,* along with an expressive sing-song intonation, marks lines 9–17 as temporally distinct from the previous lines. This projection to future events is then interrupted by my suggestion that Cynthia narrate ongoing events from the film.

In line 18, Cynthia returns to an on-line narration of events, using the phrase *I see,* as she did in line 1 of her text. In lines 18–31, she describes an ongoing scene depicted in the film, in which the gang of boys and the young boy have a type of tug-of-war with the balloon string over a high stone wall. Her narration of these ongoing events is represented both in the present tense ("they're fighting") as well as the past tense ("and he got the thing.") In line 32, however, she returns to a use of the projective verb form *gonna.* Although in lines 33–44 *gonna* appears to be used for representing ongoing events, in lines 45–54 the temporal locus of her narrative shifts back and forth between present and future events. Unlike the events narrated in lines 9–17, which were those occurring near the end of the film, the events narrated in this segment of her text seem to be those occurring in the immediate future. For instance, in line 45 Cynthia forecasts the appearance of a woman in the alleyway, and in line 48 she describes the actual occurrence of this event when the woman appears on the television screen.

Cynthia's narration of both present and upcoming events is interlaced with occasional use of evaluative commentary and with frequent use of expressive intonation. In lines 9–17, her use of *gonna* to project forward to events at the end of the film is accompanied by an expressive, sing-song intonation ("he gonna see the red^ balloon"). Also, in lines 51–53, her use of the present tense to describe ongoing events is juxtaposed with a reference to the internal motivations of the gang of boys and with a description of how the balloon appeared shiny in the dark alleyways. In summary, Cynthia's on-line narration is a montage of narrative voices: She alternates between describing ongoing events, projecting forward to future events, and commenting on the physical and internal states of characters and objects (Wolf & Hicks, 1989).

Summary

In her responses to the three narrative tasks, Cynthia displayed a wide range of narrative skills. In particular, she displayed an ability not only to list events occurring sequentially in the film, but also to manipulate temporal sequence in the service of producing contextually appropriate narratives. In her response to the news-reporting task, events were first summarized and were then presented in a manner that emphasized the conflict existing between the young boy and the gang of boys. In her story-telling narration, events were summarized from the point of view of one telling about the storybook. Finally, in her on-line narration, events were both described (actual events) and forecast (upcoming events). In Cynthia's responses to the news-reporting and on-line narration tasks, evaluative commentary and expressive intonation were also an integral part of her narratives. One might summarize her responses to the three tasks by suggesting that her narratives are interpretative renditions of the film. Events are presented in imaginative ways that highlight characters' conflicts and internal motivations ("the boys started 'cause they wanted the red balloon") and descriptive qualities of events ("and them lights was shinin").

THE NARRATIVE SKILLS OF A MIDDLE-INCOME WHITE FIRST GRADER

An examination of the three texts produced by Jessica, a middle-income white first grader, suggests a somewhat different approach to the narrative tasks. Although Jessica also shifted her "ways of telling" between tasks, all three texts were detailed descriptions of events that matched the temporal sequence of events in the film. The news-reporting text of Jessica is the first text to be examined in this section. In her response to the news-reporting task, Jessica produced what is essentially a sequential listing of events: a scene-by-scene depiction of the events in the film. Jessica appeared to organize her text around sequential groupings of events so that her narrative contains a great deal of detail from the film. She uses factual detail, thus there is little in the way of evaluative commentary in Jessica's news-reporting text.

Jessica:

Stanza 1

and all the people were amazed to see the bus // seeing the red balloon flying behind the bus

Stanza 2
and then / and then what happened was # well this man was opening the windows
and then the // his mom // the pers(on) // the little boy that owned the red balloon # his mom and him went to church
and the red balloon followed behind
and then uhm # well # they uh # got kicked out of church

Stanza 3
annnnnd # then # well uhm # when the uh # when he was going home from church # he stopped at the pastry store
and then^ __ he left his balloon outside
and it waited right there

Stanza 4
and these mean boys came
and / and stole it
and then they took it back to their hideout
and they / they almost popped it
until the little boy # uhm # uhm untied it

Stanza 5
and then he got surrounded
and then he ran up // and then he got out
and ran up on / and ran up on the hill
and then the mean boys surrounded him
and popped his balloon

and Deborah can take over

Deborah:
I'll do a little more
but then you can finish up the report
uhm # at that point # after the balloon was popped
uhm # many balloons were seen coming down to the little boy
can you finish up the report now?

Jessica:
Stanza 6
and then they // he grabbed all their strings
and he flew away for many other adventures

Stanza 1 in Jessica's narrative should be considered in the context of the scripted introduction used for each of the narrative tasks. For the news-reporting task, the final lines of this script were as follows:

he [the boy] got on the bus
and the balloon followed behind

Thus, Jessica's opening commentary may be considered a continuation of the "bus scene" depicted in my script. It is interesting to note that the opening line in her narration is a form of evaluative commentary. In fact, this comment is the only one of its kind that appears in her text. The way in which the commentary is presented is also of interest. In this particular comment, Jessica appears to adopt an eyewitness perspective in which she details "what people saw." At issue is whether or not this particular comment is a response to my own introduction to the task, or whether it represents a global approach to a particular kind of text. An examination of the remaining stanzas in Jessica's text may provide information on this question.

The beginning of stanza 2 in Jessica's text is marked by her use of a sequential phrase ("and then what happened was . . ."). The discussion of the man washing windows in this stanza seems to be a type of orientational clause for the narrative, particularly because Jessica shifts rapidly to a different "scene" in the film: the church scene. The events at the church are narrated in three completive lines, the last line being a passive construction ("they # got kicked out of church"). In stanza 2, one thus has a rapid orientation and summary of the scenes leading to the critical events in the film.

In stanzas 3–5, Jessica relates the critical scenes in which the gang of boys steals the balloon from the younger boy. In stanza 3, she provides a description of the scene in which the boy leaves his balloon outside a bakery shop. As was the case in stanza 2, the first line of this stanza can be delineated on the basis of her use of an adverbial phrase ("when he was going home from church . . ."). The last line of her stanza can be delineated on the basis of her use of a noncompletive clause ("and it waited right there"). The combined use of sequential adverbial phrases (*when, and then what happened was*) and noncompletive verb phrases is one salient means through which Jessica appears to organize her text. One set of events, or scene, is presented as the backdrop to the next set of sequentially occurring events.

I have interpreted a shift in topic, from the young boy to the gang of boys, as the beginning of a new stanza, stanza 4. This shift in topic is marked linguistically by the use of the indefinite form, *these*. In stanza 4, Jessica relates the critical stealing scene from the film. These events, as was the case with the events detailed in stanza 3, are narrated in a factual manner. The only commentary provided by Jessica is the adjective *mean*, which describes the gang of boys. A subtle form of evaluation is also presented in the final two lines of this stanza, in which Jessica states that the gang of boys were *almost* successful in their first attempts to pop the balloon, but their attempts were made futile when the boy recovered his balloon from the gang. I have interpreted these two lines as final due to the shift in topic (back to the younger boy) in the subsequent line.

Stanza 5 consists of a series of five completive statements in which Jessica swiftly relates the final climactic events seen in the film. More so than in earlier stanzas in her text, events are related in factual detail, in that no evaluative commentary is provided. The sequential discourse marker *and then* is found in three lines within stanza 5. The more extensive use of this sequential marker reflects the fact that the events in stanza 5 are presented as a list rather than subjective commentary from the perspective of the narrator.

The final stanza in Jessica's news-reporting text should, as in her opening stanza (or line), be considered in the context of my addition to her narrative. Toward the end of her narration, Jessica appeared to tire of the task, and she asked me to take over the narration. Her last lines are thus partially a response to my own phrasing of the final events from the film. She picks up on my narration, providing a completive statement about the boy taking balloon strings (a continuation of my statement: "many balloons were seen coming down . . ."). In her final statement, Jessica brings closure to the narrative with a summarizing statement ("and he flew away for many other adventures").

Jessica's news-reporting text is best characterized as a sequential listing of events. Although she does provide some evaluative commentary in stanza 4 (she describes the boys in the gang as *mean*), in the opening line of her narrative ("all the people were amazed . . ."), and in the final line of her text ("he flew away for many other adventures"), the bulk of her text is devoted to providing a sequential list of the events from the film. This is not to imply that her narration is in any way deficient of plot organization. On the contrary, Jessica organizes events according to their thematic and sequential congruencies. In her narrative, there is more focus on factual detail than on evaluation of events.

An interesting comparison can be made by examining the aforementioned narrative with one produced by Jessica for the story-telling task. As was the case with her new-reporting text, Jessica provided a great deal of detail about events in her story-telling narration, moving through the events in the film in a scene-by-scene fashion. Unlike her response to the news-reporting task, however, Jessica in her story-telling text provided more extensive evaluative commentary on events. There is a particular focus on the balloon's magical qualities. Her evaluative commentary is also linked to the stanza structure in her text. The opening lines of stanzas are frequently marked by temporal forms (*and then, what happened was*) or discourse markers (*well, so*), and final lines are often evaluative in nature. One thus finds in Jessica's story text a recurring stanza structure with the following form: (a) temporal form—discourse marker; (b) a series of narrative (completive) lines; and, optionally, (c) evaluative commentary. The following is Jessica's story-telling narrative:

Jessica:

Stanza 1
and so he climbed up the rail // well the post thing that it [balloon] was on
and # he # untied it
and brought it down

Stanza 2
and then # well he had to go to school
except there were no balloons allowed on the bus
so he made the balloon follow him
'cause it was magic!

Stanza 3
and uhm # well # he saw the man washing windows
and then he went to church with his mo / mother
and the red balloon followed
and he went in // and they both went in
and they got kicked out of church for a day

Stanza 4
and uhm # then the little boy went to a pastry shop
and heeee # uhm had something that he really liked
and it cost // and he had enough to uhm buy it [a pastry]
so he told his balloon to wait right there
'cause he was // 'cause it was magic!

Stanza 5
so then he went outside
and then all these mean! boys came along
and stole! the balloon
and they / and they took it back to the hideout
and they uhm tried to // they were uhm shooting slingshots
but they always missed

Stanza 6
and uhm then he // and then the little boy from a wall saw his red balloon
and he's // and he was saying # "red balloon come here!"
and # then # he untied it
but the boys were pulling on the string
'cause they couldn't see the balloon anymore

Stanza 7
and # then ## uhm # well all the boy // well he ran away with the balloon
and then all the boys started running after him

and thennnn ## and then they uhm cornered him
and then // but he escaped

Stanza 8
and then what happened was # they surrounded him on top of a hill
and one of 'em hit it
and it was sharp
and it made a tiny hole
and it bursted

Stanza 9
and all! of a sudden # all of these balloons were uhm flowing out of the sky
as if there was a party going on
except it was a funeral!

and ## you can take over [looks to me]

Deborah:
don't you want to finish the <story>?

Jessica:
ok [<overlap]

Stanza 10
and then they flew towards him
and he grabbed all the strings
and they took 'im for many new adventures
the end

In stanza 1, Jessica provides a narrative continuation of the opening script used for the task. In response to my opening lines, she describes the boy's actions of getting the balloon down from a lamppost. Stanza 2 illustrates a structural patterning within stanzas that appears frequently in her narrative. In the first line of this stanza, a temporal adverbial (*and then*) followed by a discourse marker (*well*) and pausing marks a shift in topic. Then, a series of lines follows, the end result of which is an explanatory/evaluative statement ('cause it was magic!). Stanza 2 consists almost entirely of evaluative lines and seems to function thematically in Jessica's story as a backdrop for the events to come. The boy wants to take the balloon with him (= friendship) and the balloon follows the boy because of its magical qualities.

Stanza 3 can be demarcated, in my view, on the basis of the discourse marker *well,* along with pausing, that appears in what I have presented as the first line of this stanza. In stanza 3, Jessica narrates a series of completive events associated with the church scene in the film. The endpoint of these events is indicated by the temporal adverbial phrase *for a day* in the final line of stanza 3. This adverbial shifts the temporal locus of the action from a series of punctuated events to an extended time period. Another shift in the action is marked by a temporal form (*and uhm then*), which I have interpreted as the beginning of a new stanza (stanza 4). This shift in temporality is also linked to a shift in the location of events. The boy moves from the church, where he has been kicked out for an extended period of time, to the pastry shop. In stanza 4, Jessica presents a series of evaluative statements about the boy's ill-fated decision to leave the balloon outside the pastry shop. As was the case in stanza 2, nearly every line in stanza 4 functions as an evaluative statement. As was also the case in stanza 2, in stanza 4 Jessica ends with a statement of the balloon's magical qualities ('cause it was magic!). This emphasis on the balloon's magical abilities appears to be a continually recurring theme in her narrative.

Against the backdrop of the ill-fated decisions in stanza 4, Jessica relates a series of critical transitional events in stanza 5. In a series of completive statements in which adverbial and verbal forms are stressed, she narrates the gang's stealing of the balloon. As was the case in stanza 3, the final line in this stanza represents a protracted event. After the gang has stolen the balloon, they take it to their hiding place (an old construction site) and shoot at the balloon for an indefinite period of time. During this indefinite period of time, they continually miss as they attempt to pop the balloon. These protracted events bring closure to stanza 5, as the protracted nature of the boy's expulsion from church also brings closure to the events in stanza 3.

As was the case in the preceding stanzas, the opening line of stanza 6 is marked by a temporal form (*and uhm then*). As a whole, this stanza represents a statement about the boy's attempt to recover his balloon. The boy's efforts are presented through character dialogue (and he was saying # "red balloon come here!"), through a completive statement (he untied it), and finally through a statement of the protracted action on the part of the gang of boys. The inability of the gang of boys to maintain their hold on the balloon is recounted through a causal statement, in which Jessica explains that the boys continued pulling on the balloon because they could not see that it had already been recovered by its owner. It is very interesting to note the similarities between the structure of this stanza and that of stanzas 2 and 4. All three stanzas end with either an explanatory statement or with evaluative commentary. This particular format alternates with stanzas 1, 3, and 5, in which a series of completive event statements are followed by a protracted event.

Stanzas 7 and 8 deviate from this pattern of alternation, in that the two successive stanzas are both primarily nonevaluative. In stanzas 7 and 8, Jessica presents the critical events occurring near the film's end. In a series of completive statements in stanza 7, Jessica narrates the chase scene. These events terminate in a partial resolution: the boy escapes for the time being. In stanza 8, however, this partial resolution proves futile. The boy is surrounded and his balloon is destroyed. Both stanzas 7 and 8 are demarcated by an initial temporal connective (*and then*), followed by either a discourse marker (*well*) or a statement of sequence (*what happened was*). Neither stanza has a statement of evaluation or protracted action in final position. Thus, these two stanzas stand out as being structurally distinct and thematically critical for the story as a whole. They suggest a turn of events.

The resolution to this critical turn of events is presented in stanzas 9 and 10. Jessica interrupts her narration in stanza 9, asking me to take over; thus it is difficult to determine the precise boundaries between these final stanzas. However, I would interpret the shift in topic, along with marked stress, which followed the balloon's bursting (and all! of a sudden # all of these balloons . . .) as indicative of the beginning of a new stanza. Stanza 9 functions partially as a presentation of new events (more balloons come out of the sky) and partially as an evaluative metaphor describing those events. The state of affairs narrated in stanzas 7 and 8 changes dramatically in stanza 9, and this change is presented metaphorically. Finally, stanza 10 brings closure to the story, through a couplet of event clauses followed by a timeless statement. Thus, the final two stanzas in Jessica's text appear to reestablish the earlier pattern of alternating evaluative and narrative groupings of lines.

It is very interesting to compare the stanza structure within Jessica's news-reporting text and her story-telling text. In both narrative texts, Jessica provides a detailed rendition of the events from the film. In fact, in some instances, events are described in similar ways in these two texts. Consider Jessica's description of the church scene in her new-reporting and her story texts:

Church Scene (News-reporting Task)

well this man was opening the windows
and then the // his mom // the pers(on) // the little boy that owned the red balloon # his mom and him went to church
and the red balloon followed behind
and then uhm well # they uh # got kicked out for a day

Church Scene (Story-telling Task)

and uhm # well he saw the man washing windows
and / and then / and then he went to church with his mom / mother
and the red balloon followed
and he went in // and they both went in
and they got kicked out of church for a day

In general, more detail is provided by Jessica in her story-telling narration than in her news-reporting text. What most distinguishes her news-reporting and story-telling texts, aside from the amount of detail provided about some events, is the more extensive evaluative commentary found in her story text. The use of evaluation, in fact, appears to play a central part in the organization of Jessica's story narrative. Descriptions of the balloon's magical qualities, causal explanations for events, and metaphorical comparisons all appear in her story-telling narrative, and these often occur in final position within stanzas.

The final text I examine in this chapter is Jessica's on-line narration. Like Cynthia, for the event-casting task Jessica produced a lengthy present-tense description of the events shown in the 3-minute segment from the film. Unlike Cynthia, Jessica limited her narrative almost entirely to events occurring in the on-line film, rather than events occurring in previous or upcoming scenes. Thus, her on-line narration is essentially a one-to-one match between verbal description and scenes displayed on the television screen.

Jessica:

1. and uhm # he has enough money for it
2. so he leaves the red balloon outside
3. 'cause there's no balloon allowed
4. and uhm # so // and then the // and then he's telling him // the balloon just to stay right there
5. and he's going into the pastry // bakery shop
6. and here come the mean boys
7. and they see him and the red balloon
8. and they go after him
9. and catch the balloon
10. and then he comes out # the boy
11. and looks for his balloon!
12. but he can't find! it
13. and # the boys are running away with it
14. and they're trying to shoot it with a . . .
15. and then // and one boy has a stick in his hand trying to pop it
16. and the little boy is still looking
17. and he can't see his balloon anywhere
18. so he's going back the way he came to see // to try the other way
19. and the bad boys are climbing over the wall with the red balloon
20. and they're running up some stairs
21. and now they're going out from this junkpile
22. the little boy is still looking for his balloon
23. walking in this dirt place
24. an' he just slipped

25. and # he's standing in one place looking now
25. and uhm the boys are trying to shoot a slingshot at the red balloon
27. 'cause they want 'im to pop

can you take over for now? [looks to me]

Deborah:
sure
and one of the gang of boys is trying to hit the balloon with a slingshot
and now the little boy is calling for his balloon

Jessica:
28. and now he is uhm # trying to open the door and go in
29. except he sees the boys are in there
30. and then he doesn't want to go in
31. so he's calling for his balloon to come down
32. so he can untie 'im
33. and / and / and he's untieing 'im
34. and the boys on the other side can't see the balloon
35. so they're pulling hard on the string
36. and they almost saw the little boy with the red balloon
37. and now the red balloon // and then the // and now the little boy with the red balloon # is running away
38. and the boys are climbing over the wall again
39. and going after 'im
40. and now he's running down this alley
41. and now he went / went // ran by this big black dog
42. and now he's gonna get surrounded
43. and uh # he's going down this alley
44. and these boy // a boy's coming from behind
45. and this old fat woman is coming from the front
46. and now all the boys are coming from there
47. and there's some // and they're pushing the woman to get out of the way
48. and / and he's still running through the aisle
49. and then these other boys are spying on 'im
50. and then these other boys that didn't know are coming down to chase 'im
51. so he is surroun^ded
52. and one boy is hiding from him
53. and all the other boys
54. and now he's climbing up to the top of the hill and . . .

Deborah:
I think that this is a great place to stop our sportscast

The most striking feature of Jessica's event-casting narrative is the amount of descriptive detail in her text. Events are narrated in rapid sequence as they occur in the film. In addition to providing factual detail, however, Jessica also provides some commentary and elaboration on events. In lines 3, 27, 31, and 32, she provides causal explanations or resultive statements that serve as an evaluation of events. In line 12, she provides a contrastive statement, which is coupled with a stressed verb, that may also be considered evaluative in nature. Finally, in line 50, she provides a clarification of the internal cognitive state of some members of the gang of boys. Thus, Jessica's primarily descriptive and factual rendition of the ongoing events in the film also includes occasional evaluative commentary.

Jessica's on-line narrative is also primarily a description of actually occurring events rather than a projection of upcoming events. The only deviation from the temporal locus of her narration is line 42, in which she projects forward to the end of the film ("and now he's gonna get surrounded"). Her adherence to the events being displayed in the film is exemplified by her consistent use of the discourse marker *now. Now* seems to function in this text much as the sequential marker *then* generally functions in past time frame narratives. Interestingly, in this respect her on-line narration is similar to her responses to the news-reporting and story-telling tasks. The temporal locus of the text has shifted from *then* to *now,* but Jessica's emphasis on detailed description and sequential event relations remains fixed. As was the case in particular with her text produced for the news-reporting task, Jessica's on-line narrative is a primarily factual description of events that is occasionally broken by a causal explanation of events or by a reference to the cognitive internal states of characters.

Summary

Like Cynthia, Jessica shifted her ways of expressing events for the three narrative tasks. For the news-reporting task, she produced a primarily factual and detailed rendition of events seen in the film. For the story-telling task, she provided a more highly evaluated rendition of the film, in which an emphasis was placed on the magical qualities of the balloon. For the on-line narration task, she produced a descriptive narration matching the actual events occurring on the television screen. Jessica's responses to the tasks differed from those of Cynthia, however, in that in all three cases she provided a detailed rendition of events that matched the sequence of events from the film. Thus, she approached all three tasks from the perspective of a reporter seeking to provide as much detail as possible. Evaluative commentary and expressive intonation were woven into her story and on-line texts, but only within the frame of a detailed account of "what happened."

GENERAL SUMMARY

Through textual analyses of the narratives produced by two first graders from different communities, I have shown that both children have the ability to shift their ways of telling according to differing task demands. Both children produced a present-tense rendition of events for the on-line narration task, and both children produced past-tense renditions of the film for the news-reporting and story-telling tasks. Each of these two children, however, interpreted the tasks in different ways. Cynthia produced a highly evaluated text for the news-reporting task, but Jessica produced a factual listing of events for this same task. For the story-telling task, Cynthia spoke about the storybook she was holding, whereas Jessica produced a detailed and highly evaluated rendition of events. Finally, for the on-line narration task Cynthia moved between both actually occurring and upcoming events, whereas Jessica adhered to the timeline of the film and narrated actually occurring events. In short, it was in part differences in the tasks and in part differences in children's interpretations of the tasks that led to shifts in Cynthia and Jessica's narrations of events.

At stake is how much these differing interpretations of the narrative tasks represent individual differences between the two children, and how much they represent broader cultural differences. In line with previous research suggesting sociocultural differences in oral narrative styles (Gee, 1986; Heath, 1982, 1983; Hymes, 1982; Michaels, 1981; Michaels & Collins, 1984; Scollon & Scollon, 1981, 1984; Tannen, 1985), perhaps Cynthia and Jessica represent differing cultural traditions. For example, Cynthia's ability to manipulate temporal sequence and her emphasis on the internal motivations of characters may stem from her participation in a culture in which telling an engaging story is on some occasions equally as important as telling the facts (Foster, 1989; Heath, 1981, 1983). Jessica's emphasis on providing a detailed description of events may stem from her participation in a community in which factual accounts of events are highly valued (Heath, 1986).

In conclusion, each of the children whose texts were examined in this chapter brings a sophisticated repertoire of genre knowledge to her first-grade classroom. I would suggest, however, that each child also brings differing sets of interpretations concerning the particular way in which one shifts the telling of events. Thus, genre knowledge is not a fixed entity that one simply learns as, for example, children acquire use of tense markers. Rather, genre knowledge is linked to a whole range of cultural values and systems of belief (Gee, 1989). To return to a theme introduced early in this chapter, I would reiterate the sociolinguistic origins of genre knowledge, in that children acquire differing ways of talking about events through their interactions in a range of social settings. Just as individual chidren develop unique ways of representing events, children also develop repertoires of narrative skills that reflect the discourse patterns of their communities.

The theoretical framework and discussions of existing literature presented in this chapter suggest that narrative development is a multidimensional phenomenon. Not only do children develop multiple ways of talking about events; children from different family and community settings also develop multiple ways of interpreting the same narrative tasks. This particular framework on narrative development points to the need for analyses of the social settings in which both preschool and elementary school children are participants. When narrative development is viewed as the acquisition of social knowledge, it seems prudent to shift from a focus on the group (community, social class, age level) to a focus on the individual child acting in an expanding social world.

APPENDIX

Event-casting Task

This is (child's name) and Deborah, sportscasters, and we're gonna say everything we see happening in the film. I'm gonna start off and then (child's name) is gonna take over.

(I start replaying a 3-minute segement from the film).

The little boy and the red balloon are going past a church steeple. And they're coming to a bakery shop. The little boy is looking inside the bakery shop. Now he's checking in his pocket to see if he has enough money to buy something to eat. Looks good. Now he's walking into the bakery shop.

Can you take over and be the sportscaster?

News-reporting Task

This is (child's name) and Deborah, and we're gonna be news reporters and tell what we saw happen in the film. I'm gonna start off and then (child's name) is gonna take over.

News Headlines: Boy Seen Flying Over City! The first thing that I saw happen was: A little boy found a red balloon on his way to the bus stop. He was seen walking with the balloon to a bus. He got on the bus, and the balloon followed behind.

Can you be the news reporter now and tell what you saw happen?

Story-telling Task

This is (child's name) and Deborah, and we're gonna be storytellers and tell the story of *The Red Balloon.* I'm gonna start off and then (child's name) is gonna take over.

(I hold in my lap a "storybook" that has on the front cover a picture from the film but which has neither words nor pictures inside)

The Red Balloon. Once upon a time there was a little boy who lived in Paris, France. One day, on his way to the bus stop, he found this big beautiful red balloon. He wanted the balloon to be his friend.

Can you take over now and be the storyteller? (I pass the storybook fascimili to the child)

ACKNOWLEDGMENTS

The research described in this chapter was made possible through a Spencer Dissertation Year Fellowship for Research Related to Education (Harvard University) and through a General University Research Grant (University of Delaware). I would like to thank Catherine Snow and Dennie Wolf for their input into this research project. I would also like to acknowledge James Paul Gee and Allyssa McCabe for their valuable comments and suggestions at various stages of research and writing. Finally, I wish to express my gratitude to the first-grade children, and their teachers, who participated in the project.

REFERENCES

Applebee, A. (1978). *The child's concept of story.* Chicago: University of Chicago Press.

Bakhtin, M. M. (1986). *Speech genres and other essays.* In C. Emerson & M. Holquist (Eds.), Austin: University of Texas Press.

Berman, R. & Slobin, D. (1986). *Coding manual: Temporality in discourse.* (rev. ed.). Cognitive Science Program, Unviersity of California, Berkeley.

Bruner, J. (1986). *Actual minds, possible worlds*. Cambridge, MA: Harvard University Press.

Chafe, W. (1980). The deployment of consciousness in the production of a narrative. In W. Chafe (Ed.), *The pear stories: Cultural, cognitive, and linguistic aspects of narrative production* (pp. 9–50). Norwood, NJ: Ablex.

Clifford, J. (1988). *The predicament of culture: Twentieth-century enthnography, literature, and art*. Cambridge, MA: Harvard University Press.

Eisenberg, A. (1985). Learning to describe past experiences in conversation. *Discourse Processes, 8*, 177–204.

Engel, S. (1986). *Learning to reminisce: A developmental study of how young children talk about the past*. Unpublished doctoral dissertation, City University of New York.

Fivush, R., Gray, J., & Fromhoff, F. (1987). Two-year-olds talk about the past. *Discourse Processes, 11*, 337–355.

Fivush, R., & Fromhoff, F. (1988). Style and structure in mother-child conversations about the past. *Discourse Processes, 11*, 337–355.

Foster, M. (1989). "It's cookin' now": A performance analysis of the speech events of a black teacher in an urban community college. *Language in Society, 18*, 1–29.

Fowler, A. (1982). *Kinds of literature: An introduction to the theory of genres and modes*. Cambridge, MA: Harvard Unviersity Press.

Gardner, H. (1982). *Developmental psychology* (2nd ed.). Boston: Little, Brown.

Gee, J. P. (1986). Units in the production of narrative discourse. *Discourse Processes, 9*. 391–422.

Gee, J. P. (1989, October). *Discourses and educational theory*. Paper presented in the 1989 Colloquium Series, University of Delaware, College of Education.

Gerhardt, J. (1988). From discourse to semantics: the development of verb morphology and forms of self-reference in the speech of a two-year-old. *Journal of Child Language, 15*, 337–393.

Heath, S. B. (1982). What no bedtime story means: Narrative skills at home and at school. *Language in Society, 11*, 49–76.

Heath, S. B. (1983). *Ways with words: Language, life, and work in communities and classrooms*. New York: Cambridge University Press.

Heath, S. B. (1986). Taking a cross-cultural look at narratives. *Topics in Language Disorders*, 7(1), 84–94.

Hicks, D. (1988). *The development of genre skills: a linguistic analysis of primary school children's stories, reports, and eventcasts*. Unpublished doctoral dissertation, Harvard University.

Hicks, D. (1990a). Narrative skills and genre knowledge: Ways of telling in the primary school grades. *Applied Psycholinguistics, 11*, 83–104.

Hicks, D. (1990b). Genre skills and narrative development in the elementary school grades. *Linguistics and Education, 2*, 43–74.

Hicks, D., & Wolf, D. (1988). Texts within texts: A developmental study of children's play narratives. In *Papers and Reports on Child Language Development*. Stanford University Press.

Hymes, D. (1981). *"In vain I tried to tell you": Essays in Native American enthnopoetics.* Philadelphia: University of Pennsylvania Press.

Hymes, D. (1982). Narrative form as a "grammar" of experience: Native Americans and a glimpse of English. *Journal of Education, 164,* 121–142.

Labov, W. (1972). *Language in the inner city.* Philadelphia: University of Pennsylvania Press.

MacWhinney, B., & Snow, C. (1985). The child language data exchange system. *Journal of Child Language, 12*(2), 271–296.

McNamee, G. (1979). The social interaction origins of narrative skills. *The Quarterly Newsletter of the Laboratory of Comparative Human Cognition, 1*(4), 63–68.

Michaels, S. (1981). "Sharing time": Children's narrative styles and differential access to literacy. *Language in Society, 10,* 423–442.

Michaels, S., & Collins, J. (1984). Oral discourse styles: Classroom interaction and the acquisition of literacy. In D. Tannen (Ed.), *Coherence in spoken and written discourse.* Norwood, NJ: Ablex.

Miller, P., & Sperry, L. (1988). Early talk about the past: The origins of conversational stories of personal experience. *Journal of Child Language, 15,* 293–315.

Nelson, K. (1978). How children represent knowledge of their world in and out of language: A preliminary report. In R. S. Siegler (Ed.), *Children's thinking: What develops?* (pp. 255–273). Hillsdale, NJ: Lawrence Erlbaum Associates.

Nelson, K. (1986). Event knowledge: Structure and function in development. Hillsdale, NJ: Lawrence Erlbaum Associates.

Nelson, K., & Gruendel, J. (1981). Generalized event representations: Basic building blocks of cognitive development. In M. Lamb & A. Brown (Eds.), *Advances in developmental psychology* (Vol. 1, pp. 131–158). Hillsdale, NJ: Lawrence Erlbaum Associates.

Ninio, A. (1988). The roots of narrative: Discussing recent events with very young children. *Language Sciences, 10*(1), 35–52.

Peterson, C., & McCabe, A. (1983). *Developmental psychology: Three ways of looking at a child's narrative.* New York: Plenum.

Preece, A. (1987). The range of narrative forms conversationally produced by young children. *Journal of Child Language, 14,* 353–373.

Rosaldo, R. (1989). *Culture and truth: The remaking of social analysis.* Boston: Beacon Press.

Rubin, S., & Wolf, D. (1979). The development of maybe: the evolution of social roles into narrative roles. In E. Winner & H. Gardner (Eds.), *Fact, fiction, and fantasy in childhood: New Directions for Child Development, 6,* 15–28.

Scollon, R., & Scollon, S. (1980). Literacy as focused interaction. *The Quarterly Newsletter of the Laboratory of Comparative Human Cognition, 2*(2), 26–29.

Scollon, R., & Scollon, S. (1981). *Narrative, literacy, and face in interethnic communication.* Norwood, NJ: Ablex.

Scollon, R., & Scollon, S. (1984). Cooking it up and boiling it down: Abstracts in Athabaskan children's story retellings. In D. Tannen (Ed.), *Coherence in Spoken and Written Discourse* (pp. 173–200). Norwood, NJ: Ablex.

Snow, C. (1983). Literacy and language: Relationships during the preschool years. *Harvard Educational Review, 53*(2), 165–189.

Sperber, D., & Wilson, D. (1986). *Relevance: Communication and cognition.* Cambridge, MA: Harvard University Press.

Stoel-Gammon, C., & Scliar-Cabral, L. (1977). Learning how to tell it like it is: The development of the reportative function in children's speech. *Papers and Reports on Child Language Development.* Stanford, CA: Stanford University Press.

Sutton-Smith, B., Botvin, G., & Mahoney, D. (1976). Developmental structures in fantasy narratives. *Human Development, 19,* 1–13.

Tannen, D. (1985). Focus on involvement in spoken and written discourse. In D. Olson (Ed.), *Literacy, language, and learning: The nature and consequences of reading and writing* (pp. 238–277). New York: Cambridge University Press.

Vygotsky, L. S. (1962). *Thought and language.* Cambridge, MA: MIT Press.

Vygotsky, L. S. (1978). *Mind in society.* Cambridge, MA: Harvard University Press.

Watson-Gegeo, K., & Boggs, S. (1977). From verbal play to talk story: the role of routines in speech events among Hawaiian children. In S. Ervin-Tripp & C. Mitchell-Kernan (Eds.), *Child discourse* (pp. 67–90). New York: Academic Press.

Wellek, R., & Warren, A. (1949). *Theory of literature.* London: Jonathan Cape.

Wells, G. (1985). *Language development in the preschool years.* New York: Cambridge University Press.

Wells, G. (1986). *The meaning makers: Children learning language and using language to learn.* Portsmouth, NH: Heinemann.

White, S. (1970). Some general outlines of the matrix of developmental changes between five and seven years. *Bulletin of the Orton Society, 20,* 41–57.

White, S., & Siegel, A. (1984). Cognitive development in time and space. In B. Rogoff & J. Lave (Eds.), *Everyday cognition: Its development in social context.* Cambridge, MA: Harvard University Press.

Wolf, D., & Hicks, D. (1989). Voices within narratives: The development of intertextuality in young children's stories. *Discourse Processes, 12*(3), 329–351.

CHAPTER 3

From Knowing to Telling: The Development of Children's Scripts, Stories, and Personal Narratives

Judith A. Hudson
Lauren R. Shapiro
Rutgers, the State University of New Jersey

What does it take to produce a coherent and cohesive narrative? We view narrative production as a cognitive and linguistic task that draws on many kinds of knowledge—for example, general knowledge about events, memories of specific episodes, knowledge about people and typical social interactions, knowledge about structural characteristics of different narrative genres, knowledge about verb tense and linguistic connectives, and knowledge about the listener's needs. The task that a narrator faces is how to coordinate this knowledge in producing a narrative. According to White (1980), "narrative might well be considered the solution to a problem of general concern, namely, the problem of translating *knowing* into *telling*" (p. 1).

Our research is concerned with how children develop different strands of knowledge and how they translate their knowledge into narratives. Our plan for this chapter is to, first, present a framework for studying narrative production focusing on the development of four types of knowledge and skill: (a) *content knowledge,* which includes generalized event representations, memories of specific episodes and stories, and knowledge about common types of social interactions; (b) *structural knowledge,* that is, macrolinguistic knowledge about the structural components of different types of narratives; (c) *microlinguistic knowledge,* including knowledge of different kinds of connectives as well as how to adjust tense, pronoun use, and anaphoric reference; and (d) *contextual knowledge,* referring to what the narrator knows or believes about the function of the narrative in the particular elicitation context. Next, we present data on children's production of three types of narrative—scripts, personal narratives, and stories—which illustrate how different event topics, drawing on different types of event knowledge, affect the content and structure of each narrative genre.

CHILDREN'S NARRATIVES: WHAT DEVELOPS?

Content Knowledge

A narrative is more than just a piece of connected discourse, it is an account of an event. In order to produce a narrative, one must have knowledge about the event that is the topic of the narrative. However obvious this point may be, it is not always the case that children are asked to produce narratives about events they know about. For example, Karmiloff-Smith (1985) asked children from 4 to 9 years to produce narratives about a sequence of pictures depicting various events such as buying balloons and going fishing. Although most are somewhat familiar with these events, it is not clear that younger and older children possess the same level of knowledge about the events. Differences in children's performance in this task may, in part, be due to differences in event knowledge. In contrast, Peterson and McCabe (1983) asked children of roughly the same ages to narrate personally experienced events such as getting stung by a bee or going to the doctor. Children were free to talk about the events they were most interested in and could initiate their own topics. In this case, the knowledge base that children drew on to produce their narratives was more similar.

Yet asking children to narrate personally experienced events does not necessarily guarantee they will have a knowledge base readily available to talk about. Research on the development of general event knowledge and memories for specific episodes has shown that general and specific event memories are part of the same interrelated memory system (Hudson, 1986). In many cases, general event knowledge can assist the retrieval of specific episodes by providing a general framework for organizing recall. In other cases it can distort memory for specific episodes by causing confusion between memories of similar episodes. Hudson and Nelson (1986) found that preschool children had a great deal of difficulty in recalling specific episodes of highly routine events, suggesting that details of routine episodes become fused into general event representations in memory. For example, memories of specific birthday parties seemed to be particularly difficult to recall and children's personal narratives for these events included a lot of general information (e.g., "you get party bags"), but few episodic details. In contrast, memories of visits to Disneyland, an event that had only been experienced once (although this is obviously a more salient event as well), were relatively rich in detail. Thus, some episodes are more accessible to recall and therefore more easily narrated. One factor influencing accessibility is the frequency of occurrence of similar episodes.

Personal narratives are not the only kind of narrative children are asked to produce. In this chapter, we discuss three types of narratives: scripts, personal narratives, and fictional stories. Each is very different in both content and structure.

Scripts

In producing a script narrative, that is, a general description of what usually happens in an event, *general event knowledge* is most salient. However, information from specific episodes can be used to illustrate the general case or to provide information about possible exceptions to the rule. General knowledge about events, organized as event schemas or generalized event representations, is acquired relatively early. Recent research has shown that children as young as 14 months demonstrate general knowledge about the organization of familiar event sequences as displayed in imitation tasks (Bauer & Mandler, 1990; O'Connell & Girard, 1985). By the age of 3, most children can verbally report what happens in events they are familiar with such as getting dressed in the morning, going to a birthday party, going grocery shopping, eating at a fast-food restaurant, and so forth.

Not only can preschoolers verbally describe events, they can also use their generalized event representations to guide recall (Hudson & Nelson, 1983), support discourse (Nelson & Gruendel, 1979), and draw inferences (Hudson & Slackman, in press). Children from the age of 5, compared to younger children, mention more actions and more complex types of actions when interviewed about their knowledge of events. Thus, there is evidence that children as young as 3 have temporally organized, general knowledge about events that is verbally accessible, although both age and increasing experience lead to more complex event knowledge (Fivush, 1984; Fivush & Slackman, 1986; Slackman, Hudson, & Fivush, 1986).

Personal Narratives

In producing a personal narrative, the narrator draws primarily on a memory of a single episode, although more general information can be included as background material.

Nonverbal evidence of memory for specific event episodes has been found in children under 1 year old by Ashmead and Perlmutter (1979, 1980) using a parental diary method. For example, they reported that one 9-month-old was able to recall the drawer where she had located some ribbons (not in their customary location) after a day's delay. A number of studies have shown that somewhere between 20 to 30 months children are able to verbally recall details of past episodes from the time they were 14 months old (Eisenberg, 1985; Hudson, 1990; Sachs, 1983). However, 2-year-olds rely heavily on cues and prompts from parents in order to recall this information. It is only around 30 to 36 months that children are able to independently report memories of past episodes without a great deal of support in the form of specific questions and cues (Fivush, Gray, & Fromhoff, 1987). During the preschool and early elementary school years children report more information and more elaborated information when asked to recall specific events (Hudson & Nelson, 1986), but there is no evidence that older children can retain more episodes in memory than younger children. Thus, there is evidence of an extensive autobiographic memory system that is verbally accessible by the age of 3.

Stories

In narrating a fictional story, the narrator must draw on some knowledge about the event occurring in the story. This could be drawn from general event knowledge, a memory of a single episode, or memory of another fictional story. In addition, to fulfill the requirement that a story develop a plot (more about this in the next section), the narrator must include some kind of problem to be resolved. Although this can be achieved by drawing on a memory of a personally experienced episode or another story plot, it can also be achieved by drawing on general knowledge about things that can go wrong, particularly with regard to social interactions. Knowledge of social roles, personality types, and typical social interactions is general knowledge that is not tied to any particular event schema. Hence, we consider this knowledge base as *general social knowledge.*

A full discussion of children's knowledge of intentions, motivations, personality types, and typical social interactions is beyond the scope of this volume (see Shantz, 1983). But, in general, research shows that preschool children have a limited concept of intentionality and that not until the years 6 to 8 is there evidence that children understand, and more importantly, take into consideration intentions in explaining the behaviors of others (Smith, 1978; Wood, 1978). Furthermore, preschool children's verbal descriptions of other people do not include psychological aspects, but focus instead on observable characteristics (Barenboim, 1981). Finally, children's understanding of authority relationships, friendship, social roles, and conflict relations is very limited during the preschool years and undergoes significant change during the middle childhood years (Damon, 1977; Selman, 1980).

These findings are primarily based on children's verbal explanations in experimental tasks and on responses to structured interviews. In more naturalistic conversations, children as young as 28 months refer to internal mental states (both their own and those of others) and the conditions that produce various mental states (Beeghly & Bretherton, 1982). McCabe and Peterson (1985) also found frequent reference to psychological causality (explicit and implicit intentions, emotions, directives, etc.) in the personal narratives of children from 4 to 6 years, indicating that preschool children display knowledge of social roles and interactions in the context of familiar situations. It is possible that preschool children's knowledge of social roles, intentions, and social conflicts is first represented as part of event schemas and specific episodes, but is not available for analyzing (or constructing) hypothetical situations until the early elementary school years.

Structural Knowledge

Structural characteristics of narratives are what give narratives *coherence,* that is, an orderly flow of information that makes sense to the listener. Although the three types of narratives discussed in this chapter are all based on the unfolding of an event over time, they do not all follow a chronological sequence beginning with the first action and proceeding in a direct chronological order to the last action. If this were the case, then narratives would only be distinguished by the content—general, specific, or fictional. In fact, each type of narrative is distinguished by both the selection of information presented (the content) and the order and manner in which it is narrated (the structure).

Scripts

Scripts are accounts of what usually happens. They are reported in the timeless present tense and often use the general pronoun *you* as in the following script for celebrating Halloween narrated by a preschooler:

(1) You have to get a costume. And you say trick-or-treat.
And you go to different houses. You get all kinds of candy.

More complex scripts include information about optional and alternative actions, as in the following script for a doctor's office visit by a third grader:

> (2) Well, you go in and wait in the waiting room. And then the doctor probably calls your name and you go in. They might give you a shot or medicine. First you have to tell them what's wrong with you or if it's your yearly check-up you would probably get a shot. Um, um, well then you say that got a good check-up and then you go. If you got a bad check-up um, then you would have to go to the hospital or something.

At the most complex level, a script can be hierarchically organized under *header acts,* as in the following excerpt from a first grader's script for going on a trip.

> (3) *You get to do fun stuff.* And you might get to go swimming, and you might get to go to the toy shop like I did, and you might get to go to Lake Champlaign where the water isn't so high.

Narrating a script is similar to giving directions or a recipe in that only the most important information is presented without embellishment, and actions are reported in the correct chronological sequence. Episodic information is only reported if it provides information about what could potentially happen again as in the previous example where the child reports, "you might get to go to the toy shop like I did."

Thus, the topic or *foreground* of the narrative is the general case, whereas episodic information is the *background* or commentary and is marked by the expressions, "one time," "once," and "except." The timeline of the narrative closely follows the chronological sequence of the event in the real world. Scripts also have a prescriptive quality in the sense that only things that should happen are mentioned, as opposed to all the things that could potentially go wrong.

The basic ability to narrate scripts is evident in young preschoolers: Three-year-olds can narrate central or core actions for familiar events in their correct temporal order using the general pronoun *you* and the timeless present tense (Nelson & Gruendel, 1986). With age, children's scripts become more complex as they mention more optional and alternative information and organize the report in a hierarchical fashion in terms of header acts and subacts (Gruendel, 1980; Hudson & Nelson, 1986; Slackman, Hudson, & Fivush, 1986).

What accounts for the development of more complex script narratives? Fivush (1984) showed that kindergarten children's school scripts become more complex with increased school experience, suggesting that increasing event knowledge contributes to more complex script narratives, independent of age. However, Hudson and Nelson (1986) found that children's script narratives, as well as their personal narratives, became more elaborated with age when familiarity with events was controlled. Moreover, a study of children's event knowledge as determined by their frequency judgments for required and optional script actions has shown that preschoolers know about optional actions, but fail to convey this knowledge in their verbal scripts presumably because they lack the necessary narrative skills (Hudson & Slackman, 1985). Development in children's script narratives can therefore be a result of both increased event knowledge and increased narrative skill.

Personal Narratives

Personal narratives are accounts of specific events that have been personally experienced. They are reported in the past tense from the perspective of a participant using personal pronouns. A coherent personal narrative is organized around a high point that is the point of the narrative. Labov and Waletzky (1967) described the structural components that serve to organize personal narratives around high points: *Abstracts* and *introducers* that occur at the beginning mark the beginning of the narrative, summarize the story, or summon the listener's attention (e.g., "You know what?"). *Orientations* provide background and setting information, whereas *complicating actions* are the actions leading up to and including the high point. The high point is marked by *evaluation* by the narrator. This is followed by a *resolution* capping the event and resolving any complications. A *coda* can be added at the end to close the story and bridge the end of the narrative proper to the present context (see Peterson & McCabe, chap. 1 in this vol., for more details).

In contrast to scripts, the topic or foreground of a personal narrative is the unfolding of a particular episode and general event information is only provided as commentary or background information. For example, in the following excerpt a first grader interjects the background information, "he's silly," to comment on the character:

(4) Well Billy was playing around in school. He's silly. I kicked Billy and then he throwed a piece of cake at me.

Breaking from a chronological sequence to insert background information also captures the listener's interest as in the following narrative by a preschooler where a deviation from the routine (i.e., screaming when you get a shot) is explicitly marked:

(5) I got a shot. When I usually scream, I didn't scream. I got a band-aid and she drew a happy face on it.

Another way in which time can be manipulated in a personal narrative to accentuate the high point is by dwelling on a particular moment either through elaboration (example 6 from a preschooler), or by using the past progressive form (example 7 from a third grader):

(6) I went yesterday. I know what my daddy's doctor's office looks like in the hospital because I went there once. Um, I, I got a shot. *It only hurted for a minute and it wasn't bleeding.* I used to have it right here and it's not there any more.

(7) One time I had to go to the doctor's office to get a shot Oh boy, I was sort of small then. *I was crying. I was running back and forth in the room.* And then after they showed me to the toy room, I was okay there. And then after a while, they said, "you are next." *Oh boy, I started crying to get inside the toy box and hide from them.* Well after they gave me the shot, she said I was good and she gave me a big E.T. poster. I hung it in my room. I still got it.

Example 7 is also noteworthy because it includes many of the structural components discussed by Labov (1972), including an abstract, "One time I had to the doctor's office to get a shot," and a coda, "I still got it."

Labov's structural analysis has been used extensively in evaluating the coherence of preschool and elementary-school-aged children's personal narratives (see McCabe & Peterson, chap. 6 in this vol). However, the structural development of personal narratives begins during the 24- to 36-month age range when children report memories of past events in conversations with adults (Fivush, Gray, & Fromhoff, 1987; Hudson, 1990; Lucariello & Nelson, 1987; McCabe & Peterson, chap. 6 in this vol.; Sachs, 1983). Eisenberg (1985) suggested that children are able to report predictable aspects of events based on general event knowledge (orientation information) before they are able to report unique or distinctive aspects of specific events. This developmental pattern was also found by Fivush and Hamond (1990) when children's adult-guided conversations about events at 30 to 36 months were compared to their independent personal narratives at age 4.

Changes in the content of early memory reports cannot be separated from changes in the adult-child conversational structure. At the same time that children report more general information, they are also more reliant on adult guidance and elicitation. If children are asked questions that they cannot respond to, they may fall back on general event knowledge as a response. When children are able to narrate a personal narrative independently, they are free to focus on the unique and distinctive aspects of experiences that are important from their own perspective and are not tied to answering questions about the events from an adult's perspective. This is an important development because, in order for a narrative to be organized around a high point, it must include some distinctive content.

Consider this first grader's narrative, which is an account of a past event reported in the past tense and does not include an explicit high point:

> (8) I went to a birthday party. When it was my birthday, I went to Chuck E. Cheese [a restaurant] and when it was one of my friends', I came over to the birthday party. We ate cake. We went to the park and played and played some games, some tricks. And we went to the mall and we had some pizza again. And that's all.

This type of chronological pattern is found at all ages and is boring at all ages (Hudson & Nelson, 1984; Peterson & McCabe, 1983). In contrast, examples 5 and 6, both by preschoolers, employ narrative devices to mark the high points. Example 7 is a fully developed high point narrative that includes all the elements of high point structure. Thus, content affects structure in that a high point must be something distinctive. But content is also shaped by structure in that a high point either can be inferred from the content or developed by the narrator.

The previous examples also illustrate the difference between what White (1980) referred to as *narrating* and *narrativizing*. In narrating the past, events are accurately reported, but there is no attempt to impose a structure on the report. An event narrative (such as example 8) is similar to a historical annal or chronicle, that is, a sequence of actions without a clear beginning, middle, and end. In narrativizing the past, the narrator structures the event report around central subjects, proper beginnings, endings, and high points (as in example 5). Actions that are not chronologically contiguous can be related and the event is given an overall coherence that was not necessarily part of the actual experience.

Narrativization is more difficult than narrating. According to White (1980), "Narrative only becomes a *problem* when we wish to give *real* events the *form* of story. It is because real events do not offer themselves as stories that their narrativization is so difficult" (p. 4). In studying the development of high point structure in children's personal narratives, we are studying the development of narrativization, which goes beyond simply reporting "what happened," to developing a plot or "story" about what happened through the use of formal structural elements.

By the early preschool years, children use introducers and abstracts to begin personal narratives in conversational contexts (Preece, 1987; Umiker-Sebeok, 1979). However, in situations when the experimenter provides the prompt for the narrative, children rarely include introducers or abstracts until the age of 8 years (Kernan, 1977; Peterson & McCabe, 1983). Thus, younger children use these devices primarily in a functional manner, to elicit attention or to mark a change in topic, whereas older children seem more aware of the narrative functions of introducers and abstracts and will include them even when they hold the floor or a shift in topic has already occurred.

Preschool children also include orientation statements in their personal narratives, although the amount and variety of orientation information children provide increases with age (Hasslett, 1986; Kernan, 1977; Menig-Peterson & McCabe, 1978; Peterson & McCabe, 1983; Preece, 1987; Umiker-Sebeok, 1979). Children's personal narratives at all ages include complicating actions, but the inclusion of resolutions seems to increase with age between the years 4 to 5 (Peterson & McCabe, 1983; Umiker-Sebeok, 1979).

The use of evaluation to mark a high point is the hallmark of a personal narrative. Children employ evaluative devices in their intraconversational personal narratives by the age of 2 (Miller & Sperry, 1988). However, young children's narratives tend to include more referential information—that is, event actions and background information—than evaluative information (Umiker-Sebeok, 1979). Miller and Sperry suggested two explanations for these findings: Either (a) the evaluative function of narratives emerges later than the referential function because personal narratives (which are evaluative) evolve from scripts (which are referential); or (b) evaluative functions in early personal narratives are first conveyed by nonverbal means, then by limited lexical means, and finally by complex syntactic structures. Miller and Sperry supported the latter explanation based on their study of 2-year-olds' personal narratives embedded in adult-child conversations that included gestural dramatizations and rudimentary lexical emphasizers such as intensifiers, quoted speech, and comparisons.

With age, the number and type of evaluative techniques increase (Hasslett, 1986; Peterson & McCabe, 1983). For example, Umiker-Sebeok (1979) found that 3-year-olds predominantly used comparison (e.g., "like I do at home") and 4-year-olds predominantly used emotional reactions (e.g., "I was scared"), whereas 5-year-olds used intensity/quantity markers (e.g., "a whole box of bandages") in addition to comparisons and emotional reactions. Kernan (1977) found that Black 7-year-olds' attitudes often were implied by their actions, whereas older children of 10 to 13 years explicitly stated their attitudes or used quoted speech.

Finally, the inclusion of codas that serve to tie a narrative together or to bring the narrative up to the present are only found in the narratives of children 8 years and above (Hasslett, 1986; Peterson & McCabe, 1983).

Thus, the basic elements of narrative structure are present in 2-year-olds' personal narratives, which are jointly constructed in conversations with adults. Skills for recounting past experience are independently applied by 3- and 4-year-olds. With age, children's use of evaluative devices expands and their narratives become more tightly connected to the degree that they include more resolutions and codas that serve to tie up loose ends in the narrative.

The evidence also suggests that scripts and personal narratives are differentiated in children's talk about events at a very early age. Although Eisenberg (1985) argued that 2-year-olds may find it easier to talk about general event characteristics than to report details of specific past episodes, there is ample evidence that 2-year-olds are able to report details of specific past episodes (Engel, 1986; Fivush, Gray, & Fromhoff, 1987; Fivush & Hamond, 1990; Hudson, 1990). It is possible that young children may report general event information if they have difficulty in recalling a specific event they are asked about. However, this does not mean that they lack the narrative skills for reporting the past. (See Nelson, 1990, for a discussion of the development of autobiographic memories in relation to the development of general event knowledge.) Rather, we propose that both narrative genres—scripts and personal narratives—emerge in their incipient forms at approximately the same time, but may develop at different rates during the preschool years.

It is important to keep in mind that the structural coherence of young children's personal narratives is very much affected by the elicitation context. Children's narratives elicited in conversations are more often coherent at an earlier age than children's narratives obtained when they are explicitly asked to tell a narrative. Many narrative devices may first be used by preschool children to establish topic in conversations and are not integrated into narratives elicited in more formal contexts. For example, in conversational contexts, 5-year-olds can include all the components of a "classic" high point narrative

(Preece, 1987; Umiker-Sebeok, 1979), but in more adult-directed situations 5-year-olds produce relatively fewer classic narratives (Hudson & Nelson, 1984; Peterson & McCabe, 1983). By age 6, children are less dependent on context and more capable of producing relatively complex and coherent narratives in directed elicitation: 35% of the longest narratives produced by 6-year-olds in Peterson and McCabe's study followed the classic pattern.

Stories

The structural characteristics of stories have been formalized into various types of story grammars. Despite some variations, there is considerable agreement on the minimally acceptable characteristics of the structure for a single episode story. It must include: (a) a *formal beginning* (e.g., "Once upon a time") and *orientation* to introduce setting and characters; (b) *initiating events,* that is, goal-directed actions; (c) a *problem* or obstacle to achieving the intended goal; (d) a *resolution* of the problem; and (e) a *formal ending device* (Botvin & Sutton-Smith, 1977; Kintsch, 1974; Mandler, 1983; Nelson & Gruendel, 1986; Stein, 1988; Stein & Glenn, 1982).

Although children as young as 4 are able to use story schemas in story comprehension (see Mandler, 1983), children are not able to use story schemas for producing stories until much later. Preschool children's story narratives lack many of the basic constituent units of a story and more closely resemble event descriptions or scripts (Applebee, 1978; Botvin & Sutton-Smith, 1977; Nelson & Gruendel, 1986). Preschool children's difficulty in producing stories may indicate that they do not have story schemas under operational control (Mandler & DeForest, 1979; Seidman, Nelson, & Gruendel, 1986) or that they are still in the process of acquiring story schemas (Poulsen, Kintsch, Kintsch, & Premack, 1979; Pradl, 1979).

Although their stories do not conform to story grammar structure, preschool children do incorporate some story elements into their narratives, including use of the past tense, introduction of fictional characters, and use of traditional fairy-tale beginnings and endings (Applebee, 1978; Kuczaj & McClain, 1984; Pradl, 1979; Shapiro & Hudson, 1989). In many cases, these elements seemed to be "tagged onto" a script, as in the following story from a preschooler:

(9) A duck went out on Halloween. When the duck dressed up like a bear. He scared people. Then went trick-or-treating.

With age, children incorporate more episodic components into their stories. By the age of 5, children include appropriate setting information (Pradl, 1979) and kindergartners include initiating actions in their stories and attempt to develop a plot (Stein, 1988). However, the inclusion of internal goals, motivations, and reactions marking more sophisticated story productions are absent from children's fictional stories before the age of around 8 years (Hidi & Hildyard, 1983; Kemper, 1984; Leondar, 1977; Stein & Glenn, 1982). (See stories 25–36 in the appendix.)

The inclusion of internal motivations and reactions corresponds with the development of more complex plots in children's stories (Gardner & Gardner, 1971; Leondar, 1977; Maranda & Maranda, 1971; Sutton-Smith, 1975). Stein (1988) asked kindergarten, third-grade, and fifth-grade children to narrate stories given an initial story stem (e.g., "Once there was a big grey fox who lived in a cave"). Kindergartners tended to tell stories revolving around either interpersonal obstacles that were resolved by force or environmental obstacles (e.g., mountains to climb), which were resolved by generating a new plan, or more frequently, by appealing for help. By third grade, there was more emphasis on interpersonal conflicts that were more often resolved by deception and counterattacks. Third graders also introduced new characters in the plot who cooperate in order to facilitate attainment of a goal in the face of obstacles. Fifth grader's plots included even more use of deception and counterattack and, for the first time, introduced compromise as a means toward goal achievement. At this age, children's plots also included intrapersonal conflicts in which the protagonist's attainment of one goal precludes achievement of another.

Interestingly, the topic stem exerted a strong influence on the content of children's stories. For example, children given the story stem, "Once there was a boy named Alan who had lots of toys," often generated stories about protecting possessions from the threats of others, whereas children given the stem, "Once there was a girl named Alice who lived by the seashore," often narrated scriptlike sequences about common actions associated with the seashore (Stein, 1986). This finding provides further evidence that the content of the narrative affects narrative structure.

Not only are children's story plots more complex with age, but children are better able to connect story elements together into a logical and coherent whole. Stein and Glenn (1982) found that second graders would logically order part of their story sequences, then randomly order subsequent actions. Fifth graders tell stories that incorporate all the episodic elements into a logical and coherent plot and their stories are more causally connected (Stein, 1988).

Similar developmental trends were found in Gruendel's (1980) research on children's stories about familiar events. Given instructions to tell a make-believe story about familiar events (baking cookies, making a fire, planting a garden, having a birthday party), preschool children were unable to generate stories: 92% of preschool children's narratives were either scripts (62%) or personal narratives (30%). Narratives incorporating aspects of story structure into either scripts or personal narratives were called *story variants.* For example, some children added a story beginning to what was basically a script narrative, changed the protagonist to a fictional character (as in example 9), or modified one of the expected actions (e.g., the oven blows up while making cookies). The most sophisticated type of story variant embedded a problem-resolution sequence within an event description. With age, children produced more story variants and fewer scripts and personal narratives. The inclusion of a problem-resolution structure that was absent from 4-year-olds' stories, accounted for 15% of the 8-year-olds' stories (yet 47% of the "stories" at this age were still scripts).

The results of both Stein's study and Gruendel's study contrast with findings of Peterson and McCabe (1983) that 5-year-olds were able to incorporate complete goal-directed episodes in 42% of their personal narratives and 4-year-olds did the same in 13% of their personal narratives. These findings show that younger children *are* able to coordinate goals, actions, and outcomes, but they seem to have difficulty coordinating this kind of episodic structure with fictional content.

Thus, children's understanding of episodic structure as demonstrated in story production undergoes considerable development during the elementary school years and it is not until around fifth grade that children are able to tell coherent, goal-based, fictional stories. Although even young children's stories are organized around interpersonal conflicts, explicit references to internal states are rare at all ages. The development of more coherent story telling can be attributed to: (a) the development of relevant content knowledge, especially social problem-solving knowledge, (b) the development of a concept of story structure based on causally organized and goal-directed actions and obstacles (Stein, 1988; Stein & Policastro, 1984), and (c) increasing ability to coordinate content knowledge and episodic structure in a fictional frame.

The Functions of Structures

It is important to keep in mind that each of these structures carries out a different function. Although the original function of a particular narrative genre may not be evident in a given elicitation context, the structural characteristics of different narratives are nevertheless derived from the functions they serve in real-world contexts.

Scripts are used to explain, to instruct, and to direct action. They must be clear and informative. In contrast, personal narratives are told to share an experience with someone else. Relating a personal experience is a way of telling someone about yourself, of disclosing personal information. Sharing personal anecdotes contributes to the development of intimacy in interpersonal relationships (Selman, 1980). A personal narrative can also instruct. Imagine a father reminiscing about kindergarten with his daughter on the eve of her first day of kindergarten. The relating of the father's personal narrative can reassure the child that her situation is not unique while providing her with information about the event to alleviate some of her anxiety.

According to Stein (1988), the relating of fictional stories serves the function of communication and representation. In oral cultures, important information is related and transmitted through storytelling. A storyteller uses stories to explain, teach, and impart moral information (Leondar, 1977). Stories are also used to help understand social events. This second function is often served by retelling personal experience in a story format.

In our culture, it is more common to narrate a personal experience or to retell a story than it is to create a fictional story. In a naturalistic observation of preschool children's spontaneous narrative productions, Preece (1987) found that only 4% of children's narratives were original fictions or fantasies: Most consisted of personal anecdotes and anecdotes of vicarious experience. Adults also have difficulty producing original fictions as can be attested to by any adult who has been asked to make up a bedtime story for a young child. Part of the difficulty children have in constructing fictional stories may be due to the fact that this narrative function is not developed in our general culture.

Microlinguistic Knowledge

Knowledge about specific narrative genres is linguistic knowledge at a macrolevel. There are also many microlevel linguistic skills that are necessary for producing well-formed narratives and for differentiating between particular narrative genres. For example, script reports are given in the timeless present tense, whereas personal narratives are cast in the past tense: To do this requires mastery of tense. General information can be included in both personal narratives and fictional stories if it is clearly marked as background information and episodic information can be incorporated into script narratives if it is distinguished from the foregrounded topic of what usually happens. To distinguish background and foreground requires mastery of expressions such as "*usually*", "*sometimes,*" and "*except.*" In addition, modulation of aspect (e.g., using the past progressive instead of the simple past) marks orientation versus complicating actions in personal narratives and stories, as in, "They were swimming (orientation). And a kid drowned (complicating action)."[1] In this way, linguistic knowledge contributes to narrative coherence.

Microlinguistic knowledge is also important for establishing narrative *cohesion,* that is, the narrative's internal connectiveness—the degree to which the propositions that constitute the narrative relate to each other. Cohesion is achieved by employing reference devices (pronominalization, anaphora) and temporal and causal connectives. Research generally shows that preschool children predominantly use the connective *and,* but with increasing age, children use more temporal, causal, and contrasting connectives, as well as intraclausal cohesion such as subordinate conjunctions (e.g., *when, after*) and prepositional phrases (Bennett-Kastor, 1986; John-Steiner & Panofsky, 1987; Peterson, 1986; Peterson & McCabe, 1987). This does not mean that older children use *and* less than younger children, but rather, older children use more varied types of connectives and also use *and* to accomplish different narrative functions (Peterson & McCabe, 1987). (See Peterson & McCabe, chap. 1 in this vol., for a more complete discussion of cohesion in children's narratives).

Contextual Knowledge

The purpose or function of a narrative will affect both its content and organization. A personal narrative related to a stranger will be different from one related to another participant. A story told to entertain a 2-year-old would be different from one narrated to a 6-year-old. A personal narrative about a camping trip might be different if a child were relating this narrative to a grandparent than if he was asked, "Can you tell me what happened one time when you went on a trip?" by an experimenter. These kinds of contextual variations reflect variations in the narrator-listener relationship, which can be considered in terms of what the narrator can assume about the listen-

[1]This distinction between orientation and complicating action is consistent with Peterson and McCabe (1983). However, Labov (1972) treated past progressive as correlative, a type of evaluation.

er's knowledge about the events and protagonists described in the narrative.

There is ample evidence that preschool children as young as 4 are aware that they need to tailor their narratives to the needs of different audiences. Four-year-olds speak in more simplified language to younger children than to same-aged children and adults (Shatz & Gelman, 1973), modify their speech to adapt to their listeners' needs (Menig-Peterson, 1975), provide necessary orienting information in personal narratives (Menig-Peterson & McCabe, 1978; Umiker-Sebeok, 1979), and report different information about past events when talking with an experimenter than when talking with their mothers (Fivush & Hamond, 1990). Thus, the ability to take the listener's perspective into consideration is already apparent in the preschool years. Failure to report critical information in a narrative cannot be attributed to children's lack of awareness of the listener's need for such information. However, knowing that background information is needed does not mean that children can consistently provide that information in a coherent and cohesive fashion (e.g., Anselmi, Sachs, & Bertrand, 1987).

Coordination of Content and Structure

These strands of knowledge are interconnected both in development and in the act of narrative production. Consider the difference in narrating a script for a very familiar event and one that has been experienced only once. Children may include more episodic information in their scripts of less familiar events because the knowledge base they are drawing from is organized as memory of a single episode (Hudson & Nelson, 1986). Consider the task of making up a story about going to a birthday party or getting stung by a bee. Clearly, the second event affords more opportunities for plot development in that the problem is already provided in the topic.

Narrativizing an event requires that the narrator shape content knowledge into a particular narrative structure. The degree to which the structure of the knowledge representations in memory matches the structure of the narrative genre will influence the overall coherence of the narrative. Greater coherence is predicted when there is less translation required from knowing to telling. Script production is improved when the narrator is familiar with the event topic and the event has a consistent chronological sequence. Under these circumstances, producing a script involves little more than simply telling what you know. Along the same lines, it is easier to produce a personal narrative if the narrator can easily recall a specific episode, and if that episode includes something unusual or distinctive that can serve as a high point. Under these circumstances, producing a high point narrative involves little more than telling what you remember. Because stories are based on problem-resolution sequence, it is easier to tell a story about an event that typically includes explicit goals and predictable mishaps (e.g., going shopping, going to the doctor). However, even under these circumstances, story construction involves more construction of events than simply relating what you know or what you remember; a plot must be developed.

We propose that narratives will be more coherent if the narrator's knowledge base that is pertinent to the particular narrative genre is accessible and is organized in a form similar to the structure of the narrative. But when the narrator must rely on less accessible knowledge and needs to restructure that knowledge in order to meet the structural requirements of a given narrative genre, we predict that the resulting narrative will be less coherent.

Furthermore, the amount of effort required to establish narrative coherence can detract from cohesion in narratives. Children may display more advanced cohesive devices such as more advanced connectives in narrative genres that they have already mastered. The structure of the event topic can also influence narrative cohesiveness (Shapiro & Hudson, 1989). Narratives about more causally connected events such as accidents and injuries requiring medical intervention may be related with more causal connectives than narratives about birthday parties in which the action sequence is not necessarily causally connected.

AN INVESTIGATION OF EFFECTS OF TASK AND TOPIC ON CHILDREN'S NARRATIVE PRODUCTION

To investigate the relationship between topic and structure in children's narratives we compared different types of narratives produced by children in nursery school, first grade, and third grade. Each child was asked to produce either scripts, personal narratives, or make-believe stories about four events—a birthday party, the doctor's office, Halloween, and a trip. Our goals were to (a) trace the development of general narrative skills common to all narratives as well as the development of skills relevant to each particular genre; (b) examine how the topic of the narrative, that is, the particular events, influenced children's ability to produce different types of narratives; and (c) explore the relationship between narrative coherence and narrative cohesion, that is, how factors influencing narrative structure also affected the connectedness of children's narratives.

Method

Thirty-seven preschool children (mean age 4;8), 38 first graders (mean age 6;7), and 34 third graders (mean age 8;7) participated in the study. Children came from lower-middle-class families in the Albany, New York area. Children in each age group were randomly assigned to one of three narrative conditions (10–13 children in each group), script, personal narrative, and story. Each child produced four narratives, one for each event (birthday party, doctor's, Halloween, and trip), with event order counterbalanced.

The interview began with the experimenter explaining that she wanted to find out what kinds of things children know about (for the script condition), could remember (the personal narrative condition), or what kinds of stories they liked to tell (the story condition). Children in the script condition were asked "Can you tell me what happens when you . . . (go to a birthday party, go to the doctors, etc.)?"; children in the personal narrative condition were asked, "Can you tell me about what happened one time when you . . . ?"; and children in the story condition were asked, "Can you tell me a make-believe story about . . . ?" To encourage children to report more, the experimenter used general probes such as "What else?" and "Then what happened?", but no specific questions were asked. All interviews were tape-recorded and transcribed verbatim for coding.

Coding

Types of Propositions

Each narrative was first coded in terms of the number of *propositions*, that is, independent clauses including a subject and predicate. Subjects could be implied as in "We went to peoples' houses (first proposition) and got candy (second proposition)." Each proposition was coded for (a) *tense*—future, present, and past; and (b) *actor*—first person (*I* and *we*), second person (*you*), and third person (*he, she, they, the doctor, my Mommy,* etc.).

Next, each proposition was coded as either an *action, elaboration, description,* or *motivation/reaction. Actions* include any type of action reported in any type of narrative:

You get candy. (script)
Mommy put a band-aid on me. (personal narrative)
A duck went out on Halloween. (story)

Elaborations are repetitions of previously mentioned information with the addition of new information:

You see animals. You see ducks and geese. (script)
I went on a trip. And I went to Hershey Park. (personal narrative)
There was all sorts of stuff there. There were ghosts, witches, vampires, bats. (story)

Repetitions of previously mentioned information that did not include any new information were eliminated from analysis. *Descriptions* are statements about what things or people looked like and information about the location or physical setting:

They have books there. (script)
There was a lot of sand there. (personal narrative)
Once there was an ostrich. (story)

Motivations/reactions included any information about emotional or physical states and reference to internal thought processes:

It doesn't hurt. (script)
We had no idea that they were going to put a bucket of water in there. (personal narrative)
Then the rabbit got real mad. (story)

Structural Characteristics

Each type of narrative was analyzed separately in terms of the structural characteristics of each narrative genre. For each type of narrative a structural checklist was constructed consisting of six to seven important structural characteristics that provided narrative coherence.

Scripts

1. Maintenance of *present tense:* 75% or more of clauses reported in present tense.

2. Second-person *perspective:* 75% or more of clauses reported using the pronoun, *you.*

3. Explicit *temporal sequencing* (e.g., some use of *then, after, next, first, last,* etc.)

4. Inclusion of some *alternative* or *optional actions* marked by *sometimes, usually, or,* etc.

5. Inclusion of *explanations,* that is background information or elaborations to further explain why or how actions are carried out.

6. Inclusion of an *ending* that signals when the script is finished, for example, "Then you go home."

Personal Narratives

1. Inclusion of a *setting statement* that signals the beginning of the narrative, usually phrased as "once . . ." or "one time."

2. Consistent use of *past tense:* 75% or more of clauses reported in the past.

3. First-person *perspective:* 75% or more clauses given from the perspective of the first person (*I* or *we*). Actions performed by someone else to the self (e.g., "He listened to my heart.") were considered as first-person perspective although the actor was a third person.

4. Explicit *temporal sequencing.*

5. Inclusion of *explanations,* that is, general background information highlighting a particular episode, provides descriptive information about the participant(s), for example, "I was 5 years old" and "I hate shots," or explains how or why actions were carried out.

6. Inclusion of a *high point* marked by stress, exclamation, attention-getters, exaggeration, contrast, and emotional reactions.

7. Inclusion of an *ending marker* to exit the narrative as in "Then we went home," "and that's all that happened."

Stories

1. Inclusion of a *setting statement* such as "Once upon a time," "once . . ." or "one time . . ."

2. Use of a *fictional character.* Here we included animals, monsters, giants, cartoon characters as well as unidentified people such as "this girl" or "a boy." In some cases, children told fictional stories about themselves and in these cases, children were credited with use of a fictional character if the story included monsters, giants, or any other fictional characters.

3. Explicit *temporal sequencing.*

4. Inclusions of a *problem* or *surprise* action.

5. Inclusion of *resolution* of a problem or *reaction* to a problem or surprise action.

6. Inclusion of *ending marker* such as "The end," "they all went home," and "they all lived happily ever after."

Note that stories can be narrated in either the past or present tense, so neither type of tense use was considered as a structural characteristic. It should also be understood that a structurally coherent narrative need not include all of these elements: One could narrate an adequate script without including explanations or could tell a good fictional story without mentioning any fictional characters. We used these as a way to differentiate the kinds of elements children incorporated into their narratives and also to track children's use of different elements with age.

Cohesive Devices

Three types of cohesive devices were coded including some of the categories used by John-Steiner and Panofsky (1987); *conjunction, prepositional phrases and relative clauses,* and *anaphoric reference.* Conjunctions were further broken down into 4 types: (a) *simple conjunction* (*and*), (b) *temporal conjunction* (*then, and then, next, first, before, after*), and (c) *adversative* (*but, except, sometimes, usually, always, or, though*) and *causal conjunction* (*because, so, if*). Prepositional phrases and relative clauses were subordinate clauses introduced by *that, who, which, with, from, in,* and *on.* The final category, anaphoric reference, included using pronouns for previously specified objects (*it*), definite reference (*the cake, that girl*) referring to previously specified information, and various anaphoric expressions such as *the other, another, more, both,* and *there.*

Predictions

If the propositional analysis maps on to different narrative functions, then we should expect to find a larger proportion of actions reported in script narratives (which are more referential) than in personal narratives and stories (which are more evaluative). Both personal narratives and stories should include a higher proportion of descriptions because this type of proposition is used to report setting information. Setting information is not necessary in script narratives because the narrator is not required to situate the event in a particular time and location (e.g., "one time," "when we went to the zoo," "the last time"). Finally, a higher proportion of motivation/reaction propositions should be evident in both personal narratives and stories because these propositions are used to provide evaluation and to report problem-resolution sequences (or more loosely, surprise-reaction sequences) that are the respective hallmarks of personal narratives and stories.

We also predicted that the structure of the event in the real world, that is the content of the narrative, would affect the overall coherence of narratives in different ways, depending on the type of event and the type of narrative produced. In general, the degree to which events are routinized, that is, follow a consistent sequence over many episodes, should produce better organized event knowledge that, in turn, would facilitate script production. Of the four events, birthday parties, visits to the doctor, and celebrating Halloween tend to be very consistent across episodes, whereas trips are extremely variable. We predicted that children's scripts for going on a trip would not be as coherent as scripts for the other events.

In contrast, it should be easier to recall specific episodes of events if the events were less routinized, that is, included more variations and were experienced less often. We predicted that memories of Halloween would be fairly easy to recall because of the limited number of Halloween experiences and the availability of distinctive episodic markers (e.g., age of the child, the child's costume) and that information about trips is more likely to be represented in memory as separate episodic memories rather than a general event schema. Thus, Halloween and trip were expected to be more easy to recall than birthday parties and visits to the doctor.

Note that the ability to recall a specific episode does not ensure that the personal narrative based on that memory will be organized in a coherent manner (e.g., leading up to a high point). Familiarity and variability of events only contrains the accessibility of specific autobiographic memories, but it is possible that if children were able to recall a single episode for each of the events, then some events support a high point structure better than others. For example Peterson and McCabe (1983) found that personal narratives about trips were relatively boring chronological lists of actions as compared to narratives about spills, wrecks, stings, fights, and injuries.

For story production, we predicted that the degree of causal structure inherent in an event would have the most influence on coherence. Children should find it easier to include problem-resolution sequences when constructing stories about events that typically include goals, initiating actions, and resolutions. Of the four events, only visits to the doctor have a built-in problem (e.g., you get sick or injured) and resolution (e.g., you are treated by the doctor and get well). This was the only event we considered to be clearly causally organized and we predicted that children's stories about this event should be more coherent than for the other three events.

We also made some tentative predictions about the relationship between coherence and cohesion in children's narratives. If children have mastered structural coherence, they may have more cognitive resources available to focus on narrative cohesion. In this case, children should use more cohesive devices in those narrative genres that are structurally more complete. Furthermore, we predicted that children would use more causal types of connectives in narratives about the more causally organized event, going to the doctor's office.

Results

Unless otherwise indicated, analyses were performed using a 3(grade; preschool, first, and third) × 3(genre; script, personal narrative, story) × 4(event; birthday, doctor, Halloween, trip) mixed model analysis of variance with repeated measures for event. Newman-Keuls posthoc tests ($p < .05$) were performed on all reported effects.

Number of Propositions

The mean number of propositions reported for each type of narrative for each age group is shown in Figure 3.1. Main effects of age [$F(2, 97) = 13.4$, $p < .001$], genre [$F(2, 97) = 3.32$, $p < .05$], and an interaction of age and genre [$F(4, 97) = 2.65$, $p < .05$] indicated that children reported more propositions with age, but this effect was due to third graders reporting more propositions than the younger age groups in personal narratives and stories ($p < .05$), but not scripts. A main effect of event [$F(3, 291) = 5.24$, $p < .01$] indicated that narratives about trips included more propositions ($M = 8.89$) than all other narratives, and narratives about Halloween and birthday parties included more propositions (mean of 7.48 and 7.12, respectively) than narratives about going to the doctor's ($M = 6.34$).

Type of Proposition

The proportions of each narrative consisting of each type of proposition were used for a 4 (type of proposition) × 3 (genre) × 4 (event) mixed model analysis of variance with repeated measures for event and type of proposition. Mean proportions for each type of proposition reported by age and condition are shown in Table 3.1. In general, children reported more acts than any other type of proposition [$F(3, 285) = 713.4$, $p < .001$ for the main effect of type]. However, an interaction of genre and type of proposition [$F(6,285) = 2.23$, $p < .05$] indicated that children tended to report more descriptions in the personal narratives than in scripts and stories. This suggests that children were sensitive to the need to provide setting information in personal narratives, but proportionally, this was a relatively small content category. There was no significant difference between the proportion of internal motivations and reactions reported in the stories and

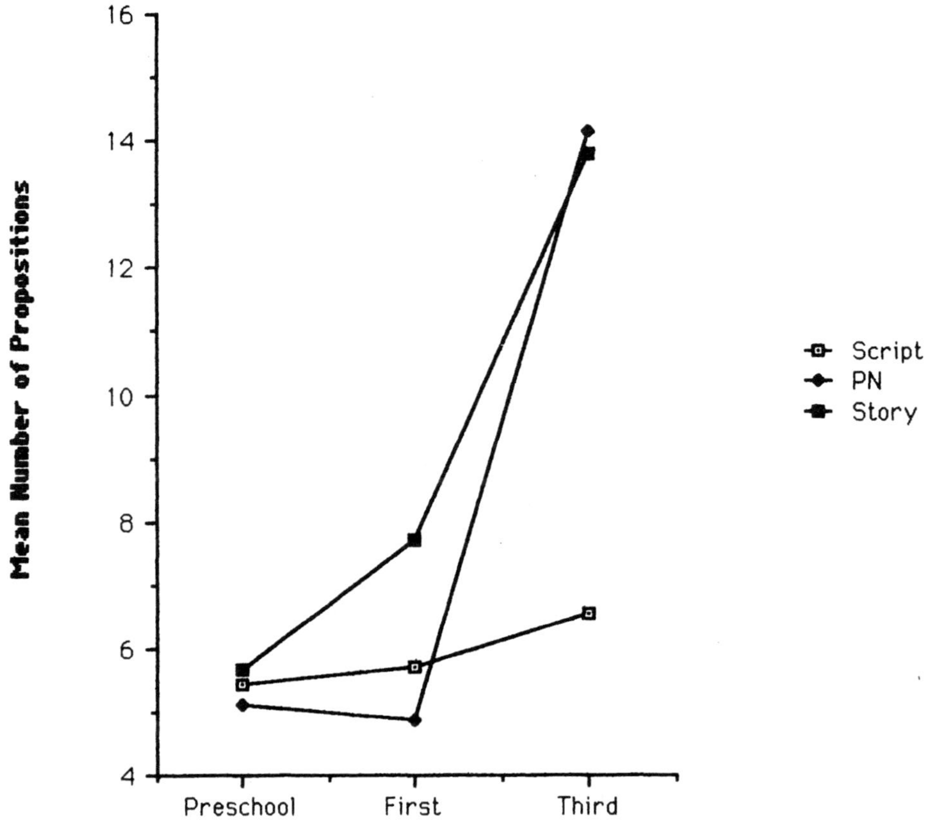

FIG. 3.1. Mean number of propositions reported by grade and type of narrative.

in the other narratives: Children did not include this important kind of information even when narrating stories.

Tense Use

Use of the past tense is an important marker that differentiates between script narratives and both personal narratives and stories (see also Hicks, chap. 2 in this vol. for further discussion of tense use in different narrative genres). As shown in Table 3.2, children reported propositions in the past tense more often in both personal narratives and stories than in scripts [$F(1, 97) = 74.31$, $p < .001$ for the main effect of genre]. Preschoolers and first graders, but not third graders, used the past tense more often in their personal narratives than in

TABLE 3.1
Mean Proportions of Each Type of Proposition Reported By Type of Narrative

	Script	*Personal Narrative*	*Story*
Act	0.74	0.67	0.70
Elaboration	0.15	0.17	0.16
Description	0.06	0.14	0.08
Motivation/Reaction	0.05	0.05	0.05

their stories, as indicated by posthoc tests on the significant interaction of age and genre [$F(1, 97) = 2.6$, $p < .05$]. Although not significant, preschool children tended to use more past tense in their script narratives than the older age groups, indicating that they were more likely to give personal narratives even when asked to produce scripts.

Actors

Another way that children differentiated the three types of narratives was in the perspective from which the narrative was told; the general *you* (script), as a participant using *I* and *we* (personal narrative) or as the narrator using the third person, *he, she,* and *they* (story). The proportion of propositions including each type of actor was analyzed in a 3 (grade) × 3 (genre) × 4 (event) × 4 (type of actor) mixed model analysis of variance with repeated measures for event and type of actor. In addition to the main effect of type of actor [$F(2, 194) \times 21.84$, $p < .001$], type of actor interacted with genre [$F(2,194) = 18.86$, $p < .001$] and there was a significant three-way interaction for type, genre, and age factors. These interactions are shown in Table 3.3.

Essentially, different patterns of usage were used by each age group depending on the genre. First consider children's scripts: Preschool and first-grade children used *you* more often than third graders in

TABLE 3.2
Mean Proportions of Propositions Reported in Past Tense By Age and Condition

	Script	*Personal Narrative*	*Story*
Preschool	0.22	0.85	0.56
First grade	0.08	0.76	0.47
Third grade	0.02	0.70	0.73
Mean	0.11	0.77	0.59

TABLE 3.3
Mean Proportions of Actor Used By Grade and Type of Narrative

	Script	*Personal Narrative*	*Story*
		Preschool	
You	0.45	0.00	0.10
I/We	0.26	0.58	0.51
Third person	0.26	0.34	0.32
		First grade	
You	0.46	0.04	0.28
I/We	0.32	0.64	0.19
Third person	0.20	0.22	0.48
		Third grade	
You	0.36	0.02	0.03
I/We	0.37	0.53	0.48
Third person	0.18	0.24	0.39

their scripts. However, third graders used a higher proportion of first-person pronouns as compared to preschoolers, which is permissable, rather than using the third-person perspective, which is inappropriate. Note that preschoolers inappropriately used a higher proportion of third-person actors in scripts than first and third graders.

Moreover, in their personal narratives, children at all ages refrained from using *you* except for the occasional background proposition. However, preschool children used the third-person actor more often than first and third graders. This pattern occurred because many personal narratives at this age involved actions performed by others rather than episodes in which they initiated most of the actions. They maintained a personal *perspective* in their personal narratives despite the fact that the actions were frequently performed by others (see section on structural elements). The lower proportion of third graders' use of *I* and *we* as compared to first graders is an artifact of the proportion measure. That is, third graders reported more propositions consisting of setting/orientation information (21% of all propositions) that did not contain any actor (e.g., "It was very dark.") so their proportion scores for actors decreased.

Children's selection of actors for their stories varied widely by age. Both preschool and third-grade children predominantly told stories about themselves. However, third graders' stories were often marked as fictional by the introduction of an additional fictional character (e.g., a witch, a monster, a doctor with magical powers). In contrast, almost half of first graders' stories were appropriately narrated about a third person or persons. Preschool and first-grade children used *you* more often than third graders, indicating that they tended to confuse stories and scripts; this was more evident for first graders than for preschoolers.

There was also a significant interaction of type of actor with event [$F(6,582) = 17.59$, $p < .001$]. Results of posthoc tests showed that children used first-person actors more often in talking about a trip ($M = 0.64$) than in the other three events (birthday = 0.44, doctor = 0.40, Halloween = 0.55) and the third person was used more in doctor narratives ($M = 0.55$) than in narratives about birthdays (0.34), Halloween (0.26), and trips (0.22). These data support the hypothesis that knowledge about trips is represented as autobiographic memories of specific episodes (i.e., from a personal perspective) and suggest that visits to the doctor include more actions performed by a third person (the doctor) on a participant.

Structural Elements

An analysis was performed on the proportions of structural elements included in each narrative. (Proportion scores were used because there were more coding categories for personal narratives than for scripts and stories). With age, children included more elements in all types of narratives ($F(2, 97) = 14.56$, $p < .001$ for the main effect of age]: Preschool children's narratives included 33% of all structural elements, first graders' narratives included 40% and third graders' narratives included 56%. To further illustrate age differences in inclusion of different types of structural elements, Fig. 3.2 shows the percentage of children in each age group who incorporated the various structural elements into their narratives.

In producing script narratives, use of the present tense and the appropriate perspective was evident in even the preschool children's narratives. First graders and third graders usually incorporated an additional element into their scripts, most likely the mention of optional actions or explicit temporal sequencing. Explanations and ending actions were relatively infrequent at all ages and except for explicit sequencing and mention of an ending act, there was little development past first grade. Interestingly, the oldest subjects did not organize their scripts hierarchically and rarely used header acts, in contrast to results obtained by Gruendel (1980). In personal narratives, tense and perspective were, once again, mastered by the youngest children. But there was little differentiation between preschool children and first graders in their use of high point structural characteristics. However, the inclusion of setting and background information, explicit sequencing, and inclusion of a high point generally surpassed the comparable structural "embellishments" for scripts at the same ages. Thus, pre-

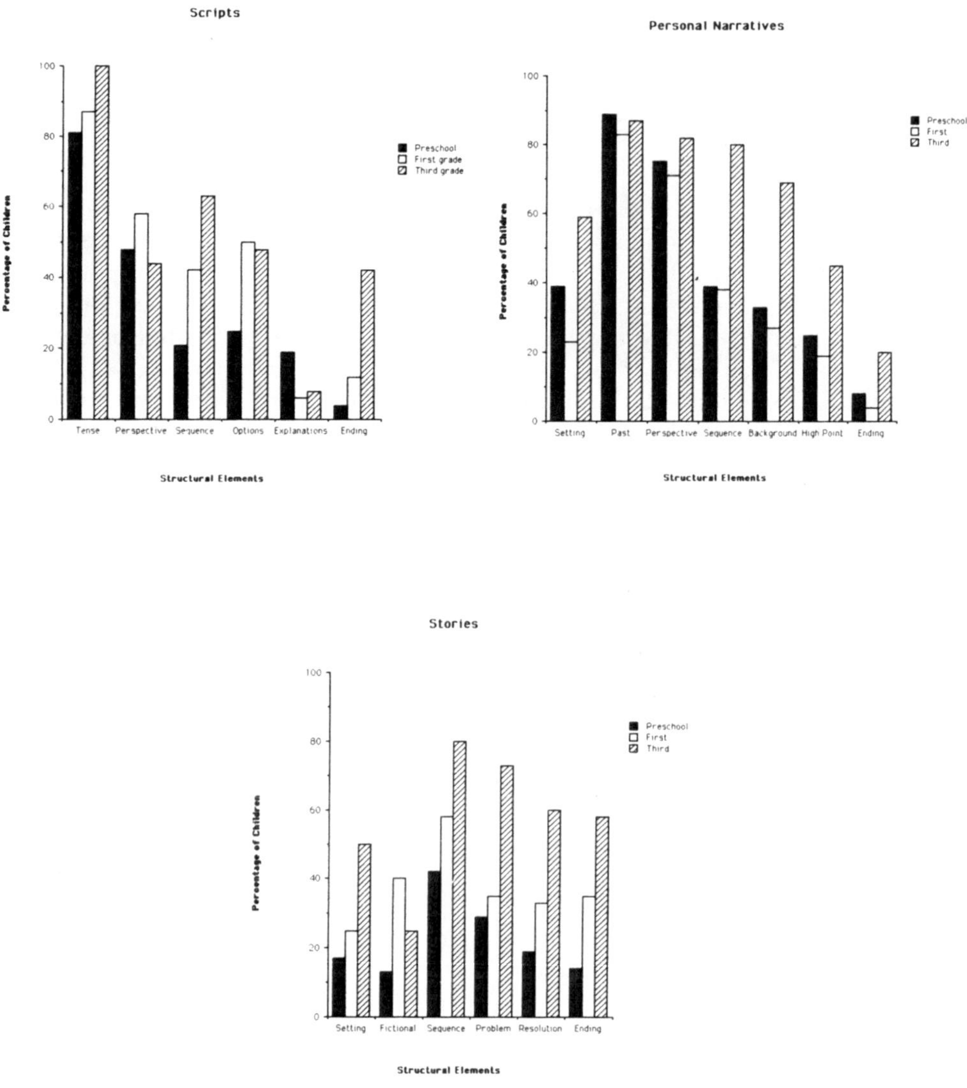

FIG. 3.2. Percentage of children in each age group including structural elements into each type of narrative.

schoolers and first graders showed some differentiation between the two narrative structures in other than simply tense and perspective, but the third graders far surpassed both of the younger age groups in their use of high point organization.

Not surprisingly, preschool children included relatively few elements of story grammars into their story narratives. The only element evident in more than 25% of their narratives was explicit temporal sequencing, a characteristic also found at the same rate in their personal narratives. But the inclusion of a setting statement fell below the use of setting markers in preschoolers' personal narratives. The finding that almost 25% of their narratives included a problem suggests there was some early appreciation of the structural requirements of stories, but, as is discussed later, this could be accounted for somewhat by the structure of the events used as topics, in particular the problem-resolution structure of the doctor's office event topic.

First graders showed improvement in all structural elements, indicating that they were aware of the structural properties of stories although they may not have mastered the narrative skills for story production. Finally, third graders were relatively skilled at incorporating key story elements into their story narratives. The infrequent use of fictional characters is due to the fact that children often used themselves as protagonists. The relatively high inclusion of explicit endings indicates that ending markers are more of a necessary component of stories than scripts and personal narratives. In addition, Pradl (1979) suggested that children reach the end of their "inventiveness span" fairly quickly and will abruptly finish stories with tag endings (e.g., "the end").

As predicted, narrative structure was influenced by the event topic of the narrative [$F(3, 219) = 3.22, p < .05$ for the main effect of event]. The mean proportion of structural elements included in each type of narrative for each event topic are shown in Table 3.4. An interaction effect for event and genre [$F(6, 291) = 3.69, p < .05$] showed that, contrary to expectations, going to the doctor's office produced the best scripts, and the difference in proportion of elements reported for birthday and doctor was significant. Inspection of children's scripts showed that going to the doctor's office was a highly routinized event with relatively fewer variations than the other events (see examples 2 and 10 in the appendix).

The most structural elements for personal narratives were found in the trip narratives. The proportion of structural elements found in these narratives was significantly higher than in narratives about birthdays and going to the doctor, but not Halloween. We had predicted that children could easily recall single episodes of trips that

TABLE 3.4
Mean Proportions of Structural Characteristics by Event and Type of Narrative

	Script	*Personal Narrative*	*Story*	*Mean*
Birthday	0.36	0.45	0.38	0.39
Doctor	0.48	0.44	0.46	0.46
Halloween	0.45	0.48	0.34	0.42
Trip	0.40	0.55	0.34	0.43
Mean	0.42	0.47	0.39	

would help them in their personal narrative production. However, we had also predicted that Halloween celebrations would be easily recalled. Apparently, children did not have any trouble recalling Halloween episodes, but Halloween personal narratives tended to include more scriptlike sequences (see examples 15, 19, and 23 in the appendix) as compared to personal narratives about trips that included more evaluation (e.g., "I had lots of fun," example 20), high points (e.g., "and then finally we got there . . .," example 24), and explicit endings (e.g., "and then we went home," example 16).

As predicted, the causal structure of the doctor event allowed children to tell better stories about this event than the other three event topics (see examples 26 and 30) although only the difference in proportion of structural elements for doctor and birthdays (the least causally organized event) was significant.

Cohesion

A good narrative does more than just include the necessary components; cohesion is created by weaving the elements together. To what degree is children's use of cohesive devices determined by the type of narrative they are reporting and the topic of that narrative? Children's use of each type of device was computed by dividing the frequency of use for each type by the total number of propositions in each child's narrative. These proportions are displayed in Table 3.5. Use of the three types of *conjunction* was analyzed in a 3 (grade) × 3 (genre) × 4 (event) × 3 (type of conjunction) mixed model analysis of variance with repeated measures for event and type of conjunction. Use of *relative clauses and prepositional phrases* and *anaphoric reference* were each analyzed in separate 3 (grade) × 3 (genre) × 4 (event) mixed model analyses of variance with repeated measures for event.

With age, children used more connectives, $F(1, 97) = 7.18, p < .01$,

TABLE 3.5
Mean Proportions of Cohesive Devices by Condition

	Script	*Personal Narrative*	*Story*
Conjunction:			
Simple (*and*)	0.24	0.34	0.36
Temporal	0.17	0.22	0.22
Adversative and causal	0.20	0.11	0.15
Relative clauses and prepositional phrases	0.45	0.57	0.45
Anaphoric reference	0.14	0.17	0.16

(means of 0.17, 0.22, and 0.26 for preschool, first-grade, and third-grade children, respectively). There was also a main effect for type of conjunction [$F(2, 194) = 29.17, p < .001$] and an interaction of type with condition [$F(2, 194) = 4.42, p < .01$]. The overall pattern was as follows: *And* was used most frequently, followed by temporal connectives, which were used more frequently than adversative and causal connectives (see Table 3.5). However, children used fewer simple conjunctions and more adversative and causal conjunctions in scripts than in personal narratives and stories.

The event topic also influenced children's use of connectives as indicated by a main effect of event [$F(3, 291) = 2.9, p < .05$] and a significant interaction of event and type of conjunction [$F(6, 582) = 4.18, p < .01$]. These data are displayed in Fig. 3.3. Narratives about birthday parties, the least temporally or causally organized event, included the least number of connectives and mostly the simple conjunction, *and*. Narratives about the doctor's office, the most causally organized event, included the least amount of simple conjunction and a relatively high amount of adversative and causal conjunction. Connective use in Halloween and trip narratives were very similar and generally conformed to the overall pattern except that the level of adversative and causal connective use was relatively higher in the trip narratives.

The differences in the use of relative clauses/prepositional phrases and anaphoric reference by narrative type were not significant (see Table 3.6). Nor did use of these cohesive devices vary by age. However, there was a main effect of event for use of relative clauses and prepositional phrases [$F(3, 291) = 4, 78, p < .01$]: The highest proportion of use was found in children's narratives about going on a trip (M = 0.58), which was significantly greater than use in narratives about

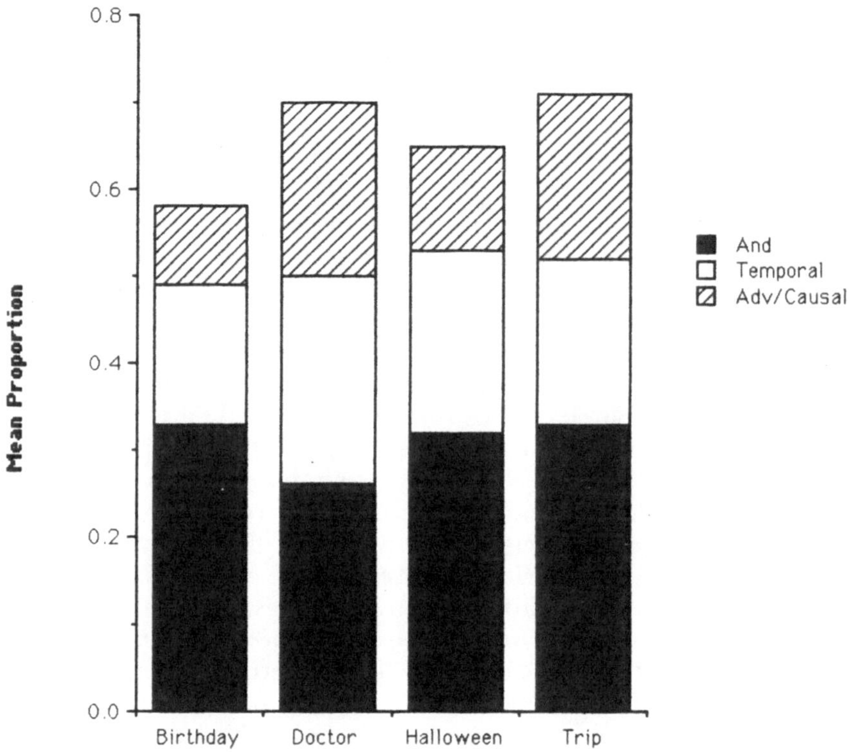

FIG. 3.3. Mean proportions of connectives used by event topic and type of connective.

going to the doctor's (M = 0.51), which, in turn, was significantly greater than use in narratives about Halloween (M = 0.45) and having a birthday party (M = 0.42).

Discussion

In order to impose coherence on the results of our study, we present three stories about those findings. The first story is about how children's understanding of narrative genre develops. The second story details the effects of event topic on the production of different narrative genres. The third story is an account of how event topic and narrative genre affect children's ability to produce cohesive narratives.

Development of Narrative Genres

First consider the development of children's scripts. There were no age differences in amount of information reported but, with age, children included more types of structural elements. Specifically, children were more likely to explicitly sequence their scripts, add more optional information, and provide clear endings. These developments suggest that older children, particularly third graders were more aware of scripts as *narratives,* in that they were more likely to make the sequence and ending explicit (see examples 6, 11, and 12 in the appendix). Younger children followed closely the temporal sequence of the event in their reports but did not explicitly mark sequence, relying instead on shared knowledge between themselves and the experimenter about the usual sequence of events (see examples 1 and 2 in the appendix). They were reporting general knowledge about what happens, but were not constructing a narrative.

Another difference between younger and older children's scripts was that preschoolers included more episodic information using the past tense and personal pronouns. In some cases, episodic information was presented as an explanation or example (see example 4 in appendix), but in other cases children's scripts were more episodic than general (example 3 in appendix). Preschool children seemed to have a looser conception of a script than first and third graders. This is consistent with the interpretation that they were simply reporting what they knew about the event, and if they happened to recall some relevant episodic information in the process, they reported that as well. Older children seemed more aware that they were constructing a narrative requiring them to edit out episodic information.

Consider the development of personal narratives. Third graders' personal narratives were significantly longer than both preschoolers' and first graders' and also included more types of structural elements. In particular, they included more setting statements, explicit sequencing, background information, high points, and endings. Both preschool and first-grade children showed less awareness of the structural characteristics of personal narratives as compared to third graders despite the fact that they had mastered the necessary discourse conventions for referring to past events in their use of past tense and personal reference. The use of setting statements by 38% of the preschoolers and 22% of the first graders indicates that they were aware of some of the discourse markers for narrating personal narratives before they were able to structure their accounts around a high point.

These findings, especially the performance of first graders, contrast with reports in the literature of preschool and first-grade children's ability to produce coherent high point narratives (Peterson & McCabe, 1983; Preece, 1987; Umiker-Sebeok, 1979). There are a number of reasons for this discrepancy.

First, as discussed in the introduction, children's personal narratives are more often coherent at an earlier age in conversational contexts than when they are explicitly asked to produce a narrative. In an ongoing conversation, abstracts and introducers are necessary to capture the listener's attention, whereas in an experimental elicitation context, the experimenter is already attending to the subject.

Furthermore, the spontaneous relating of personal narratives is motivated by the desire to communicate something interesting, novel, or unusual. The high point of the narrative is the point that the narrator is most interested in communicating. In an experimental elicitation context, the subject only has to relate "what happened" to fulfill the experimenters' request and there is no intrinsic motivation to narrativize, that is, organize their accounts around a high point or plot.

More important, we selected the topic of the narrative for the children and 75% of the event topics were familiar events. Familiarity tends to increase general event knowledge while decreasing the accessibility of episodic memories (Hudson & Nelson, 1986).

For these reasons, we do *not* conclude that preschool and first-grade children cannot incorporate high point structure in their personal narratives, but rather, they are less likely to do so when the topic and context are not conducive to narrativizing. Our data, and those of others already cited, indicate that preschool and first graders seem to be aware of genre differences, but are not always able to produce a specified genre.

Third, consider the development of stories. Here, there was a gradual developmental increase in the number of story elements included. Preschool children's stories were often indistinguishable from scripts and personal narratives because they often used first- and third-person actors, were frequently reported in the present tense (see also Hicks, chap. 2 in this vol.), and only included a problem in 24% of the stories (which could be due to the fact that 25% of the stories were about going to the doctor's office). They were very capable in reporting what they knew or could remember about the events, but could not restructure that knowledge into a story format.

First graders showed some awareness of story characteristics in that they used more third-person and fictional actors and included more problems, resolutions, and endings. However, only a little more than a third of their stories included a problem-resolution structure. They seemed to recognize that stories were different from general event accounts and reports of specific personal episodes and that stories typically included problems, but they had difficulty restructuring their knowledge into a problem-resolution structure.

In contrast, setting statements, problems, resolutions, and endings were found in more than half of the third graders' stories. Interestingly, third graders more than first graders used themselves as the protagonist of their stories, but followed the appropriate problem-resolution structure. This is most likely because most of the event topics were events frequently experienced by children.

Thus, first graders' narratives were more differentiated than preschoolers', indicating an increased awareness of narrative genre, but a limited ability to integrate structural elements into coherent narratives. By the third grade, children were able to produce structurally coherent and differentiated scripts, personal narratives, and stories, indicating a general understanding of narrative structure as well as the particular structural requirements of each narrative genre.

However, third graders' stories still lacked explicit reference to internal states, goals, and reactions. This finding is consistent with research showing that goal-based stories are not produced until the late elementary school years (Gruendel, 1980; Hidi & Hildyard, 1983; Kemper, 1984; Leondar, 1977; Stein & Glenn, 1982). Thus, the development of narrative structure in scripts and personal narratives is relatively complete by the third grade, but the narrative structure in children's stories continues to develop.

Interaction of Task and Topic

The event topic exerted a strong influence on all narratives. Children's scripts about going to the doctor's office included the most structural elements because going to the doctor's office is a highly familiar, very routine, and causally organized event. Well-structured general event knowledge seemed to interfere with children's ability to tell good personal narratives. The event topic that included the most structural elements for personal narratives was going on a trip—a less familiar and more variable event. The event topic that produced the best stories, as for scripts, was about going to the doctor's office. This event routinely involves a problem and resolution so children did not have to construct new problems in order to tell a good story.

Cohesion in children's narratives was also affected by event topic. Narratives about the more causally organized events, going to the doctor's and going on a trip included more connectives and a higher proportion of adversative and causal connections than the less causally structured events, going to a birthday party and celebrating Halloween.

The Development of Narrative Cohesion

With age, children used more connectives in their narratives. However, use of cohesive devices was strongly influenced by the topic of the narrative and the type of narrative produced (see section on interaction of task and topic). Children used more of the *more* advanced adversative and causal connectives when narrating scripts and more simple conjunctions when narrating personal narratives and stories.

These findings supported our prediction that children would use more advanced types of cohesive devices in narrative genres for which the structural requirements have been mastered. That is, children expend relatively less cognitive effort to achieve narrative coherence when they have mastered narrative structure and when the event topic requires little restructuring for narrative production. When the cognitive effort needed to achieve coherence is decreased, more effort can be applied to the creation of narrative cohesion (Pratt & MacKenzie-Keating, 1985). Because children at all ages had acquired the necessary components for script coherence—present tense and third-person perspective—they may have been able to focus more on connecting propositions in a more coherent manner. Children's use of various types of cohesive devices was therefore more dependent on the interaction of narrative genre and topic than on age of the narrator.

CONCLUSIONS: KNOWING, REMEMBERING, AND NARRATING

In our introduction, we proposed that narrative production is very much influenced by what knowledge is used in producing the narrative and how the structure of that knowledge does or does not match the structural requirements of the particular narrative genre, that is, the amount of translation involved between knowing and telling. The results of our investigation support this proposal. They also raise some important issues about the development of knowledge and its role in cognitive development.

Recent research has emphasized the role of children's knowledge representations in the development of memory and cognition (see Fivush & Hudson, 1990). In general, this approach has shown that children's knowledge representations, especially knowledge about familiar events organized as generalized event representations, provide children with a *cognitive context* to support various cognitive and discourse tasks (Nelson, 1986).

However, our research shows that performance is enhanced only when the subject has the relevant knowledge base to apply to a task and that knowledge is organized in a way that facilitates the particular kind of performance required. Brown (1975) referred to this match between knowledge and task performance as "headfitting." The results from our study show that a relevant knowledge base is necessary but not sufficient to produce coherent narratives. For young children, the fit between the structure of knowledge and memory and the structure of the narrative genre is critical in determining narrative coherence. Older children are better able to restructure knowledge into different types of narrative structures, perhaps because those narrative structures are well-developed and easily accessible, and are therefore less dependent on headfitting in narrative production. What this means is that we cannot simply ask children to talk about things that they know about and assume that this will facilitate their performance; we need to take into account the structure and accessibility of their knowledge and its relevance to the task at hand.

Our focus on the relationship between what children know and how they are able to access and weave their knowledge into different narrative genres is somewhat similar to Young's (1984) discussion of the relationship between the *taleworld* and the *storyrealm* of narratives, that is, between the world of the events conjured up by the narrative—what we call narrative content—and the framework of understanding that is invoked by different kinds of genres (personal narratives, fictional stories, legends, myths, jokes, etc.). However, in Young's formulation, content is not separate from structure, but rather, when viewed from different perspectives (i.e., within different "realms"), the same narrative elements provide different kinds of content.

Young (1984) also discussed a third perspective, the *realm of conversation* in which narrative production is embedded. Considered from this perspective, narrative elements can be viewed as contributions to the ongoing conversations and social interactions they are plucked from for the purpose of analysis.

Young's characterization of narrative reminds us that not only do we need to consider the cognitive context in which children's narratives are produced, but we must also consider the *social context* of narrative production (see McCabe & Peterson, chap. 6 in this vol.). As discussed earlier, different narratives serve different communicative functions and the structures that define narrative genre are a result of those communicative functions. By altering the communicative function of narrative production, we necessarily alter the coherence of the narrative produced.

This is not to say that experimental elicitation is invalid: In fact, it is very necessary to make the kinds of comparisons we made in our study; to tease apart the effects of age, task, and topic in the development of narrative skill. But we need to consider the communicative context as another factor influencing narrative coherence (or in Young's formulation, as another perspective from which to evaluate coherence). This forces us to go beyond discussion of what is the best or most appropriate context for studying narrative production, and to develop a model of how context affects narrative production, a model that can encompass narratives elicited by experimenters, narratives spontaneously produced in conversation, narratives elicited by teachers in normal classroom activities (see Dickinson, chap. 8 in this vol., and Michaels, chap. 9 in this vol.), narratives created in play and narratives told to reminisce (see McCabe, Capron, & Peterson, chap. 5 in this vol.).

Narrative skill cannot be considered as a general skill applicable to all narrative genres and elicitation contexts; nor can we treat narrative genres as static schemas that children do or do not have available for narrative production. Rather, different narrative genres can be viewed as different frames for rendering experience into narrative (Wolf, 1990). Our research suggests that there are many ways of knowing and many ways of telling. Thus, the nature of the experience, how it is represented to the narrator, and how the narrator chooses to relate that experience, all play important roles in narrative production.

ACKNOWLEDGMENTS

The research reported in this chapter was supported by a grant to Judith A. Hudson from the Research Foundation of the State University of New York. We are grateful to MaryBeth Hagreen for her assistance in data collection and transcription. We also thank Roni Avedon, Rosa Bianco, and Carolyn Guarino for their help in coding.

REFERENCES

Anselmi, D., Sachs, J., & Bertrand, J. (1987). *Presuppositional knowledge in children's narratives.* Paper presented at the Fourth International Congress for the Study of Child Language, Lund, Sweden.

Applebee, A. N. (1978). *The child's concept of a story: Ages two to seventeen.* Chicago: University of Chicago Press.

Ashmead, D. H., & Perlmutter, M. (1979). *Infant memory in everyday life.* Paper presented at the American Psychological Association, New York.

Ashmead, D. H., & Perlmutter, M. (1980). Infant memory in everyday life. In

M. Perlmutter (Ed.), *Children's memory: New directions for child development* (No. 10, pp. 1–16). San Francisco: Jossey-Bass.

Barenboim, C. (1981). The development of person perception in childhood and adolescence: From behavioral comparisons to psychological constructs to psychological comparisons. *Child Development, 52,* 129–144.

Bauer, P. J., & Mandler, J. M. (1990). Remembering what happened next: Very young children's recall of event sequences. In R. Fivush & J. A. Hudson (Eds.), *Knowing and remembering in young children* (pp. 9–29). New York: Cambridge University Press.

Beeghly, M., & Bretherton, I. (1982). Talking about internal states: The acquisition of an explicit theory of mind. *Developmental Psychology, 18,* 906–921.

Bennett-Kastor, T. L. (1986). Cohesion and predication in child narrative. *Journal of Child Language, 13,* 353–370.

Botvin, G. J., & Sutton-Smith, B. (1977). The development of complexity in children's fantasy narratives. *Developmental Psychology, 13,* 377–388.

Brown, A. L. (1975). The development of memory: Knowing, knowing about knowing, and knowing how to know. In H. W. Reese (Ed.), *Advances in child development and behavior* (Vol. 10, pp. 103–152). New York: Academic Press.

Damon, W. (1977). *The social world of the child.* San Francisco: Jossey-Bass.

Eisenberg, A. R. (1985). Learning to describe past experiences in conversation. *Discourse Processes, 8,* 177–204.

Engel, S. (1986, April). The role of mother-child interaction in autobiographic recall. In J. A. Hudson (Ed.), *Learning to talk about the past.* Symposium conducted at the Southeastern Conference on Human Development, Nashville, TN.

Fivush, R. (1984). Learning about school: The development of kindergarteners' school scripts. *Child Development, 55,* 1697–1709.

Fivush, R., Gray, J. T., & Fromhoff, F. A. (1987). Two-year-olds talk about the past. *Cognitive Development, 2,* 393–410.

Fivush, R., & Hamond, N. R. (1990). Autobiographic memory across the preschool years: Towards reconceptualizing childhood amnesia. In R. Fivush & J. A. Hudson (Eds.), *Knowing and remembering in young children* (pp. 223–248). New York: Cambridge University Press.

Fivush, R., & Hudson, J. A. (1990). *Knowing and remembering in young children.* New York: Cambridge University Press.

Fivush, R., & Slackman, E. (1986). The acquisition and development of scripts. In K. Nelson (Ed.), *Event knowledge: Structure and function in development* (pp. 71–96). Hillsdale, NJ: Lawrence Erlbaum Associates.

Gardner, H., & Gardner, J. (1971). Children's literary skills. *Journal of Experimental Education, 39,* 42–46.

Gruendel, J. M. (1980). *Scripts and stories: A study of children's event narratives.* Unpublished doctoral dissertation, Yale University.

Hasslett, B. (1986). A developmental analysis of children's narratives. In D. G. Willis & W. A. Donahue (Eds.), *Contemporary issues in language and discourse processes* (pp. 87–109). Hillsdale, NJ: Lawrence Erlbaum Associates.

Hidi, S. E., & Hildyard, A. (1983). The comparison of oral and written production of two discourse types. *Discourse Processes, 6,* 91–105.

Hudson, J. A. (1986). Memories are made of this: General event knowledge and the development of autobiographic memory. In K. Nelson (Ed.), *Event knowledge: Structure and function in development* (pp. 97–118). Hillsdale, NJ: Lawrence Erlbaum Associates.

Hudson, J. A. (1990). The emergence of autobiographic memory in mother-child conversation. In R. Fivush & J. A. Hudson (Eds.), *Knowing and remembering in young children* (pp. 166–196). New York: Cambridge University Press.

Hudson, J., & Nelson, K. (1983). Effects of script structure on children's story recall. *Developmental Psychology, 19,* 625–635.

Hudson, J., & Nelson, K. (1984). Differentiation and development in children's event narratives. *Papers and Reports on Child Development Research, 23,* 50–57.

Hudson, J. A., & Nelson, K. (1986). Repeated encounters of a similar kind: Effects of familiarity on children's autobiographic memory. *Cognitive Development, 1,* 232–271.

Hudson, J. A., & Slackman, E. A. (in press). Children's use of scripts in inferential text processing. *Discourse Processes.*

Hudson, J. A., & Slackman, E. A. (1985, August). *Developmental differences in script complexity: Fact or artifact?* Paper presented at the meetings of the American Psychological Association, Los Angeles.

John-Steiner, V. & Panofsky, C. (1987, April). *The development of cohesion in children's retold narratives.* Paper presented at the meetings of the Society for Research in Child Development, Baltimore.

Karmiloff-Smith, A. (1985). Language and cogitive processes from a developmental perspective. *Language and Cognitive Processes, 1,* 61–85.

Kemper, S. (1984). The development of narrative skills: Explanations and entertainments. In S. A. Kuczaj (Ed.), *Discourse development: Progress in cognitive development* (pp. 99–122). New York: Springer-Verlag.

Kernan, K. T. (1977). Semantic and expressive elaboration in children's narratives. In S. Ervin-Tripp & C. Mitchell-Kernan (Eds.), *Child discourse* (pp. 91–102). New York: Academic Press.

Kintsch, W. (1974). *The representation of meaning in memory.* Potomac, MD: Lawrence Erlbaum Associates.

Kuczaj, S. A., McClain, L. (1984). Of hawks and moozes: The fantasy narratives produced by a young child. In S. A. Kuczaj (Ed.), *Discourse development: Progress in cognitive development.* New York: Springer-Verlag.

Labov, W. (1972). *Language in the inner city.* Philadelphia: University of Pennsylvania Press.

Labov, W., & Waletzky, J. (1967). Narrative analysis: Oral versions of personal experiences. In J. Helm (Ed.), *Essays on the verbal and visual arts,* pp. 12–44. Seattle: University of Washington Press.

Leondar, B. (1977). Hatching plots: Genesis of storymaking. In D. Perkins (Ed.), *The arts and cognition* (pp. 172–191). Baltimore: Johns Hopkins University Press.

Lucariello, J., & Nelson, K. (1987). Remembering and planning talk between mothers and children. *Discourse Processes, 10,* 219–235.

Mandler, J. M. (1983). Representation. In J. H. Flavell & E. M. Markman (Eds.), *Handbook of child psychology, Vol. 3: Cognitive development* (4th ed., pp. 420–494). New York: Wiley.

Mandler, J. M., & DeForest, M. (1979). Is there more than one way to recall a story? *Child Development, 50,* 586–589.

Maranda, E., & Maranda, K. (1971). *Structural models in folklore and transformational essays.* The Hague: Mouton.

McCabe, A., & Peterson, C. (1985). A naturalistic study of the production of causal connectives by children. *Journal of Child Language, 12,* 145–159.

Menig-Peterson, C. L. (1975). The modification of communicative behavior in preschool-aged children as a function of the listener's perspective. *Child Development, 46,* 1015–1018.

Menig-Peterson, C. L., & McCabe, A. (1978). Children's orientation of a listener to the context of their narratives. *Developmental Psychology, 14,* 582–592.

Miller, P. J., & Sperry, L. L. (1988). Early talk about the past: The origins of conversational stories of personal experience. *Journal of Child Language, 15,* 293–316.

Nelson, K. (1986). Event knowledge and cognitive development. In K. Nelson (Ed.), *Event knowledge: Structure and function in development* (pp 1–19). Hillsdale, NJ: Lawrence Erlbaum Associates.

Nelson, K. (1990). Remembering, forgetting, and infantile amnesia. In R. Fivush & J. A. Hudson (Eds.), Knowing and remembering in young children (pp. 301–316). New York: Cambridge University Press.

Nelson, K., & Greundel, J. M. (1979). At morning it's lunchtime: A scriptal view of children's dialogues. *Discourse Processes, 2,* 73–94.

Nelson, K., & Gruendel, J. M. (1986). Children's scripts. In K. Nelson (Ed.), *Event knowledge: Structure and function in development* (pp. 21–46). Hillsdale, NJ: Lawrence Erlbaum Associates.

O'Connell, B., & Girard, A. (1985). Scripts and scraps: The development of sequential understanding. *Child Development, 56,* 671–681.

Peterson, C. (1986). Semantic and pragmatic uses of "but." *Journal of Child Language, 13,* 583–590.

Peterson, C., & McCabe, A. (1987). The connective 'and': Do older children use it less as they learn other connectives? *Journal of Child Language, 14,* 375–381.

Peterson, C., & McCabe, A. (1983). *Developmental psycholinguistics: Three ways of looking at a child's narrative.* New York: Plenum.

Poulsen, D., Kintsch, E., Kintsch, W., & Premack, D. (1979). Children's comprehension and memory for stories. *Journal of Experimental Child Psychology, 28,* 379–403.

Pradl, G. M. (1979). Learning how to begin and end a story. *Language Arts, 56,* 21–25.

Pratt, M. W., & MacKenzie-Keating, S. (1985). Organizing stories: Effects of task difficulty on referential cohesion in narrative. *Developmental Psychology, 21,* 350–356.

Preece, A. (1987). The range of narrative forms conversationally produced by young children. *Journal of Child Language, 6,* 91–109.

Sachs, J. (1983). Talking about the there and then: The emergence of displaced reference in parent-child discourse. In K. Nelson (Ed.), *Children's language* (Vol. 4, pp. 1–28). Hillsdale, NJ: Lawrence Erlbaum Associates.

Seidman, S., Nelson, K., & Gruendel, J. M. (1986). Make-believe scripts: The transformation of event representations in fantasy. In K. Nelson (Ed.), *Event knowledge: Structure and function in development* (pp. 231–247). Hillsdale, NJ: Lawrence Erlbaum Associates.

Selman, R. L. (1980). *The growth of interpersonal understanding.* New York: Academic Press.

Shantz, C. U. (1983). Social cognition. In J. H. Flavell & E. M. Markman (Eds.), *Handbook of child psychology, vol. 3): Cognitive development* (pp. 495–555). New York: Wiley.

Shapiro, L. R., & Hudson, J. A. (1989, April). *Coherence and cohesion in preschool children's picture-elicited narratives.* Paper presented at the meetings of the Society for Research in Child Development, Kansas City.

Shatz, M., & Gelman, R. (1973). The development of communication skills: Modifications in the speech of young children as a function of listener. *Monographs of the Society for Research in Child Development, 38* (5, Serial No. 152).

Slackman, E. A., & Hudson, J. A. (1984, October). *Filling in the gaps: Inferential processes in children's comprehension of oral discourse.* Paper presented at the Boston University Conference on Language Development, Boston.

Slackman, E. A., Hudson, J. A., & Fivush, R. (1986). Actors, actions, links, and goals: The structure of children's event representations. In K. Nelson (Ed.), *Event knowledge: Structure and function in development* (pp. 47–69). Hillsdale, NJ: Lawrence Erlbaum Associates.

Smith, M. C. (1978). Cognizing the behavior stream: The recognition of intentional action. *Child Development, 49,* 736–743.

Stein, N. L. (1986, October). *A model of storytelling skills.* Paper presented at the Boston University Conference on Language Development, Boston.

Stein, N. L. (1988). The development of children's storytelling skill. In M. B. Franklin & S. Barten (Eds.), *Child language: A book of readings* (pp. 282–297). New York: Oxford University Press.

Stein, N. L., & Glenn, C. G. (1979). An analysis of story comprehension in elementary school children. In R. O. Freedle (Ed.), *New directions in discourse processing, Vol. 2,* pp. 53–120. *Advances in discourse processes.* Norwood, NJ: Ablex.

Stein, N. L., & Glenn, C. G. (1982). Children's concept of time: The development of a story schema. In W. J. Friedman (Ed.), *The developmental psychology of time* (pp. 255–282). New York: Academic Press.

Stein, N. L., & Policastro, M. (1984). The concept of a story: A comparison

between children's and teacher's perspectives. In H. Mandl, N. L. Stein, & T. Trabasso (Eds.), *Learning and comprehension of text* (pp. 113–155). Hillsdale, NJ: Lawrence Erlbaum Associates.
Sutton-Smith, B. (1975). The importance of the storytaker: An investigation of the imaginative life. *The Urban Review, 8,* 82–95.
Umiker-Sebeok, D. J. (1979). Preschool children's intraconversational narratives. *Journal of Child Language, 6,* 91–109.
White, H. (1980). The value of narrativity in the representation of reality. In W.J.T. Mitchell (Ed.), *On narrative* (pp. 1–49). Chicago: University of Chicago Press.
Wolf, D. (1990). *The development of genre: What does it mean?* Discussion presented in J. A. Hudson (chair), Evaluating structure in different narrative genres. Symposium presented at the Conference on Human Development, Richmond, VA.
Wood, M. E. (1978). Children's developing understanding of other people's motives for behavior. *Developmental Psychology, 14,* 561–562.
Young, K. (1984). Ontological puzzles about narrative. *Poetics, 13,* 239–259.

APPENDIX

The following narratives began after the experimenter asked the general question, "What happens when you . . .?" (script); "What happened one time when you . . .?" (personal narrative); or "Can you tell me a make-believe story about . . .?" (story). Nondirective prompts (e.g., "what else?", "then what happened(s)?") are marked by "/"

1. Preschool: Script: birthday

You get to sing. / You get cake. / You eat ice cream.

2. Preschool: Script: doctor's office

You have to wait until your turn. / When they say your name then you go in. / He checks you out.

3. Preschool: Script: Halloween

You get pumpkins. / You eat candy. On the last one I dressed up into a witch. / I hadn't even dressed up into my costume because it got my hair and I couldn't see. I had a very good one. / Sometimes I can eat special food and can go trick-or-treating. And the last one was at fire engine house. And they had juice and doughnuts. And we got a doughnut.

4. Preschool: Script: Trip

You get to swim at the ocean. I swam very good. / ' Cause I went on swimming lessons. / You get to camp. / You get to cook outside, on your barbecue. / But when it's real summer, me and my mommy and daddy and my sister go outside to cook a barbecue.

5. First grade: Script: birthday

You get toys. / And you get bags of candy and toys. / Yeah, and you get stuff to eat. And they give you cake. And you get to watch the person open up presents. / There could be magic men coming to show you a show. / You have a lot of fun.

6. First grade: Script: doctor's office

If you are sick or something, they give you medicine and tell you to keep it for a few weeks or a few days and then come back after four or five days or something. / If you have bug bites like I did once, I went to the doctor's and they gave me a different kind of medicine that's special. / After you, um, you get stickers and then you have to go sign up, and then go pay, pay for it, and then go home.

7. First grade: Script: Halloween

You go to parties. And you get costumes. And sometimes you get candy and go trick-or-treating. And sometimes you knock on people's doors and they give you candy.

8. First grade: Script: trip

Well, you ride on the bus or you fly in a plane or you take a train. / You go to (pause) / Go play with a friend. / And you might go on a train and take another ride.

9. Third grade: Script: birthday

Well you just go to the party and you have fun times. You have cake, play games, and have a lot of fun. / Kids get gifts. And people give you cards for your birthday. You play on your birthday and you play all the games that you get sometimes. / Some kids, if they are at your party, they would want to play, too.

10. Third grade: Script: doctor's office

You have a check-up to see how healthy you are and if you're sick or have an ear infection. / Well, for regular check-ups you have to have a shot.

11. Third grade: Script: Halloween

You go trick-or-treating. You go around the neighborhood and um, ring each doorbell. / Then people give you candy. And you could go with your friends if you wanted to. Just to be safe. And then you could go home. But your parents have to check the candy before you eat it.

12. Third grade: Script: trip

First you pack. And then you drive to wherever you are going. And then, say if you are going to the beach or something, well you unpack first, and then you um, might um, well you could go down to the beach. And, um, you could go swimming and stuff like that.

13. Preschool: Personal narrative: birthday

Well there was a cake. And there were people and presents and cards on the presents. / And there was candles on the cake. And they light. And we sing Happy Birthday.

14. Preschool: Personal narrative: doctor's office

I got a shot. / I didn't cry though. / Then I went home.

15. Preschool: Personal narrative: Halloween

Well, me and my mommy, and we went outside for Halloween. And I remember that I was a fairy princess. And I got a lot of stuff in my bag. And I remember my sister was a clown. And we went to some houses with my mommy to get a lot of stuff together. And that's all I remember.

16. Preschool: Personal narrative: trip

We went on a hike and we saw turtles on a log. We saw alligators/ / We saw fish. We saw birds and birds' houses and holes in the ground that squirrels lived in. And then we had a picnic. And then we went home.

17. First grade: Personal narrative: birthday

My mom said not to go in the backyard because there was a new bike for me in the backyard. / I rided it all day.

18. First grade: Personal narrative: doctor's office

I had pneumonia and I had to go to the doctor's office. And they had to check my throat and stuff. And I felt a little better. And they gave me a sticker and a card. / This other doctor, he had to check my heart. / He listened to my heart. / And then he checked to see if there were any pains in it.

19. First grade: Personal narrative: Halloween

I had to dress up and stuff. And then I went out with my mother. And some people were trying to scare us with the Halloween stuff on. / And we knocked on the door and say trick-or-treat.

20. First grade: Personal narrative: trip

A long time ago my daddy used to live with me. And he took me to the beach. / I swimmed in the water and I had lots of fun. / I think that's it.

21. Third grade: Personal narrative: birthday

Well, I went to a birthday party at my friend, Lisa's and she, we were having a sleep-over. And we had a pillow fight and all that. And it was really funny, too, because when we went to bed, everyone started throwing animals at me. / We went to Pizza Hut and stuff after that. And when they brought me home, I was having somebody sleep over then, too.

22. Third grade: Personal narrative: doctor's office

Can it be me going to the dentist? Can that count? / Once I went to the dentist and he checked me and I was fine. And then I went out in the car to wait. And then he called me back in. And then he pulled out one of my teeth. And he said that, well, he was talking but I couldn't hear him because he put me out. So I just had to, I was sleeping. And then I felt scared like an astronaut floating. And then when I woke up I got scared because this lady, she was drilling into my teeth. And finally they just told me where I was.

23. Third grade: Personal narrative: Halloween

One time when I was celebrating Halloween, we went trick-or-treating with my friends. And we saw, we saw a witch on the other side of the street. And she was trick-or-treating, too. And there was this one lady, we knocked on her door, and um, she answered the door and she was dressed up as a soldier.

24. Third grade: Personal narrative: trip

Once I went to Ohio with my grandparents. And it's really long. And that's, we stopped at a diner and that's the first time I've ever been to a diner. And we got lost and it rained so we couldn't see the road so we made a lot of wrong turns so it took about two hours extra. / Well, we were asking everybody where to go. And then finally we got there at ten o'clock at night. / I learned how to play pool once I got there.

25. Preschool: Story: birthday

Um, well, I pretend that one of my friends is going to have a birthday party. Let me see, what's next? / And the cake was uh, white and it with ice cream. / Well we played a game that I know and it's called Candyland. / Well then we went home and uh, I had some ice cream. That's the end.

26. Preschool: Story: doctor's office

I broke my arm. / Because I falled off of the chair. / Um, he put a cast on me. / People wrote their names on my cast.

27. Preschool: Story: Halloween

You dress up. / In costumes, like a witch. / You go to the firehouse. / And have a party. That's what I do.

28. Preschool: Story: trip

Once there was an ostrich and he couldn't fly but he walked all the way to Florida. / And then he found it was too hot there so he went back to here and it was too cold. / He just stayed here thinking of where he could go where it wasn't too hot and it wasn't too cold. / Then he just said, "Let's stay here."

29. First grade: Story: birthday

There was this birthday party. And I was supposed to go to the birthday party. And it was late. And then my mother, she had to hurry up to go to the birthday party. When we came, it wasn't there; it was at another place. So we went to the other place and we saw the birthday party. And when we came in, it was dark. And then they said surprise.

30. First grade: Story: doctor's office

Somebody was sick so they had to go to the doctor's. And when he got back, he felt better.

31. First grade: Story: Halloween

A duck went out on Halloween. / Well, then the duck dressed up like a bear. / He scared people. / Then went trick-or-treating.

32. First grade: Story: trip

You can make pretend you have a car. And you can make pretend you're driving. / You have to get your hat and coat on and your boots. / Let me see, then you can go out the door. / Then you can go, go all the way out till you find it. And you get out and then you can, maybe if there's some mountains, maybe you can climb them.

33. Third grade: Story: birthday

At my cousin's birthday party we had pies and soda. In the middle of the party people started throwing pies all over. / And I threw one at my friend. And he threw it back. And then he started throwing soda. / Then some more kids came. And our big neighbor came over and said,

"What's going on?" And then a boy threw a pie at her face. Then she started throwing them back. / And then some more people came. And then, they, too, got pies on their face and they started throwing back. / At the end they all went home dirty.

34. Third grade: Story: doctor's office

Once I went to the doctor's office and the doctor wasn't in because he was sick. And (pause) my mother and I left. / And then we went to K-Mart and bought anything there. / Well, I was so sick that I turned into a parakeet. / Um, that's when we went to K-Mart—no wait, that would be embarrassing. / So we went home. And my brother laughed at me and my two sisters did, but my father didn't. / I had to stay home from school for a week until it went away and I got to fly around the house.

35. Third grade: Story: Halloween

One day on Halloween I um, I went out for Halloween with my mother and my sister and my friends. And we went around blocks saying trick-or-treat. One house, um, was a haunted house. And we heard noises like a witch. And um, well we knocked on the door 'cause we were afraid and Frankenstein opened the door. / Well, he invited us in and he asked us if we wanted anything to eat or drink and we go, "No, thanks." Well, we just took a treat and then we sat down for one minute. And then we, um, got, uh, something got us down in the seats. And then he said, "Now you have to meet my company." There was all sorts of stuff. There were ghosts, witches, vampires, bats. / And there was pictures and they moved around. And we sorta got kinda scared. And we said, "Can we leave now?" So we did. And we went all the way home. And we checked out the, we checked the treats they gave us real, real good so we wouldn't be poisoned.

36. Third grade: Story: trip

Once upon a time I went on a trip and I brought my dog along. And then I got onto the train, um plane, and then the plane crashed. And the dog went out on the thing and he got everybody out on time. And then they went into a parachute, one of those air balloons, and then they landed where they wanted to. And the next day they were at the beach and they were swimming and a kid drowned. And the dog started to swim into the ocean. And then he got her out. And then he brought her on the thing. And then he bit her. And then she was alive again.

CHAPTER 4

The Voice of Experience: The Recall of Early Childhood and Adolescent Memories by Young Adults

Allyssa McCabe
Harvard University, and Tufts University

Earl Capron
Southeastern Louisiana University

Carole Peterson
Memorial University of Newfoundland

Narrative and memory have a complicated relationship. Ever since Bartlett (1932) used a narrative, specifically an Indian folktale, to demonstrate the reconstructive nature of remembering, work on the linguistic structure of narrative has overlapped with work on memory. This is particularly true of work in episodic or autobiographical memory, namely memory for personal experience.

There have been a number of approaches to the study of narratives and early childhood memories, as well as to the intersection between narrative and memory. Various approaches to the study of narrative are reviewed elsewhere (see Peterson & McCabe, 1983, chap. 1 in this vol.; Hudson & Shapiro, Chap. 3 in this vol.; Kemper, 1984), as are approaches to the study of early childhood memories (Bruhn & Last, 1982; Pillemer & White, 1989) so this chapter briefly examines approaches to autobiographical memories and concentrates on reviewing intersections between narrative and memory. We then report an investigation of early childhood and adolescent personal narratives from young adults. We compare these two types of memories with each other, and also consider ways in which adults' early childhood narratives compare to the personal narratives of children much closer to the time when some event was experienced. Our principal concern is to document some important ways in which one must always consider the language of memory, which we define as narrative, as something other than a transport window to memory for personal experience.

AUTOBIOGRAPHICAL MEMORIES: THEORETICAL AND EMPIRICAL APPROACHES

First, consider previous approaches to early childhood memories. Many (e.g., Freud, 1905/1953; Schactel, 1947) have been struck by what adults do not remember from their childhood. Children seem to forget the specifics of the first 3 or 4 years of their life, despite the formative nature of these years. This phenomenon has been dubbed *childhood amnesia*. Freud (1916/1971) believed that during latency, the content of any remaining childhood memories were displaced and otherwise distorted to protect the individual from becoming upset by awareness of childhood psychic trauma. Freud considered early memories "screen memories" because the actual experiences were unconsciously hidden or "screened" from awareness. Originally, Freud believed that once the disguised "manifest content" of the memory was properly analyzed, the hidden actual experience would become evident; later revisions suggested that analysis would reveal the person's general perception of large periods of psychosexual development condensed into a single "event" (e.g., Kris, 1956).

Whereas Freud conceived of early memory content as deceptive and concealing, Alfred Adler (1931) considered such content as *revealing* and directly interpretable. For Freud early memories contain disguised clues of the person's past, but for Adler, such memories contain relatively direct information concerning the person's present view of life. Adler maintained that out of the almost infinite number of experiences available, individuals unconsciously select to remember only those things that are consistent with their current framework. Adler (1931) wrote, "Thus his memories represent his 'Story of My Life': a story he *repeats to himself* [emphasis added] to warn him or comfort him, to keep him concentrated on his goal, to prepare him, by means of past experiences, to meet the future with an already tested style of action" (p. 73).

Thus, we remember only that which fits and reinforces our current world view, that which helps us move toward our life goals. Finally, there is an important difference between Freud and Adler concerning the causal role of childhood memories. Freud considered early memories to reflect real events or traumas that are retained in disguised form because they represent important causal events—events that influenced later personality development. Adler placed no causal significance on the events remembered. In fact, actual memory content need not necessarily reflect real events experienced in the person's life. "Personal" recollections, in his view, may concern entirely fictitious events that are, nevertheless, unconsciously retained because they are congruent with the person's current framework (Ansbacher, 1947). Fictitious events cannot have true causal significance. Autobiographical memories (whether true or imagined) simply reflect current psychological functioning; they have not caused it. Adler and his followers have pursued the use of early recollections as a projective technique (Mosak, 1958), examining what subjects claim as their earliest childhood memory for what it reveals about their personality.

The notion that reality is recapitulated in language has provided many researchers with a tempting truth criterion for memories in narrative form that is not in place for other discourse genres (e.g., opinions, jokes). However, this idea that we can assess the truthful content and adequacy of an adult's or a child's personal account by reference to some external set of "facts" may well be an illusion. When we read stories to adults or children and ask them to recall these stories, we still have the original stimulus to which we can compare their versions—the developmental equivalent of Bartlett's paradigm and one that has been used extensively in research on story grammar reviewed later. When someone has a personal experience, however, what are the "facts" that are comparable to the original story stimulus?

Personal narratives seem primarily factual but are occasionally spiced with fiction, most obviously in childhood. For example, the first author's son (age 32 months) informed his parents one night that "I go to school, I went on a different bus," which surprised his parents as well as his babysitter, who stays home with him all day every weekday. In a footnote to *Play, Dreams, and Imitation,* Piaget (1952) recounted in remarkable detail one of his most vivid early memories, a memory of being kidnapped in his second year. He and his parents were informed when he was 15 years old of the fact that his nurse had made up the whole story, but Piaget claimed still to experience the memory as a personal, real one. Todd and Perlmutter (1980) tape-recorded spontaneous rememberings in the homes of 4-year-olds and found them to recall clearly fictional events as if they were real 3% of the time. Preece (1987) found that fictitious narratives about real people occurred approximately 4% of the time in the conversation of 5- and 6-year-olds with each other. Such narratives are often creative exaggerations. But although clear departures from truth are relatively rare, they do draw our attention to the fact that personal narratives are "versions of reality" (Peterson & McCabe, 1983, p. 195), if only by selection of the set of events mentioned in sequence.

Empirical work in psychology has largely forgotten Adler's point of view, has confirmed an early period of childhood that is forgotten, but has not otherwise verified Freud. For example, childhood amnesia usually encompasses the first 3 or 4 years instead of the first 6 or 8 as Freud claimed (see Pillemer & White, 1989). The psychoanalytic framework in general has been abandoned in favor of a cognitive framework.

In a classic investigation of childhood amnesia, Waldevogle (1948) studied 48 male and 76 female college students. The average age of the first memory they could recall was between 3 and 4 years, which supported prior reports by Dudycha and Dudycha (1933) and Gordon (1928). Waldevogle also noted that half of these memories were pleasant, 30% unpleasant, and 20% neutral. The relatively large number of unpleasant memories reported does not support Freud's notion that early memories invariably "screen" bad experiences.

Amnesia for the first 3 years of life occurs despite the fact that 3-year-olds are in fact capable of remembering both routine and novel experiences that they had when they were two (Nelson & Ross, 1980). This discrepancy between adults' and children's recall of early childhood could be due to cueing differences or to issues involved in adult reconstruction of the time an event occurred during their childhoods (Pillemer & White, 1989). It could also be due to extensive revision of world knowledge; knowing what happens in general versus what happened one time. Hudson and Shapiro (chap. 3 in this vol.) extensively review the relationship between routine scripts and personal narratives in children, so we do not do so here. Suffice it to say that several studies have demonstrated that preschool children are more liable to report routine scripts than older, school-aged children (Hudson & Nelson, 1983; Mistry & Lange, 1985). However, it is important to note the work of Fivush and Hamond (in press), who found that at age 2½ years, children recount typical and distinctive information in about equal parts in their narratives, while by age 4 they are recounting significantly more distinctive information about events. At age 4, children reported different, yet still accurate, information about events they experienced when they were 2½ years than they did when they recalled those same events at the age of 2½, shortly after experiencing them. Younger children also were more reliant on specific prompting than older children; their narratives were largely responses to specific adult questions. This experiment stands as a notable exception to the tendency noted by Bartlett (1932) for people to abbreviate, but remain true to a gist of, memory formulated shortly after exposure to a narrative. More germaine to the present point, beginning at 2½ years, Fivush and Hamond (in press) documented the gap between autobiographical memory and narrative, or, in other words, between what is available for recall and what is in fact encoded in a narrative, the language of specific recall.

Nelson (in press) argued that childhood amnesia is overcome through the sharing of memories between parents and children, the kind of talk that is the topic of investigation by McCabe and Peterson (chap. 6 in this vol.). Nelson purported that the age of onset of autobiographical memory is consistent with the age of learning to talk about memories, that mothers vary in the way that they engage their children in memory talk, and that the fact that some individuals have much earlier onset of autobiographical memories than others may be attributable to the fact that they had more of the "right kind" of memory talk at that early age. Perhaps, as Pillemer and White argued (1989, p. 328), "a new memory system is constructed in the preschool years, with language as the primary medium of expression."

Turning to autobiographical memories beyond early childhood, we find that episodes of personal experience that occur during times of transitions, such as the first month of college, and that tend to be rated as intensely emotional persist in memory for many years (Pillemer, Goldsmith, Panter, & White, 1988; Pillemer, Rhinehart, & White, 1986). Such memories are usually of specific, unique experiences. Alumnae rated their own memories for freshman year as positive (34%), negative (27%), mixed positive and negative (35%) but rarely neutral (4%) (Pillemar et al., 1988), proportions that are almost identical to such ratings of freshman year memories by current college students (Pillemer et al., 1986). The discrepancy between the low incidence of neutral memories in these studies and the results already reported for early childhood memories could be due to the fact that the latter did not include a "mixed positive and negative" category so that, for want of a more appropriate category, subjects registered bittersweet memories as neutral (Pillemer & White, 1989).

Regardless of the exact proportions of neutral personal memories reported, autobiographical memories are not simply a cognitive phenomenon. Most memories of any stage of life investigated to date are classified by subjects as emotional. The present authors argue, with Adler, that the objective truth of the original experiences we report may never be determined and is somewhat irrelevant. It is important to note that our subjects believe in the truth of the experiences they report, and that truth has emotional as well as cognitive components.

Subjective versions of reality are worthy of study in their own right and on their own terms and should not simply be seen as degradations of an objective set of facts, all the more problematic for scientific study because the original stimulus was not under an experimenter's control. It is in this spirit that this chapter draws attention to the voice of experience.

INTERSECTIONS OF NARRATIVE AND MEMORY

Turning now to the specific intersections of work on narrative and work on memory, we again find several diverse antecedents from diverse disciplines. To begin with, in literary studies there is the famous Perry–Lord hypothesis, which held that formulaic language aided the memory of oral composers when they reconstructed their fictional narratives to entertain their audiences. Lord (1960) found examples of such formulaic language in the *Iliad* and the *Odyssey,* which were presumably narratives from an oral tradition that found their way into print early on but bore the imprint of oral composition, including such formulaic language as repeated reference to "the wine-dark sea." Thus, memory requirements arguably affect the language used to express such memories of fictional stories. Analyses of personal memories collected in the present project did not reveal such formulaic, repetitious language, so this approach is not dealt with further.

In psychology, language has also been found to facilitate memory for sequences of events. Provision of a connective narrative or of a logical sequence of actions facilitates the reconstruction of fictional events by preschoolers (Brown, 1975; Brown & Murphy, 1975). Provision of explicit evaluation by children facilitates adults' recall of children's personal narratives, so long as the experiences narrated are not sensational, in which case explicit evaluative language does not enhance the likelihood of recall (McCabe & Peterson, 1990). Sensational experiences were those that involved deaths, injuries, or acute embarrassments—the kind of experiences that need no comment in order to serve as warnings about what to do or not to do.

If language can shape memories and memory can shape expressive language, memory can also affect perceived language. Early experimental work established that memory filters perceived language when people recall fictional stories composed by others. In adults, propositions or statements in a narrative rated as more important than other propositions are more likely to be recalled (see Kintsch & van Dijk, 1978 for review). While third- and fifth-grade students are unable to differentiate propositions of fairy tales in terms of their relative importance to the text, nonetheless their recall is predicted by adults' ratings of structural importance (Brown & Smiley, 1977).

A number of investigations have specified this work on memory for fictional stories, documenting what has come to be called the *story category effect* (Glenn, 1978; Mandler & Johnson, 1977; Thorndyke, 1977). The story category effect refers to the fact that when listening to stories, children, as well as adults, recall the setting, the beginning, and the consequence of a protagonist's attempt to reach a goal substantially more frequently than that character's motivating state or reaction to the outcome of such an attempt. When encountering scrambled presentations, school-aged children, even more than adults, adhere to the logical ordering of events captured by story grammar analysis (Bischofshausen, 1985; Mandler & DeForest, 1979; McClure, Mason, & Barnitz, 1979). It has been established that verbal presentation of material is not essential; the story category effect has been found with reference to events that are simply presented pictorially (e.g., Day, Stein, Trabasso, & Shirey, 1979). Omanson (1982, p. 335) related this story category effect back to the experimental work discussed earlier with his finding that the centrality of story content, as identified by an analysis focusing on the causal, purposeful, and componential relations connecting story events and states, accounted for "nearly three-quarters of the story category effects." Among other recent critics of the story grammar approach, Lehnert (1981) cautioned that memory representation of intentional problem solving, the focus of story grammars, is only one of a number of types of complex plot units to be found in conversational narratives. In other words, work that has endeavored to efface the language of narrative in an attempt to document the structure of memory has not gone unchallenged. In a number of different ways, narrative, the language of memory, is often more complicated than a story grammar analysis can adequately describe.

PERSPECTIVE

One of the ways that attention has been drawn previously to the language of memory is in work on perspective. Personal narratives take place in specific conversations to specific audiences, and the nature of those interactions affects the language used to recall an experience. Young (1984) distinguished the realm of conversation, into which personal narratives are woven, from what she termed the *storyrealm* (narrative) and the *taleworld* (the events being narrated). Evaluation of taleworld events occurs in narrative language (Labov, 1972; Peterson & McCabe, 1983), or the storyrealm, which suggests one sort of perspective from a narrator. But a different type of perspective occurs in the interface between the storyrealm and the larger realm of conversation, one more clearly making explicit the presence of a specific narrator and a specific listener.

Preschool children are capable of recognizing the perspective of their listeners in narratives (Menig-Peterson & McCabe, 1978), providing more information in narratives to a naive than an informed listener (Menig-Peterson, 1975), and generating more exophora (references outside the text) to an informed versus a naive listener while generating more endophora (references of a discourse to itself) to a naive than to an informed listener (Pellegrini, 1984). Preschool children do not, however, have a mature perspective. Thus, the present investigation focuses on the presence of a mature perspective in adult recollections of early childhood experiences.

GOALS OF THIS INVESTIGATION

We document a distinction between *autobiographical memories* and *narrative,* the language used to encode such memories. The language of memory—narrative—will be shown to be a composite of various things, including the urge to embroider experience previously noted, explicit recognition of the perspective of the listener, as well as explicit recognition of the perspective of the narrator looking back, selecting which memories to report and the language in which to report them.

In addition, the present investigation examines the relationship between early childhood and adolescent memories and narrative structure. If narrative structure is some attribute of the memories described, one would predict a significant developmental change from early childhood to adolescence, reflecting maturity in encoding experiences. If, however, narrative structure is a way of understanding the language used to encode memories, as McCabe (preface in this vol.) suggests, then one would not necessarily expect such a developmental change, because one would expect adults to produce adult language regardless of the age of an experience being narrated.

In contrast to such structural description, a content analysis is expected to reveal a developmental change both in terms of the specific sorts of experiences described, as well as more general tendencies to revise experience in light of one's present stage of development.

METHOD

Subjects

Eight male and eight female students participated in this interview for credit toward an introductory psychology course. They ranged in age from 18 to 22 years of age (M = 19.9 years). All were white and lived in the Southern United States.

Procedure

Subjects were individually interviewed to obtain their three earliest childhood memories and their three earliest adolescent memories. Childhood memories were defined as any specific, clearly visualized recollection of a single personal experience occurring between the ages of 2 and 8. Adolescent memories were defined as any specific, clearly visualized recollection of a single personal experience occurring between the ages of 12 and 18. The experimenter followed a standardized interview format in which she attempted to secure a complete description of a memory for a single (not generalized or repeated) experience and then asked a series of follow-up questions about that memory before asking for the next memory. The experimenter maintained a nonjudgmental and nondirective attitude throughout the interview, refraining from any comment about or personal evaluation of any memory or of the subject. The interview was tape-recorded. Subjects signed an informed consent form prior to participation in the interview.

Specifically, the experimenter asked the subject, "Please describe in detail your very *earliest* memory of an experience that you had when you were between the ages of 2 and 8 (or 12 and 18) years old. Remember it must be of a *specific* experience that you can *clearly visualize* even today." Initial comments during the person's recounting were limited to "uh huh" or repetitions of what he or she just said. When the subject seemed to be through, the interviewer asked, "Did anything else happen concerning this particular experience?" Once a person responded, "No," to this question, the interviewer asked, "What stands out most about this memory, for example, some feeling, some thought, some feature of the environment, some action, whatever?" And then, finally, "How old were you at the time this happened?" After this, the interviewer went on to ask, "All right, now please tell me your next earliest memory of something that happened to you before you were the age of 8/18." Occasionally, even after extensive requests to be specific, participants persisted in recounting general experiences. Such scripts for routine events have received considerable attention, as reviewed earlier (e.g., Hudson & Shapiro, chap. 3 in this vol). It was judged more ecologically valid to include these scripts for study than to exclude them because of our a priori definition of childhood memories as specific recollections of single personal experiences.

Scoring

Early memories were scored for their conformance to story grammar structure and to high point structure (see Peterson & McCabe, 1983; McCabe & Peterson, chap. 6 in this vol; also see appendix a for a description of these structures). Additionally, stories were scored according to whether the overall affect of the story was neutral, positive, negative, or bittersweet, with the latter referring to stories that contained a mixture of positive and negative affect. Finally, the stories were catalogued for content, with categories induced to be mutually exclusive, and examined for explicit articulation of adult perspective. The latter was defined as saying something that a child/adolescent would not have said if recalling the experience shortly after it had happened or for evidence of lessons learned from experience.

Reliability

All memories were scored for high point and story grammar structure by one experimenter, trained on both systems using an extensive corpus of stories collected previously. Twenty (21.0%) of the 96 memories also were scored independently on both systems by a second experimenter, and the proportion of agreements to combined agreements plus disagreements was 85.0% for high point analysis and 80.0% for story grammar analysis. Two experimenters scored all memories for affect, and their proportion of agreements to decisions was 92.7%. Disagreements in all three categorization systems were analyzed and found not to be consistently due to differential interpretation of a few categories. Other examinations of the memories are qualitative, and the evidence is presented later. In other words, other examinations of memory content did not call for reliability estimations.

RESULTS AND DISCUSSION

General Descriptive Information: Replicating the Infantile Amnesia Effect

The mean age of the earliest memory recalled was 4;0, ranging from two memories at the age of 2;0 (one of which was of an experience that was made into a family movie) to 5;0. The earliest memory was not always the one recalled first, as requested. But overall, the means of the memories in order of recall did increase, as requested, 4;8, 5;6, 6;3, 13;7, 15;1, and 15;9 years. In general, this study replicates prior studies reviewed in the introduction in that the age of earliest episodic memory is between 3;0 and 4;0 years.

No Development of Story Grammar Structure

Table 4.1 presents the results of an analysis of story grammar structure. There was no association of age and sophistication of structure from this point of view, chi-square (6, $N = 47$) = 2.69, n.s.[1] Peterson and McCabe (1983) argued that in children's personal narratives there was substantial development in terms of increased narration of experiences that contained complete episodes of motivated behavior. Specifically, the incidence of such motivated episodes in personal narration increased dramatically between the ages of 5 and 6, and again between the ages of 6 and 7. How can one reconcile that developmental picture with the adevelopmental picture presented here, which is most notable for the prevalence of what story grammarians term *unsophisticated structures* even in adolescent memories? The answer to this question requires individual consideration of each supposedly primitive structure.

The Persistance of Scripts (Descriptive and Action Sequences)

First of all, despite extensive prompting to be specific, some individuals have a strong tendency to reminisce about general, habitual, repeated events—scripts, to use Hudson and Shapiro's terminology (chap. 3 in this vol.)—and this tendency is not confined to memories for early childhood experiences. Consider the following exchange, a descriptive sequence despite many requests to be specific: (A prompt for second earliest memory between the ages of 12 and 18 years.)

> *Subject* (Female, 21 years): Uh, that would probably be when I started high school. Is that, you said before you didn't want us to say things over and over again.
>
> *Interviewer:* That's fine.
>
> *Subject:* That's fine, when I started high school—just the confusion and the differentness of the atmosphere from grammar school to high school. I went to a Catholic grammar school, and then a Catholic high school, and we didn't change classes or anything in grammar school. The teachers always did the changing. And it was a big change going, when I started in high school, having to, um, adjust to moving from

---

[1]Note that although chi-square analysis assumes independent observation, and that that assumption was violated here (the same subjects produced more than one memory), no other statistical analysis was more appropriate. Such statistical analysis as we did is congruent with inspection of the data. Furthermore, no subject contributed disproportionately to this pattern. This disclaimer holds throughout this chapter.

TABLE 4.1
Frequency of Story Grammar Structures as a Function of Age at Time of Experience

	Early Childhood	*Adolescence*
Descriptive sequence	9	8
Action sequence	1	2
Reactive sequence	10	6
Abbreviated episode	1	3
Complete episode(s)	15	16
Complex & interactive episodes	10	13
Incomplete episode	1	0

Note. One miscellaneous structure in the memories of early childhood was omitted. Note also that 15 of 96 memories contained multiple structures and were tabulated here only in terms of the most sophisticated of those structures. Six of those multiple structure narratives were from early childhood recollections, 9 from early adolescent recollections.

place to place, teacher to teacher, um, getting myself, my bearings straight. And the different atmosphere of people because it wasn't just people that I went to grammar school with now; it was people from all over, from three different parishes, but, um, just adjusting to all that. That's I think the next, that would be the next memory that I had, walking through the hall and being scared because I was unfamiliar with the surroundings, and we had so many people, older people who were so sure of themselves and we were just these little freshmen that had to go around and try to find, find your own way around things and that, stuff like that.

Interviewer: You had to go and find your way around stuff?

Subject: um hum.

Interviewer: Did anything else happen concerning this particular experience?

Subject: No, I guess that said it all.

Interviewer: So the particular incident that you remember is your first day going?

Subject: The first day, the first week, you know, adjusting that first week.

Interviewer: Can you narrow it down to a more particular incident of one thing that happened concerning the beginning of high school?

Subject: I remember how crowded things were, you know, people going through the halls. You had to push your way through and you had five minutes to get from one end to the other, and there was just like clutters of people everywhere. That's one of the main things that I remember about when I first started school. It seemed like so much chaos and turmoil.

Interviewer: You have the general idea, but I have the impression that what you just gave is an overall description of that whole time period. I would like it if you could narrow it to one particular incident that happened concerning this time period.

Subject: Um, I don't, I don't really know how to narrow it down to one particular incident, but the main, the thing that most sticks with me is, you know, like the first week where just the crowding, the crowding, the chaos of the, you know, I mean, I don't know how, how more narrow I can get as far as, um, because I was comfortable in my classes, and I was comfortable, um, you know, when I would get to class, I was comfortable with my teachers and my surroundings in the classrooms, but it was just in the hallways between classes, having to try and find your way and get there on time and things like that. It was only about the first week that I was, is that better?

Interviewer: That's okay.

Such a tendency to reminisce about a series of events, does, indeed, appear strong. In fact, descriptive sequences constituted 19.0% of the childhood and 16.7% of the adolescent recollections. Conversely, 81.0% and 82.3% of all memories were specific, respectively, a rate comparable to the 67.0%–79.0% range of specific memories of freshman year by college students (Pillemer et al., 1986), though higher than the 55.0% of memories of freshman year by alumnae (Pillemer et al., 1988). The fact that our percentage of specific memories is higher than those in the other studies looking at this issue reflects our repeated requests to be specific; in other words, our methodology probably to some extent underestimates the extent of production of descriptive sequences in personal narratives. In any case, there is continued production of descriptive sequences, such as the one presented earlier, in personal narratives over the life span.

There is also the occasional action sequence, such as the following:

Subject (Female, 20 years): My first date. I went to a junior high dance. And I remember I was so nervous. And when I went to the dance, it was really nice. We went out to eat, went to the dance, and then when we came home, and he had met my parents and everything. It was really nice.

Such an action sequence is very little more than a script one would write for any first date. Nothing particular, no personal detail is mentioned.

Victim Stories (Reactive Sequences): The Limitations of Experience

The persistance of the reactive sequence, narratives in which characters simply react to events without forming goals, is also of interest. Peterson and McCabe (1983) found that, contrary to the predictions of story grammarians regarding the production of fictional narratives, reactive sequences did not show a strong developmental decrease in the personal narratives of 4- to 9-year-old children. Freedman (1987) found that reactive sequences were common in fictional stories written by advanced high school seniors.

Peterson and McCabe (1983) also argued that some experiences do not lend themselves to forming goals. Some problems cannot be solved; they can only be commiserated with. Scrutiny of our present corpus of narratives allows us to amplify this point. Of the 10 early memories that were classified as reactive sequences, 8 were stories in which someone was injured. Of the 6 adolescent memories classified as reactive sequences, 5 were stories in which someone was injured.

Looking at this point the other way around, there are 17 early memories in which someone was injured. In 6 of these, the victim was taken to the doctor or a hospital, and so the incident was classified as at least a complete episode. Three injuries resulted in a motivated goal—getting punished or getting angry for some deliberate injury or becoming phobic about riding bicycles and having to overcome this phobia. The 8 remaining injury incidents involved no trip to doctor or hospital, nor any motivated slowdown, and hence were classified as reactive sequences. Similarly, with adolescent memories, there were 11 victim or injured party stories, 5 of which did not involve treatment, or, in other words, precipitated no goals, and were thus reactive sequences. Of the remaining 6, some incidents precipitated caring from doctors or boyfriend (multiple complete episodes), others precipitated moral/motivational consequences. These observations are summarized in Table 4.2. A chi-square analysis of those results was not possible due to an expected frequency of fewer than five in one cell, as well as to violations of independence. However, 54% of victim or injury stories were reactive sequences, whereas 81% of reactive sequences were about victims or injured parties. Descriptions of hurt were associated with the production of reactive sequences.

Thus, the reactive sequence was strongly characteristic of victimization or injury experiences. It is the nature of what happens to victims,

TABLE 4.2
Observed (and Expected) Frequency of Reactive Sequences as a Function of Victimization

	Story Grammar Classification	
Content of Experience	*Reactive Sequence*	*Other*
Victims described	13 (4.0)	11 (20.0)
No victims described	3 (12.0)	69 (60.0)

rather than the sophistication of the narrator, that determines whether such a narrative is classified as sophisticated or unsophisticated from a story grammar point of view. In documenting the contribution of characteristics of experience to narrative structure, we complement the results of Hudson and Shapiro (chap. 3 in this vol). The reactive sequence is not a developmentally primitive structure; it is the hallmark of victimization at any age.

No Development of High Point Structure

The results of Table 4.3 were submitted to analysis, and no association was found between the sophistication of high point structure and the age at which the experience recalled was said to have occurred χ^2 $(4, N = 47) = 3.87$, n.s., see footnote 1). As was the case with story grammar, but much less frequently, there are some supposedly primitive high point structures in adolescent memories. Five of these were the descriptions, or scripts, discussed earlier. Five of these were chronological narratives, which Peterson and McCabe (1983) found reflective of relative noninvolvement with telling a particular story. Perhaps chronology is an alternative form of narration present to some extent in narratives of all ages; one has only to reflect on the travel narratives of many adults to think of outstanding examples of such laundry lists of actions that should be more exciting than they are. Two others were two-event narratives, where action was overwhelmed by a preoccupation with descriptive orientation or evaluation, as in the following:

> Subject (Male, 19 years): Getting, just getting your [sic] driver's license at fifteen. I was, you know, I was like, "I can't wait, I can't wait." It finally came, and it was, and I had to get it on the first day too, and I remember that clearly. My mama didn't want to take me. I missed school that day so Mama could take me. That's about it.

There were six adolescent memories that were classified as what Peterson and McCabe (1983) termed "Ending at the High Point Narratives," found to be characteristic of 5-year-old narrators. This represents 13% of this sample of adolescent memories. Peterson and McCabe (1983) found this structure to dwindle from 29% of the productions at age 5 to 17% of the productions at ages 7, 8, and 9 years. Perhaps it is yet another persistent alternative form; there was no commonality in terms of content to explain its persistence. Soap operas are one of the most common examples of such structure in the stories of adults.

However, this picture of no development is misleading. Recall that

TABLE 4.3
Frequency of High Point Structures as a Function of Age at Time of Experience

	Early Childhood	*Adolescence*
Classic structure	26	30
End at high point structure	12	6
Chronology structure	4	5
Description only	2	5
Two-event narratives	3	2
Disoriented	1	0

the mean age of earliest memory recalled here was 4 years. At 4 years, Peterson and McCabe found that the dominant structure of the most advanced narratives of children could best be described as leapfrogging, a disordered recapitulation of several events. Only 12% of the 4-year-olds' narratives were what we termed *classic narratives*. Yet in this corpus, we see that a little over half of the earliest memories can be categorized as classic narratives, and we found no examples of leapfrogging. Development has occurred behind the scenes.

The most striking thing about the high point analysis, then, is the anachronistic overrepresentation of sophisticated high point forms in the narratives of early childhood experience. Contrast the following two narratives about experiences at the age of 3½ years:

> *Subject* (male, 18 years): I remember when I was probably about 3 and a half, 4 years old. The first house we ever lived in was a big house, but we had a pond right next to it in the next lot. And my favorite thing was for my brother to pull me around in a wagon. He'd pull me all over the yard. And he kinda acted like it was a little racecar, you know. And he was, he was 10 years older than I was, but he had fun pulling me around, you know, because I enjoyed it. We really, you know, we got along real well. I remember going around the pond one time, and he cut a little bit close and happened to hit like a root or something. And I fell into the pond. [High point] And the pond never was necessarily deep, it probably wasn't any more than 2 feet deep. And um, I remember, I mean I went completely under. I remember him pulling me out. And I remember they had me in the washtub in the garage washing me off since I was just real little, and um, for about a month or 2 months, I swore that my brother had tried to drown me. And I didn't want to have anything to do with him. That was really the last time I ever, you know, was pulled around in a wagon, or anything. [Classic high point structure; abbreviated episode in story grammar analysis]
>
> *Subject* (female, 3;8): My sister had, she's had [to have a cast on]. She broke a arm when she fell in those mini-bike. She broke her arm. She had, she went to the doctor, so I, My dad gave me spanking, and I

> *Interviewer:* You dad gave you what?
>
> *Subject:* A spanking to me.
>
> *Interviewer:* A spanking?
>
> *Subject:* Yeah, and she had to go to the doctor to get a cast on. She had to go get it, get it off and, and it didn't break again.
>
> *Interviewer:* And then it didn't break again?
>
> *Subject:* No. She still got it off. She can't play anymore . . . She can't play we, she can play rest of us now.
>
> *Interviewer:* Oh good . . . Have you ever had a shot? [the next prompt scheduled]
>
> *Subject:* Mm, she has cast on. When she was home. When she came *back* and she, and she, and she hadda go back and take off the cast.
>
> *Interviewer:* She had to go back and take off the cast?
>
> *Subject:* Yeah. The doctor. [Leapfrog high point structure; complete episode in story grammar analysis]

Aside from obvious development in terms of command over negatives and pronominal specification, longer sentences, and more words per narrative, there is dramatic contrast in terms of discourse-level skill. Once you are capable of chronologically ordering events (or logically, if chronology is departed from), you do not mentally undo such organization. If you know what major events must be included to make sense of an experience, you do not leave them out of your earliest recollections. Would it even be possible for many neurologically intact adults to tell disordered versions of early childhood experiences? Furthermore, if you are accustomed to resolving action in narratives, you do not usually leave off at a high point, even though you almost certainly would have had you narrated the event shortly after it had happened. In other words, there are more classically structured early childhood memories from adults than one would expect given the age they reported having had the experience and what we know of the narratives produced by children at that age. From the perspective of high point analysis, memories have been revised in the process of being expressed in adult language.

The Voice of Experience

Recall that the most central question of this chapter is the extent to which narrative and memory coincide. In the following examples, the section(s) reflecting an adult perspective have been capitalized.

Sometimes, one has the sense of hearing the unvarnished memories of young children from the mouths of young adults:

> *Subject* (Female, 18 years): Okay, it [sic] was about 2 years old, and um, it was back whenever it was snowing in Louisiana, which is very, not very often, which is, I guess, the reason that I remember it. And um, me and my brother, we lived on like a slope. The house was on top of it and down below. We, um, had socks for mittens and we went down at the bottom of the slope and was playing in the snow and building a snowman.
>
> *Interviewer:* You'all were playing down at the bottom building a snowman?
>
> *Subject:* Um hum. I just remember playing with my brother.
>
> *Interviewer:* What stands out about that particular experience?
>
> *Subject:* The snow, mainly because it does not really snow all that often in Louisiana.

As McCabe and Peterson point out (chap. 6 in this vol.), 2-year-olds usually string only a couple of events together at most, much as this narrator is doing about an experience she had when she was 2. However, she embellishes the two events—she "went down at the bottom of the slope" and was "playing" and "building a snowman"—with more orientation than 2-year-olds would provide, along with explicit discussion about why she is remembering such an event.

In other cases, such embellishment is considerably more extensive:

> *Subject* (Female, 19 years): Um, oh, this is a good one. Um, um, we grew strawberries. We had a garden, a big garden. This is, we were still in Ponchatoula. We, um, we had, my dad farmed pretty much, but we had a um, we were growing strawberries. I think it was our first year to even try and grow strawberries, that year. They had never did it before. And we were out putting the, um, that black, that's that black, um, shiny kinda, um, vis-, not visquain, I don't know what's it called, but you put over the and over the, the, um, rows of stuff in the garden, but um. And we were all out there planting and picking and whatever we were doing. And we had like a little shopping cart, like a buggy towards this set, towards like the far left end of the pasture. And my mom said, you know, for my brother to get it. Well, I didn't, I figured well he just didn't hear her or whatever. So about a little while after that, after awhile, I figured she was wondering why he didn't go get it, I'm going to get it. So when I sent to go get it, and they had grass around it where it had, you know, the grass just had grown around it. And the, um, but I didn't know that they had a big big bee nest at the, um, buggy. And, um, I didn't see that. Well, he had saw it, and he had told Mama that there was a big bee nest, whatever. So me, I'm pushing, trying to get it out of

> the grass. And I'm going back and forth, I must have been 7, I guess, at the time. I was just going, I couldn't get it out. Well, all of a sudden, I looked down and I see this gigantic, I'm talking gigantic bee nest, bees everywhere, and all of a sudden they start coming out, and I start running. And they, I mean I could look back, and I could see some following me. Well, they were yellow jackets. I got stung *seven* times that day. I mean, all over me, on my face, on my arms, everywhere. An um, I swoll up like a balloon. They had to bring me to the, a hospital. It was terrible. I WAS AN ACCIDENT PRONE CHILD, LET ME TELL YOU. But, um, I remember running to the house trying to get inside before they came, but they caught me. But, um, that's all I remember, just, I don't even remember the hospital, though. I remember she told me they brought me to the hospital. I just remember running. That's all I remember about it. [Classic high point structure; two complete story grammar episodes]

Although the nature of this experience is very much typical of the stories we collected from children aged 4 to 9 years (Peterson & McCabe, 1983), it is much more elaborated in terms of the evaluation and orientation provided.

The Voice of Experience in Early Childhood Recollections

In addition to extensive elaboration, the fact that an adult is narrating these experiences is often made explicit. In a variety of ways, our adult narrators stand back from the storyrealm to make it clear that they are no longer children. Sometimes they make *specific mention of the age difference:*

> Subject 1: And we was just being, just typical kids. Real bad. . . . How childish I was back then.
>
> Subject 4: Not too many people get baptized at that young age and really know what they were doing and I thought I knew what I was doing.
>
> Subject 11: And I don't remember what we were fighting about . . . just silly little things all the time. [And in another early memory:] I guess it was just kind of silly, I mean, we were slamming the dolls into the pool like they would really dive.
>
> Subject 14: . . . I was just real little, . . .

Sometimes they comment on their *changed physical perspective:*

> Subject 2: I saw it [field] a couple of years ago, and it can't be no more'n 200 yards long, but at the time it looked like it was a mile long.
>
> Subject 14: And I fell into the pond. And the pond never was necessarily deep, it probably wasn't anymore than 2 feet deep. . . . (BUT) for about a month or 2 months, I swore that my brother had tried to drown me . . .

One subject's entire narrative is an articulation of the *different emotional perceptions* of members of his family regarding a Christmas tree. Because this poignant difference of perception is the point of the narrative, I quote it in full:

> Subject 10: I can remember a Christmas time when we didn't have much money. And I can remember wanting a Christmas tree, and my parents were real upset about not getting a tree. And then my dad came in and tried to walk through the door pretending like he had this huge tree and he had this little bitty tiny tree, and everybody was so happy, you know. It's just the thought behind it. But I can remember everyone, you know, teasing him and everything. Well my mom was mad about it. She thought that he was, you know, making fun of Christmas, you know, bringing home something like that when we all wanted a big tree, but we were all happy with the tree we got . . .

Adult perspective is sometimes revealed by the *attribution of causality or understanding beyond what one would expect of a child* (subjects 3 and 16). Children's encoding of causal relationships in their personal narratives, although frequent and most often psychological, tends over half of the time to be the encoding of unremarkable relationships (McCabe & Peterson, 1985).

> Subject 1: And I feel that the race car brought, brought my father and I closer together . . .
>
> Subject 3: He [coach] was giving me a chance . . .
>
> Subject 8: But then he (brother) used to drop her (sister) on her head all the time because he was jealous that we were spending all our time with her.
>
> Subject 16: I thought that it [blowing a cap gun up with fireworks] was pretty interesting, and, at the same time, I really didn't like it because it was my favorite cap gun . . . That was the first time that I had seen that so it really seemed interesting at the time.

Sometimes adult *vocabulary* reveals aspects of an event that a child would not have encoded, particularly in the case of psychoanalytical vocabulary:

Subject 2: The more I used the box, the more PLIABLE it would become.

Subject 4: She (mother) came there HYSTERICAL . . .

Subject 5: She (grandmother) LURED us down . . .

Subject 6: Cause I was really PARANOID about it and my, my very close ROLE MODEL, which was my mom, was hurt . . .

Subject 7: She (mom) had to spank me again. I didn't, I don't ever want to start school, but nothing TRAUMATIC.

Subject 8: That was one of my first really big, uh, you know, happy feelings inside when I was younger . . . That was the last time that I had been in the hospital for that, so it was kind of LIKE A GRADUATION, I guess, from all of it, you know.

Subject 9: (see "ACCIDENT-PRONE" example) & "She (mother) PANICKED"

Subject 12: . . . that was my first TRANSVESTITE dress-up . . . I guess I was really worried about other kids picking on me because we had to dress up like girls and all. It was three or four of my friends had to do it too. And so we kind of carried on for years after that, and plus we pull out the pictures and laugh about it because we all had to dress up like girls and stuff.

Subject 13: I just remember it because of the IMPACT it had on my family.

In only 1 of our 16 cases, was adult perspective never explicitly marked. That person did comment on the *habituality* of something:

Subject 15: I remember one time when my little brother used to be, used to like to play with matches.

But mention of typical reactions is not specific to the narratives of adults recalling childhood experiences; even young children at times mention the typicality of behaviors. For example, one 8-year-old girl in the Peterson and McCabe (1983) sample addressed her brother's typical behavior, "Whenever we get home from school, he starts an argument," as well as her own, "I get so mad I punch him in the stomach but not that hard." This is very close to what Subject 15 had to say, and contrasts to Subject 9, who diagnosed herself as accident-prone; whereas that term denoted typical behaviors, it also seemed to draw on a wider perspective, the perspective of an adult summarizing herself as a child.

The Voice of Experience in Early Adolescent Recollections: The Lessons I Have Learned

In searching for the voice of experience in young adults' early adolescent recollections, certain types of reflections would not logically be found. Vocabulary differences between these two ages are not clear. Physical perspective has not changed remarkably. We do not have enough relevant evidence of developmental change from 12 to 18 in terms of causal understanding to see differences. The only possible similar articulation of how things have changed would be specific mention of an age or stage difference, which happened twice:

> Subject 10: I guess I was kinda insecure.
>
> Subject 14: At that age (13) they all thought I was pretty good too, I did too, But you know, I guess I was just showing off.

These young adults have yet to shift much from the perspective of their early adolescent years. In the words of one, they are still "just trying to get everything into perspective." Instead, what one does find as the voice of experience in recent memories is the presence of what might be termed lessons learned from experience. Six out of 16 of our subjects explicitly turned their adolescent experiences into personal parables, denoted by use of the second person instead of first person or by use of "I learned," "I will never again," or "I will always." Some of these lessons are mundane, some address the profound issues of life:

> Subject 2: They say that when you have wind blowing out of the east, it's bad luck and the fish don't bite and all that. Well it blew out of the east most of the day, and we caught a lot of fish.
>
> Subject 4: Uh, well, as far as I'm concerned I learned not to trust what a person says off the bat, cause that's the type of experience that I got from him as far as that time because I believed a lot of things this particular girl was telling me about him, and I threw it in his face, but it wasn't true.
>
> Subject 7: (c) I worked hard at something that I really wanted and I got it; (d) I never did that again. I never ever spray-painted my name anywhere again; (e) I would never have thought about taking a car again before I was of age to drive.
>
> Subject 9: (d) People are strange; (e) And I mean anytime, I guess, you have a high speed chase like that through a small town or whatever, I guess innocent people are going to get hurt. . . . [and another lesson from same narrative] I guess trying to focus on the fact that you know

that they really were dead because that's something you just can't accept like in a minute, you know. You've got to kinda, And I still didn't want to believe it until I actually saw them. And I mean, I don't know, I guess just trying to get everything into perspective, trying to say, hey, you know, you got to accept it, you [sic] cousins are gone, you know.

Subject 12: I never let him (brother) drive my car again;

Subject 13: (c) That taught me how to do it (kill deer); (d) Yeah, I continued dumping girls, but I think I'm through with that now, though.

The transience of the last lesson quoted suggests that many of the lessons we learn from life apply only for a while, something that is corroborated by considering the transience of lessons learned from early childhood experience:

Subject 6: (a) I stopped riding my bike for about year . . . (c) I guess these two experiences really got me steered away from my bike because it was really dangerous.

Subject 10: It took me a little while to like horses again, you know, cause I was scared of them for a while.

Subject 14: (a) That was really the last time I ever, you know, was pulled around in a wagon or anything; (c) I said that I'd never ride a bike again, but they got me on one again.

Only a few lessons learned in early childhood endure for these young adults, at least on this very explicit episodic level:

Subject 2: I never rolled in another box again.

Subject 4: I learned afterwards how to hold a scissors right.

Subject 15: She said put them (cold hands) under the *cold* water and we thought, you know, why should we put them under the cold water, they're already cold and, um, we just put them under the cold water and they felt better.

Subject 16: You have old friends, but new friends you always look forward to.

Even some of these, such as rolling in a box, seem of limited relevance to young adults. One wonders how much of our accumulated life wisdom from adolescence, young and middle adulthood undergoes similar revision, becoming obsolete at later stages.

Explicit Talk of Remembering

In a trivial sense, our subjects recalled events because we asked them to; there was no reason that they needed to justify telling us personal memories when that was the explicit requirement. Yet they frequently talked about remembering, the act itself as well as how well they remembered, and even why they remembered. To give a sense of how common such references were, first consider all references from three subjects to remembering. [In the following excerpts, the presence of "..." indicates that we have deleted parts of the narrative and the small letters indicate which of a subject's six narratives the excerpts came from. If a letter is skipped, it is because there were no references to remembering in that narrative.]:

Subject 1: (a) The best thing that I remember is like we all went out one time to a birthday party . . . I just remember the times that my friend and I, we had together; (b) . . . there wasn't nothing major, as far, as far as I can remember except for a bicycle accident.

Subject 2: (a) I remember when I was about (false start) . . . But I remember distinctly the way each time she hit the glass, the glass would shatter . . . and for the most part, I remember all the blood . . . I remember the blood; (b) . . . I remember my brother having to pull his little friends around in the wagon . . . And I remember Mama and Daddy coming to the door and just watching me; (c) . . . And I remember my brother dragging an old refrigerator box out into the field . . . And I remember one day I was out there flipping in the box. . .

Subject 3 (a) . . . Okay, I remember the incident that was my first time (pitching) when I was about 7, 7 or 8 years old . . . That's about the only thing that I remember . . . Like I remember being disappointed . . . I remember too much; (b) I remember, I think, remember my building, I think I was about 6, building a snowman the year it snowed . . . All I remember is my next door neighbor said 'come on' . . . I don't remember nothing. I remember having a picture of it; (c) Do you find it hard to remember things like that or do you just . . . It's hard, you know, like I don't remember. Okay, I remember moving from my old house to my new house . . . I remember moving cause we was in my car, I remember, in the car, and we were driving over there. For some reason, that's the only part I remember, though, the ride in the car. I think it was the last trip, but I remember sitting in the back of the seat . . . I feel like they had a rack of something, I remember, of some shoes or something that I was laying next to . . . I think that's all I remember.

Recent memories:
Subject 1: (c) . . . I can remember, remember driving it home . . . that was the biggest thing that really stands out a lot is me bring, bringing it

> (car) home for the first time; (e) . . . And just, just the look on the lady's face I will never forget.
>
> Subject 2: (c) . . . I can't remember the exact type and all, but I do remember the ten speed. . . . And I remember lifting it out of the back of the trunk . . . I just distinctly remember lifting the bike out of the trunk of the car and the colors and the type of seat . . .; (d) . . . And I remember climbing up in the top where we had kinda like an attic and then walking across the crossties, the rafters. I can, I can, I can remember the smell of the place . . . I remember inside the shed is when I kissed my first Louisiana girlfriend. That shed holds fond memories before we tore it down though . . . ; (e) . . . I remember my father always coming back from these fishing trips with my uncle and saying 'Yeah we caught this and this and this.' . . . But I can distinctly remember the description of the cork . . .
>
> Subject 3: (c) . . . And I remember, I remember hitting the ball and everything, you know. I remember hitting one of them; I don't remember hitting the second one for some reason . . . ; (d) . . . I kinda just, you know, I remember that good because I know I didn't want to go . . . I was scared. I remember being scared . . .; (e) . . . And I had to get it on the first day too, and I remember that clearly . . .

To a limited extent, all this talk of remembering echoes the language of the interviewer's requests. There are occasional times such as when subject 5 said, "I remember New Year's Eve when we went to Monopoly's" in response to the interviewer's request, "Do you remember like one specific night that ya'll went out?"

But most of the references were not in direct response to the interviewer. Rather, they are the sort of verbs introducing verb phrase complements noted by Deese (1984) as potential vehicles for carrying aspect in English. In effect, our subjects were acknowledging the reconstructive nature of their memories by specifically underlining that which they were really certain they were remembering and telling us occasionally why they were certain that they were remembering these events.

By implication, events not introduced by "I can remember" are not to be given as much weight, are more likely to be speculative. Hence we can understand why subject 3 in effect corrects himself: "I was scared, I remember being scared." He does not want us to suspect that this is simply a posthoc inference on his part. And sometimes subjects comment explicitly on the fact that they know something must have happened but they do not feel like they know it: "I don't remember hitting the second one for some reason." Finally, comments such as "I will never forget the look on the lady's face" are really telling listeners not only that the listeners can rest assured that this is really remembered but are also telling them that such an event was quite significant.

To give you a sense of the way that subjects distinguish between what they really remember, what they do not remember, and what they are guessing at, consider the (embellished) narrative at the outset of this section about getting stung while picking strawberries; we could really use almost any of our corpus as examples. The narrator says that "I think it was our first year to even try and grow strawberries" and "we were all out there planting and picking and whatever we were doing" and "I must have been 7, I guess, at the time." She says, "They had to bring me to the hospital," but then she goes on at length about what she does and does not really remember: "I remember running to the house . . . I don't even remember the hospital, though, I remember she told me they brought me to the hospital. . . ."

Or consider another excerpt:

> . . . She (mother) brought me to the, um, to the hospital and um, and they had to put, to deaden it and everything, cause it was just like two little stitches or something they needed. And I wouldn't keep still for nothing. They had like four nurses, two doctors. They put me in one of those child, where they strap down your hands and your neck and everything, and I mean my feet. I was just, I was wild. When I saw the needle coming, I was dying. And, but I remember that like yesterday. That was weird. *I can still see the shot coming at em, me* [emphasis mine] screaming and stuff. I had a black eye for a little while. That's, I mean I don't really remember too much more.

In other words, the voice of experience itself makes explicit the distinction between memory and narrative in its talk about remembering. But to forestall using comments introduced by "I remember" as the "real memories," consider all examples not listed above of people providing or trying to provide a rationale for why they remember something:

> Subject 4: I still remember that (injury) because I still have a little scar there.
>
> Subject 5: (a) . . . it was snowing in Louisiana, which is very, not very often which is I guess the reason that I remember it . . . I just remember playing with my brother; (b) I remember my grandmother was babysitting me for my mom . . . That was just one of my few memories of her coming down there; (c) I remember going to, my grandparents used to have a fruit stand in the middle of Albany, . . . This is one of the few memories of him [grandfather] . . . And that's about the only thing I can remember about him . . . I don't know why I remember so much

about that particular thing. It's about the only memory I have of my grandfather because he died when I guess when, whenever I was about 6 or 7 and that's about the only memory that I have of him.

Subject 6: And this was going on during, this is while my parents were getting a divorce, so I guess that was kind of, that's why I guess I remember it the most—because it was divorce time.

Subject 12: I remember that specifically because that was my favorite breakfast . . . it was just an impact that something that, I guess, drastic happened on my birthday just makes it stick out.

Subject 13: I remember, you know, that real well because shortly after that he, he (godfather) passed away . . . I just remember it because of the impact it had on my family.

Subject 14: I remember that because it was another cold morning.

Subject 15: I guess that's (the embarrassment) why I remember it (meeting)

Such rationale for remembering things suggests that subjects are reconstructing even what they feel sure they are almost "seeing" to use the words of one subject above. In some cases they know what they are using to reconstruct the facts, thus they mention such scaffolds in order to indicate that of all things they remember and say that they do, these are the things they are most sure of, those for which in a way they can specify objective corroboration.

Talk about remembering is significantly more common in early childhood recollections (M = 10.75 for three recollections together) than in adolescent recollections [(M = 4.94), $t(15) = 4.88$, $p < .001$], two-tailed, although no firm generalizations can be made regarding this difference because early recollections occurred prior to adolescent recollections. Order effects cannot completely account for this difference, however, because the first early memory contained no more references to remembering (M = 3.44) than did the third early memory [(M = 4.00), $t(15) = -.67$]. Evidently, people are more explicit about the reconstructive nature of early childhood recollections than of adolescent ones, indicating perhaps greater awareness of their active efforts to reassemble their past with the passage of more time.

A scan of the 1,124 children's narratives (aged 4 through 9 years) in the Peterson and McCabe (1983) corpus revealed only four uses of the "I remember" construction, all by 9-year-old children. This occurred despite the fact that even the 4-year-old children in our sample occasionally produced sentences just as syntactically complex (e.g., "I told my Dada and Mommy I bumped it."). One 6-year-old even used the construction within the storyrealm: "I hided it and couldn't remember where I hided it." But not until 9 years did children ever say, "I don't even remember what it's called," "I remember I was writing with a pen," or "I remember it's crutches." This could mean that children do not monitor the degree of their remembering until sometime after the age of 9, or that individuals of all ages need to be more than a few years removed from an experience in order to recognize their own reconstructive efforts, or that the difference in the tasks was great enough to cause more explicit metamemory in the present case. The latter interpretation seems unlikely between the 9-year-olds who did (rarely) produce the "I remember" construction participated in a procedure identical to that of the younger children, who did not. What is more, use of the "I remember" introducer is rare in adult nonnarrative discourse despite abundant use of many other introducers (Deese, 1984). Thus, the "I remember" introducer may be a distinguishing characteristic of adult narrative discourse.

Initiations

In contrast to the lack of development in structure explicitly documented in this chapter, analysis of content reveals a striking change in terms of the experiences encoded in early childhood versus adolescent memories. Table 4.4 presents the results of our content analysis. It is striking that narratives of injury events are characteristic early childhood memories by adolescents, corroborating an emphasis on the negative documented in children's narratives of real experience (Miller & Sperry, 1988) as well as fantasy (Ames, 1966; Pitcher & Prelinger, 1963). Bicycle injuries give way to car injuries in early adolescence. Miscellaneous events drop out, reflective perhaps of greater consensus, standardization, socialization in terms of what events are seen as worthy of being remembered, at least out loud. But the most surprising result is that 29 (60%) of 48 adolescent memories were of initiations of one sort or another. These were of events (such as getting car licenses) that could not have happened at the earliest age we were prompting for (12 years), which means that subjects reconstructed the task. They were not recounting the *earliest* things that happened to them between the ages of 12 and 18 (our explicit and repeated wording). Rather, they were recounting the most *important* things—initiations. Initiations are one sort of transitional life experience, and an increased memory for life transitions has also been found in college students (Pillemer et al., 1986) and college graduates as long as 22 years after graduation (Pillemer et al., 1988). As literature and movies on adolescent initiation are popular—some even claim a genre of Bildungsroman—our data document what might be the basis for

TABLE 4.4
Content of Memories as a Function of Age at Time of Experience

	Early Childhood	*Adolescence*
Injury/death	10	2
House burned down; property damage	2	2
Bicycle wrecks	5	1
Car wrecks	1	5
Operations	1	1
Shames & guilty deeds	6	3
Gifts	1	2
Weather (snows; floods)	3	1
Family moves	2	2
Initiations (totals)	(4)	(29)
Religious ceremonies	2	0
Shaving	0	1
Getting license	0	3
Starting school	1	5
Hunting/fishing firsts	1	5
Out late	0	1
Intoxications	0	2
Sexual incidents	0	5
Leaving home	0	2
Accomplishments	0	6
Miscellaneous*	13	0

Note. Content categories are mutually exclusive.

* Miscellaneous memories were the following: clubhouse activity, being pulled around in a little red wagon, almost being run over by a combine, getting a dog, being visited in the hospital by a kindergarten class, having a sister come home from the hospital, being chased by a horse, having a little Christmas tree, taking fake photographs on a trip, throwing dolls in a pond, an experience in transvesticism, drinking hot milk, learning to swim.

such popularity. Perhaps transitional events are key autobiographical narratives after childhood because it is such events themselves, rather than arbitrary chronological ages, that mark the passage to new stages of life.

Developmental Change of Affect: Content Analysis

Table 4.5 displays the results of an analysis of affect. Early memories are less often positive, more often negative, whereas adolescent memories are more often positive, less often negative than one would expect due to chance alone [chi χ^2 (2, N = 96) = 8.84, $p < .025$, but see footnote 1]. This finding runs counter to G. Stanley Hall's (1904) recapitulation theory of adolescence as a time of Sturm und Drang; our finding is much more congruent with more modern empirical

TABLE 4.5
Observed (and Expected) Frequency of Affect as a Function of Age at Time of Experience

	Early Childhood	*Adolescence*
Positive	7 (13.5)	20 (13.5)
Bittersweet or neutral*	13 (11.5)	10 (11.3)
Negative	28 (23.0)	18 (23.0)

* Five neutral memories of early chldhood were combined with bittersweet memories in order to be able to perform a chi-square test of the hypothesis of association between age and affect; there were no neutral memories of early adolescence.

research that does not find adolescence to be an especially stormy time for most teenagers (e.g., see Atwater, 1983, pp. 35–38 for a review).

Nor is childhood an ontological garden of Eden. Young adults recount memories of early childhood experiences that tend to be painful, shameful, unflattering to the self. Contrast the following two narratives from the same subject:

Interviewer: Please describe in detail your very earliest memory of an experience you had when you were between the ages of 2 and 8 years old.

Subject (Male, 19 years): Okay, playing baseball would be one. One specific incident is when I was pitching, and uh, my first time pitching, and I walked in the winning run. Is that?

Interviewer: um hum.

Subject: Okay, I remember the incident, that was my first time when I was about 7, 7 or 8 years, 7 years old, I guess. Uh, first time I was pitching, that's the memory, just going to the mound and pitching and walking the guys and they ended up taking me out. That's all, that's about the only thing that I remember.

Interviewer: Did anything else happen concerning this particular experience?

Subject: What you mean, like . . . like I remember, uh, being disappointed. Is that what you mean?

Interviewer: Um hum. What stands out most about this memory?

Subject: Just the idea of the first time getting to, to pitch. Because, you know, I was like, I was really young. That was my first year, and um, he was giving me a chance, and I went up there and walked two guys, and he come pull me out. That's about it. That's all I remember, too much. [a classic high point narrative that is also a complete episode in story grammar analysis]

The same subject recalled the following as his earliest memory of adolescence:

Subject: You know like what kind, what kind of incident, like just?

Interviewer: Anything that you remember, the earliest memory.

Subject: The earliest? It probably has to pertain to baseball again, you know. That's all right? Cause, uh, it was, 12 years old, I played baseball in Hammond. I live in Gonzales, and, uh, it was allstars playing in Hammond. And uh, I hit two homeruns in one game, and that was a big incident, I guess. You know, we won the game over Hammond. And I remember, I remember hitting the ball and everything, you know.

Interviewer: You remember hitting it?

Subject: Yep, I remember hitting one of them. I don't remember hitting the second one for some reason. One of them went over in right center.

Interviewer: Anything else?

Subject: Uh the second one was, uh, helped us win the game.

Interviewer: What stands out most about that memory?

Subject: It was, they put your in the book because if you hit two homeruns in a game, you know, it tied a record. That's uh, so they put your name, that's what I remember most. [a classic high point narrative that is an abbreviated episode in story grammar analysis]

Here the childhood loser has become the adolescent hero despite the fact that content has remained the same. Playing baseball—or any game—is the occasion for many positive and negative experiences at any particular age. The narrator might have recalled his satisfaction at first hitting a ball in early childhood or of dropping a ball or striking out sometime in adolescence. Yet that was not his choice. In a way, this subject's pair of narratives is representative of the combined autobiographical memories of our subjects: painful childhood experiences are overcome and give way to thrilling but often positive initiations into and participation in powerful adult experiences during adolescence. Perhaps, as Adler suggested, we have a tendency to revise our autobiographical memories over time to conform to our current sense of self. In any case, we confirm previous research documenting the tendency for personal memories to be of intense, emotional, transitional experiences (Pillemer et al., 1986, 1988).

SUMMARY

This project compared young adults' memories for early childhood experiences with comparable memories for early adolescent experiences in terms of structure, language, and content of the memories.

Were structure to reflect the way these young adults encoded personal experiences, one would have expected significant differences in the structure of their reminiscences reflective of the age they were when they had the experience. Yet such was not the case: There were no structural differences at the discourse level between the two sorts of memories, even though two different approaches to assessing structure were used. This lack of structural development was attributed to a combination of persistent alternative structures for telling a personal narrative (i.e., descriptive and action sequences, ending at the high point, chronological, and two-event narratives), aspects of the original event itself (i.e., reactive sequences), and development of narrative ability prior to young adulthood (i.e., leapfrog narratives disappear).

Next, attention was called to aspects of the language used to reminisce. Such an examination revealed explicit acknowledgment of the present perspective of the narrator, though the way in which that perspective was marked showed some differences reflective of the age of the narrator at the time of the experience itself. Specifically, young adults mark their perspective on early childhood memories by perceptive causal or otherwise embellished inferences, actual mention of their age change, comments regarding changed physical perspective, acknowledgement of different emotional perceptions of a childhood event, or adult vocabulary. In contrast, these young adults mark perspective on early adolescent memories by means of the lessons they have drawn from such experiences. The rare lesson drawn from early childhood experience seems outdated; explicit lessons drawn from life experiences may not endure throughout all subsequent developmental stages. To what extent this lesson extraction reflects a basic human impulse rather than a continued schooling in our culture to talk about "One important thing" (see Michaels, chap. 8 in this vol.) requires research on narratives from adults of other cultures to determine. In any case, we argue that we should not confer a uniquely formative role for early childhood experiences without also considering what people *say* they have learned from experiences during various developmental stages.

We also highlighted the frequent explicit talk about remembering itself. Such talk was common in memories of early childhood and adolescence, although it was significantly more common in the former. We interpret this usage as a sign that young adults monitor themselves in the act of remembering, marking what they feel really happened in contrast to what they are inferring, embellishing in the particular conversation. That contrast may seem more apparent with greater lapse of time from the time of the original experience; memories of early adolescence as well as early childhood collected from middle-aged and elderly adults could determine whether the greater frequency of explicit mention of remembering is peculiar to early childhood recollections, or whether it is, in fact, reflective of greater time lapse between experience and recall.

Finally, we considered the content of memories. There was a remarkable trend toward standardization of the content of memories in adolescence versus childhood, with adolescence memories largely recounting initiations, first experiences. Negative memories are relatively more common in childhood, whereas positive memories are relatively more common in adolescence. Memories from both times were of emotional, not neutral, events.

In conclusion, this chapter has attempted to demonstrate that memory is certainly the cloth of which personal narrative is made but that the language of narrative reflects the nature of the event, as well as the perspectives of both listener and narrator, including the age of the narrator during the narration. The age of narrators during narration is, in some respects, more important than their age at the time of experiences themselves. The voice of experience, among other things, is an indication of the omnipresent discrepancy between autobiographical memory and the language of memory, which is narrative.

APPENDIX

Structural Patterns of Narratives in Story grammar

Descriptive sequence: describes character(s), surroundings, and habitual actions with no causal relationships.

Action sequence: a list of actions that are chronologically rather than causally ordered.

Reactive sequence: a set of changes that automatically cause other changes with no planning involved.

Abbreviated episode: describes aims of a protagonist, but planning generally must be inferred.

Complete episode: also describes aims but exhibits more evidence of planning.

Complex episode: an elaboration of a complete episode in one of four ways:

1. by an embedded reactive sequence
2. by an embedded complete episode
3. by a multiple plan application (i.e., repeated attempts)
4. by a multiple plan application with an embedded complete episode

Interactive episode: describes one set of events from two perspectives, where both people have goals and influence each other. There are two primitive variants of this pattern that involve interchange between characters, although they are not truly interactive:

1. A shifting perspective narrative describes contiguous, not coextensive, events from alternative perspectives.
2. An interactive reactive sequence describes extensive interactions with no evidence of planning.

Incomplete episode: gives all components of a complete, complex, or interactive episode except the requisite consequence.

Multiple structure narratives may be complex or they may be compounds of simpler structures.

Structural Patterns of Narratives in High Point Analysis

Classic pattern: Narrative builds up to a high point, evaluatively dwells on it, and then resolves it.

Ending-at-the-high-point pattern: Narrative builds up to a high point and then ends; there is no resolution.

Leap-frogging pattern: Narrative jumps from one event to another within an integrated experience, leaving out major events that must be inferred by the listener.

Chronological pattern: Narrative is a simple description of successive events.

Two-event pattern: Narrative consists of too few sentences for any other high point pattern to be recognized, or the narrative extensively reiterates and evaluates only two events.

Disoriented patterns: Narrative is too confused or disoriented for the listener to understand.

Miscellaneous patterns: Narrative that does not fit into one of the previous categories.

REFERENCES

Adler, A. (1931). *What life should mean to you.* Boston: Little, Brown.

Ames, L. B. (1966). Children's stories. *Genetic Psychology Monographs, 73,* 337–396.

Ansbacher, H. L. (1947). Adler's place today in the psychology of memory. *Journal of Personality, 3,* 197–207.

Atwater, E. (1983). *Adolescence.* Englewood Cliffs, NJ: Prentice-Hall.

Bartlett, F. C. (1932) *Remembering.* Cambridge, England: Cambridge University Press.

Bischofshausen, S. (1985). Developmental differences in schema dependency for temporally ordered story events. *Journal of Psycholinguistic Research, 14,* 543–556.

Brown, A. L. (1975). Recognition, reconstruction, and recall of narrative sequences by pre-operational children. *Child Development, 46,* 156–166.

Brown, A. L., & Murphy, M. D. (1975). Reconstruction of arbitrary logical sequences by preschool children. *Journal of Experimental Child Psychology, 20,* 307–326.

Brown, A. L., & Smiley, S. (1977). Rating the importance of structural units of prose passages: A problem of metacognitive development. *Child Development, 48,* 1–8.

Bruhn, A. R., & Last, J. (1982). Earliest childhood memories: Four theoretical perspectives. *Journal of Personality Assessment, 46,* 119–127.

Day, J., Stein, W., Trabasso, T., & Shirey, L. (1979, March). *A study of inferential comprehension: The use of a story schema to remember picture sequences.* Paper presented at the meetings of the Society for Research in Child Development, San Francisco.

Deese, J. (1984). *Thought into speech: The psychology of a language.* Englewood Cliffs, NJ: Prentice-Hall.

Dudycha, G. J., & Dudycha, M. M. (1933). Some factors and characteristics of childhood memories. *Child Development, 4,* 265–278.

Fivush, R., & Hamond, N. R. (in press). Autobiographic memory across the preschool years: Towards reconceptualizing childhood amnesia. In R. Fivush & J. Hudson (Eds.), *Knowing and remembering in young children.* New York: Cambridge University Press.

Freedman, A. (1987). Development in story writing. *Applied Psycholinguistics, 8,* 153–170.

Freud, S. (1953). *Three essays on the theory of sexuality.* In J. Strachey (Ed.), *The standard edition of the complete psychological works of Sigmund Freud* (Vol. 7, pp. 135–243). London: Hogarth Press. (Original work published 1905)

Freud, S. (1971). *A general introduction to psychoanalysis* (J. Riviere, Trans.). New York: Pocket Books. (Original work published 1916)

Glenn, C. (1978). The role of episodic structure and of story length on children's recall of single stories. *Journal of Verbal Learning and Verbal Behavior, 17,* 229–247.

Gordon, K. (1928). A study of early memories. *Journal of Delinquency, 12,* 129–132.

Hall, G. S. (1904). *Adolescence* (Vols. 1–2). New York: Appleton.

Hudson, J., & Nelson, K. (1983). Effects of script structure on children's story recall. *Developmental Psychology, 19,* 625–635.

Kemper, S. (1984). The development of narrative skills: Explanations and entertainments. In S. Kuczaj (Ed.), *Discourse Development* (pp. 99–124). New York: Springer-Verlag.

Kintsch, W., & van Dijk, T. (1978). Toward a model of text comprehension and production. *Psychological Review, 85,* 363–394.

Kris, E. (1956). The recovery of childhood memories in psychoanalysis. *Psychoanalytic Study of the Child, 11,* 54–88.

Labov, W. (1972). *Language in the inner city.* Philadelphia: University of Pennsylvania Press.

Lehnert, W. G. (1981). Plot units and narrative summarizations. *Cognitive Science, 4,* 293–331.

Lord, A. B. (1960). *The singer of tales.* Cambridge, MA: Harvard University Press.
Mandler, J., & Johnson, N. (1977). Remembrance of things parsed: Story structure and recall. *Cognitive Psychology, 9,* 111–151.
Mandler, J., & DeForest, M. (1979). Is there more than one way to recall a story? *Child Development, 50,* 886–889.
McCabe, A., & Peterson, C. (1990). What makes a narrative memorable? *Applied Psycholinguistics, 11,* 73–82.
McCabe, A., & Peterson, C. (1985). A naturalistic study of the production of causal connectives by children. *Journal of Child Language, 12,* 145–159.
McClure, E., Mason, J., & Barnitz, J. (1979). An exploratory study of story structure and age effects on children's ability to sequence stories. *Discourse Processes, 2,* 213–249.
Menig-Peterson, C. (1975). The modification of communicative behavior in preschool-aged children as a function of the listener's perspective. *Child Development, 46,* 1015–1018.
Menig-Peterson, C., & McCabe, A. (1978). Children's orientation of a listener to the context of their narratives. *Developmental Psychology, 74,* 582–592.
Miller, P. J., & Sperry, L. L. (1988). Early talk about the past: The origins of conversational stories of personal experience. *Journal of Child Language, 15,* 293–315.
Mistry, J. J., & Lange, G. W. (1985). Children's organization and recall of information in scripted narratives. *Child Development, 56,* 953–961.
Mosak, H. H. (1958). Early recollections as a projective technique. *Journal of Projective Techniques, 22,* 302–311.
Nelson, K. (in press). Remembering, forgetting, and childhood amnesia. In R. Fivush & J. Hudson (Eds.), *Knowing and remembering in young children.* New York: Cambridge University Press.
Nelson, K., & Ross, G. (1980). The generalities and specifics of long-term memory in infants and young children. In M. Perlmutter (Ed.), *Children's memory: New directions for child development* (No. 10, pp. 87–101). San Francisco: Jossey-Bass.
Omanson, R. C. (1982). The relation between centrality and story category variation. *Journal of Verbal Learning and Verbal Behavior, 21,* 326–337.
Pellegrini, A. D. (1984). The effect of dramatic play on children's generation of cohesive text. *Discourse Processes, 7,* 57–67.
Peterson, C., & McCabe, A. (1983). *Developmental psycholinguistics: Three ways of looking at a child's narrative.* New York: Plenum.
Piaget, J. (1952). *Play, dreams, & imitation in childhood* (M. Cook, Trans.). New York: International Universities Press.
Pillemer, D. B., & White, S. H. (1989). Childhood events recalled by children and adults. *Advances in Child Development and Behavior, 21,* 297–340.
Pillemer, D. B., Goldsmith, L. R., Panter, A. T., & White, S. H. (1988). Very long-term memories of the first year in college. *Journal of Experimental Psychology: Learning Memory, and Cognition, 14,* 709–715.

Pillemer, D. B., Rhinehart, E. D., & White, S. H. (1986). Memories of life transitions: The first year in college. *Human Learning, 5,* 109–123.

Pitcher, E. G., & Prelinger, E. (1963). *Children tell stories.* New York: International Universities Press.

Preece, A. (1987). The range of narrative forms conversationally produced by young children. *Journal of Child Language, 14,* 353–373.

Schactel, E. (1947). On memory and childhood amnesia. *Psychiatry, 10,* 1–26.

Thorndyke, P. W. (1977). Cognitive structures in comprehension and memory of narrative discourse. *Cognitive Psychology, 9,* 77–110.

Todd, C. M., & Perlmutter, M. (1980). Reality recalled by preschool children. In M. Perlmutter (Ed.), *Children's memory: New directions in child development,* (No. 10, pp. 69–85). San Francisco: Jossey-Bass.

Waldevogle, S. (1948). The frequency and affective character of childhood memories. *Psychological Monographs, 62,* (Whole No. 291).

Young, K. (1984). Ontological puzzles about narrative. *Poetics, 13,* 239–259.

CHAPTER 5

The Oral Monologue as a Form of Emergent Reading

Elizabeth Sulzby
Liliana Barro Zecker
The University of Michigan School of Education

During the last 2 decades, influenced by the findings in the area of cognitive and oral language development, investigators of literacy have started to look at young children (infancy to age 6–7) in their everyday encounters with the print in their environments (Bissex, 1980; Clay, 1975, 1979; Chomsky, 1971; Dyson, 1985a, 1985b; Ferreiro & Gómez Palacio, 1982; Ferreiro & Teberosky, 1982; Goodman, 1980; Graves, 1975; Gundlach, McLean, Stott, & NcNamee, 1985; Harste, Woodward, & Burke, 1984; Sulzby, 1983, 1985a, 1985b, 1986a, 1986b, 1986c, 1988; Teale, 1981, 1984, 1986; Teale & Sulzby, 1986). This area of research has come to be known as *emergent literacy*.

We are approaching emergent literacy as the study of the literacy behaviors and concepts of young children that precede and develop into conventional literacy. We assume that some aspects of literacy will remain common and some will vary across cultures.

One of the main tasks facing young children in becoming literate is discovering the interrelationships between oral and written language within their culture. That is, within a culture, how do children develop the ability to differentiate and use *oral* and *literate* strategies? What are the characteristics of emergent literacy knowledge? How do children start marking their developing knowledges of oral and written language in their speech? The present study addresses some of those issues by comparing the linguistic features that differentiate reading attempts judged to be oral-language-like and written-language-like in nature, according to Sulzby's (1985a) emergent storybook reading classification scheme (explained later). These reading attempts were exhibited by a group of incipiently bilingual preschool and kindergarten children "reading" in Spanish from a favorite storybook that had been read to them repeatedly in both English and Spanish.

EMERGENT LITERACY RESEARCH

Research in the development of literary or *emergent literacy* (Teale & Sulzby, 1986) has followed the general principles that characterized the investigation of oral language development after the challenge posed to behaviorism by Chomskian theory in the 1960s, and the later emphasis in the fields of psychology and linguistics on cognition/psycholinguistics (Shatz, 1984) and pragmatics/sociolinguistics (Halliday, 1975). In general, investigators of literacy development view literacy learning as a hypothesis-testing process in which the conventional forms of written language are learned through the exercise of its different functions. Children are viewed as active participants in the construction of their literacy knowledge, which is also strongly influenced by environmental forces. Interactions with others (parents, peers) provide models and feedback and, only rarely, direct tuition.

Emergent literacy researchers have approached the study of young children's literacy development through many disciplines and methodologies. Many studies in emergent literacy are ethnographic in character (Heath, 1983, 1986; Taylor, 1983; Scollon & Scollon, 1981); some use other types of naturalistic observations (Bissex, 1980; Dyson, 1985a, 1985b, in press; Gundlach, McLean, Stott, & NcNamee, 1985), and others combine these techniques with experimental designs to a greater (Bus & van IJzendoorn, 1988; Sulzby, 1985a, 1985b) or lesser degree (Ferreiro & Gómez Palacio, 1982; Ferreiro & Teberosky, 1982; Harste et al., 1984). Some are more strictly framed within a Vygotskian (Dyson, 1985a, 1985b; Gundlach et al., 1985; Luria, 1978) or a Piagetian developmental perspective (Ferreiro & Gómez Palacio, 1982; Ferreiro & Teberosky, 1982). Furthermore, studies have varied by unit of analysis (e.g., word, sentence, paragraph, story), literacy tasks (e.g., reading storybooks vs. own compositions, writing from dictation vs. spontaneous writing), and settings (classroom, laboratory, home environment).

However, regardless of the discipline observing the literacy phenomena, three methodological trends characterize most research activity in the field of emergent literacy. First, there has been a general emphasis on naturalistic observations that highlight the pragmatic functions of language, and, second, a systematic consideration for the role played by individual differences. A few researchers (Heath, 1983;

Sulzby, 1987; Sulzby & Teale, 1987) have also viewed emergent literacy from the vantage point of cultural differences within oral and written language organization.

Within the emergent literacy framework proposed by Sulzby (1985a, 1985b), any direct and necessary ties between speech and oral language and writing and written language are questioned. Both oral and written language are considered to co-occur, in an interrelated fashion, with aspects of both developing simultaneously rather than sequentially. Signs of oral language will be found in the child's performances in written situations and, certainly, written characteristics are found when children speak. Thus, development in written language is believed to influence development in oral language and vice versa. Similarly, the child is considered to develop as a writer/reader, acquiring skills and strategies in both aspects of literacy at the same time, long before becoming conventionally literate (Ferreiro & Teberosky, 1982; Sulzby, 1983; Teale & Sulzby, 1986). Reading and writing are viewed as mutually influential and interwoven aspects of the process that becoming literate entails and both reflect the child's developing understandings of oral and written language. Finally, for any given child, the nature of emergent literacy will vary according to how literacy is used within the culture and how it is communicated to the young.

Many earlier investigations approaching literacy development as emergent (Chomsky, 1979; Henderson & Beers, 1980; Read, 1971, 1975) were primarily concerned with children's products involving conventional letter forms and the graphophonemic analysis of print. The more recent investigations in emergent literacy show that children develop many literate knowledges, skills, and strategies before they can read and write conventionally. Such "roots of literacy" (Goodman, 1980; see also Goodman & Goodman, 1979) are related to both the form and functions of print, and include reading and writing behaviors such as parent-child storybook reading, reading from pictures, scribbling, writing via pseudo letters, syllabic spelling, and awareness of the differences and correspondences between oral and written language (Clay, 1975; Ferreiro & Gómez Palacio, 1982; Ferreiro & Teberosky, 1982; Harste et al., 1984; Sulzby, 1985a, 1985b, 1986a, 1986c; Sulzby & Otto, 1982).

EMERGENT STORYBOOK READING

Children's emergent literacy capacities can be characterized by increasing awareness of the differences between oral and written language. Young children show evidence of their emergent literacy knowledge when dictating stories to adults, reading favorite storybooks, and writing their own compositions (Sulzby, 1985a, 1985b, 1986a, 1989; Sulzby, Barnhart, & Hieshima, 1989). Their orally delivered speech has been used as one of the primary sources of data and is subsequently analyzed for features of both oral and written language. Here we focus on emergent storybook reading.

Storybook reading is a particularly fruitful place to study narrative structure. In storybooks, writers relate events that carry familiar content to children in familiar form. However, that content is transformed into a linguistic structure that explains past or nonpresent events in a way that young children can understand. Authors of children's storybooks may reflect general understandings of the standards that society enforces about how oral and written language are expected to be related and conveyed to the young. Such storybooks, according to the stereotypical description, are fairly decontextualized and autonomous (Olson, 1977), but, in fact, they can vary quite widely (Street, 1984). Children's emergent storybook reading attempts for any given book, however, have been interpreted (Sulzby, 1985a, 1988) as reflecting their abstractions of what such a genre should contain. In other words, children are interpreted as working out what the oral and written standards are within their culture.[1]

In highly literate societies, parent-child storybook reading is among the earliest and most common literacy events in which children participate. It is not uncommon to observe very young children reenacting and "pretending" to read familiar stories. Sulzby (1985a, 1988) studied patterns of emergent storybook reading in English monolingual children. Based on story reading attempts by middle-income U. S. kindergarten children, Sulzby (1985a) proposed a classification scheme for emergent reading of favorite storybooks and tested it through a yearlong study of low- and middle-income children of mixed ethnicity at a day-care center in which storybook reading was an habitual practice. Both groups confirmed the existence of the major categories and the subcategories of the classification scheme but one subcategory, monologic storytelling (or the oral monologue), was underrepresented. We present the major features of the classification scheme, then return to discuss the oral monologue and its significance in investigating possible cultural differences in children's developing understandings of oral/written language relationships.

---

[1]A *standard* is a form of linguistic usage enforced by society's members. Standards can be as formal as a Royal Society, as a publishers' stylesheet, or as informal as habitual parental or peer "corrections" of a child's speech. (e.g., parents in the southern United States may correct the child's use of *ain't* but not *runnin'*).

The Sulzby studies use a very simple technique. Either a teacher reads a set of books repeatedly to children or children select favorites from a classroom collection or from home. Researchers then ask individual children to "Read me your book." Children typically begin an "independent reenactment" in which they say the words of the book in their own way. Occasionally, children refuse to read independently and are encouraged to read, first, interactively, and, later, independently, using prompts such as, "Now it's your turn. You read to me." The resulting speech is transcribed and classified using the *Sulzby Classification Scheme.*

The Sulzby Classification Scheme is organized into four major categories and eleven subcategories that include a wide range of behaviors, from labeling items in pictures without forming a story to reading the storybook text conventionally. Children reading via the first three categories (e.g., "attempts governed by pictures") do not use print in their reading attempts. Instead, they rely on the pictures to "read" the story.

1. Attempts governed by pictures, story not formed.
2. Attempts governed by pictures, story formed (oral language-like).
3. Attempts governed by pictures, story formed (written language-like).
4. Attempts governed by print.

On the surface, this scheme appears to depict a simple transition from oral to written language, which Sulzby (1985a) has rejected. Such a simple transition is clearly not found in children's attempts to compose emergently and to reread from their writing (Sulzby, 1985b; Sulzby, et al., 1989). The uneven distribution of the subcategories, even with English-speaking children, prompted further studies of cultural differences to which we return later.

Oral Monologues

Two types of reading attempts fall into the second category of oral-language-like readings: *dialogic storytelling* and *monologic storytelling.* In oral-language-like reenactments, the child uses speech in such a way that the listener can interpret that the child is interpreting the storybook reading situation to call for speech appropriate in oral, face-to-face interactions such as conversation or storytelling.[2]

---

[2]*Storytelling* is a misleading term because the child is reading, or responding to a request to read; instead the term refers to the nature of the speech used. It *sounds* like storytelling rather than *being* storytelling.

The dialogic storytelling subcategory describes those readings that are conversational or dialogic in nature; this subcategory typically can take two different forms. Text itself can contain dialogue, of course, but when it does, in the first form of dialogic storytelling, the child converts it to a particular kind of dialogue. When dialogue appears within the text the child is reenacting, the child often replaces the dialogue carriers (such as "he said," or "said the baby bird") with the use of different "voices" for different characters. Narrative ties between stretches of dialogue are also often omitted. The listener is thus more dependent on paralinguistic features such as intonation than on the lexical choices and syntactical structures. The second form of dialogic storytelling involves the child interactively addressing the adult during the reading and seeming to be dependent on such interactions. Both types of dialogic reenactments are characterized by conversational prosody and contextualized wording (e.g., overabundance of deictic terms without clear reference) that make it difficult for listeners to understand the story unless they can see the book.

Sulzby (1985a, 1988) referred to the subcategory of monologic storytelling as being an oral monologue given as a reading attempt in a reading situation. Oral monologues are characterized as being complete stories delivered in storytelling intonation (in contrast to reading intonation). They seem to be stories told orally to captivate a listener. As with the dialogic storytelling, oral monologues are governed by pictures and the listener usually needs to see the book to follow the story. (In the corpus analyzed herein, some of the stories were "autonomous" in that the listener was given sufficient context in the speech to follow the story of the "reader," but this degree of specification is unusual for a storybook reading attempt. As Peterson and McCabe (1983) pointed out, it is not unusual in children's real-life narratives.) The intonation and syntax are characteristic of informal, face-to-face speech. Paralinguistic features, including sound effects, may be used to enhance personal involvement. However, the story is basically monologic rather than dialogic in nature (Sulzby, 1985a, 1988).

Written Monologues

Written-language-like reading attempts constitute the third major category in the Sulzby Classification Scheme. Within this category, there are three types of reading attempts: (a) reading and storytelling mixed, (b) reading similar to original story, and (c) reading verbatimlike story or written monologues. Readings in the first group include oral-language-like parts mixed with portions that have more written language characteristics. The reading-similar-to-original-story subcategory includes those readings that have patterns of written language but which depart somewhat from the original story.

Both reading-similar-to-original-story and reading verbatimlike story are written monologues. In both, children use reading intonation in contrast with storytelling or conversational intonation. Children seem to take the storybook reading situation as just that, a *reading* rather than talking situation. We focus here on the subcategory of reading verbatimlike story as the most stereotypical form of the written monologue. In written monologues, children recite the entire story as if they were reading from a book. According to Sulzby (1988), in the extreme case of reading verbatimlike children use "overgeneralized patterns of written language . . . such as overly specified dialogue carriers" (p. 57). They seem to be attempting to retrieve the actual story of the book verbatim or show signs of an active effort to reconstruct the story according to some internal model. This attempt is seen through many self-corrections.

To summarize, reading attempts classified as oral or written monologues are complete stories that children "read" by looking at the pictures in the storybook. Oral monologues are characterized by oral-language-like intonation patterns, wording, and syntactical structure. Written monologues, on the other hand, include primarily written-language-like patterns of intonation, lexical choice, and syntax.

In the previous studies (Sulzby, 1985a, 1988), the oral monologue as a subcategory was found to be proportionately underrepresented. It was hypothesized that oral monologues might be given more readily by children coming from cultures in which storytelling was more predominant as a means of interacting with the young and in which storybook reading was less dominant. In exploratory studies (Sulzby & Teale, 1987) with low-income white children whose families had moved to the Midwestern United States from the rural South, more children gave what appeared to be oral monologues, but these were scanty in nature and difficult to judge reliably. Judges found that they were able to make these judgments by disregarding dialectical differences and characteristics of immature syntax. The current study extends this work more systematically to a corpus of storybook reading attempts about which judges were able to make reliable distinctions.

It should be noted that the Sulzby Classification Scheme (1985a, 1988) is based on a holistic judgment about the nature of the entire discourse. Judges have consistently had difficulty when they try to take single linguistic characteristics from the subcategory descriptions and look for their presence or absence. For example, oral monologues are described as having characteristics of oral storytelling, and the presence of the initial conjunctions *and* and *and then* are given as examples. Many written monologues contain these conjunctions; and yet the overall judgment is that they were intended as readings (they have reading intonation) and they contain features of written language. To overrely on the presence of the conjunctions (or any other isolated feature) leads judges to make erroneous placements of transcripts. Yet many researchers have catalogued such linguistic features as differentiating oral and written discourse. In the present study, we examined the distribution of such features once the initial holistic judgments were made. This practice is consistent with other research such as Chafe's (1982, 1985) in which speech has been gathered from oral or written situations and then classified. In our corpus, all of the speech has been taken from an ostensibly written (storybook reading) situation and then judged for oral or written features. Before we proceed, however, we investigate some of the issues concerning oral and written language relationships, particularly as they pertain to young children.

ORAL AND WRITTEN LANGUAGE RELATIONSHIPS

> If a coherent theory of literacy is to be developed, it will have to account for the place of written language, both in relation to the forms of spoken language, and also in relation to the communicative functions served by different types of language in different social settings in our culture. (Stubbs, 1980, p. 16)

Many researchers have investigated the similarities and differences between oral and written language (Chafe, 1982, 1985; Ochs, 1979; Olson, 1977; Scinto, 1986; Scollon & Scollon, 1981, 1984; Tannen, 1982a, 1982b, 1983, 1985, 1987). Most of the investigations comparing oral and written language from a sociolinguistic/pragmatic perspective have adopted the terms spoken and written discourse to refer to "spoken or written language that has actually been produced and used by people in real contexts" (Tannen, 1983, p. 79). This section presents views that emphasize the similarities between oral and written discourse and the importance of considering contextual variables such as goal of communication, genre, and situational constraints. The following section describes the differences between both modes of discourse that are relevant for the present study.

Similarities

As discussed earlier, the type of relationship between oral and written discourse has long been in question. Often, this relationship was described as one of primacy of oral language over written language. For years, written language was commonly assumed to be parasitic on oral language, both developmentally and structurally (Stubbs, 1980; see also Sulzby, 1987). In other cases, oral and written discourse were thought to be separate systems, each of them with its own syntactic and semantic rules.

More recently, research in written language and written language development has adopted a different position that refutes both the primacy and the separate-systems arguments (Lakoff, 1981; Scinto, 1986; Sulzby, 1985b, 1988, 1989; Tannen, 1982a, 1982b, 1983, 1987). Investigators of oral and written language view the two types of discourse not as opposite and structurally unrelated systems of communication, each with its own exclusive and static characteristics, but rather as alternative modalities or norms falling on a single communicative continuum. The structural differences between oral and written language are determined by the different communicative functions that their various forms (e.g., narrative, expository text, lecture, informal conversation) serve in different situations (Scinto, 1986; Tannen, 1982a, 1982b, 1983, 1987). As Scinto (1986) stated: "The oral norm and the written norm of language do not constitute monolithic, unitary phenomena but are themselves further differentiated into functional types. [I]t is indeed incorrect to assume that any singular notion of a written norm and its associated practice stands in opposition to an oral norm and its associated practice" (p. 92).

Stubbs (1980) discussed at length the arguments that led to the notion of the primacy of oral over written language. There are, in his opinion, different aspects of the primacy relationship to be considered. He distinguished three different planes at which the primacy of one mode over the other can be analyzed: *chronological* primacy, *social* primacy, and *logical* primacy. Chronological primacy relates to the time of onset of orality and literacy phylogenetically as well as ontogenetically. Social primacy refers to the relative standing of oral and written language as social means of communication. Issues in logical primacy address the relation between oral and written symbols (e.g., Is there a perfect logical correspondence between oral and written symbols?).

Stubbs (1980) claimed that the position classifying oral language as primary (and written language parasitic on it) is based on a number of different claims about the supposed priority of oral language. From all existing evidence—most of which is inferential—oral language came first in the history of the human race, in individual societies as well as for individuals. Speech is also biologically based. Initial vocal activity in babies seems to be instinctive, not dependent on imitation, and the investigations that show that human vocal organs have evolutionarily transformed in order to accommodate speech all give support to the claim that the development of oral communication was first.

Literacy, on the other hand, is a historically recent widespread phenomenon, and although some cultures have an old literate tradition, high proportions of the world population have remained and still remain relatively illiterate. (Here Stubbs has many detractors who would argue that literacy levels and types have shifted and that few or no societies are illiterate.) That is, ontogenetically and phylogenetically, at the individual and social level, oral language development temporarily precedes, in the very early stages, the development of written language. Stubbs (1980) argued, however, that the chronological primacy and its biological basis should not be extended to issues of social and logical primacy.

Societies differ in their emphasis on written forms of language and their functions. Writing is not as universal a phenomenon as spoken language. Many societies have developed writing systems quite recently. However, Stubbs (1980) observed that, in literate communities, it is usually the written forms that have increased the communicative power of a given language and are used as the major vehicle of cultural transmission through schooling and carry more social prestige. Socially, then, written language seems to have, if not total, at least considerable primacy over spoken language.

Finally, Stubbs (1980) argued that in terms of logical primacy, even when written language represents units of spoken language, it does not represent them directly, in a one-to-one correspondence fashion. The two systems are partially autonomous in that there are distinctions in one that are not made in the other (e.g., some words that are pronounced the same are spelled differently: fined/find, and vice versa: wind/wind). Also, their change over time proceeds at different rates. Once a writing system develops it seems to "[t]ake on a life of its own, . . . along partly independent lines, [to be] used for different purposes." (Stubbs, 1980, p. 30). In the logical sense, then, written and spoken language seem to have comparable levels of standing.

The primacy argument is not the only source of disagreement among researchers. Several investigators refute the view of oral and written language as totally independent modes of communication characterized by exclusive syntactic, semantic, and pragmatic structures (Lakoff, 1981; Scinto, 1986; Scollon & Scollon, 1981, 1984;

Sulzby, 1985b, 1988; Sulzby & Teale, 1987; Tannen, 1982a, 1982b, 1983, 1987). According to Tannen (1982a, 1982b, 1987), the position that believes in a clearcut distinction between oral and written language characteristics is an artifact of the types of oral and written language that have been compared and contrasted. She claimed that many of the characteristics described as typical of oral and written discourse are often found to be a trait of each type of discourse respectively; they result not from the nature of the discourse as such (oral or written), but rather from the genres that have been selected for analysis (e.g., narratives vs. academic prose). For the most part, genre differences have not been taken into account and most of the comparisons leading to the description of the distinctive features of oral and written discourse have been made looking at oral narratives in contrast to expository text. In Tannen's (1983) opinion, "[by] limiting our analysis to these genres, we are likely to draw conclusions about spoken and written language that are incorrect" (p. 80)

A similar claim is made by Torrance and Olson (1985) when they affirmed that the structural differences between oral and written discourse "should not be attributed to modality, rather they should be attributed to intent or function" (p. 238). Chafe (1982, 1985) and Ochs (1979), as well as other researchers, discussed the importance of considering different oral and written discourse types before making generalizations about the characteristics of both modes. Lakoff (1981) claimed that discourse analysis should be based on a taxonomy of discourse types.

Tannen (1982a, 1982b, 1983, 1985, 1987) argued that in fact there are many lexical and structural forms that oral and written discourse share if the comparison is done on a similar type of genre. Written narratives, for example, often conserve many traits characteristic of informal oral language. On the other hand, the literate style that infuses oral discourse of the type used in academic lectures, some radio and television broadcasts, and so forth, is widely recognized.

Tannen (1983) proposed the study of discourse types should be done on a continuum. In her opinion:

> differences in discourse types spring out not from their status as oral or written but out of communicative goals and levels of involvement: I suggest that the distinction between writing and speech, literacy and orality, is not primary but that the differences between them may in fact grow out of other factors: specifically, communicative goals and relative focus of involvement. (p. 80)

In other words, Tannen (1983, 1985, 1987) claimed that oral and literate strategies are used in different kinds of discourse, regardless of their oral or written nature, to mark the writer or speaker's level of involvement and communicative goals. The function of a determined piece of discourse serving the specific communicative intent of the speaker/writer determines the discourse form or structure.

Scollon and Scollon (1981, 1984) proposed a similar frame of reference to approach the study of literacy and literacy strategies across cultural groups. They claimed that differences between what is often defined as oral or literate styles should be analyzed in terms of the focus of the communicative situation. Scollon and Scollon (1984) differentiated between *focused situations,* in which negotiation of meaning is limited due to different variables (e.g., distances, medium of communication, unknown audience, etc.), and *nonfocused situations* in which the emphasis of the communicative event is on "mutual sense making among participants" (p. 183). Oral traditions of the type observed within the Athabaskan culture that the Scollons studied, in which storytellers and listeners "construct" the story together, lie at the nonfocused end of the continuum. On the other hand, essayist literacy and some radio or television broadcastings are examples of highly focused communication in which there is no negotiation of meaning. Other kinds of literate and nonliterate communicative interchanges (e.g., personal letters or "formulaic" oral traditions) can be placed at some point between the two extremes of the continuum, according to the degree of participation of the speaker/listener or writer/reader.

Tannen (1980, 1985, 1987) looked at the conversational patterns displayed by individuals of different cultural backgrounds (e.g., Greeks, Jewish-Americans, Americans) and discovered differences in the amount of literate and oral strategies used. She called attention to the fact that even when Jewish-Americans and Greeks used more oral strategies than their American partners, both ethnic groups have highly literate traditions as well as rich oral traditions. It would not be accurate to attribute the conversational style of Greeks and Jewish-Americans to lack of literate strategies in their cultural groups. "Thus, individuals and groups are not either oral or literate. Rather, people have at their disposal, and are inclined to use, based on individual habits as well as cultural conventions, strategies associated with literacy and orality both in speech and writing" (Tannen, 1983, p. 88). Street (1984) also called attention to ethnocentric discussions in the writings of many scholars who have tagged various cultural groups as being either oral or literate in tradition.

Finally, Heath (1982, 1983) also proposed the use of an oral-written language continuum with a "social reality" for the study of literacy. Like the Scollons and Tannen, Heath (1982) emphasized the fact that the relationship between oral and written language is an evershifting one, and such a relationship responds to, but also creates, "the individual and societal meanings of literacy" (p. 115). After having examined literacy practices in different cultural groups, Heath (1982) concluded that "all peoples have their uses of literacy in the context of their societal needs" (p. 108).

Differences

However, even when oral and written language are considered to fall on a single communicative continuum and to adapt their forms according to the communicative functions that they serve at different times and in different contexts and cultures, it is clear that there are certain structural traits that are more characteristic of one form of discourse than of the other, within a given culture. The works of Chafe (1982, 1985) and Ochs (1979) are especially relevant for the purpose of this study.

In his comparison of oral and written discourse, Chafe (1982, 1985) proposed four sets of dichotomies under which the differences between the two modes can be summarized: (a) *integration/fragmentation,* (b) *innovation/conservativism,* (c) *involvement/detachment,* and (d) *evidentiality.* Under each category Chafe described the linguistic features that he found to differentiate both discourse modes for English adult speakers.

Different units of analysis have been used in the study of oral and written discourse (e.g., sentence, proposition, T-unit, clause, utterance). According to Chafe (1982, 1985), some of the differences between oral and written language are only understood when analyzing discourse in terms of idea units. An idea unit is always a clause, that is, it contains a verb phrase and either a noun, prepositional, adverbial, or other appropriate phrase. In oral discourse, each idea unit is spoken with a single intonation contour and is preceded by some type of hesitation that marks the beginning of a new idea to be communicated. In oral discourse, idea units are typically chained, with little subordination between them. In writing, writers combine several idea units in one sentence. Chafe (1982, 1985) proposed that written discourse is characterized by a high degree of integration, as opposed to the fragmented nature of oral discourse. Chafe (1982, 1985) argued that idea units in written discourse are longer and more comprehensive. This expansion of idea units in written discourse, he proposed, is attained by means of various linguistic devices such as:

- Nominalization
- Increased use of participles and adverbial clauses

- Attributive adjectives
- Conjoined phrases and series of phrases
- Sequences of prepositional phrases
- Complement clauses
- Relative clauses
- Indirect questions and quotations (e.g., The little bird asked if he had a mother, as opposed to "Do I have a mother?" asked the little bird)

In spontaneous oral communication, speakers produce text on-line, in face-to-face interaction. Chafe (1982, 1985) claimed that given the faster and on-the-spot production characteristic of oral discourse, speakers are forced to monitor the information output and control its flow through the use of different devices. These flow-monitoring devices act as fillers (e.g., *anyways, well, now,* etc.) that help the speaker organize the information. Disfluencies in the form of hesitations, repetitions, and rephrasings are also output-control devices that speakers use to make on-line corrections. These flow-monitoring devices contribute to the fragmented nature of oral discourse.

The second dichotomy (innovation/conversativism) proposed by Chafe to describe the differences between oral and written discourse results from the evanescent nature of oral discourse on the one hand, and the permanence that characterizes written discourse on the other. Oral discourse is less permanent and more permeable to rapid change. Written discourse changes less rapidly and is more conservative. These characteristics, according to Chafe, result in lexical and grammatical forms that are typically oral or written. He called attention to the existence of a "colloquial" as well as a "literate" lexicon (e.g., say/state; guy/man; stuff/material). Some grammatical forms are also more characteristic of either oral (e.g., contractions) or written mode (e.g., the subjunctive NO used as an adjective, dialogue carriers following direct quotations.)

Chafe (1982, 1985) argued that oral and written discourse also differ in the level of involvement or detachment that speakers/writers adopt in relation to (a) their audience, (b) the subject matter, and (c) themselves as they relate to the information presented. In Chafe's opinion, oral discourse is characterized by considerable involvement on the part of the speaker, whereas detachment is a fundamental characteristic of written discourse.

Involvement of the speaker in oral discourse is marked by the frequent use of first-person pronouns (e.g., *I, we, my*). The presence of emphatic particles like *just* and *really* mark the involvement of the speaker with the subject matter. Speakers also mark and seek involvement with their audiences through the use of second-person pronouns, addressing hearers by their names, and pausing and asking for confirmation by means of intoned words like *OK?*, *right?*, and so forth. A higher incidence of direct quotations in oral discourse is also indicative of the involvement of the speaker with the message and the audience. The detachment of written discourse, on the other hand, is by the frequent use of passives, abstract noun phrases and clauses, and indirect quotations, among other constructions.

Finally, Chafe (1982, 1985) pointed out that oral and written discourse differ in terms of evidentiality, that is the attitude speakers/writers' adopt toward the content of their messages, the source and validity of the information presented, and the reasoning that led to it. Oral discourse is more prone to appeal to sensory evidence and nonscientific sources of information as marked by introductory phrases such as "I heard . . . ," or "It looks as if . . ." Written discourse presents information in a more noncategorical fashion, and is more concerned with the reliability of its content (e.g., citing literature) and relativity of statements, which are marked with hedges, modals, or other qualifiers (e.g., *generally, should, presumably*).

In summary, Chafe (1982, 1985) proposed that written discourse is characterized by a high level of integration and detachment. By contrast, the rapid pace of oral discourse forces the speaker to monitor its flow on-line, and, as a result, ideas are presented in a more fragmented fashion with less subordination and economic connections than in written discourse. Oral discourse assumes a higher degree of involvement of the speaker with both the audience being addressed and the information being communicated. Written discourse is supposedly more conservative and resistant to innovations. Oral discourse is less permanent and thus supposedly more permeable to change.

Ochs (1979) compared the linguistic features of *unplanned* oral discourse of casual conversations and personal narratives to those present in the *planned* written discourse of academic lectures. Overall, her findings agree with Chafe's. Ochs (1979) claimed that the presence of morphosyntactic structures learned early in life characterizes unplanned discourse. She described in particular the following ones:

- Reliance on immediate context to express relationships between propositions (e.g., referent deletion)
- Preference for deictic modifiers (e.g., here, there, this, that, the)
- Avoidance of relative clauses
- Preponderance of repair mechanisms
- Verb voice (e.g., active voice rather than passive voice; direct quotations rather than indirect speech)

- Verb tense (e.g., present tense rather than past tense)
- Use of parallelism (e.g., repetition of phonemes, lexical items and syntactical constructions)

Like Chafe, Ochs (1979) described written discourse as being more compact or integrated. In her analysis, planned written discourse is characterized by the presence of complex morphosyntactic structures learned later in life:

- Lexicalization of relationships between propositions, informal cohesive devices, and topic sentences
- Use of relative clauses
- Absence of repair mechanisms
- Tendency to use past tense in narrative

There are many other positions concerning the relationships between oral and written language. Our position is closer to that of Street (1984) who held that different cultures have devised different relationships between oral and written means of discourse than to that of authors, such as Olson (1977), who seem, at least in part, to interpret oral and written language differences as being characteristics of deeply seated cultural, cognitive differences. We use Olson's (1977) view of written language as autonomous and decontextualized as a useful heuristic means to view language users' general stances rather than being a reflection of a dichotomy between oral and written language. Thus, investigations like those conducted by Chafe (1982, 1985) and Ochs (1979) may be interpreted as implying that in certain contexts of situation certain paralinguistic and linguistic features (syntactical and grammatical structures) are more characteristic of one mode of discourse than the other.

Thus in our work in storybook reading, we turned to a set of emergent storybook reading transcripts that might yield the greatest differences between features of oral and written language coming from a group of children for which cultural differences could be predicted. Previously we had studied paralinguistic features (e.g., intonation) proposed to differentiate oral speech from written monologues (Reuning, 1986). After the wording of the reading attempts had been masked so that judges could rely only on intonation patterns, the storytelling intonation of dialogic storytelling or oral monologues was judged different from reading intonation of written monologues. In the present study, we analyzed linguistic features internal to previously classified oral monologues and written monologues in transcript form, in Spanish. The analysis focused on whether the specific linguistic features that have been described as being characteristic of written language in English (Chafe, 1982, 1985; Ochs, 1979; Scinto, 1986; Tannen, 1982a, 1982b, 1983, 1985, 1987) significantly differentiate the oral and written monologues produced by Spanish-speaking children when attempting to read a well-known storybook, even though the initial selection of passages was based on a more holistic system.

INFORMAL ANALYSIS OF EMERGENT STORYBOOK READINGS

Sulzby and Teale (1987) reported that children from rural Mexico who immigrated with their parents to an industralized suburban area outside a large Midwestern U. S. city gave a large proportion of oral monologues among their emergent reading forms. This was predicted from the accounts that these children had come from an area in Mexico where there is little tradition of storybook reading but a tradition of much oral storytelling. Also school records from home visits, teacher contacts by a well-known bilingual teacher, and parental notes indicated that parents' written language usage was very minimal. The children were from low-income families living predominantly in two large apartment complexes.

Our first step was to conduct a more in-depth but informal analysis of these oral monologues (the method is described later). The first step was a confirmation that trained linguists who spoke Mexican Spanish fluently would concur in our classification. Then an informal analysis of internal linguistic features was made and predictions drawn for a subsequent detailed analysis.

As the examples that follow illustrate, an informal analysis of oral monologues and written monologues (OMs and WMs, hereafter) seemed to indicate that WMs contained a higher incidence of some specific syntactical and grammatical constructions, such as explicit subjects, dialogue carriers, and marked introduction of characters into the story via undetermined articles, that are considered more characteristic of written discourse than of oral discourse (Chafe, 1982, 1985; Ochs, 1979; Padilla & Lindholm, 1976). The preliminary informal comparison between WMs and OMs also seemed to reveal varied degrees of "fragmentation" (Chafe, 1982) marked by an overabundance of coordinating conjunctions introducing clauses (e.g., Y *se iba allí.* Y *dijo que se fue. . . .* Y *se quebró el huevo.* Y *miró para arriba y para abajo y no la vio; And* was leaving there. *And* said that (she) left. . . . *And* the egg cracked. *And* looked up and down and did not see her.).

Following are two complete transcripts with English translations. Anastacio's written monologue is given first so that the contrast with Ermelinda's oral monologue is more vivid. All judgments were made in the Spanish version but the English is included for reader convenience.

Anastacio (6;3):
¿Tú eres mi mamá?
Una pájara calentaba un huevo.
El huevo saltó y saltó.
"!Oh, no! Mi pajarito pronto volará.
¿Que querrá comer?"
Se fue y. . . "Pronto volveré."
El huevo saltó y saltó y quebró y salió un pajarito.
"!Oh, oh! ¿Dónde está mi mamá?" dijo el pajarito.
Miró arriba, miró para abajo.
No la vio.
"Yo voy a buscarla," dijo.
Se cayó del árbol.
Del árbol había, un trecho hacia abajo.
No podía volar.
No podía volar, pero podía andar.
El pajarito siguió, pero no la vio.
Y, ya se encontró con un gatito.
"¿Tú eres mi mamá?" dijo el gatito.
"¿Cómo cree-?" Tsk.
El gatito no más miraba y miraba.
El gatito no dice nada.
Se encontró con un. . . Ahora se encontró con una gallina.
"¿Tú eres mi mamá?"
"No, yo soy una gallina."
El gatito no era su mamá.
La gallina no era su mamá.
Así que siguió su camino.
Se encontró con un perro.
"¿Tú eres mi mamá?"
Dijo, "¿Cómo crees que yo sea tu mamá?
Yo soy una vaca, un perro."
El gatito no era su mamá.
La gallina no era su mamá.
El perro no era su mamá.
Así que siguió su camino.
Ahora se encontró con una vaca.
"¿Tú eres mi mamá?"
"No. ¿Cómo crees que yo soy tu mamá?

Yo soy una vaca."
El gatito no era su. . . , el gatito y la gallina no eran su mamá.
El perro y la vaca no eran su mamá.
"Yo tuve mamá," dijo el pajarito.
"La, la encontraré, la encontraré."
Así que el pajarito no andaba, nomás que corría y corría.
Muy abajo, abajo, un trecho hacia abajo, vio un,
¿cómo se llama?
Barco. Hacia arriba, muy arriba,
miró un avión.
El avión no se detuvo, siguió adelante.
En ese momento, se encontró con una cosa grande.
"¡Ahí está!" dijo el pajarito.
"Ahí está mi mamá!"
Ella se le acercó y dijo,
"[Indecipherable] tú no eres mi mamá.
Tú eres. . . , tú bufas."
[ind.] subió y subió y subió y subió [ind.].
Dijo el pajaro, "Oh, ¿Qué me va a hacer esta cosa grande?
"¡De. . . , sálvenme!"
Pero la, la cosa grande, el pajarito dijo, dijo,
"¡Quiero irme pa' mi casa!
Quiero ver mi mamá!"
[Ind.] dejó al pajarito en el árbol.
[Ind.] la pájara volvió al árbol.
"¿Tú sabes quién soy yo?"
"Sí. Tú no eres un gatito.
Tú no eres una, un, una, una [sigh] una gallina.
Tú no eres un perro.
Tú no eres una vaca.
Tú no eres un cascajo de automóvil.
Tú no eres un barco.
Tú no eres un avión, ni una cosa grande.
Tú eres una pájara,
tú eres mi mamá."
Colorín colorado, este cuento se ha acabado.

Translation[3]

Anastacio:

You are my mother?

[3]Translations into English were done adapting some syntactical structures so that the meaning was conserved. Immature syntactical constructions were translated as such (e.g., question forms that do not use S-P inversion like "You are my mother?"). Subject deletion in Spanish was conserved in the English translation because it is a relevant feature for the purpose of this study (e.g., Miró para arriba; Looked up). Reflexive particles in Spanish (e.g., *se*) are translated as personal pronouns in parenthesis to indicate that person was marked but not via explicit subject (e.g., Se cayó; (It) fell). It

A bird was warming an egg.
The egg jumped and jumped.
"Oh, no! My baby bird will fly soon.
What will he want to eat?"
(She) left and, "Soon will be back."
The egg jumped and jumped and broke
and a baby bird came out.
"Oh no! Where is my mother?" said the baby bird.
Looked up, looked down.
Did not see her.[4]
"I am going to look for her," said.
(He) fell from the tree.
From the tree there was, a long way down.
Could not fly.
Could not fly but could walk.
The baby bird went on but did not see her.
And, now he came to a kitten.
"You are my mother?" said the kitten,
"How do you thin . . . ?" Tsk.
The kitten just looked and looked.
The kitten does not say anything.
(He) came to a . . . Now (he) came to a chicken.
"You are my mother?"
"No, I am a chicken."
The kitten was not his mother.
The chicken was not his mother.
So went on his way.
(He) came to a dog.
You are my mother?"
Said, "How do you think I could be your mother?
I am a cow, a dog."
The kitten was not his mother.
The chicken was not his mother.
The dog was not his mother.
Then he went on his way.
Now (he) came to a cow.
"You are my mother?"
"No. How do you think I could be your mother?
I'm a cow."
The kitten was not his . . . the kitten and the chicken were not his mother.

---

should be noted that such marking of person is somewhat ambiguous because the same reflexive particle (e.g., *se*) is used for third-person feminine and masculine as well.

[4]In the translations in English, the use of contractions would sound more appropriate; however, we have not used them because there is no equivalent in the Spanish. Hence the translations in English sound more formal in nature than is appropriate for the child's speech. All scoring was done with the Spanish versions.

The dog and the cow were not his mother.
"I had a mother," said the baby bird.
"Will,. will find her, will find her."
So the baby bird did not walk, just ran and ran.
Very far down, down, a long way down, saw a. . what do you call it?
Boat. [ind.]
Up, very high up, saw an airplane.
The plane did not stop, went on.
At that moment, he (came) to a big thing.
"There it is!" said the baby bird.
"There is my mother."
She came close to him and said "[ind.] you are not my mother.
You are . . . , you snort."
[Ind.] went up and up and up and up. [ind.]
Said the bird, "Oh. What is this big thing going to do to me?"
"Lea- . . . , save me!"
But the, the big thing, the little bird said, said, "Want to go home!
Want to see my mother!"
[Ind.] left the baby bird in the tree
[Ind.] the mother bird returned to the tree.
"You know who I am?"
"Yes. You are not a kitten.
You are not, a, a, a, a [sigh] a chicken.
You are not a dog.
You are not a cow.
You are not a wrecked car.
You are not a boat.
You are not a plane, or a big thing.
You are a bird,
you are my mother."
Colorín, colorado, este cuento se ha acabado [common ending to children's stories in Spanish].

Emerlinda (5;9):
La mamá calentaba un huevo.
"Debe comer mi ni- mi baby."
Debía que comer porque, él no debía que- él no comía.
"Yo ahorita venía."
Y se fue.
Se fue a buscarlo y, y le fue- y no lo encon- y se fue.
Saltó, saltó, saltó.
Y estaba entero primero y luego, se quebró.
"¿Dónde está mi mamá?
Yo voy a ir a buscarla."
Miró arriba y no la vio.
Miró pa' 'bajo y no la vio.
"Yo voy allá a encontrarla."

Y se fue.
Cayó y cayó hasta el techo.
Se cayó y cayó.
El no podía volar, pero podía cam-, andar.
El fue a su camino y no la vio.
No sabía cómo era su mamá.
Se fue a su camino y se encontró a un gatito.
"¿Tú eres mi mamá?"
"¿Cómo?"
Nomás el gatito miraba y miraba.
El gatito no era su mamá.
Se fue a su camino, y, y no la vio.
Se encontró con una gallina.
Eh, "¿Tú eres mi mamá?"
"¿Cómo crees que voy a ser tu mamá?"
El, el, el gato no era su mamá, o la gallina no era su mamá.
"Todavía tengo que encontrarla.
Tengo que encontrarla."
Se encontró con un perro.
Le dijo, "¿Tú eres mi mamá?"
"Yo no soy tu mamá.
¿Cómo crees que yo soy [ind.] tu mamá si yo soy un perro?"
El gatito no era su mamá, la gallina no era su mamá, el perro no era su mamá.
Se fue a su camino.
Se encontró con una vaca.
"¿Tú eres mi mamá?"
"¿Cómo crees que yo soy tu mamá si yo soy una, una vaca?"
El gatito no era su mamá, la gallina no era su mamá, el perro no era su mamá, la vaca no era su mamá.
"Yo tengo mamá.
Tengo que buscarla.
Yo tengo mamá.
Yo debo [ind.] buscarla.
Yo debo encontrarla.
Debo de encontrarla."
Se encontró con una cosa vieja.
Y él, él no paraba y él no más se fue.
Se encontró con una cosa vieja.
Y bien abajo, abajo se encontró con una lancha.
"¡Acá estoy, mamá! Acá estoy."
No más se fue y no paró.
Miró bien arriba, "¡Acá estoy, mamá!"
No más el avión no se detuvo, nada más se fue.
Se encontró con una cosa grande.
"¡Acá estoy, mamá!"

No era su mamá.
Se de- se, se puso arriba de esa cosa grande, y se le-, y esta-
"¡Acá estoy, mamá!"
Y no se paró.
"Esto no es-", gritó, "¡Acá estoy, mamá!"
Y la cosa se- "¿Qué me va a hacer esta cosa?"
Y, y esta vez se detuvo.
Esta vez se detuvo más.
Y luego, "¿Qué me va a hacer esta cosa?"
Y estaba haciendo más pa' 'rriba y pa' 'rriba.
"Esto es- ¿Qué me va a hacer esta cosa?
¡Yo me quiero ir pa' mi casa!
¿Qué me va a hacer esta cosa vieja?
¡Algo me va a hacer!
¡Sálvenme de aquí!
Yo me quiero ir pa' mi- con mi-, a mi casa."
Se fue a su casa, y, una cosa le iba a agarrar.
Se lo quería llevar, y esta-
"¿Tú sabes quién soy yo?"
"Claro, es, tú no eres un- tú no eres un gatito,
tú no eres una gallina,
tú no eres un perro,
tú no eres . . . algo grande."
Colorín colorado, se acaba este cuento.

Translation

Ermelinda:
OK. [Span.] The mother was warming an egg.
"My ba- my baby [Eng.] must eat."
Must eat
because, he should not, he did not eat.
"I was coming right now."
And (she) left.
(She) went looking for him and, and wen- and did not fin-
and (she) left.
Jumped, jumped, jumped.
And was whole first
and then, (it) broke.
"Where is my mother?
I am going to go look for her."
Looked up and did not see her.
Looked down and did not see her.
"I am going there to find her."
And (he) left.
Fell, fell, to the roof. [Note: techo, "roof" is similar to the word *trecho* (way) used on that page of the text.]

(He) fell and fell.
He could not fly but he would wal- walk.
[He] went to his way and did not see her.
Did not know what his mother was like.
(He) went to his way and met a kitten.
"You are my mother?"
"What?"
The kitten just looked and looked.
The kitten was not his mother.
He went on his way, and, and did not see her.
(He) met a chicken.
Uh, "You are my mother?"
"How can you think I am your mother?"
The, the, the, cat was not his mother, or the chicken was not his mother.
"Still have to find her.
Have to find her."
(He) met a dog.
Told him, "You are my mother?"
"I am not your mother.
How do you think that I am [ind.] your mother if I am a dog?"
The kitten was not his mother, the chicken was not his mother, the dog was not his mother.
(He) went on his way.
(He) met upon a cow.
"You are my mother?"
"How can you think that I am your mother if I am a, a, cow?"
The kitten was not his mother, the chicken was not his mother, the dog was not his mother, the cow was not his mother.
"I have a mother.
Have to look for her.
I have a mother.
I must [ind.] look for her.
I must find her. Must find her."
(He) met an old thing.
And he, he did not stop
and he just left.
(He) met an old thing.
And way down, down (he) met a boat.
"Here I am mother, here I am!"
Just left and did not stop.
Looked way up,
"Here I am, mother!"
The plane just did not stop,
(it) just left.
(He) met a big thing.

"Here I am, mother!"
Was not his mother.
(He) st- (he), (he) got up on top of that big thing,
and (he) we- and wa- "Here I am, mother!"
And (it) did not stop.
"This is not . . . ," yelled.
"Here I am, mother!"
And the thing wa-
"What is this thing going to do to me?"
And, and this time (it) stopped.
This time it stopped more.
And then, "What is this thing going to do to me?"
And he was doing more up and up.
"This is- what is this thing going to do to me?
I want to go to my house!
What is this old thing going to do to me?
Going to do something to me!
Save me from here!
I want to go to my, with my, to my house!"
(He) went to his house,
and, a thing was going to grab him.
(It) wanted to take him, and wa-
"Do you know who I am?"
"Sure, is, you are not a, you are not a kitten,
you are not a chicken,
you are not a dog,
you are not . . . something big."
Colorín, colorado, se acaba este cuento [common ending to children's stories in Spanish].

Following the informal analysis, it was hypothesized that written monologues would present a significantly higher incidence of linguistic devices characteristic of written language. A more formal quantitative comparison was planned. All transcripts were compared in Spanish; two trained Spanish-speaking analysts did the primary scoring. A number of expectations were articulated prior to analysis.

First, it was expected that WMs would present a higher incidence of subject-predicate clauses than predicate-only clauses. Subject-predicate clauses have an explicitly stated subject (e.g., *El pajarito miró para arriba;* The little bird looked up.). Predicate clauses are clauses in which the subject is deleted and the referents of prepositions have to be inferred from previous or immediate context (e.g., *Miró para arriba;* Looked up.). Deletion of the subject is very common in oral Spanish, and it is considered a structural characteristic of conversational or informal speech (Clark, 1985; Padilla & Lindholm, 1976), in which communication relies heavily on immediate context.

In addition, WMs were expected to present a higher incidence of dialogue carriers. Dialogue carriers constitute linguistic devices that provide the receiver of the message with explicit and clear information about the participants in a dialogue (e.g., *La gallina* digo, "No! Yo soy una gallina"; The hen *said,* "No! I am a hen."). While in oral communication, dialogue is often marked via changes in intonation and pitch, the presence of dialogue carriers makes context more explicit.

Besides differences in the number of dialogue carriers included in OMs and WMs, it was predicted that the position of the dialogue carriers with respect to the direct quotations would differ significantly between the groups. Following Chafe's (1982) description of the typical final position of dialogue carriers in written discourse, it was also predicted that WMs would present a higher incidence of dialogue carriers following the direct quotations (e.g., "*Yo no soy tu mamá,*" dijo *la vaca;* "I'm not your mother," *said* the cow.) as opposed to preceding them (e.g., *La vaca* dijo, "*Yo no soy tu mamá*"; The cow *said,* "I'm not your mother.") a feature more common in informal speech. Moreover, it was expected that more characters in the WMs would be introduced by indefinite articles (e.g., *a, an*) than by definite articles (e.g., *the*) and determiners (e.g., *this, that, these*). Indefinite articles are used to mark information as newly introduced. On the other hand, definite articles and determiners, also considered deictic terms, are used to mark contextually "shared" information. Introducing characters with definite articles assumes shared context and ignores the receiver's need for more explicit information. Deictic terms function as anchors of discourse, as ties relating new parts of discourse to previous referents, or "shared context" (Fillmore, 1975). According to Wales (1979); "Deictic expressions serve to direct the hearer's attention to spatial or temporal aspects of the situation. . . . [T]o interpret them the interpreter not only needs context independent semantic information but also information which is contingent on an actual (or construed) context" (p. 241).

Fourth, oral monologues were expected to present a higher degree of fragmentation marked by a higher incidence of coordinating conjunctions at the beginning of clauses. This expectation was tempered somewhat by the knowledge that young children typically use many initial coordinating conjunctions even in quite formal speech, and we had noted many in our informal analyses of emergent readings that had been classified as written monologues. Nevertheless, because our initial scoring had been based on holistic, structural judgments rather than analyses of discrete linguistic features at the syntactical and lexical levels, we awaited results of our comparisons.

METHOD

Data Base

Twenty-eight reading attempts by preschool and kindergarten children were compared in this study. These reading attempts were part of a data base from a larger study of emergent storybook reading (Sulzby & Teale, 1987). The original study was organized in two cohorts of children attending public school in a large suburban school district near a large midwestern city in the United States. Cohort 1 was a 1984–1985 bilingual kindergarten group, and cohort 2 was a billingual preschool group followed into bilingual kindergarten in the fall of 1986. These children were the children in this district with the lowest scores on a test of English and Spanish proficiency (most Spanish-speaking children attended regular classrooms and were given pull-out instruction in English as a Second Language, or ESL).

Students in both cohorts were from low-income homes. Almost all were from two large apartment complexes that housed a large number of recent Mexican-American immigrants. The same data collection procedure was used for the two cohorts. The classroom teacher read parallel versions (in Spanish and English) of storybooks to the children repeatedly during group storytime. These books had been used in previous studies (Sulzby, 1983a, 1983b, 1985a, 1988; Sulzby & Reuning, 1984). They had been surveyed by experts in linguistics and bilingual education and judged to be appropriate for each culture and to have relatively equivalent forms of translation. Each book was read to the children by their classroom teacher five times in each language version. The teachers were asked to use their ordinary reading style and to audiotape their readings.

On the third to fifth day following the final reading of the book by the teacher, each child was taken from the classroom individually by a researcher to a quiet spot in a nearby room. The researchers had visited the classrooms many times, and the children were familiar with them. Directions were given in English unless the child did not seem to respond to English, in which case they were given in Spanish. Each child received the same request: "Read me your book." The children were asked to choose which way they wanted to read the book first, "in English or in Spanish, in Spanish or in English?" The order chosen by the child was indicated on a record sheet, along with notes about nonverbal behaviors and preliminary judgments about the features of the reading and the subcategory of the overall reading according to the Sulzby Classification Scheme for Emergent Reading of Favorite Storybooks (1985a). All sessions were audiotaped. The transcripts used for this analysis were from sessions conducted from 4 to 7 months into the study, so the children were quite familiar with the procedures and had read a number of books in this manner. All transcripts for this study were taken from the same storybook, *Are You my Mother? /¿Eres Tú mi Mamá?* (Eastman, 1967).

Each tape was transcribed and translated by a trained Spanish-speaking transcriber/translator and double-checked by a different transcriber/translator for accuracy. Typed versions of the transcripts and translations were classified by two independent judges using the Sulzby Classification Scheme. Particular care was taken in the classification of the Spanish rereadings. First judgments were made by two independent raters using the English translations of the Spanish readings (Sulzby & Teale, 1987). A second analysis/reclassification of the data was conducted by a Mexican-American linguist and an English-speaker with moderate reading knowledge of Spanish (Sulzby & Vazquez, 1987). Agreement was high across both sets of judgments. The second analysis confirmed the first classification of the Spanish-speaking children's rereading attempts into oral and written monologues. Furthermore, the second analysis was able to identify a group of rereadings that best fit and were most representative of the OM and WM categories.

Analysis

Eighteen OMs (N = 18) and 10 WMs (N = 10) that had been identified as being among the most representative of the OM and WM categories (Sulzby & Vazquez, 1987) were analyzed in the present study. The children who produced the OMs ranged in age from 4–6 to 6–1 (M = 5–5). The age range in the WM group was 5–3 to 7–1 (M = 5–9).

The OM and WM transcripts were further analyzed into clauses. The clause (e.g., a predicate phrase with a corresponding subject phrase and prepositional, noun, or adverbial phrases complementing the predicate) was used as the unit of analysis, given the fact that many of the differences between oral and written discourse have been described at that level (Chafe, 1982, 1985; Ochs, 1979). Because deletion of the subject is common in the Spanish language, many clauses only included the predicate phrase with other complement phrases but no subject phrase (e.g., *Siguió su camino;* Continued his way.). The total number of clauses, number of subject-predicate (SP) clauses, and predicate-only (P) clauses were tallied. Interscorer agreement was 91%.

The OMs and WMs were also analyzed in terms of number of direct quotations (DQ), number of dialogue carriers (DC), position of dialogue carriers (preceding and following the direct quotations), and the number of initial coordinating conjunctions (ICC). Interscorer agreement was 87% for direct quotations and dialogue carriers, and 90% for initial coordinating conjunctions. For all categories, reconciled scores were used in the final analysis.

WMs were significantly longer than OMs, $t(26) = 3.2$, $p < .01$ (two-tailed). The mean number of clauses in WMs was 90 (range from 68 to 107; Md = 95). In the OMs, the mean number of clauses was 63 (range from 22 to 109; Md = 60.5). It should be noted that these story productions are quite lengthy for children of this age range. However, such long productions are common to emergent storybook studies, using books of up to 64 pages. In order to provide relative measures of the compared features independent of the overall production (length of output), the proportion of each linguistic feature in the entire monologue for each child was calculated (e.g., proportion of SP clauses over total number of clauses) and used in the comparisons. The incidence of written language features in any given text is, to a certain extent, a function of its genre (Tannen, 1982a, 1985, 1987), thus the Spanish version of the storybook was subject to the same analysis in order to obtain a baseline to which the OMs and WMs could be compared.

Results

Oral Monologues and Written Monologues differed significantly in a number of the linguistic features under analysis. As predicted, WMs had a significantly higher incidence of SP clauses over P clauses: $t(26) = 2.09$, $p < .05$ (one-tailed). Clauses with stated subjects (*El pajarito no sabía cómo era su mamá;* The little bird did not know what his mother looked like.) were significantly more common in WMs than in OMs. In fact, the average proportion of SP clauses to total number of clauses was higher in WMs (M = 50, Md = 54.5) than in the storybook text itself (SP = 48), a finding that indicates that children were applying and overgeneralizing their knowledge of critical features of written language (Sulzby, 1985b, 1988) rather than simply memorizing the text. On the other hand, in spite of these differences, several of the

OMs nonetheless presented large sections of text without any subject reference:

Y después se fue, le estaba trayendo la comida.
And then (she) left, was bringing him the food.
Después saltó y, y quebró.
Then jumped and, and cracked.
Y es que va a buscar a su mamá.
And that is going to look for his mother.
Vio para arriba y para abajo.
Looked up and down.
"Voy a buscarla"
"Am going to look for her"
Se cayó.
(He) fell down.
Y no quería, no, no, no quería caminar.
And did not want, not, not, not, want to walk.
Después se-, se-. siguió su camino
Then con, con , continued his way
y encontró un gato.
and met a cat.
Dijo "Su mamá?"
Said *Your mother?"*
Encontró el. . . una gallina.
Met the. . . a hen.
(Darío, 5–9)

We had not expected the number of direct quotations to differ, but rather the positioning of these quotations in relation to dialogue carriers. Indeed, direct quotations were equally frequent in OMs and WMs: $t(26) = 1.32$, $p = .19$ (two-tailed). Given the characteristics of the story (DQ constitute 33% of the text), it is not surprising that this feature did not differentiate OMs from WMs. It is worth mentioning, however, that some children in the WMs group attempted to use indirect quotations (e.g., *Y el pajarito dijo que él ten-. . . . , "Yo tengo mamá";* And the little bird said that he ha- . . . , "I have a mother.") but reverted to the direct speech form before they finished their utterance. It could be the case that those children had not yet achieved the language development level that would allow them to use such indirect speech constructions with complete ease. It could also be hypothesized that their emergent literacy knowledge already included the awareness of the characteristic higher incidence of indirect quotations in written language and that they were trying to apply it but then reverted to the actual style of the storybook.

In spite of the fact that the frequency of direct quotations was similar in WMs and OMs, the number of dialogue carriers accompanying direct quotations in WMs and OMs was significantly different. WM had more dialogue carriers than the OM: $t(26) = 2.33$, $p < .05$ (one-tailed). That is, in WMs, dialogue was marked by linguistic devices (e.g., *"Tú eres mi mamá?" le dijo a la gallina. "Yo no ero tu mamá," dijo la gallina;* "Are you my mother?" (he) asked the hen. "I'm not your mother," said the hen). In OMs, on the other hand, children seemed to rely more on intonation, reenacting the dialogue: *"Eres tú mi mamá?" "No! Cómo voy a ser yo tu mamá? Yo soy una vaca'.";* "Are you my mother?" "No! How could I be your mother! I'm a cow.") and omitting dialogue carriers.

Furthermore, when the position of dialogue carriers in reference to the direct quotations was compared in WMs and OMs, results indicated that WMs had a higher incidence of dialogue carriers *following* the direct quotations: $t(26) = 2.65$, $p < .01$ (one-tailed). The two following portions of an OM from Estela and a WM from Ernesto illustrate that difference:

Estela (5;4):
Dijo, "¿Tú eres mi mamá?"
Y el gato no más miró y no dijo nada.
Miró y miró.
El gato no era su mamá.
Dijo, "¿Tú eres mi mamá?"
Y dijo, "No." [pause] El gato no era su mamá y la gallina no era su mamá.

Estela:
Said, "Are you my mother?"
And the cat only looked and did not say anything.
Looked and looked.
The cat was not his mother.
Said, "Are you my mother?"
And *said,* "No." [pause] The cat was not his mother and the chicken was not his mother.

Ernesto (7;1):
[. . .] Pasó por un. . . , a un gato.
"¿Tú eres mi mamá?"
le *preguntó* al gato.
Y el gato no dijo nada.
Y se-, y, y, llegó una gallina.
"¿Tú eres mi mamá?"
le *dijo* a la gallina.
"Yo no ero tu mamá,"
dijo la gallina.

El gato no era la mam. . . , la mamá.
La gallina no era su mamá.
Y se fue. Llegó un perro.
"¿Tú eres mi mamá?"
preguntó al perro.
Yo no ero tu mamá" le *dij*. . .La gallina no era su mamá.
El perro no era su mamá.
se fue. Llegó una vaca.
"¿Tú eres mi mamá?"
le *preguntó* a la vaca.

Ernesto:
[. . . .] Passed by. . . , a cat.
"You are my mother?"
asked to the cat.
And the cat did not say anything.
And it-, and, and a chicken came
"You are my mother?"
said to the chicken.
"I am not your mother,"
said the chicken.
The cat was not the moth. . . , the mother.
The chicken was not his mother.
And (he) left.
A dog came.
"You are my mother?"
asked to the dog.
"I am not your mother,"
he *sai*. . .
The cat was not his mother.
The chicken was not his mother.
The dog was not his mother.
And (he) left.
A cow came.
"You are my mother?"
asked to the cow.

We speculated that introduction of characters would be important because of the children's choices of proper names, nouns, or pronouns in referring to these characters. There are 12 occasions in the storybook text in which new characters are introduced. The number of characters included in OMs and WMs was not significantly different: $t(26) = 1.68, p > .05$ (two-tailed). Children producing OMs and WMs included a comparable number of characters in their reading attempts, regardless of length differences. However, the use of indefinite articles to introduce characters was significantly more frequent in the WMs (e.g., *Una pájara calentó un huevo;* A bird warmed an egg.) than in the OMs: $t(26) = 2.20, p < .05$ (one-tailed). In OMs the first appearance of characters in the story was often not marked as new information. Rather, a definite article (e.g., *the*) was used when a new character was introduced: *Se encontró a la gallina;* (He) met the chicken.

Finally, the use of coordinating conjunctions at the beginning of clauses was not found to differ significantly between WMs and OMs: $t(26) = 1.25, p > .05$ (one-tailed). This finding is not surprising because overuse of coordinating conjunctions is typical of young children's language. Situational constraints might also have influenced these results. Ochs (1979) and Chafe (1982, 1985) claimed that coordinating conjunctions at the beginning of clauses or phrases constitute one type of flow-monitoring device that communicators use as a filler or repair mechanism when the situational constraints force them to construct their messages on one (but see Peterson & McCabe, chap. 1 in this vol. for a contrasting viewpoint). It could be the case that the frequent use of coordinating conjunctions in both OMs and WMs was a result of the demands that the experimental situation placed on the subjects. The nature of the task (e.g., oral delivery), even when some children were constructing a written-language-like piece, might have forced them to resort to flow-monitoring devices in order to control their output.

Case Studies

Among the subjects in Sulzby and Teale's study (1987) there were four children whose reading attempts during the school year included both an OM and a WM. Each of them produced an OM during an early data collection session and a WM later during the year when the last readings were elicited. Those OMs and WMs were not included in the analysis already reported in order to maintain the independence of the compared groups. However, the differences between them are interesting to observe because they provide some idea of development from OM into WM within each child.

The incidence of the same variables previously described was compared for each child's OM and WM. Overall, the results agree with the findings of the group comparisons (Table 5.1). WMs present more SP clauses, a greater number of dialogue carriers, and a higher proportion of dialogue carriers following direct quotations. The introduction of characters in the WMs is more frequently done via indefinite articles.

Three out of the four children used more SP clauses in their WMs than in their earlier OMs. All four included more dialogue carriers in

TABLE 5.1
Comparison of linguistic features in oral monologues and written monologues produced by four case-study children

	SP Clauses		*Total DC*		*DC after DQ*		*Characters introduced as new information*	
	OM	*WM*	*OM*	*WM*	*OM*	*WM*	*OM*	*WM*
Anastacio	53	60	6	9	0	3	10	10
Maria A.	46	53	9	13	0	1	4	6
Rogelio	54	45	1	3	0	2	9	9
Victor	41	45	9	16	4	8	11	12

Values reported for SP clauses are proportions of SP clauses over total clauses to compensate for differences in the length of the monologues.

their WMs. Furthermore, a greater proportion of their dialogue carriers appeared in final position. Finally, two out of the four children increased the number of characters that were introduced as new information (preceded by indefinite articles) in their WMs in contrast to their OMs.

DISCUSSION

This study extends the work in emergent storybook reading and helps to explain the nature of the forms that have previously been found with English-speaking children. First, these children (as did the other children in the full study from which this subset of data were drawn) gave emergent storybook readings after they were read to repeatedly in their classrooms in both English and Spanish. In addition, many of the children in the study showed immature speech articulation and syntax patterns in relation to those typical of their age (the two examples given here do not illustrate this point). When those immaturities were ignored, raters were able to classify their readings appropriately by structural features.

The primary contribution of this study is to confirm by using methods developed by Chafe (1982), that the Sulzby Classification Scheme had differentiated oral and written monologues appropriately. It also implies that these children gave oral monologues in situations where children from a different culture tended to bypass that subcategory. Does this mean that these children are somehow less well-developed than U. S. English-speaking children, who bypass oral monologues to engage in reading and storytelling mixed? Our answer is no, that their development is different. The subcategory of "reading and storytelling mixed" that succeeds the oral monologue, or "monological storytelling," is a more disorganized subcategory that has less coherence than the oral monologue. This study seems to indicate that, in a reading situation, these children have not decided that an oral monologue is inappropriate. The structural complexity of the oral monologues is rich, as is the lexical choice.

However, we do not think that these oral monologues are totally similar to stories told in an oral situation. We think that these children, as have the English-speaking children, have already made linguistic adaptations to the reading situation. They already make distinctions between oral and written language that are in some ways similar to those of English-speaking children and in a few minor ways different. In a subsequent study with low-income black and white children in an urban area of Michigan, we (Sulzby, 1989) are pursuing a comparison of orally told stories in oral situations with storybook reading.

One conclusion drawn from the larger study (Sulzby & Teale, 1987) needs to be repeated here. These children were able to listen to complete stories in two languages and gave emergent storybook readings in both languages. Yet these were the children with the lowest measured English and Spanish proficiency in a large district and, heretofore, had been given a curriculum focusing on learning isolated vocabulary in English. Their teachers subsequently were able to adapt the curriculum to build on their knowledge of emergent literacy and allow the children to practice and demonstrate their proficiency.

ACKNOWLEDGMENTS

The research reported in this chapter was supported in part by grants from the Spencer Foundation to Elizabeth Sulzby and by support to both authors from the Center for Research in Learning and Schooling (CRLS) of The University of Michigan.

REFERENCES

Bissex, G. L. (1980). *GNYS AT WRK: A child learns to write and read.* Cambridge, MA: Harvard University Press.

Bus, A. G., & van IJzendoorn, M. H. (1988). Mother-child interactions, attachment, and emergent literacy. *Child Development, 59,* 1262–1272.

Chafe, W. (1982). Integration and involvement in speaking, writing, and oral literature. In D. Tanen (Ed.), *Spoken and written language* (pp. 35–54). Norwood, NJ: Ablex.

Chafe, W. (1985). Differences between speaking and writing. In D. Olson, N. Torrance, & A. Hildyard (Eds.), *Literacy, language and learning* (pp. 105–123). New York: Cambridge University Press.

Chomsky, C. (1979). Approaching reading through invented spelling. In L. B. Resnick & P. Weaver (Eds.), *Theory and practice of early reading* (Vol. 2, pp. 43–65). Hillsdale, NJ: Lawrence Erlbaum Associates.

Clark, E. (1985). The acquisition of romance, with special reference to French. In D. Slobin (Ed.), *The crosslinguistic study of language acquisition, Vol. 1: The data* (pp. 687–782). Hillsdale, NJ: Lawrence Erlbaum Associates.

Clay, M. (1975). *What did I write?* Auckland, New Zealand: Heinemann.

Clay, M. M. (1979). *Reading: The patterning of complex behaviour.* Exeter, NH: Heinemann.

Dyson, A. H. (1985a). Second graders sharing writing: The multiple social realities of a literacy event. *Written Communication, 2,* 189–215.

Dyson, A. H. (1985b). Research currents: Writing and the social lives of children. *Language Arts, 62,* 632–639.

Dyson, A. H. (in press). Unintentional helping in the primary grades: Writing in the children's world. In B. Rafoth & D. Rubin (Eds.), *The social construction of written communication.* Norwood, NJ: Ablex.

Eastman, P. D. (1967). *Are you my mother?* New York: Random House.

Ferreiro, E., & Teberosky, A. (1982). *Literacy before schooling.* Exeter, NH: Heinemann.

Ferreiro, E., & Gómez Palacio, M. (1982). *Análisis de las perturbaciones en el proceso de aprendizaje de la lectoescritura.* México, DF, Mexico: Dirección General de Educación Especial.

Fillmore, C. J. (1975). Santa Cruz lectures on deixis: Summer Program in Linguistics monograph. Bloomington: Indiana University Linguistics Club.

Goodman, Y. M. (1980). The roots of literacy. In P. M. Douglas (Ed.), *Claremont reading conference forth-fourth yearbook* (pp. 1–32). Claremont, CA: Claremont Reading Conference.

Goodman, K., & Goodman, Y. M. (1979). Learning to read is natural. In L. B. Resnick & P. Weaver (Eds.), *Theory and practice of early reading* (Vol. 1, pp. 137–154). Hillsdale, NJ: Lawrence Erlbaum Associates.

Graves, D. (1983). *Writing: Teachers and children at work.* Exeter, NJ: Heinemann.

Gundlach, R., McLean, J., Stott, F., & McNamee, G. (1985). The social foundations of children's early writing development. In M. Farr (Ed.), *Advances in writing research, Vol. 1: Children's early writing development* (pp. 1–58). Norwood, NJ: Ablex.

Halliday, M. A. K. (1975). *Learning how to mean: Explorations in the development of language.* New York: Elsevier North Holland.

Harste, J., Woodward, V., & Burke, C. (1984). *Language stories and literacy lessons.* Portsmouth, NH: Heinemann.

Heath, S. B. (1982). Protean shapes in literacy events. In D. Tannen (Ed.),

Spoken and written language: Exploring orality and literacy (pp. 91–117). Norwood, NJ: Ablex.
Heath, S. (1983). *Ways with words: Language, life, and work in communities and classrooms.* Cambridge, MA: Cambridge University Press.
Heath, S. (1986). Separating "things of imagination" from life: Learning to read and write. In W. Teale & Sulzby, E. (Eds.), *Emergent literacy: Writing and reading* (pp. 156–172). Norwood, NJ: Ablex.
Henderson, E., & Beers, J. (1980), *Developmental and cognitive aspects of learning to read and write.* Newark, DE: International Reading Association.
Lakoff, R. (1981). Persuasive discourse and ordinary conversation, with examples of advetising. In D. Tannen (Ed.), *Analyzing discourse: Text and talk* (pp. 25–42). Georgetown University Round Table. Washington, DC: Georgetown University.
Luria, A. R. (1978). The development of writing in the child. In M. Cole (Ed.), *Selected writings of A. R. Luria* (pp. 31–62). White Plains, NY: Sharpe.
Ochs, E. (1979). Planned and unplanned discourse. In T. Given (Ed.), *Discourse and syntax* (pp. 51–80). New York: Academic Press.
Olson, D. R. (1977). From utterance to text: The bias of language in speech and writing. *Harvard Educational Review, 47,* 257–281.
Padilla, A., & Lindholm, K. (1976). Acquisition of bilingualism: An analysis of the linguistic structures of Spanish/English speaking children. In G. Keller, R. Teschner, & S. Viera (Eds.), *Bilingualism in the bicentennial and beyond* (pp. 108–123). Jamaica, NY: Bilingual Press.
Peterson, C. L., & McCabe, A. (1983). *Three ways of looking at a child's narratives: A psycholinguistic analysis.* New York: Plenum.
Read, C. (1971). Preschool children's knowledge of English phonology. *Harvard Educational Review, 41,* 1–34.
Read, C. (1975). Lessons to be learned from preschool orthographers. In E. Lenneberg & E. Lenneberg (Eds.), *Foundations of language development* (Vol. 2, pp. 329–346). New York: Academic Press.
Reuning, C. (1986, June). *Prosodic features of reading intonation: An exploratory study.* Master's thesis in Linguistics and Language and Cognition. Northwestern University, Evanston, IL.
Scinto, L. F. M. (1986). *Written Language and psychological development.* Orlando, FL: Academic Press.
Scollon, R., & Scollon S. (1981). *Narrative, literacy, and face in interethnic communication.* Norwood, NJ: Ablex.
Scollon, R., & Scollon, S. (1984). Cooking it up and boiling it down: Abstracts in Athabascan children's story retellings. In D. Tannen (Ed.), *Coherence in spoken and written discourse* (pp. 173–197). Norwood, NJ: Ablex.
Shatz, M. (1984). A song without music and other stories: How cognitive-process constraints influence children's oral and written narratives. In D. Schiffrin (Ed.), *Meaning, form, and use in context: Linguistic applications* (pp. 313–324). Washington, DC: Georgetown University Press.
Street, B. (1984). *Literacy in theory and practice.* Cambridge: Cambridge University Press.

Stubbs, M. (1980). *Language and literacy: The sociolinguistics of reading and writing.* London: Routledge & Kegan Paul.

Sulzby, E. (1983). *Beginning Readers' developing knowledges about written language.* Final Report to the National Institute of Education (NIE-G-80-0176). Evanston, IL: Northwestern University.

Sulzby, E. (1985a). Children's emergent reading of favorite storybooks: A developmental study. *Reading Research Quarterly, 20,* 458–481.

Sulzby, E. (1985b). Kindergartners as writers and readers. In M. Farr (Ed.) *Advances in writing research, Vol. 1: Children's early writing development* (pp. 127–199). Norwood, NJ: Ablex.

Sulzby, E. (1986a). Writing and reading: Signs of oral and written language organization in the young child. In W. H. Teale & E. Sulzby (Eds.), *Emergent literacy: Writing and reading* (pp. 50–89). Norwood, NJ: Ablex.

Sulzby, E. (1986b). Young children's concepts of oral and written texts. In K. Durkin (Ed.), *Language development during the school years* (pp. 95–116). London: Croom Helm.

Sulzby, E. (1987). Children's development of prosodic distinctions in telling and dictating modes. In A. Matsuhashi (Ed.), *Writing in real time: Modeling production processes* (pp. 133–160). New York: Longman.

Sulzby, E. (1988). A study of children's early reading development. In A. D. Pellegrini (Ed.), *Psychological bases for early education* (pp. 39–75). Chichester: Wiley.

Sulzby, E. (1989). Emergent writing, with and without the computer. Proposal (funded) to the Spencer Foundation. Ann Arbor, MI: Center for Research in Learning and Schooling of the University of Michigan.

Sulzby, E., Barnhart, J., & Heishima, J. (1989). Forms of writing and rereading from writing: A preliminary report. In J. Mason (Ed.), *Reading-writing connections* (pp. 31–63). Needham Heights, MA: Allyn & Bacon.

Sulzby, E., & Otto., B. (1982). "Text" as an object of metalinguistic knowledge: A study of literacy development. *First Language, 3,* 181–199.

Sulzby, E., & Teale, W. H. (1985). Writing development in early childhood. *Educational Horizons, 64,* 8–12.

Sulzby, E., & Teale, W. H. (1987). *Young children's storybook reading: Longitudinal study of parent-child interaction and children's independent functioning.* Final report to Spencer Foundation.

Sulzby, E., & Reuning, C. (1984, December). *Emergent reading abilities in high and low literacy background children.* Paper presented at the National Reading Conference, St. Petersburg, FL.

Sulzby, E., & Vazquez, M. (1987, December). *Differences in emergent storybook reading: The role of oral monologues.* Paper presented at the National Reading Conference, St Petersburg, FL.

Tannen, D. (1980). Implications of the oral/literate continuum for cross-cultural communication. In J. Alatis (Ed.), *Current issues in bilingualism* (pp. 326–347). Georgetown University Round Table. Washington, DC: Georgetown University Press.

Tannen, D. (1982a). The oral/literate continuum in discourse. In D. Tannen (Ed.), *Spoken and written language: Exploring orality and literacy* (pp. 1–16). Norwood, NJ: Ablex.

Tannen, D. (1982b). Oral and written strategies in spoken and written narratives. *Language, 58,* 1–21.

Tannen, D. (1983). Oral and literate strategies in spoken and written discourse. In R. W. Bailey & R. M. Fosheim (Eds.), *Literacy for life: The demand for reading and writing* (pp. 79–96). New York: Modern Language Association.

Tannen, D. (1985). Relative focus of involvement in oral and written discourse. In D. Olson, N. Torrance, & A. Hildyard (Eds.), *Literacy, language, and learning* (pp. 67–88). New York: Cambridge University Press.

Tannen, D. (1987). The orality of literacy and the literacy of conversation. In J. Langer (Ed.), *Language, literacy, and culture: Issues of society and schooling* (pp. 67–88). Norwood, NJ: Ablex.

Taylor, D. (1983). *Family literacy: Young children learning to read and write.* Exeter, NH: Heinemann.

Teale, W. H. (1981). Parents reading to their children. What studies of early readers tell us. *Language Arts, 55,* 902–910.

Teale, W. H. (1984). Reading to young children: Its significance in literacy development. In H. Goelman, A. Oberg, & F. Smith (Eds.), *Awakening to literacy* (pp. 110–121). Exeter, NH: Heinemann.

Teale, W. H. (1986). Home background and young children's literacy development. In W. H. Teale & E. Sulzby (Eds.), *Emergent literacy: Writing and reading* (pp. 173–206). Norwood, NJ: Ablex.

Teale, W. & Sulzby, E. (1986). Emergent literacy as a perspective for looking at how children become writers and readers. In W. H. Teale & E. Sulzby (Eds.), *Emergent literacy: Writing and reading* (pp. vii–xxv). Norwood, NJ: Ablex.

Torrance, N. & Olson, D. (1985). Oral and literate competencies in the early school years. In D. Olson, N. Torrance, & A. Hildyard (Eds.), *Literacy, language, and learning* (pp. 256–284). New York: Cambridge University Press.

Wales, J. (1979). Deixis. In P. Fletcher & M. Garman (Eds.), *Language acquisition* (pp. 241–260). New York: Cambridge University Press.

PART II:

SOME WAYS TO DEVELOP NARRATIVE

CHAPTER 6

Getting the Story: A Longitudinal Study of Parental Styles in Eliciting Narratives and Developing Narrative Skill

Allyssa McCabe
Graduate School of Education
Harvard University, and
Eliot-Pearson Department of Child Study
Tufts University

Carole Peterson
Department of Psychology
Memorial University of Newfoundland

The structure of children's personal narratives reflects their culture (Michaels, chap. 8 in this vol.; Schieffelin & Eisenberg, 1984) and their age (Peterson & McCabe, 1983). In this chapter, we intend to show that it also reflects habitual interactions with their parents. We intend to establish evidence supporting a social interactionist account of narrative development.

DEVELOPMENT OF STRUCTURE IN CHILDREN'S PERSONAL NARRATIVES

As documented in the preceding chapters, narrative structure develops in many ways. It moves from scriptlike accounts to increasingly specific recollections between the ages of 2 and 3 years (Eisenberg, 1985; see Hudson & Shapiro, chap. 3 in this vol. for details). Spontaneous classroom narratives of 3- to 5-year-olds increase in length, and in the variety of elements of narrative structure included (Umiker-Sebeok, 1979).

Peterson and McCabe (1983) studied over 1,000 personal narratives about real experiences told to a familiar but unrelated adult experimenter by 96 White children ages 3½ to 9½. There was an age-related development of overall narrative structure, with children moving from temporally disorganized lists of actions at age 4 to narratives that followed the temporal sequence of experienced events but that ended prematurely at the high point of the story at age 5. By the age of 6, most children told personal narratives that conformed to Labov's (1972) description of what makes a good narrative, a finding confirmed by Kemper (1984). In other words, 6-year-olds oriented their listeners to who, what, where, and when something happened, gave complicating action building to a climactic event that was evaluated in some way, went on to resolve the action, and sometimes provided a coda updating the events in the narrative.

Narratives serve two functions, one is *referential* and the other *evaluative*, meaning that narrators tell the listeners what the events meant to them (Labov & Waletzky, 1967). Children aged 4 to 9 years evaluated about half of their narrative comments (Peterson & McCabe, 1983). Extensive and varied evaluation in the narratives of 2- to 2½-year-old children has also been found (Miller & Sperry, 1988).

The study of narratives provides a good means of studying an aspect of decontextualized language, or language that relies minimally on listener inference, language that is argued to be an important prerequisite for literacy (e.g., Snow, 1983). Orientation of the listener to the context of the narrative is a hallmark of good narration (Labov, 1972), and has been demonstrated to become more complete and better placed (i.e., at the outset of a narrative) with age (Menig-Peterson & McCabe, 1978), a sophistication that increases at least through the age of 14 (Kernan, 1977). It was a hypothesis of the present study that children develop this ability to orient their listener in anticipation of parent questions that were experienced during the telling of previous narratives.

At every age and in every aspect of narrative development, individual differences in skill exist (Peterson & McCabe, 1983, 1985, 1987a, 1987b). Structural description of the development of narration consists of age-related averages in performance, which leaves such individual differences unexplained. It is important to address such individual differences because there is some evidence that children who, relative to cultural peers, do not tell long or frequent narratives may have subtle language delays (Evans, 1987), and, conversely, that children who have learning disabilities have difficulties with narration (see Roth, 1986, for review). In drawing such conclusions, however, it is critical not to mistake cultural differences in narrative structure for narrative deficits, as has sometimes happened (see Michaels, chap. 8 in this vol.). We turn now to attempts to account for individual differences in culturally similar children by examining habitual parental conversation to young children.

FROM STRUCTURALISM TO SOCIAL INTERACTIONISM: HOW DOES NARRATIVE STRUCTURE DEVELOP?

In contrast to what is known about the structure of children's narratives, little is known about differences in parental styles of eliciting narratives from children. There is abundant evidence (e.g., Nelson, 1973, 1981; Smolak & Weinraub, 1983) that different parents adopt different styles in speaking to 1- and 2-year-old children, and these differences are associated with differences in the verbal style and/or ability of their young children. Specifically, a positive cognitive style is comprised of frequent questions by the mother, few directives, few overt corrections of the child's behavior, and more expansions of what the child says. In contrast, what Nelson (1973) called the negative social style is comprised of frequent directives and negation of the child's behavior. The positive cognitive style is generally associated with better articulation, faster vocabulary acquisition, and more genuinely complex sentences (see also Bretherton, McNew, Snyder, & Bates, 1983; Lieven, 1978; Nelson, 1981 for review of relevant studies). During the 22- to 27-month period, optimum syntactic growth is associated with talking at length about one topic either with simple recasts, which involve limited structural changes in a sentence related to the prior sentence, or with new statements extending a topic, resulting in few topic changes and few outright imitations of the child (Nelson, Denninger, Bonvillian, Kaplan, & Baker, 1984).

But this evidence pertains to young children at the one- and two-word stages of development. One might expect, then, that parents would exhibit different styles of eliciting narratives from their somewhat older children, and that these would have an impact on the development of narrative structure.

In a first step in this direction, Eisenberg (1985) studied the dialogic nature of conversations of two 21- to 38-month-olds with their parents. She found three phases of development: (a) most of a conversation was supplied by an adult, and children responded with "yes," "no," or a one-word nominal answer, (b) children became much less dependent on the scaffold provided by an adult's questions, only half of the descriptions being elicited by adults; events were primarily general scripts, as described by Nelson, and (c) few descriptions of the past had to be elicited, with the child providing much new information to the conversation. Eisenberg's sample, however, consisted of only two children, both Spanish-speaking. Thus, little information could be gained about the effects of systematic differences in style of elicitation of narratives.

As a second step in the direction of a social interactionist account of narrative development, Fivush and Fromhoff (1988) recorded 30 minutes of conversation about the past from 10 white, middle-class mothers of 2½-year-olds. Half of the mothers talked significantly more than the other half. The first group asked more memory and elaborative questions. Mothers did not differ in response to children's lack of response, nor did they differ when their children recalled something. Instead, the more talkative mothers differed from the others only when their children indicated a willingness to talk about a topic but did not succeed in recalling anything about it. Talkative mothers continued questioning at such points in the conversation, whereas the less talkative mothers tended to drop the topic. Talkative mothers provided more information about the events discussed, and such information was much more richly descriptive—animals were not just "animals," but instead were "real mean old animals." Children of the more talkative mothers recalled more than children of the less talkative mothers. Although, as usual, one is tempted to attribute causality to maternal style, Fivush and Fromhoff recognized that one cannot do so on the basis of relationships observed at a single point in time. Talkative mothers were termed *elaborative* in contrast to the less talkative mothers, who were called *repetitive.* The authors concluded that the real difference in style was quantitative rather than qualitative. Some mothers are much more persistent than others in demanding that their children remember some event.

In a third step in the direction of providing a social interactionist account of narrative development, Snow and Tabors (personal communication) collected dinner-table conversations from 40 low-income families of 3-year-olds. In a separate session, mothers were asked to elicit personal event narratives from their 3-year-olds. Three styles of elicitation were identified: *Passive* (showing interest but making no attempts to elicit more information), *collaborative* (asking many leading questions, posing information-rich clarification questions, and providing summaries and evaluations), and *confrontational* (demanding that the child be clear and conventional, providing little information in clarifying questions).

In a general way, Fivush and Fromhoff's *elaborative* style resembles Snow and Tabors's *collaborative* style, and seems the past-tense version of Nelson's (1973) *positive cognitive* style of conversation about the present. Less certain is an analogy between Fivush and Fromhoff's *repetitive* style and Snow and Tabors's *passive* style, or an analogy between Snow and Tabors's *confrontational* style and Nelson's *negative social* style.

Although not directly relating to narration of personal experiences, Snow and Goldfield (1981) conducted a preliminary investigation of the way in which fictional narrative conversation develops between a mother and child when they repeatedly read the same book between the ages of 2;5 and 3;4. There was a shift in such conversation: Discussion of items, item elaborations, events, and event elaborations at the outset was accompanied by a striking increase in discussion of motives and causes at the end of that period. The child gradually assumed increased responsibility for introducing various story-grammar-like categories of information (item labels, then events, then motives, and causes). Providing informative content lagged somewhat behind introduction of such categories; at the end of the observations, for example, the boy had come to introduce most of their discussion of motives and causes (something his mother had done 83% of the time at the outset), but his mother still provided most of the information in these discussions. In other words, the child first learned from his mother what questions to ask, and then how to answer them.

Also with reference to fictional narrative form, Pratt, Kerig, Cowan, and Cowan (1988) investigated the way in which parents of 3-year-olds intervened in a story-retelling task. Most of the stories produced by the children were very uninformative and incoherent. The most common type of parental strategy in this task was to ask general story questions (e.g., "Tell me your story"), followed by specific information questions ("What was the dog doing?"), and the even more structured tactic of suggesting information by means of yes/no questions ("Was the bike broken?"). Children's provision of information showed the inverse pattern: They provided most information in response to the suggested information questions, least in response to the vague general story questions. Parents of more advanced story retellers made significantly greater use of the intermediate level of intervention than other parents, though direction of causality could not be determined from this single time of observation. The authors relate such Vygotskian scaffolding techniques to Baumrind's concepts of effective parenting style, as well as to rate of success. More *authoritative* parents were more likely to be sensitive to their 3-year-old's abilities. In contrast, relatively uninvolved parents tended not to provide their children with the support they needed on this story-retelling task, which was difficult, perhaps even too difficult, for most of them.

Vygotsky (1986) argued that intrapersonal processes are transformed interpersonal processes, a broad theoretical position that meshes nicely with the social interactionist approach to language. As far as narrative is concerned, we hypothesize that narrative structure develops as a response to others, primarily mothers. In other words, the development of an internal sense of audience, expressed by increasingly decontextualized language, would be accomplished first by responding to a real audience. Along these lines, Michaels (1987, chap. 8 in this vol.) presented a Vygotskian account of the development of written narratives by elementary school children in response to questions and comments by teachers and classmates. Also, Sachs (1979, 1982) examined her daughter's initial acquisition of conversation about the past and concluded that successful conversation with children about the past depends more on the skill of the adult in guessing and/or probing than it does on the skill of the child in supplying relevant information. However, parental questioning could reach a point of diminishing returns; parents who ask too many questions could end up discouraging narration just as much as parents who ask too few. The former could be perceived as too inquisitive or unaccepting of information volunteered by the child, and the latter as uninterested in what the child has to say.

More can be said about question-driven discourse in general. Mishler (1984) examined interviews between doctors and patients driven by doctors' questions. Such interviews consist of "sequence structures," which include a request/question from the physician, a response from the patient, and a postresponse assessment/acknowledgment by the physician. Such request/questions control the conversation. When these questions do not meaningfully relate to previous responses by the patient, the patient's discourse becomes dysfluent, characterized by considerable hesitation, then one-word replies. Such an analysis may be applicable to parents and children; sensitive parents would relate follow-up questions to something children have just said in order to further the coherence and fluency of their discourse.

In addition to sensitive questioning, parents may display other means of facilitating narrative conversation. For example, there is abundant evidence that *modeling* results in learning many behaviors other than narrative (e.g., Bandura, 1969). Children are exposed to models of narrative in imaginary stories that are read to them. More relevant to the present project is the issue of what models of personal narratives are presented to them by adults in middle-class white American homes: How often do adults tell children narratives about what happened to them in the past or during temporary separations? Is the presentation of adult personal narratives one of the components of successful parental strategies for eliciting narratives? (Peterson &

McCabe [1983] found this tactic to be very successful for experimenters to get relatively unfamiliar children to tell them narratives.) The present project attempted to answer such questions. Similarly, the role of reinforcement in maintaining behavior in general is well-known (Bandura, 1969) and might also be expected to play a role in encouraging narration.

Again, although not directly relevant to narrative development, it is important to consider the probable role of corrective feedback. The field of child language in general has recently revised its view of the role of corrections in language acquisition. Previously, it was thought that explicit corrections of developing language do not happen often (Brown & Hanlon, 1970), are largely ignored by a child if they do occur (McNeill, 1966), and, if unusually frequent in parent-child discourse, may actually be associated with delay in language acquisition (Nelson, 1973). However, Ninio and Bruner (1978) noted a number of maternal corrections of one child's incorrect labels in a book-reading session. Although this led to no immediate repetition by a child, in the long run it increased the chances of that word being used again. Other researchers find that although explicit negative feedback is indeed rare, *implicit* feedback in the form of requests for clarification is more frequent after syntactically and phonologically ill-formed, as opposed to well-formed productions from children (Bohannon & Stanowicz, 1988; Demetras, Post, & Snow, 1986), as is implicit feedback in the form of expansions or repetitions with changes (Bohannon & Stanowicz, 1988; Penner, 1987). Well-formed child productions are more likely than ill-formed productions to be repeated verbatim (Bohannon & Stanowicz, 1988) or to be followed by statements extending the topic (Penner, 1987). Finally, several studies have found that children will not learn a form unless its approximations are corrected (Chapman, Leonard, & Mervis, 1986; Platt & MacWhinney, 1983; Whitehurst & Valdez-Menchaca, 1988). Although all such studies explored corrections of phonology or sentence syntax rather than corrections at the discourse level, they do primarily pertain to the age group to be examined in the present study: 2 to 3½-year-olds (e.g., Bohannon & Stanowicz, 1988; Brown & Hanlon, 1970; Demetras et al., 1986; Penner, 1987). What then can one predict about the effect of corrections on a discourse level, corrections of facts, really? What can one say about parents who insist that a child "get the story straight?" Taking the previous research together and extending it to the discourse level, we predict that overt correction of fact will be effective only if used judiciously, and that a more effective tactic will be gentle, implicit correction in the form of clarifying questions or accurate, informative expansions of what a child has incorrectly or incompletely stated. The latter tactics provide the opportunity for self-correction to children while demonstrating interest in the content of what was said.

One substantial difficulty has emerged from the social interactionist study of young children's language in general. A number of investigators attest to the difficulties of sorting out cause-and-effect relationships from the naturalistic observation of mothers' and (very young) children's speech (e.g., Furrow & Nelson, 1986; Hoff-Ginsburg & Shatz, 1982; Schwartz & Camarata, 1985). This difficulty was addressed in the present study by means of looking at development longitudinally, which allowed time-lagged correlations of mother's speech patterns with child's prowess in narration approximately 11 and 15 months later. In fact, it was a major goal of the present project to extend prior research by providing a quasi-causal account; specifically, we were interested in examining the effects of variations in parental input at one time on child narrative discourse at two later times.

In reviewing the previous work in this area, an exclusive focus on very young children, often observed at a single point in time interacting with their mothers, and very small sample sizes severely curtail the extent to which a social interactionist account of the development of personal narrative structure has been provided. Behaviors viewed at one point in time are likely to correlate for many reasons besides causal ones. The sample size of the present project was a modest 10, so this study, too, will remain in the exploratory range. However, such a sample does permit analysis of individual differences across time, unlike prior accounts. If parental behaviors are in any sense affecting child behaviors, then correlations of parental behaviors at time one with child behaviors at time two should exceed correlations of child behaviors at time one with parental behaviors at time two (see Campbell & Stanley, 1963, p. 69 for discussion of this design).

SHARED VERSUS UNSHARED EXPERIENCES

Mothers in middle-class American homes ask their children to talk both about events that they experienced together and about those they experience during separations, but the former are more prevalent in daily conversation (Sachs, 1979; Schieffelin & Eisenberg, 1984). The former—joint narration of shared experiences—allow for more maternal scaffolding, which Bruner (1978) described as the way in which the difficulty of tasks is reduced so that children can concentrate on the acquisition of a particular skill.

But eliciting narratives about unshared experiences may also be an important arena for the acquisition of decontextualized language. Parents would have more incentive to demand more complete information from their children in these cases because they often would not know what the child is leaving out. Parental desire to know what happened would be complemented by the probability that children would be more explicit in narrating about unshared relative to shared experiences. Children as young as 3 years related abbreviated and disorganized narratives with much less orienting information when talking to listeners already knowledgeable about the events being described as opposed to listeners not present at those events (Menig-Peterson, 1975). Pellegrini (1984) found greater intersentential cohesiveness in stories that were retold to naive versus knowledgeable listeners.

Thus, the two groups of studies motivate contradictory predictions regarding the quality of young children's responses to probes about shared versus unshared experiences: Shared experiences lend themselves to more effective parental scaffolding whereas unshared experiences are likely to bring forth better performances from children. Although no specific hypothesis may be formulated in the absence of further information, the two types of narratives are tracked in the present project.

In short, the present study addresses the hypothesis that the acquisition of narrative skill is associated with parental strategies for eliciting narratives.

RESEARCH DESIGN AND METHOD

Subjects[1]

Ten white, middle-class Canadian children participated in this study, along with their parents. Half were boys, half were girls. With the exception of one boy who was 31 months at the outset of the study, all other children were 25 to 27 months old at the outset of the study. All mothers had attended college.

[1]Note that while M.L.U. (Mean Length of Utterance) and other aspects of language differentiated the children at the outset, these may well be ecologically valid confounds with narrative complexity due to the already mentioned generally informative effect of clarifying questions (among other aspects of parental input) about syntax, phonology, and discourse. In any case, a detailed study of the interelationship of M.L.U., vocabulary comprehension, and narrative complexity is beyond the scope of this chapter.

Procedure

Parents were supplied with tape-recorders and blank 1-hour cassette tapes and asked to record at home occasions when their children liked to tell them narratives, defined as "stories about personal experience, about real events that have happened in the past." Parents were asked to do this in as natural a way as possible—"like you ordinarily behave when you ask your child to talk about past events." No more specific instructions were given.

Parents were originally asked to supply one tape every other month for 18 months. All tape-recordings were transcribed. However, because so few did this consistently, only two tapes from each parent were submitted to statistical analysis: one at the outset of the study, when the children were, on the average, 27 months old (time 1), and one when the children were 31 months old (time 2). There was one exception: In the case of one boy, a parent tape was not available prior to the age of 32 months, so a tape at 33 months was substituted for the earlier age. Most of the time, only mothers supplied tapes, or tapes revealed mothers doing most of the conversing with fathers occasionally chiming in. Maternal input was examined exclusively with one exception. In the case of that one child, only his father supplied tapes, and so paternal input was used exclusively for this child. Presumably, such variation reflected habitual interactions in the home.

When the children were 42 months old (time 3), they were interviewed at home by an experimenter, who prompted them for narratives using the procedure developed by Peterson and McCabe (1983). That is, the child was given a drawing task to minimize self-consciousness, whereas the experimenter talked in a minimal way about something that had happened to her (e.g., "I have a band-aid on my finger because I cut myself while peeling potatoes. Did anything like that ever happen to you?"). While the child was narrating, the experimenter was confined to saying "Unhuh" or "And then what happened?" or repeating verbatim what the child said. This allowed for assessment of narrative skill in the absence of adult scaffolding. This third assessment was independent of the other two previous assessments, which were based on transcripts of interaction with parents, both in terms of time of assessment and in terms of the person to whom narration was directed. The experimenter had not heard the parent tapes and was blind to our hypothesis about which parental styles might be preferable.

Transcripts of the parent's speech at time 1 and time 2 were scored according to Dickinson's (Chap. 7 in this vol.) system: Open-ended questions initiating new topics (e.g., "What did you do at school today?), open-ended questions extending a topic (e.g., "What did you see there?), closed-ended questions initiating a new topic ("Did you play with Alex today?"), closed-ended questions extending topics ("Was Joseph with you when you read that book?"), echoes ("You hit Pete?" after child's "I hit Pete."), clarifying questions ("What?"), statements initiating a topic, statements extending a topic, statements showing attention ("Umhumm"), clarifying questions that were partial echoes ("*Who* had to clear it all away?" after the child had mentioned something about someone clearing it all away), and appreciations of the child's narratives. In a separate analysis, parental speech was identified for direct corrections of discourse ("No way, you weren't swimming, you just got wet."). In addition, narrative exchanges were scored according to whether they concerned an experience that parent and child did or did not share. Children's speech was also scored for instances where they refused to answer a parent's specific questions or respond in any way to a topic proposed by a parent.

Note that the sequence structures discussed by Mishler (1984) are captured here in terms of coding for whether a question or statement extends the discourse, whereas Eisenberg's (1985) distinction between *yes/no questions* versus *wh-questions* is clarified here in terms of the open-ended versus close-ended distinction; specifically, some wh-questions (e.g., "What color was it?") are scored as close-ended, although most are open-ended, and some yes/no questions (e.g., "Do you remember what you did yesterday?") are scored as open-ended, although most are close-ended. Open-ended questions are also analogous to what Fivush and Fromhoff (1988) referred to as "memory questions."

Children's productions in conversations with their parents were scored for the number of clauses containing a verb, as well as for high point structure, namely whether those clauses were orientation ("I was in the grass"), evaluation ("Because it's hot"), or complicating action ("I throw sand there"). Comments such as "I don't know" or "You tell me," or codas ("The other time, can I bring my shovel?") were not common and were tracked separately.

Children's three most complex narratives at time 3 were scored for the number of propositions per narrative, a measure of overall complexity. In order to provide comparable data from identical tasks, propositions in this analysis were defined as in Peterson and McCabe (1983): any verb in an independent clause (e.g., "He ran and fell" contains two propositions). On the basis of this measure, the child's three longest narratives were identified and scored for overall high point structure (see McCabe, Capron, & Peterson, chap. 4 in this vol. for a description of such structures; Peterson & McCabe, 1983). Few subordinate clauses were produced by these young children, so scoring of propositions in the longest three narratives was virtually identical to scoring of verbs in conversational narratives at times 1 and 2.

Reliability

There was one principal coder of the parent conversational data, but 15% of the transcripts were scored by a second person. Reliability of scoring all pertinent variables is presented in Table 6.1. All rates of agreement were estimated as better than 80%. All of the children's conversational data were scored by a different experimenter. A second person also scored 16% of the conversations. Rates of agreement again were always in excess of 80%. The parents' behavior at times 1 and 2 was compared to the children's behavior at time 3 (with experimenter).

Language data are often corrected for talkativeness by forming

TABLE 6.1
Mean Frequencies, Standard Deviations, Correlations over Time, and Reliability of Scoring All Parent and Child Variables

	Mean (S.D.) 27 Mos.	*Mean (S.D.) 31 Mos.*	*Correlation 27 w/31 Mos.*	*Reliability (%)*
Parent variables:				
Open-ended questions				
Initiating topics	2.8 (2.6)	3.1 (2.5)	−.32	83
Extending topics	25.8 (23.9)	20.4 (16.7)	.51*	86
Closed-ended questions				
Initiating topics	2.9 (2.4)	3.5 (3.3)	.29	96
Extending topics	21.9 (23.2)	19.7 (8.8)	.34	92
Clarifying questions	6.2 (9.1)	5.4 (3.6)	.64**	81
Clarifying questions/echo	1.6 (1.6)	3.8 (4.8)	.23	88
Statements				
Initiating topics	0.4 (0.7)	0.4 (.5)	−.18	86
Extending topics	5.4 (5.6)	9.0 (6.5)	.30	96
Echoes	2.0 (1.8)	2.0 (2.6)	.14	93
Shows attention verbally	3.0 (6.0)	3.4 (5.0)	.20	98
Child variables:				
Number of narratives	6.2 (3.7)	6.3 (3.5)	.05	85
Propositions/narrative	4.4 (2.1)	4.1 (2.7)	.72**	89
Orientative comments	3.4 (2.6)	4.1 (4.1)	.04	90
Complicating actions	14.2 (9.6)	15.1 (13.3)	−.36	90
Evaluations	5.3 (4.9)	5.6 (5.9)	.69***	88
Number of propositions/Top 3 narratives (42 mos) 9.5 (1.8)				

*$p<.06$
**$p<.05$
***$p<.01$

proportions of total language produced that falls into a particular category. This was done, and most (15 out of 20) of the resulting proportions were strongly and significantly correlated with the corresponding raw frequencies of parental input. At best the proportions were redundant and actually less informative than the raw frequencies, consequently they were not submitted to further analysis. In the case of developing narrative structure, more frequent prompting is assumed to be more effective than less frequent prompting.

RESULTS AND DISCUSSION

Quantitative Results: Topic-extension Versus Topic-switching

We were unable to construct a model for parent-child discourse effects a priori because of the paucity of prior research on input to discourse development. The kinds of input that are beneficial for vocabulary and syntax may not necessarily be beneficial for discourse development (see Nelson et al., 1984 for discussion of such phenomena at other levels of discourse). Thus, we selected a statistical analysis that simply reduces complex data sets without requiring a priori hypotheses—principal components analysis. Principal components analysis requires estimation of the sample mean vector and the covariance matrix, and this can be done on the basis of 10 subjects, although such a sample size would not yield an efficient estimation of location and scale (Mardia, Kent, & Bibby, 1979).

A principal components analysis followed by a varimax rotation was performed on the correlated frequencies of parental input categories at 27 and 31 months and children's narrative complexity scores at 3½ years. Two principal components were extracted, and the variable loadings on these components are given in Table 6.2. The first principal component is a *topic-extension component,* comprised of average number of propositions per narrative (child to experimenter, time 3), and clarifying questions, closed- and open-ended questions extending a topic by parents at times 1 and 2. Open-ended questions introducing a topic loaded negatively onto this first component. The other principal component was basically a *topic-switching* (or *topic-introduction*) *component,* comprised of open- and closed-ended questions introducing topics as well as statements introducing new topics (all at time 1 only). Open- and closed-ended questions extending a topic at time 1 also loaded rather highly on this component. Note that the average length of narrative of the child at time 3 loaded negatively onto this second

TABLE 6.2
Variable Loadings on Principal Components

	Component 1		Component 2	
	27 mos.	*31 mos.*	*27 mos.*	*31 mos.*
Parent variables:				
Open-ended questions				
Initiating topics	−.5026	.2529	.6085	−.1737
Extending topics	.4821	.8614	.6107	.1903
Closed-ended questions				
Initiating topics	−.0832	.2023	.9248	.0143
Extending topics	.5172	.8576	.7176	−.0494
Clarifying questions	.7739	.8318	.2540	−.0347
Clarifying questions/echo	−.3242	.3131	.1027	−.1572
Statements				
Initiating topics	.1177	−.2572	.9550	−.2452
Extending topics	.2202	.1469	.1465	.1489
Echoes	−.0084	.0832	−.0009	−.2972
Shows attention verbally	−.0439	−.0773	.0237	.0509
Child variable (42 mos):				
Number of propositions /top 3 narratives		.4342		−.1788

component. Thus habitual parental extension and clarification of children's narratives at 27 and 31 months was associated with the later provision of longer narratives to a familiar experimenter, whereas attempts to initiate new topics, regardless of form, were not beneficial to the child, especially at 27 months.

The principal components analysis gives us the picture of two different parental techniques for conversing with 2-year-olds: initiating a lot of topics in the hope that one will catch their fancy, or extending some topic, often of the parent's own choosing. These two techniques are independent and not simply a function of greater talkativeness on the part of some parents. Whereas components might have revealed parental preference for certain types of questions or other syntactic forms instead of revealing, as it did, content-related correlations, this did not prove to be the case. For example, consider the following nonsignificant correlations of propositions related formally: the frequency of parental close-ended questions extending a topic was not correlated with the frequency of close-ended questions initiating topics at either time of observation. Similarly, the frequency of open-ended questions extending a topic was never correlated with the frequency of open-ended questions initiating topics. The frequency of statements extending a topic was not correlated with the frequency of statements initiating a topic at 27 months and significantly was negatively correlated with the frequency of statements initiating a topic at 31 months [r (10) = −.60, $p < .05$].

The topic-extending technique was the more successful of the two in terms of the principal outcome measure—the child's conversation at 42 months. As is shown in Table 6.3, the average number of propositions per narrative in the longest three narratives produced by children at 42 months was significantly correlated with parental statements extending a topic at 27 and at 31 months and with closed-ended questions extending a topic at 31 months.

Synchronic Correlations Between Parents' and Children's Behavior

At 27 months, there were seven significant correlations between parents' and children's behavior. The number of narratives produced by the children correlated, sensibly, with the number of closed ques-

TABLE 6.3
Significant Time-lag Correlations of Behavior From Parent-Child Study

	Child Behavior				
	31 months				*42 months*
	Average Propositions	*Orientations*	*Evaluations*	*Actions*	*Ave. props./ longest 3*
Parental behavior:					
27 months					
Statements extending topic					.66
Verbal attention			.59		
Clarifying questions		.68			
Open-ended questions introducing topics		−.55			−.60
Closed-ended questions introducing topics	−.60				
Statements introducing topics	−.53				
31 months					
Statements extending topic					.53
Closed-ended questions extending topic					.63

Note. For all correlations: $p < .05$

tions introducing new topics [$r(10) = .81$, $p < .005$] and the number of parental statements introducing new topics [$r(10) = .69$, $p < .02$]. The frequency with which children provided complicating actions also correlated with parental closed questions introducing topics [$r(10) = .70$, $p < .01$] and with statements introducing topics [$r(10) = .60$, $p < .05$]. The number of evaluative clauses provided by the child correlated with clarifying questions [$r(10) = .56$, $p < .05$], with statements extending the topic [$r(10) = .67$, $p < .05$], and with the number of times parents simply showed attention verbally to what their children said [$r(10) = .74$, $p < .01$].

At 31 months, the pattern of correlations was somewhat different: Here, the number of narratives produced by the child correlated with parental topic introduction, but with the open-ended form only [$r(10) = .57$, $p < .05$], and with clarifying questions [$r(10) = .61$, $p < .05$]. The frequency of complicating actions provided by children correlated also with the frequency of parental clarifying questions [$r(10) = .67$, $p < .02$]. Here, as opposed to previously, orientative comments from children correlated with several parental measures: the number of closed-ended questions extending a topic [$r(10) = .65$, $p < .05$], the number of clarifying questions [$r(10) = .81$, $p < .005$], and the number of echoes that function as clarifying questions [$r(10) = .62$, $p < .05$]. Evaluation provided by children also correlated with the latter parental measure [$r(10) = .62$, $p < .05$]. The only exactly replicated correlation was between evaluation and parental frequency of clarifying questions [$r(10) = .63$, $p < .05$].

Thus, the more topics initiated by parents in a given conversation, the more different narratives the children provide in response, with such narratives comprised primarily of complicating actions. Clarifying questions at times provoke evaluations of experience, at other times complicating actions, orientations, or even more narrative.

Diachronic Correlations: Effects of Parents on Children

Of greater interest than these synchronous correlations are the time-lag correlations between parental behavior at 27 months and child behavior at 31 months. These demonstrate a depressive effect of frequent topic introduction by parents that complements findings from the multivariate principal components analysis, where topic extension was shown to have a positive time-lag association with discourse extension and topic-switching was shown to have no effect. As shown in Table 6.3, the frequency of parental open-ended questions introducing topics at 27 months was significantly negatively correlated with the frequency with which the 31-month-old child provided orientation and complicating actions. Also, as is shown in Table 6.3, the frequency with which parents asked close-ended questions introducing topics, as well as made statements introducing topics, both negatively correlated with the average number of clauses per narrative later on. Children's evaluation of their narratives had only one significant time-lag correlation—with the number of times parents showed verbal attention at 27 months.

Perhaps of greatest interest is the fact that parental clarifying questions correlated with children's subsequent provision of orientative clauses. Such questions may have a beneficial effect on discourse development, as well as providing informative feedback about incorrect phonology and syntax (Bohannon & Stanowicz, 1988; Chapman, Leonard, & Mervis, 1986; Demetras et al., 1986). The present project began as an attempt to demonstrate that some middle-class parents are better than others at facilitating the use of language in a decontextualized way. As hypothesized, children develop this ability to orient their listeners in anticipation of parent questions, and the questions that serve this purpose best are clarifying questions. The long-term beneficial effect of clarifying questions on the provision of orientation accompanies short-term synchronic benefits on discourse: Recall that clarifying questions are associated with the immediate provision of evaluation both times and with the provision of complicating action, as well as orientation, at 31 months.

Diachronic Correlations: Effects of Children on Parents

Although there were six significant correlations of parents' behavior with subsequent children's behavior during parent-child conversations, there were four significant correlations of children's behavior at 27 months with parents' behavior at 31 months. The more clauses per narrative provided by children at 27 months, the fewer open-ended questions extending the topic and the more statements introducing a new topic were provided by parents 4 months later [$r(10) = -.57$ and $+.57$, $p < .05$, respectively]. The more complicating actions provided by children at 27 months, the fewer the echoes provided by parents at 31 months [$r(10) = -.71$, $p < .01$]. Finally, the more evaluations provided by children at 27 months, the more parents produced clarifying questions that echoed their child later on [$r(10) = .60$, $p < .05$]. In several subtle ways, parents fine-tune their input in response to their children's narrative conversation.

What the Parents Elicited

The average number of clauses containing a verb in the children's productions to their parents was 4.36 at 27 months and 3.75 at 31 months. Although our parents seem to have pushed their children to talk a little longer, our findings are not markedly different from past research on narratives of 2- to 3-year-old children, which found such narratives to average approximately two clauses in length (Eisenberg, 1985; Miller & Sperry, 1988; Umiker-Sebeok, 1979).

Development?

There was little development from time 1 to time 2 in terms of what the children produced. At 27 months, 13% of their 252 clauses was orientation to the context of the narratives, 56% was complicating action, and 21% was pure evaluation of what happened. There were also a few codas, and a number of "I don't knows", as well as, in one case, several "You tell mes". At 31 months, there were slightly fewer of these other comments; 15% of the 241 clauses was orientation, 56% was complicating action, and 21% was evaluation. Parents were principally attempting to get their children to tell them what happened at this age range. Orientation was often supplied by the children in terms of one-word (i.e., nonclausal) responses to specific parental questions. This lack of development is confirmed by *t*-tests of the children's behaviors from time 1 to time 2, none of which were significant; children produced just as many narratives, just as many clauses per narrative, just as many orientations, complicating actions, and evaluations at 27 as at 31 months. Lack of a time effect with the children dovetails with a comparable lack of a time effect with parents in those conversation. None of the *t*-tests comparing parents behaviors at time 1 with the same behaviors at time 2 were significant.

Means, standards deviations, and correlations over time of all parent and child behaviors are presented in Table 6.1. On the part of the parents, the most stable behaviors (i.e., significant correlations between behaviors at times 1 and 2) appear to be asking clarifying questions and open-ended questions that extend a topic. On the part of children, the average number of clauses produced per narrative and the provision of evaluations are the most stable behaviors.

As is indicated in Table 6.1, the most frequent tactics parents use are closed- and open-ended questions extending discourse. Converting to percentages, at 27 months open-ended questions extending a topic account for 34.3% of parental discourse, close-ended questions extending a topic account for 24.5%; at 31 months, the comparable percentages are 27.9% and 29.8%, respectively. These tactics were considerably more frequent than the others. Only statements extending a topic at 31 months accounted for more than 10% of the rest of parental discourse.

Most parental discourse consists of topic-extension. However, as we have also seen, there are considerable individual differences among parents. Taking the previous analyses together, open- and closed-ended questions extending a topic and statements extending a topic, along with clarifying questions are the most optimal types of input to narrative development, especially at 31 months. We calculated the percentage of parental comments that fell into these categories. At the highest extreme was Harriet; in her case 87% of her mother's discourse was optimal topic-extension. At the lowest extreme was Terry; only 64% of his father's discourse was such optimal extension. With this qualitative backdrop, we turn now to a qualitative examination of such variations in style.

Qualitative Analysis: Parental Styles

First we consider samples of several stylistic aspects of conversation about the past: topic-switching, repetitive, topic-extension, confrontational, modeling, and reinforcement aspects. Then we address the issue of prompting for shared versus unshared experiences. Finally, we return to a consideration of the structure of very young children's narratives.

Topic-switching

There were many abrupt changes of topic in the following short excerpt—from talk of boats to talk of Mommy's supper to talk of ducks. This father is an example of the type of parent whose main conversational tactic in the face of a child's resistance was to shift topics. Among adults, switching topics is an appropriate means of repairing conversational breakdowns; specifically, if an adult to whom you are speaking fails to relate a story similar to the one you have narrated, and you wish to get them to speak, changing the topic is often a successful means of restoring formal turn-by-turn talk (Maynard, 1980). It is not a particularly successful tactic for 2-year-old children who have yet to learn how to extend conversation about the past. Terry, a 30-month-old boy, was among the least advanced of our sample in terms of a variety of measures of language development.

Father: What did we see down in the harbor?
Terry: Boat.

Father: Yeah.
Terry: (Mumbles unintelligibly)
Father: Many?
Terry: One boat there.
Father: Which boat?
Terry: (Unintelligible) boat.
Father: Did you bring supper to Mommy yesterday?
Terry: Aaa.
Father: Yeah.
Terry: Man cook it.
Father: Who did?
Terry: Man.
Father: What did he do?
Terry: Man cooking supper Mommy.
Father: The man cooked supper for Mommy.
Terry: Aaa.
Father: Oooh. And who gave it to her?
Terry: Mommy.
Father: Who gave supper to Mommy?
Terry: That mom, that mom.
Father: But who brought supper to her?
Terry: (unintelligible)
Father: Did you bring it in?
Terry: Aaa.
Father: Did you give supper to Mommy?
Terry: Aaa.
Father: Did you see any ducks this morning?
Terry: (Screams; tape-recorder is turned off at this point.)

Topic-switching is not a style of parental input to narration identified in previous research. Recall that other researchers noted a passive, repetitious style that was contrasted to a more optimal style (Fivush and Fromhoff, 1988; Snow & Tabors, personal communication). These two pictures of less-than-optimum input do not coincide. That is, a parent who habitually switches topics does not necessarily display the repetitiousness noted by Fivush and Fromhoff (1988), and vice versa.

Repetitive

We found examples of repetitiousness, as well as topic-switching. The mother in the following excerpt seems to fit the style called repetitive by Fivush and Fromhoff (1988), or passive by Snow and Tabors (personal communication). The mother directly corrects one statement by the child about the presence of Sarah, but supplies very little information other than that, and she never asks her daughter something to which the daughter does not know the answer. Whereas one repetition is a recast of the sort that Nelson and colleagues (1984) found beneficial to syntax development in younger children, most of the repetitions are not informative in any way. This exchange was longer than, but otherwise typical of, exchanges between Kelly and her mother at that age. At 42 months, Kelly would have the shortest average narratives in our sample. Consider the following early exchange:

> Mother: Do you remember when we were on the farm at Christmas?
> Kelly: I liked Grandpa.
> Mother: You liked grandpa?
> Kelly: Huh-huh.
> Mother: Yea.
> Kelly: I love chocolate.
> Mother: You love chocolate? Did you have chocolate at Grandpa's house? Yes.
> Kelly: There are cows at his house.
> Mother: There are cows at his house. That's true.
> Kelly: And . . . and . . . and
> Mother: What? Who was at the farm when we were there?
> Kelly: Ummm, Grandpa.
> Mother: Grandpa and who else?
> Kelly: Ummm, Granny.
> Mother: Yea, and who else?
> Kelly: Ummm, Sarah.
> Mother: Sarah! Sarah wasn't there. Who else was there?
> Kelly: Ummm, Samuel.
> Mother: And what happened to Samuel?
> Kelly: Ummm . . . cold.
> Mother: He got a bad cold, didn't he. And what did he do when he had that bad cold?
> Kelly: Ummm, he fell asleep.
> Mother: He fell asleep, yea. Poor Samuel. Where did he sleep?
> Kelly: On the couch!
> Mother: Yea that's right.

Repeating her child's comments with very few changes or additions did keep her daughter talking, but it did not provide information to help her daughter better her narrative abilities. We suggest that repetitive parental feedback falls somewhere between topic-switching and topic-extension in terms of value for a novice narrator.

Topic-extension

Contrast the topic-switching and repetitive exchanges already presented with the following exchange between Harriet, a 27-month-old girl, and her mother. It was the longest recorded exchange on one topic at the time, and stands as a good example of topic-extension. Some parents are willing and able to extend a topic despite the limitations of their 2-year-olds' narrative contributions. Note that the parent picks a topic likely to be of interest to young children, though not one traditionally considered exemplary polite conversation:

Mother: And did you get sick at school Harriet?
Harriet: Yeah.
Mother: What made you sick?
Harriet: I got (unintelligible) my pants fall, fall down.
Mother: You got wee-wees in your pants and you fell down. Is that what you said? And who looked after you when you got sick?
Harriet: Helen.
Mother: Helen did. Did Helen look after you when you were sick?
Harriet: Yeah.
Mother: Did you lie on the mat? Heather put a blanket over you?
Harriet: Yeah.
Mother: Did you fall asleep?
*Harriet: I can't close my eyes.
Mother: But you didn't close your eyes?
Harriet: No.
Mother: And what happened when you got sick, who came for you?
*Harriet: Tommy gone.
Mother: Yeah Tommy was sick too. And who came for you when you were sick and brought you home?
Harriet: Mom.
Mother: And where did you go before you went home? Did you visit anybody else?
Harriet: Yes.
Mother: Who did you visit? Did you visit Ann?
Harriet: Yeah.
Mother: And who else?
Harriet: Mindy.
Mother: Mindy. And what did you do at Auntie Mindy's house? Do you know?
Harriet: (unintelligible) gone.
Mother: What's gone?
Harriet: Mindy's gone.
Mother: Where did Mindy go? Oh she went for a nap.
Harriet: Yeah.
Mother: Did you sleep when you were there?

Harriet: Yep.
Mother: And then what happened when you woke up?
*Harriet: I don't want it.
Mother: Who came for you then? Did Daddy come for you?
Harriet: Yeah.
Mother: He did? And where did he take you?
Harriet: Mom. At my Mom's.
Mother: And where did Daddy take you? Whose house did you visit then?
*Harriet: Look.
Mother: Did you visit Andrea's?
Harriet: Yep.
Mother: And who else was there?
*Harriet: Look. Look.
Mother: Who else was there besides Andrea?
*Harriet: Look, this is Sadie's.
Mother: And what did you do at Andrea's house, Harriet? Harriet? Did you sleep at Andrea's house?
Harriet: (unintelligible)
Mother: You want to put that on.
Harriet: Yeah.
Mother: So what did you do at Andrea's house? Do you know? Did you go to sleep there?
Harriet: Mm-mm.
Mother: You did? You went to sleep at Andrea's house?
Harriet: Mm-mm.
Mother: And who else was there besides Andrea?
*Harriet: (whimpering sounds)
Mother: And who else was there besides Andrea? Was your brother there?
Harriet: Yeah.
Mother: And what's his name?
Harriet: Oow—Ben.
Mother: Ben. And what did Ben do when you were there? Did he go to sleep too?
Harriet: Yes.
Mother: And did you wake him up?
Harriet: Yeah.
Mother: You did. Why did you wake him up? Did you watch T.V.?
Harriet: Yep.
Mother: And did you watch a special movie?
*Harriet: (whimpering sounds)
Mother: What else did you do, Harriet? Did you do anything else?
*Harriet: I need this.

This is obviously a much longer exchange than the previous examples of topic-switching and repetitive input. The topic-extending mother occasionally echoes her child, but usually engages in repeated questions, often moving from general, open-ended questions to progressively more specific questions in the face of nonresponsiveness, in the manner outlined by Pratt and colleagues (1988). Such a technique provides information to a child when that child is focused on a topic and perhaps in the kind of receptive state that will enable her to tell a more complete narrative next time. See, for example, Harriet's mother's questions about Harriet's brother, Ben, to get a flavor for the information a parent can provide about a topic. The reader should note that if the mother's contributions are eliminated, there is virtually no story left:

> Yeah. I got (XXX). My pants fall down. Helen. Yeah. Yeah. I can't close my eyes. No. Tommy gone. Mom. Yes. Yeah. Mindy. (XXX) gone. Mindy's gone. Yeah. Yup. I don't want it. Yeah. Mom. At my Mom's. Look. Yep. Look. Look. Look this Sadie's. (XXX). Yeah. MM-mm. Mm-mm. (whimpers). Yeah. Oow-Ben. Yes. Yeah. Yep. (whimpers). I need this.

This would be classified as an two-event narrative (formerly "impoverished") in Peterson and McCabe's (1983) system, as would most of the narratives produced by even the most talkative children at this age.

Harriet's mother is very persistent in her questioning. For example, she asks what happened at Andrea's house six times before she finally is rewarded with an answer; she then repeats that question and the successful response. The asterisks in the previous example note places where Harriet either seems to be or is clearly trying to change the subject; her mother brings her back to the subject seven of the eight times. At 42 months, Harriet had the second longest narratives of our sample of ten children.

Parental persistence is necessary in view of young children's apparent resistance. Resistance to telling narratives is characteristic of all our narrators at this age, even the most advanced ones. At 26 months, Carl, the boy who at 42 months would become our most expansive narrator engaged in exchanges like the following:

> Mother: Can you remember Christmas?
> Carl: No.
> Mother: What did we do for Christmas?
> Carl: Put (unintelligible)
> Mother: Put decorations on the Christmas tree? Can you say 'decorations'?

Carl: Yep.
Mother: What is it? What did we put on the Christmas tree?
Carl: Decorations.
Mother: Decorations.
Carl: And put a big star.
Mother: A big star up top, right. What else? What was under the Christmas tree? (Pause) Presents?
Carl: Open the presents.
Mother: And then you opened the presents.
Carl: Some neat presents.
Mother: Some neat presents.
Carl: Tub toys.
Mother: Tub toys. What else?
Carl: Bubba.
Mother: Bubba. Who is Bubba?
Carl: (unintelligible).
Mother: What kind of an animal is Bubba.
Carl: Bubba bear.
Mother: Bubba bear.
Carl: Yes.
Mother: Bubba the Bear.
Carl: No.
Mother: No. What else was under the Christmas tree?
Carl: (unintelligible)
Mother: Were there any presents for other people too or just for Carl?
Carl: Just for Carl.
Mother: Just for Carl! Did Mom and Dad get something?
Carl: Ah, maybe something too.
Mother: Maybe something too.
Carl: Yeah.
Mother: Did you like Christmas?
Carl: Yes.

Carl's mother literally will not take "no" for an answer.

Confrontational Topic-extension

Note that in the previous exchange Carl's mother does correct him when he claims to be the only recipient of presents, but in an indirect, questioning sort of way. Other parents are less accepting. Recall the introductory comments regarding direct corrections of syntax, phonology, and vocabulary in young language-learning children. Direct negative feedback on these levels was found to be rare, whereas indirect negative feedback was considerably more common. One of our questions in this project was whether or not such direct negative feedback exists at the level of discourse, how common it was, and its probable effect, a question about which we now have some information.

Direct corrections of discourse do exist, but they are rare. What is more, direct corrections of narrative facts seem a risky means of extending conversation about the past. Consider the following interchanges between 32-month-old Paul and his mother. One only gets a feel for the cumulative effect on Paul by considering a number of such interchanges from the same general conversation:

Narrative A:

Mother: Where did you see them?
Paul: At the field.
@Mother: *In* a field.
Paul: And they ate some hay.
Mother: And they ate some hay.
Paul: And they took the doggy and they cuddled in, to a doggy.
Mother: They cuddled in to a doggy.
Paul: And he was asleep in the field.
@Mother: *When* the dog was asleep in the field.
Paul: And a real dog came.
!Mother: Oh they didn't cuddle into a *real* dog did they? It was a *toy* dog.
Paul: They cuddled into the toy dog and then a real dog came.
Mother: And then a real dog came.
Paul: And woked them up.
Mother: Yeah. Was that those rude rabbits you're talking about?
Paul: Yeah. I saw them in the field.
Mother: What else did those rude rabbits do?
Paul: You help me with those rude rabbits.

Narrative B:

Mother: And what's she going to do about that rotten tooth?
Paul: Nothing.
Mother: Nothing. Did she show you the rotten tooth?
Paul: Yes. Grandma's teeth fell out, flew on the floor.
Mother: Grandma's teeth flew out across the floor. That was funny wasn't it, when she sneezed?
Paul: Yea.
!Mother: *Nanny* that was, not Grandma. Her teeth flew across the floor.
Paul: She sneezed and then her teeth fell out.
Mother: *False* teeth.
Paul: On the floor.

Narrative C:

Paul: Through the gap. One day.
Mother: One day?

Paul: A boy dropped his mitten through that gap.
?Mother: Dropped his?
Paul: Mitten through that gap.
Mother: Mitten through that gap. What gap is that? (Laughs)
Paul: (unintelligible) inside that bus.
Mother: Oh, inside that bus. What happened to the mitten?
Paul: A rat ate it.
Mother: A rat ate the *mitten.*
Paul: One day I dropped my mitten through the gap and I was sitting.
@Mother: *When* you were sitting. And what building was this?
Paul: Stadium.
Mother: You dropped your mitten through a gap at the stadium.
Paul: And a lady said there could be rats under there.
!Mother: Well a lady told me there *could* be rats under there. She told me to hurry in there and get the mitten and come out again cause she once saw a rat down there because there's lots of garbage and food scraps that people drop under the risers. Those benches that we were sitting on are called risers. And you can go underneath the risers. You discovered that yesterday.
Paul: And, and rats.
Mother: She said that one time there was a rat down there, eating the garbage, eating the garbage, eating bits of things people dropped down there. I don't think a rat would eat a mitten though. He wouldn't eat your mitten.
*Paul: I wouldn't eat snow or ice.
Mother: Probably not. They like to eat little leftover bits of apple and potatoes, things like that, that people drop down. Popcorn, people drop popcorn. (End of exchange)

Narrative D:

?Mother: Well we started last night. We had a failure here didn't we? We were whipping some?
Paul: Cream.
?Mother: And it didn't?
Paul: Work.
Mother: Why? Do you remember why?
Paul: Because the machine was broken.
?!Mother: We didn't think it was the *machine.* We thought it was the cream. So this morning you and I decided to?
*Paul: No, you tell me.
Mother: No, I want you to tell me.
Paul: Whip it.
?!Mother: Whip it. And we didn't whip it this morning. What did we do? Where did we find the cream this morning? It was in the refrigerator in a?
Paul: Gla, in a glass.

Mother: Um-mm, so what did we do to make butter?
*Paul: Tell me.

First of all, note that Paul's mother engages in a fill-in-the-blank style of questioning (marked by a ? in the left margin) that is very atypical of parents. It is much more typical of teachers' classroom discourse (Cazden, 1988). In fact, after the first author wrote these observations, the second author, who was responsible for data collection and hence knew the parents, informed her that Paul's mother is a primary school teacher and the only teacher in our sample of parents.

Paul's mother might be said to display a get-the-facts-straight, confrontational style of discourse to her son, concerned as she is with teaching him how to tell a correct narrative. The exclamations (!) note the direct corrections of fact this mother makes during her son's narrations, corrections that are present in virtually all their narrative exchanges. The comments preceded with an @ are corrections of his word choice. It does not seem unrelated to such extensive correction that her son tells his mother to tell the story herself (see asterisks). In narrative C, she retells the whole story in such a corrective fashion that it does not seem to us or to the child at the time that it is his story to tell any longer. At 3½, Paul is an above-average narrator, so this strict drill has its usefulness, but one wonders about the overall effect of such repeated lack of acceptance of a child's version of experience.

Such pervasive correctiveness was unique to this parent-child pair. Three parents never directly corrected their child during either conversation; three directly corrected their child once or twice; three corrected their child during fewer than half of the narratives. Paul's mother directly corrected her child at least once during virtually every narrative exchange, several times at length, as in narrative C. Although the previous examples are narratives about shared experiences, Paul's mother did not confine her corrections to events she personally witnessed. For example, consider narrative E from a conversation recorded when he was 40 months (not included in data previously analyzed):

Narrative E:

Mother: What did you see in our harbor?
Paul: In the other harbor?
Mother: No, in St. John's harbor.
Paul: Nothing. Right Daddy? Nothing.
Father: We saw a big pile of something.
Paul: We saw a big pile of something. It was, it was a pile of salt and it was for the street to get to make the cars rusty.

!Mother: Well they don't actually get it in just to make the cars rusty. That's not the purpose.
?Father: It's on the roads to melt the?
*Paul: I don't know.
Father: Ice.

Once again, Paul reluctantly was drawn into talking about something only to be corrected by his mother in his account of an event she did not even experience.

Providing the Opportunity for Self-correction

The aforementioned discussion pertains to direct corrections at the discourse level, corrections that are really contradictions of facts mentioned by the child. Indirect corrections, however, were more common, and far more varied in form. In fact it is the case that most parental statements extending the topic of discussion could be construed as indirect correction of a novice narrator's incomplete recounting of events. However, the following example shows one parent's very delicate way of handling correction of a 27-month-old child's more obvious confusions (Note that Harriet and her mother are quoted at length, because her mother is among those who extended their child's discourse the most, and that Harriet is the second most expansive narrator in our sample):

Mother: Did we buy a card for Dad when we were out today? Why did we buy a card for him?
Harriet: 'Cause was his birthday again.
Mother: His birthday again. And how old is he?
Harriet: Two.
Mother: He's two? That's how old you are. You don't think Dad's the same age as you, do you?
Harriet: Yep.
Mother: He is?
Harriet: I was five. I was five.
Mother: You were five?
Harriet: Yep.
Mother: But Harriet, Sally [older sister] is going to be five. She's going to be five in July.
Harriet: I be five too.

In other words, information may be offered in such a way that its status as a correction is not what strikes the child. Perhaps it is the very ambiguity of such indirect factual corrections that makes them successful in a way that more direct corrections are not.

Modeling and Reinforcement?

Although we had expected that parents of the best narrators would themselves model narratives to their children, this did not occur. We recorded no examples at any time of parents telling their children narratives about their own experience. Perhaps this reflects parents' interpretation of our task as one in which we were interested in the children's narratives only, and so is not reflective of their normal interaction.

In view of the fact that the parents had been fully informed of our interest in narratives, we had also expected parents to show explicit appreciation of their children's better efforts. We never recorded any instances, however, of a parent saying something to the effect of, "That's a good story." Instead, parents occasionally called for evaluation of the events of the story they had just collaboratively told. See, for example, Carl's mother who closes their story with, "Did you like Christmas?"

Shared Versus Unshared Experience

Some, though certainly not all, of Paul's extreme resistance may pertain to the fact that at 32 months his mother is still primarily prompting him for narratives about shared experiences, a tactic that may have outlived its usefulness. A chi-square analysis of the relationship between successful elicitation of a narrative by a parent and whether the parent prompted for discussion of shared versus unshared experiences resulted in no relationship between success and mutuality of experience at 25 months. However, prompts for unshared experiences were associated with significantly greater success in getting a child to narrate at 31 months [χ^2 (1) = 4.16, $p < .05$]. Thus, prompting a child to talk about shared experiences is not always successful as a means of scaffolding child language at all ages.

Back to Structure

At 42 months, during a conversation with a familiar experimenter, the children's three longest narratives were assessed for qualitative high point structure (Peterson & McCabe, 1983). Sixty percent of the 30 narratives were classified as *Two-event Narratives,* meaning that they consisted of too few sentences for any high point pattern to be recognized or the narrative extensively reiterated and evaluated only two events, a pattern termed *impoverished* by Peterson and McCabe (1983). Twenty percent of the 42-month narratives were classified as *chronology,* meaning that the narrative was a simple description of successive events. Ten percent displayed a *leap-frog pattern,* jumping from one event to another within an integrated experience but leaving out major events that must be inferred by the listener. There was one narrative that *built up to a high point* and ended there, prematurely, with no resolution. Finally, there was one *classic* narrative, one that built up to a high point, evaluatively dwelt on it, and then resolved it.

That classic narrative was provided by Carl, the child who produced the longest discourse in terms of propositions per narrative:

Experimenter: Okay. What color should I use?
Carl: There's lots of different colors.
Experimenter: I'll say you have a lot of different colors, don't you?
Carl: Of course, because Grandma bought them.
Experimenter: Grandma bought all those crayons for you?
Carl: Yeah.
Experimenter: She did?
Carl: Cause Grandma thought that there wasn't enough so we thought if Grandma didn't think it was enough, she should bought some. [HIGH POINT] So then we went. There was a package of it. So we bought it.

Another impressive narrative was provided by Leah, whose mother engaged in considerable topic-extension when Leah was 27 and 31 months. This narrative was produced at 41 months and so was not included in the previous summary, but it is also a classic narrative and the longest and best one we observed from any of the children during our 18 months of tapings:

Experimenter: So you were hiding on your mommy, were you?
Leah: Yeah.
Experimenter: What happened?
Leah: Um, ah, She looked in the neighbourhood and she looked everywhere. She thought I was killed and she thought a man had stealed me.
Experimenter: Somebody had stealed you. She thought somebody had stealed you?
Leah: Yeah, but I didn't, cause I was hiding that.
Experimenter: You were hiding behind that, were you?
Leah: Cause, cause I didn't know that she was getting, she said, 'Leah, get your shorts' and then I was lying down, then, then she couldn't find me. Then that's what, and then, and then, then I came out.
Experimenter: You did?
Leah: But they find me, but I was saying, 'No, I don't want to go in there. I don't want to go in there.' (LOUD) I was shouting, so she smacked me. And then I was in my shorts. I was hiding under there and Mommy didn't know where I are so that's what she did, see. And she didn't know where I was, where, so I was over hiding in that chair, but

it was raining out first, cause I was crying. Then I went in there to hide. Then I was hiding under there and then . . . then, and then she gave me a smack on the hand and she thought that somebody had stealing me, and then, and then . . .
Experimenter: She thought somebody was stealing you.
Leah: Yeah, but, but I thought I was going down the street with M and J.
Experimenter: Mm.
Leah: So I wasn't, I was hiding under there.

Contrast these two narratives, produced with little prompting from the experimenter, with the following exchange, at 42 months, between Terry and the experimenter. It is Terry's longest exchange:

Experimenter: Did you go around the bay before?
Terry: Yes.
Experimenter: Yeah?
Terry: And see the calf.
Experimenter: You saw a calf?
Terry: Yes.
Experimenter: You did?
Terry: And he was bad.
Experimenter: He was bad?
Terry: No.
Experimenter: No, he wasn't bad?
Terry: No, not at Bernard's place.
Experimenter: What?
Terry: Down home.
Experimenter: He what?
Terry: Not down home.
Experimenter: Not down home.
Terry: Yes down home.
Experimenter: What happened?
Terry: Just down home.
Experimenter: Down home. What happened?
Terry: I gave Moo-moo a big hug.
Experimenter: You gave a moo-moo cow a big hug?
Terry: And went home.
Experimenter: And then you went home?
Terry: Here.
Experimenter: Then you came home here?
Terry: I (long pause) . . .
Experimenter: When you were out around the bay, you gave a moo-moo cow a hug?
Terry: Yes. And I came back home. Me.

Even at his best, and with extensive prompting, Terry was unable to produce a very expansive narrative, whereas Carl and Leah produced nicely formed narratives rather spontaneously. Behind the scenes of these performances we have seen different parental strategies for getting stories from their children. Carl's mother, like Leah's and Harriet's, extended her child's discourse regularly and effectively by providing statements extending a topic and by asking information-rich, closed-ended questions also relevant to what was being discussed. Rather than switching the topic frequently, Leah's mother, as well as Harriet's and Carl's mothers, asked many clarifying questions in both samples, which was associated with the immediate provision of all aspects of narration at 31 months, and showed a time-lag relationship at 27 months with the child's provision of orientation at 31 months. Such tactics were significantly associated with the quality and extent of their children's discourse to others at 42 months.

In contrast, Terry's father changed the topic of conversation almost as often as he tried to extend it, a tactic inversely associated with the frequency of various narrative comments 4 months later. (Recall that his mother never provided us with a tape during the 18 months of this study, despite her assent to doing the study.) Parents ($n = 6$, including Terry's father) of our less expert narrators provided little input of any sort, switched the topic a lot, and/or were repetitious rather than informative in their feedback during narrative conversations with their children.

Paul's mother was unique, as we also have seen; she very frequently extended narratives with her child but she often did so in a way that was counterproductive. She directly corrected her child so much that he became openly resistant to telling her narratives and, although above average, was not among our top three narrators. Paul, like all the other children we have recorded at 3½ years of age (Peterson & McCabe, 1983), often produces narratives that are confused in some way. There is a need for correction. But we suggest that correction will be more effective if indirect. Too much concern for getting the story straight may interfere with getting the story at all.

As children grow older, resistance to telling a narrative may be due to many things other than an inability to tell any kind of narrative at all. Children may develop temporary stuttering problems or embarrassment about discussing certain kinds of experiences, for example. Parents would be wise, in such circumstances, to drop the subject at times. In other words, we still believe that too much pushing at certain ages may be counterproductive.

In conclusion, the ability of 3½-year-olds to produce an extended personal narrative to an interested but relatively uninvolved listener reflects an earlier interpersonal process in which some parents extend their children's incipient narrations by means of statements and specific questions relevant to what is being discussed rather than proposing a series of topics in the hopes that one will catch a young child's fancy.

Summary

A Vygotskian social interactionist account of the development of personal narratives was proposed and tested. Children develop personal narratives in anticipation of habitual parental interaction. Children were studied from the age of 27 months, the onset of conversation about the past (Sachs, 1979, 1982). Conversations between 10 white middle-class children and parents were recorded at 27 months and 31 months. Parents were specifically requested to elicit personal narratives from their children, and parental input to the resulting interactions was scored for the number of closed- versus open-ended questions posed to their children either initiating or extending the topic of conversation, for the repetitions of what the child said, for the statements introducing versus extending the conversation, for the number of clarifying questions, and the number of times parents simply showed verbal attention. At the age of 3½ years, children were asked to produce narratives to a familiar experimenter, and their three longest narratives were assessed for overall complexity. Although all parents engaged in topic-extension during narrative conversations to their young children, some parents engaged in considerably more topic-extension than others. Parental topic-extension proved predictive of longer child narratives over time, whereas topic-switching was associated with subsequent relatively shorter narratives. However, one type of topic-extension—direct negative feedback—was identified as rare and problematic. Furthermore, prompting for unshared experiences was eventually more successful than prompting for shared experiences. We did not find any "natural storytellers" at age 2. We only found parents who differed in the extent to which they tried to get their children's stories and in the manner in which they went about such collaboration.

REFERENCES

Bandura, A. (1969). *Principles of behavior modification.* New York: Holt, Rinehart & Winston.

Bohannon, J. N., & Stanowicz, L. (1988). The issue of negative evidence:

Adult responses to children's language errors. *Developmental Psychology, 24*(5), 684–689.

Bretherton, I., McNew, S., Snyder, L., & Bates, E. (1983). Individual differences at 20 months: Analytic and holistic strategies in language acquisition. *Journal of Child Language, 10,* 293–320.

Brown, R., & Hanlon, C. (1970). Derivational complexity and order of acquisition in child speech. In J. Hayes (Ed.), *Cognition and the development of language* (pp. 11–54). New York: Wiley.

Bruner, J. (1978). The role of dialogue in language acquisition. In A. Sinclair, R. Jarvella, & W. Levett (Eds.), *The child's conception of language.* New York: Springer-Verlag.

Campbell, D. T., & Stanley, J. C. (1963). *Experimental and quasi-experimental designs for research.* Boston: Houghton Mifflin.

Cazden, C. B. (1988). *Classroom discourse: The language of teaching and learning.* Portsmouth, NH: Heinemann.

Chapman, K. L., Leonard, L. B., & Mervis, C. B. (1986). The effect of feedback on young children's inappropriate word usage. *Journal of Child Language, 13,* 101–117.

Demetras, M. J., Post, K. N., & Snow, C. E. (1986). Feedback to first language learners: The role of repetitions and clarification questions. *Journal of Child Language, 13,* 275–292.

Eisenberg, A. R. (1985). Learning to describe past experiences in conversation. *Discourse Processes, 8,* 177–204.

Evans, M. A. (1987). Discourse characteristics of reticent children. *Applied Psycholinguistics, 8,* 171–184.

Fivush, R., & Fromhoff, F. A. (1988). Style and structure in mother-child conversations about the past. *Discourse Processes, 11,* 337–355.

Furrow, D., & Nelson, K. (1986). A further look at the motherese hypothesis: A reply to Gleitman, Newport, and Glietman. *Journal of Child Language, 13,* 163–176.

Hoff-Ginsberg, E., & Shatz, M. (1982). Linguistic input and the child's acquisition of language. *Psychological Bulletin, 92,* 3–26.

Kemper, S. (1984). The development of narrative skills: Explanations and entertainments. In S. Kuczaj (Ed.), *Discourse development* (pp. 99–124). New York: Springer-Verlag.

Kernan, K. T. (1977). Semantic and expressive elaboration in children's narratives. In S. Ervin-Tripp & C. Mitchell-Kernan (Eds.), *Child discourse,* (pp. 91–102). New York: Academic Press.

Labov, W. (1972). *Language in the inner city.* Philadelphia: University of Pennsylvania Press.

Labov, W., & Waletzky, J. (1967). Narrative analysis: Oral versions of personal experience. In J. Helm (Ed.), *Essays on the verbal and visual arts* (pp. 12–44). Seattle, WA: University of Washington Press.

Lieven, E. V. M. (1980). *Language development in young children.* Unpublished doctoral dissertation, Cambridge University.

Mardia, K. V., Kent, J. T., & Bibby, J. M. (1979). *Multivariate analysis.* New York: Academic Press.

Maynard, D. W. (1980). Placement of topic changes in conversations. *Semiotica, 30,* 263–290.

McNeill, D. (1966). Developmental psycholinguistics. In F. Smith & G. Miller (Eds.), *The genesis of language* (pp. 15–84). Cambridge, MA: MIT Press.

Menig-Peterson, C. (1975). The modification of communicative behavior in preschool-aged children as a function of the listener's perspective. *Child Development, 46,* 1015–1018.

Menig-Peterson, C., & McCabe, A. (1978). Children's orientation of a listener to the context of their narratives. *Developmental Psychology, 74,* 582–592.

Michaels, S. (1987, October). *Discourse, ideology, and appropriation: What we learn about learning to write by studying teacher talk and student texts.* Paper presented at the 12th Annual Boston University Conferences on Language Development, Boston, MA.

Miller, P. J., & Sperry, L. L. (1988). Early talk about the past: The origins of conversational stories of personal experience. *Journal of Child Language, 15,* 293–315.

Mishler, E. G. (1984) *The discourse of medicine.* Norwood, NJ: Ablex.

Nelson, K. (1973). Structure and strategy in learning to talk. *Monographs of the Society for Research in Child Development, 38.*

Nelson, K. (1981). Individual differences in language development: Implications for development and language. *Developmental Psychology, 17,* 170–187.

Nelson, K. E., Denninger, M. S., Bonvillian, J. D., Kaplan, B. J., & Baker, N. D. (1984). Maternal input adjustments and nonadjustments as related to children's linguistic advances and to language acquisition theories. In A. D. Pellegrini & T. D. Yawkey (Eds.), *The development of oral and written language in social contexts* (pp. 31–56). Norwood, NJ: Ablex.

Ninio, A., & Bruner, J. (1978). The achievement and antecedents of labeling. *Journal of Child Language, 5,* 1–16.

Pellegrini, A. D. (1984). The effect of dramatic play on children's generation of cohesive text. *Discourse Processes, 7,* 57–67.

Penner, S. G. (1987). Parental responses to grammatical and ungrammatical child utterances. *Child Development, 58,* 376–384.

Peterson, C., & McCabe, A. (1983). *Developmental psycholinguistics: Three ways of looking at a child's narrative.* New York: Plenm.

Peterson, C., & McCabe, A. (1985). Understanding 'because': How important is the task? *Journal of Psycholinguistic Research, 14,* 199–218.

Peterson, C., & McCabe, A. (1987a). The connective 'and': Do older children use it less as they learn other connectives? *Journal of Child Language, 14,* 375–382.

Peterson, C., & McCabe, A. (1987b). The structure of *and* coordinations in children's narratives. *Journal of Psycholinguistic Research, 16,* 467–490.

Platt, C. B., & MacWhinney, B. (1983). Error assimilation as a mechanism in language learning. *Journal of Child Language, 10,* 401–414.

Pratt, M. W., Kerig, P., Cowan, P. A., & Cowan, C. P. (1988). Mothers and fathers teaching 3-year-olds: Authoritative parenting and adult scaffolding of young children's learning. *Developmental Psychology, 24,* 832–839.

Roth, F. P. (1986). Oral narrative abilities of learning-disabled students. *Topics in Language Disorders,* 7(1), 21–30.

Sachs, J. (1979). Topic selection in parent-child discourse. *Discourse Processes, 2,* 145–153.

Sachs, J. (1982). Talking about the there and then: The emergence of displaced reference in parent-child discourse. In K. E. Nelson (Ed.), *Children's language* (pp. 1–28). Hillsdale, NJ: Lawrence Erlbaum Associates.

Schieffelin, B. B., & Eisenberg, A. R. (1984). Cultural variation in children's conversations. In R. L. Schiefelbusch & J. Pickar (Eds.), *The acquisition of communicative competence* (pp. 378–420). Baltimore, MD: University Park Press.

Schwartz, R. G., & Camarata, S. (1985). Examining relationships between input and language development: Some statistical issues. *Journal of Child Language, 12,* 199–207.

Smolak, L., & Weinraub, M. (1983). Maternal speech: Strategy or response. *Journal of Child Language, 10*(2), 369–380.

Snow, C. E. (1983). Literacy and language: Relationships during the preschool years. *Harvard Educational Review, 53,* 165–189.

Snow, C. E., & Goldfield, B. A. (1981). Building stories: The emergence of information structures from conversation. In D. Tannen (Ed.), *Analyzing discourse: Text and talk* (pp. 127–141). Washington, DC: Georgetown University Press.

Umiker-Sebeok, D. J. (1979). Preschool children's intraconversational narratives. *Journal of Child Language, 6,* 91–109.

Vygotsky, L. (1986). *Thought and language.* Cambridge, MA: MIT Press.

Whitehurst, G. J., & Valdez-Menchaca, M. C. (1988). What is the role of reinforcement in early language acquisition. *Child Development, 54,* 430–440.

CHAPTER 7

Teacher Agenda and Setting: Constraints on Conversation in Preschools

David K. Dickinson
Department of Education
Clark University

During the preschool and early school years children become members of their culture as they acquire the patterns of acting, speaking, and thinking used by their parents and peers. Following Vygotsky, we can view this acquisition process as involving internalization of the culture's modes of thought, action, and consciousness. In the course of development, interpsychological processes become intrapsychic processes and begin to order the internal cognitive and emotional life of the child (Vygotsky, 1962, 1978). According to current Vygotskian theorizing, development should be viewed as a semiotic process in which children move from acquisition of external forms toward grasp of the significance they carry for their culture. The structures acquired may be individual words (Wertsch & Stone, 1985), or, as Bakhtin argued, they could be forms of discourse (Cazden, 1989; Emerson, 1983; Holquist, 1983).

The process of becoming literate is one aspect of development where recent research suggests that this Vygotskian approach to understanding development may be of particular value. Anthropological (Goody & Watt, 1962–1963; Heath, 1983; Scollon & Scollon, 1981; Street, 1984), historical (Olson, 1977; Pattison, 1982), and psychological (Scribner & Cole, 1981; Vygotsky, 1978) research indicates that acquisition of literacy involves internalization of modes of discourse required for engaging texts in ways consistent with those required by the culture in which the acquisition occurs. Furthermore, depending on the context, the acquisition of literacy may profoundly affect intellectual functioning (Ehri, 1985; Olson, 1986; Scribner & Cole, 1981) and social interactions (Scollon & Scollon, 1981).

LITERACY AND ORAL LANGUAGE

Reading and writing are specialized techniques for using language. Whereas there are several types of relationships between oral and written language (Dickinson, 1987), it is clear that one important aspect of becoming literate is acquiring the discourse forms required by one's society for reading and writing. Historically, the degree of similarity in structure and vocabulary of spoken and written language forms has varied dramatically (Pattison, 1982), with greater distance between oral and written forms serving to exclude less privileged members of society from access to literacy. Currently, in Western industrialized societies, there are distinct discourse modes associated with different uses of language. Informal, conversational exchanges can be distinguished from the more formalized discourse of lectures or essays along a number of quantifiable dimensions (Chafe, 1982; Tannen, 1982, 1984) related to factors such as information density, amount of ambiguity, and amount of negotiation of meaning between speaker and hearer (see Dickinson, 1987; Sulzby & Barro Zecker, chap. 5 in this vol. for more complete reviews).

Differences in communicative demands made of interlocutors can be placed on a continuum ranging from settings where conversational partners know each other, are familiar with the topic under discussion, and are free to engage in mutual negotiation of meaning, to occasions when novel information must be communicated to a partner who shares indeterminant amounts of background information and who is unable to provide feedback regarding his comprehension of the message. The former, contextualized language skills, are honed through informal conversations with intimates. It also may be that the later skills, often called decontextualized skills, can be developed through conversations when topics discussed require communication of novel, cognitively demanding information (e.g., explanations, recall of past events, recounting experiences not shared by one's conversational partner). Additionally, occasions when adults read and discuss books with children are contexts that are especially conducive to fostering development of decontextualized skills (Cochran-Smith, 1984; Goldfield & Snow, 1984).

Oral Language-literacy Links

Contextualized language skills have been found to be distinct from decontextualized skills, and decontextualized skills have been found to be more predictive of academic success (Cummins, 1983; Davidson, Kline, & Snow, 1986; Snow, 1987). This finding of dissociation between two clusters of skills may help explain why correlational research has had difficulty linking oral language abilities to literacy (Groff, 1978; Hammill & McNutt, 1980; reviewed by Dickinson, 1987) and why experience with books during the preschool years is more predictive of school success than typical sentence-level measures of oral language development (Wells, 1985).

Additional evidence suggesting the importance of decontextualized language skills to literacy success comes from research with language-impaired and learning-disabled children. Learning-disabled and normally developing children have been found to be distinguished in tasks requiring recall of scripts (Feagans & Short, 1984), narratives (Graybeal, 1981; Weaver & Dickinson, 1982), and procedural information (Feagans & Short, 1986), and in tasks requiring constructions of complete narratives (Roth & Spekman, 1986). Qualitative differences on recall and production tasks between language-disabled and normally developing children point to differences at the inter-sentential level. Weaver and Dickinson (1982) found that disabled readers tended to omit causal and temporal markers. Similarly, Roth and Spekman (1986) found language-impaired children used *and* and causal links less often. Using an episodic level analysis, they found that language-impaired children omitted information needed to provide complete episodic information. They interpreted this finding as reflecting a failure to realize the need to provide listeners with complete background information.

Links between discourse skills and reading also have been identified. Kindergarten children's ability to tell complete narratives has been found to predict later schooling success (de Hirsch, Jansky, & Langford, 1966). Similarly, moderate correlations have been found between script recall and reading of normal and reading disabled 6- and 7-year-olds (Feagans & Short, 1984).

ACQUISITION OF DECONTEXTUALIZED ORAL LANGUAGE

Converging lines of research indicate that decontextualized oral language skills provide linguistic resources that are critical for successful reading development. Unfortunately, we know very little about how children acquire the discourse skills that appear to be linked to later literacy. In this section I briefly review relevant research and propose two models that describe distinct ways of conceptualizing the relationship between preschool literacy-related experiences and later literacy.

One body of research relevant to determining the early sources of literacy deals with emergent literacy (reviewed by Sulzby & Barro Zecker, chap. 5 in this vol.; Teale & Sulzby, 1986). In general, this work has demonstrated that, prior to formal literacy instruction, children construct knowledge about the uses and forms of print (e.g., Dyson, in press; 1984; Ferreiro & Teberosky, 1982; Harste, Woodward, & Burke, 1984; Sulzby, 1985), acquire language patterns associated with written language, and can shift between conversational and written language styles (Sulzby & Barro Zecker, chap. 5 in this vol.).

A second relevant body of research with implications for support for literacy during the preschool years is study of bookreading at home (e.g., Snow & Goldfield, 1982; Snow & Ninio, 1986; Teale, 1984, 1986) and in the school (Cochran-Smith, 1984; Dickinson & Keebler, 1989; Teale & Martinez, 1984). This work has demonstrated the multiple ways in which adults help children learn to take meaning from text, thereby helping to explain why previous correlational research has found such strong links between being read to and later academic success (Goldfield & Snow, 1984).

The Direct Influence Model

Work on early literacy development has concentrated on describing children's print-related knowledge and the nature of their contacts with print, but efforts to specify critical sources of early literacy knowledge have been limited. An implicit assumption of much of the emergent literacy work and much of the book-reading research seems to be that direct contact with print is what builds literacy skills. This model, to be called the *direct influence of print model* of the role of early experience on literacy development, is most clearly articulated by Harste, Woodward, and Burke (1984), who postulate that it is the amount of experience with literacy that determines the timing of early literacy development. Others are less explicit about causal mechanisms, but two assumptions regarding probable sources are suggested by the research emphases: (a) incidental exposure to print in the home and at school fosters literacy development (e.g., Anderson & Stokes, 1984; Taylor, 1983), and (b) opportunities to be read to and to reread familiar books support literacy development (e.g., Brown, Cromer, & Weinberg, 1986; Dickinson, 1989; Feitelson, Kita, & Goldstein, 1986; Goldfield & Snow, 1984; Lartz & Mason, 1988). According to the direct influence of print model, literacy emerges from the child's active construction of print-related knowledge and acquisition of written language structures. The knowledge acquired that supports literacy includes knowledge about the forms and functions of print (e.g., Bissex, 1980; Ferreiro & Teberosky, 1982; Harste, Woodward, & Burke, 1984; Lartz & Mason, 1988; Mason, 1980, in press; Mason & Allen, 1986) and acquisition of written language forms as they are revealed in children's story reenactments (Pappas & Brown, 1987a, 1987b; Purcell-Gates, 1988; Sulzby, 1986) and story telling (Sulzby, 1986, Sulzby & Barro Zecker, chap. 5 in this vol.). Work consistent with the direct influence model has been confined to the early stages of literacy development.

Work consistent with the direct influence model is distinct from traditional approaches to early reading development in three critical respects: (a) early writing is emphasized and the connections between writing and reading are emphasized, (b) children's rule-governed constructive efforts are emphasized (i.e., less emphasis is placed on direct instruction), and (c) acquisition of language forms associated with written language is seen as being one aspect of emergent literacy development. Despite these important differences, the direct influence model and more traditional views (e.g., Chall, 1983) share an emphasis on print-related experiences and skills needed for initial decoding.

It is important that we gain clarity about assumptions about the relationship between early experience and later literacy, because different models suggest different approaches to intervention. Intervention programs (Allen & Mason, 1989) and books providing advice to teachers (e.g., Loughlin & Martin, 1987; Morrow, 1989) that draw inspiration from work on early literacy are beginning to appear. There are differences in emphasis in these programs. Some programs (e.g., Holdaway, 1979) stress motivational factors and the importance of opportunities to use print for a variety of functions, whereas others stress print-specific knowledge (McCormick & Mason, 1989). Despite their differences, in much of this work the importance of two areas of agreement with traditional views of reading development are evident: (a) concern with children's movement toward control of skills and concepts needed for initial decoding, and (b) an almost exclusive focus on experiences with printed materials.

The Communicative Needs Model

A contrasting model of the relationship between early experience and later literacy, the *communicative needs model,* emphasizes the importance of children's language competence to later literacy development. It differs from the direct influence model in two respects: (a) it sees nonprint experiences as making important contributions to acquisition of decontextualized language competence, and (b) it is concerned with including consideration of reading development well after initial decoding skills are mastered. This model draws on work emphasizing the importance of language to later literacy (e.g., Dickinson, 1987, 1989; Gee, 1987; Heath, 1983, 1986; Olson, 1984; Snow, 1983; Tizard & Hughes, 1984; Torrance & Olson, 1985).

The specialized language-using competencies hypothesized to support literacy will be referred to as *decontextualized language strategies* (Dickinson, 1987; Snow, 1983). This term should not be taken as meaning that we see any language as being used outside of a context, rather as a shorthand way to refer to specialized uses of language strategies that arise in response to the communicative need to convey and interpret messages apart from the contexts in which they are crafted. Over time, such needs have most often been seen as affecting communication patterns in literate societies (e.g., Goody, 1977). However, recent anthropological research (Denny, in press; Feldman, in press) has shown that language uses associated with literacy (e.g., decontextualization, talk about language) also can occur in oral cultures where codified bodies of oral language can be reflected on and used in ways comparable to written language. However, it is in technological societies where advanced literacy skills are required rather than elective. It is in these settings that a premium is placed on the ability to understand and communicate large amounts of novel abstract information with considerable precision.[1] In these societies information exchanges occur between interlocutors who are distant from each other in space and who may not even know each other. Language that successfully copes with these demands relies minimally on resources such as gesture, intonation, and allusions to shared knowledge, resources typically available in face-to-face conversational settings.

The communicative needs model assumes that competence using decontextualized language results from interactions that require explicitness and communication of novel information. It sees experiences like book reading as facilitative because they provide ideal settings for development of decontextualized skills, but it does not assume that print-based experiences *per se* are essential for critical literacy. Instead, it assumes that, given appropriate topics and conversational moves, similar facilitation also might be provided by conversations with moth-

---

[1] See Ogbu (1988) for a similar argument linking ecological demands to intellectual development in diverse cultures.

ers, fathers, and teachers. Similar to the direct influence model, it assumes that print-related knowledge results from experiences with print and instruction related to its use, and that acquisition of this knowledge is essential for initial decoding.

The communicative needs model draws on much current work on reading development in assuming that, in addition to specialized discourse skills, literacy draws on other subskills including print-related knowledge (e.g., names of letters, sound-symbol correspondence knowledge, print concepts) and metaphonemic awareness (see Dickinson, in press; Snow & Dickinson, in press, for elaboration).

Implications of the Communicative Needs Model

Work consistent with the communicative needs model is relatively new and has not yet generated much in the way of advice to teachers (but see Dickinson, 1990a, 1990b) or intervention programs. However, experimental work in the book-reading tradition has demonstrated effects on language development resulting from attention to how books are read and discussed in the home (Whitehurst et al., 1988) and in school settings (Elley & Mangubhai, 1983). Such work also has been shown to have beneficial effects on early literacy (Brown, Cromer, & Weinberg, 1986)—a finding also consistent with the direct influence model.

Experiences around books provide a rich opportunity for children to practice constructing new meanings from language, but these are not the only settings where there may be opportunities for children to construct and interpret connected text with the characteristics of more decontextualized language. Such opportunities also may arise when children recount for parents their daily experiences at school, when explanations are provided for puzzling phenomena, when plans are laid for future activities, and when children engage in pretend play that includes verbalization of plans, roles, and dramatic actions. Practice supported by an adult who is sensitive to a child's current discourse abilities, and is capable of working in the child's zone of proximal development, is most likely to result in production of the most complex language of which a child is capable (Pratt, Kerig, Cowan, & Cowan, 1988). Facility producing such discourse probably develops with practice; therefore, in the long run, practice producing decontextualized discourse likely translates into skills that support later literacy functioning.

EXPLAINING VARIATION IN LITERACY LEVELS

A satisfactory model of literacy development should help explain variance in children's success acquiring literacy; it should help us understand why some homes and some schools are more likely to have children who acquire high literacy levels than others. No doubt, much of the variance in literacy development across ethnic and economic levels can be attributed to motivational factors tied to complex societal and historical factors (e.g., Erickson, 1984; Ogbu, 1988). In addition to understanding the impact of such factors, we also need cognitive models that can help us describe the constellation of experiences that nurture literacy development.

Home Experiences

Evidence is contradictory regarding the question of whether homes vary significantly in the extent to which children are provided opportunities to engage in sustained discourse of the type posited to be related to literacy. In a study of home and school language experiences of working- and middle-class children, Tizard and Hughes (1984) found few significant class-related differences in indices of conversational complexity (e.g., length of turns, topic, length of conversations). In contrast, Heath's ethnographic study (1983) of three communities found major differences in adult-child conversations. Subsequently, Heath (1986) recorded conversations between three mothers of children from different backgrounds and found that the white middle-class child had many more sustained conversations than either the working-class white or Black children.

Little is known about the effects of home language environments on decontextualized language and literacy development. McCabe and Peterson's finding (chap. 6 in this vol.) of differential effectiveness of different narrative elicitation strategies indicates that analysis of decontextualized language development must take into consideration parental strategies for supporting children's language. There also is some evidence hinting at the possibility that home language affects literacy. In a study of the effects of out-of-school factors on literacy development, Anderson, Wilson, and Fielding (1988) found that length of mealtimes was positively correlated with reading growth. This finding might reflect beneficial effects of opportunities to construct and understand connected discourse. On a somewhat less speculative note, Snow, Barnes, Chandler, Goodman, and Hemphill (in press) found that contact with adults and family practices such as taking trips are associated with vocabulary development and improvements in reading comprehension.

It should be noted that prior research does not give any clear reason to believe that one type of connected discourse has a privileged position relative to others. However, with the exception of work reported in this volume (e.g., Hicks, chap. 2; Hudson & Shapiro, chap. 3), little attention has been given to this question. The communicative needs model would predict that performances on tasks requiring high information transfer are most strongly associated with later literacy. Thus, a hierarchy of predictiveness would be anticipated, with explanations being most highly correlated with literacy measures, followed by narrative competence, with ability to produce scripts being least predictive.

Effects of Preschool Experiences

Many young children also spend considerable amounts of time in group care settings. These early schooling experiences have been found to be related to language development using global measures, such as amount of time spent in preschool (Wadsworth, 1986) and indices of overall language experience (McCartney, 1984). McCartney's results indicate that the amount of talk by teachers of a representational rather than controlling nature is an important variable affecting children's language growth in preschool. Peer interaction in preschools also may facilitate language growth. This is indicated by the fact that intensive efforts to increase the level of dramatic play have been found to result in increases in vocabulary (Levy, Schaefer, & Phelps, 1986) and correlational research suggests links between symbolic play and literacy (Pellegrini, 1984).

Unfortunately, we know relatively little about the details of children's typical language experiences in preschool classrooms. The best evidence comes from Tizard and Hughes' (1984) comparison of children's home and school language experiences in British infant schools. They found that schools compared relatively poorly with the home, especially for working-class children. Compared with the home, in school settings adult-child conversations tended to occur less often, to be shorter, and children tended to demonstrate less curiosity and engage in less complex and less cognitively demanding discussions.

Structural differences place teachers at an inherent disadvantage relative to parents. Children far outnumber adults, making it difficult to engage in sustained conversations and increasing the difficulty of forming deep relationships with each child. As a result, teachers lack a parent's knowledge of a child's interests, knowledge, and experiences, impeding their ability to build on and extend children's interests.

Despite these structurally based difficulties, there are aspects of the school setting under the control of the teacher that have a bearing on teacher's interactions with children. The nature of experiences planned is one such variable. One study of six classrooms serving 3- to 5-year-olds (Innocenti et al., 1986) found considerable variation across activities in teacher presence. Teachers were usually absent during free play (96% of the time) and lunch (92% of the time). Often teachers were absent during individual activity periods (80% absence), but were usually present during group times (12% absence). If teachers rarely are present during many activities, children obviously have fewer opportunities to engage in the type of interactions that McCartney (1984) found to be most facilitative of development.

We also have some clues regarding ways in which the content of talk varies by setting. Group times seem to be relatively rich. Cochran-Smith (1984) found that decontextualized talk about print was concentrated in group times, and McCartney (1984) found a positive correlation between amount of time spent in groups and amount of representational talk. Tizard and Hughes's work (1984) provides insight into how interactional content during nongroup times is affected by organizational factors. They found extended conversations to be more common when adults were in one place and children could approach them than when adults were circulating. It was at these times that children were most likely to approach teachers with questions and engage in the type of sustained conversations more commonly found in the home.

RESEARCH QUESTIONS

The research to be reported assumes that discourse development arises from opportunities for supportive interactions with adults and, to a lesser extent, peers. We assume that the content and structure of teacher-child talk is affected by organizational features of classrooms such as the nature of the activities engaged in by children and teachers and the number of participants. In particular, we anticipated that occasions when teachers are stationary and psychologically available would be most likely to be times when extended conversations appear. Research in the home has found lunch to be a time conducive to such talk (Heath, 1986; Tizard & Hughes, 1984), but the most detailed classroom study, that done by Tizard and Hughes (1984), could not observe children during lunch at school because they were at home.

This present study included lunch observations because the absence of lunchtime talk—a potentially rich time for language—might have led Tizard and Hughes to underestimate the potential of preschools to provide rich language environments.

Personal variables such as conversational strategies and pedagogical beliefs related to language use also were expected to help shape the nature of classroom conversations. Controls provided by the nature of the data (i.e., same children, same general program, similar general educational philosophy) created a setting that could potentially allow us to distinguish effects of contextual variables from personal variables. We reasoned that, if situational variables help structure conversations, then we should see similar patterns of talk across different settings across all teachers. On the other hand, if variables linked to teacher-specific differences (e.g., styles of relating to children, beliefs about language facilitation) have a major impact on the shape of teacher-child dialogue, then we should see variation among teachers in patterns of teacher-child relationship even within the same setting.

We were interested in the general question of whether setting affects the likelihood of teachers engaging in sustained dialogue of the type posited to support decontextualized language. If such settings can be identified, it may be possible to plan classroom activities that are most likely to provide opportunities for rich teacher-child interaction. If teacher-specific variables are found to affect the likelihood of such interactions, teacher education efforts might enable teachers to adopt beliefs or to develop strategies that are likely to support discourse development. These issues are addressed first by taking a detailed look at talk between three teachers and the same group of children. Next, we review less detailed analyses of teacher-child talk in eight different preschool classrooms.

STUDY ONE

The first study to be discussed was designed to provide detailed information regarding ways in which context shapes teacher-child interaction in preschools. Opportunities for decontextualized language use were of central interest because of their theoretical link to later literacy. Given Tizard and Hughes' (1984) and Heath's (1986) finding that lunch is a time when mothers and children are likely to engage in sustained discussions, we collected speech samples during lunch at school. This was especially interesting because, as noted, Tizard and Hughes were unable to assess talk during mealtimes in school because children were home for lunch. We also collected speech during activity periods because these occupy a large portion of the time spent during classroom days in many day-care centers. We examined activity time for variation depending on the role of the teacher because of Tizard and Hughes's (1984) finding that teachers most often engaged children in extended talk when they were situated in one location for an extended period of time.

Two central questions were tested: (a) Does teacher-child interaction vary systematically during activity time depending on whether the teacher is stationary or circulating? and (b) Does teacher-child talk vary systematically between lunchtime and activity time?

Methodology

A university-related day-care center in a northeastern metropolitan area was the setting for the research. The classroom served 22 children between the ages of 3;6 and 4;2 in October. Eleven children were from professional homes, three were children of university students, and eight were from working-class homes. English was the first language of all but one. One child was Black and the rest were White.

The classroom was visited by a research assistant who was known by the group because she also was collecting recordings of book reading during group times. Each of the three teachers who were present during the bulk of the day were audiotaped on separate days. Each was recorded during a typical lunch and during an activity period. The recording was made using a wireless microphone worn by the teacher. A research assistant made context notes concerning her activities. The length of recorded interactions varied by teacher, with a range for lunchtime being from 20 to 30 minutes and for activity periods from 40 to 55 minutes. Recording sessions occurred from mid-October to mid-November.

Coding

Audiotapes were transcribed onto computer disks in the format required for analysis using the Child Language Data Exchange System (CHILDES) (MacWhinney & Snow, 1985). Transcriptions were spot-checked to ensure accuracy. Speech was broken into utterances and each child and teacher utterance was coded using three coding systems that were adapted from systems provided by the CHILDES system and from a previous study of book reading (Dickinson & Keebler, 1989). It should be noted that the microphones were worn by the teachers, thus child talk coded is that which was directed to the teacher, not talk among children.

A *topic-coding* system analyzed the topic of talk. Topic was of interest because it was assumed that talk restricted to the present would be more likely to support contextualized language growth, whereas more analytical talk and talk about the past and present would require more decontextualized strategies. Topics coded included discussion restricted to the present (talk about ongoing activities, present objects, and feelings and preferences), analytical talk (about states of knowledge, talk about language, explanations of causality or motivation), talk about past or future actions or nonpresent objects, and didactic talk designed to convey knowledge (see appendix 1 for details). Interrater agreement was estimated on the basis of 100 successive codes in three transcripts and averaged 84%. For this, as well as the other two coding systems, disagreements were discussed and resolved.

The second coding system focused on *speech acts*. It was important to discover the functions utterances were serving because this provided information regarding the social meaning of topics. Certain speech act codes such as explanations and speculation were expected to result in more efforts to make referents clear and to communicate novel information, resulting in more decontextualized talk (see appendix for details). On the other hand, control-oriented talk (commands and suggestions) was deemed unlikely to have such value. This coding system also allowed us to identify frequency of different kinds of questions, to determine the frequency of questions requesting information unknown to the hearer (real questions) as opposed to questions requiring display of information already known to the hearer. Information related to patterns of questioning was interesting because we assumed that a higher proportion of real questions would be associated with more extended, information-rich interactions. Interrater agreement, estimated on the basis of 100 utterances in three different transcripts, averaged 90%.

The third coding scheme, the *topic development* system, traced the introduction and development of topics according to whether comments were initiations or extensions and coding these according to whether they were statements or questions (see appendix). Considerable previous research on classroom discourse during the school years (e.g., Cazden, 1988) has found it to be heavily dominated by teacher's talk. Research at the elementary and preschool level (Tizard & Hughes, 1984) also has found that the range of questions asked is limited and tends to consist of many questions asked by teachers designed to test rather than extend children's knowledge.

Decontextualized language skill requires opportunities to construct meaning at the level of discourse, which requires several utterances or multiple speaker turns addressing the same topic. Development of extended topics is likely to be encouraged if children can initiate topics of interest to them, because these are more likely to be topics about which they have the kind of detailed knowledge that lends itself to creation of extended texts. Topic development is also likely to be encouraged if both teachers and other children ask questions, because the presence of child questions suggests that children are functioning as full conversational partners. Question-asking is most likely to promote development of elaborated topics if the type of questions asked is varied (i.e., open-ended as well as limited response yes/no style questions). Interrater reliability of the topic development coding scheme was based on coding of 100 utterances in each of three transcripts. There was an average of 89% interrater agreement.

Results

The data could not be analyzed statistically because of the small number of subjects (the three teachers). Instead, analysis was based on frequencies of different codes, which indicate overall characteristics of the speech environment as well as qualitative examination of teacher-child interactions. First I report quantitative analyses from the three coding systems for activity times. Next I discuss qualitative aspects of activity time speech. The same pattern is followed for discussion of lunch time. A comparison of lunch and activity time conclude the section.

Activity Periods: Topic Coding

For initial analyses, topic codes were collapsed into two categories, present and nonpresent. Present topics are those that deal with immediate ongoing actions, personal feelings or preferences, and rules governing behavior. Nonpresent topics deal with past and future actions, objects not in the immediate vicinity, and analytical and instructional talk. Examination of the teacher's talk during portions of the activity period when the teacher was stationary revealed remarkable consistency across teachers in the amount of time spent discussing present as opposed to nonpresent topics (see Table 7.1). In each case, the proportion of teachers' comments dealing with present topics ranged from 50% to 58%. Children's talk typically followed the same pattern (though see section on Petra presented later for a counterexample). For the most part, present talk was concentrated on discussions of immediately present actions and objects. Nonpresent talk was more varied, with the most heavily used categories being discussion of non-

TABLE 7.1
Proportion of Children's and Teacher's Talk Addressing Different Topics During Acti

	Connie		*Terri*		*Petra*	
	Con.	*Ch.*	*Ter.*	*Ch.*	*Pet.*	*Ch.*
	(n = *172)*	(n = *106)*	(n = *122)*	(n = *56)*	(n = *118)*	(n = 5
	Times When the Teacher Was Stationary					
Present focus						
Actions/obj.	.45	.39	.43	.45	.35	.22
Feelings/ownership	.09	.12	.07	.07	.08	.06
Rules	.03	.01	.02	.00	.07	.04
Total prop.	.58	.52	.52	.52	.50	.31
Analytical						
World/motivation	.19	.14	.08	.07	.09	.13
Cognition	.02	.01	.03	.04	.02	.00
Language	.02	.03	.19	.14	.00	.00
Total	.23	.18	.30	.25	.11	.13
Past, future, & absent						
Non-present actions/objects	.10	.17	.11	.09	.30	.46
Future	.07	.12	.05	.14	.09	.09
Narrative	.00	.00	.00	.00	.01	.00
Total	.17	.29	.16	.23	.40	.56
Didactic						
Preschool knowledge	.01	.01	.02	.00	.00	.00
Symbols/books	.00	.00	.01	.00	.00	.00
Total	.00	.00	.02	.00	.00	.00
Total Non-present	.42	.48	.48	.48	.51	.69
Total Present	.58	.52	.52	.52	.50	.31

TABLE 7.1
(continued)

	Connie		*Terri*		*Petra*
	Con.	*Ch.*	*Ter.*	*Ch.*	*Pet.*
	(n = *101)*	(n = *38)*	(n = *226)*	(n = *93)*	(n = *19)*
	Times When the Teacher Was Circulating				
Present focus					
Actions/obj.	.49	.61	.43	.38	.42
Feelings/own	.28	.21	.16	.16	.16
Rules	.08	.02	.12	.09	.26
Total	.85	.84	.71	.62	.84
Analytical					
World/human	.09	.02	.06	.01	.10
Cognition	.01	.02	.01	.04	.00
Language	.01	.01	.00	.00	.00
Total	.11	.05	.07	.05	.10
Past, future, & absent					
Actions/obj.	.01	.02	.10	.20	.10
Future	.01	.07	.10	.04	.05
Narrative	.00	.00	.02	.08	.00
Total	.02	.09	.22	.32	.16
Instructional					
Preschool K.	.01	.02	.00	.00	.00
Symbols	.00	.00	.00	.00	.00
Total	.01	.02	.00	.00	.00
Total Non-P.	.14	.16	.29	.37	.26
Total Pres.	.85	.84	.71	.62	.84

present actions and objects and analysis of human motivations and physical causation.

A comparison of when teachers were stationary with times when they were circulating, reveals that topic selection was consistently more focused on the present when teachers were circulating. Instead of spending about half their time engaged in present-focused talk as they did when they were stationary, between 71% and 85% of the teacher's talk was bound to the present when they were circulating. Children's talk followed a similar pattern and no category of nonpresent talk appeared with much frequency.

Activity Periods: Speech Act Analyses

For the purposes of initial analyses, several speech act codes describing techniques for controlling behavior were collapsed. The remaining codes describe diverse aspects of more informationally rich interaction (e.g., informative comments, nonpresent talk). These exchanges, which also were more mutual than the control interactions, were collapsed under the heading of *positive engagement* (see Table 7.2).

Comparison of the relative frequency of control-oriented talk across the three teachers revealed considerable consistency, with between 18% and 25% of all teacher comments dealing with control issues. Children's talk was more variable, but roughly shadowed that of the teachers. Naturally, consistency also was observed in the proportion of positively engaged talk across teachers. The subcategories that were combined in the overall positive engagement category (e.g., nonpresent, test-questions and responses) varied by teacher. In general, information giving, real-question-asking and test-question-asking were the most frequent categories. Children's talk was dominated by information giving, but significant amounts of question asking also appeared.

As anticipated, during the time when teachers circulated, there was relatively more concern for maintaining order (an average of 37% control comments compared with an average of 21% during the stationary periods), and a reciprocal decrease in positive engagement. The control category displaying the greatest increase was that of indirect control. Positive engagement was dispersed in a manner roughly similar to that found during the stationary periods of activity time. No single category displayed noteworthy declines relative to that observed during the stationary periods.

Activity Periods: Topic Development Analyses

Teacher-child conversations also were analyzed to determine how topics were introduced and extended using the topic development coding system. It is interesting to note that children had a slight

TABLE 7.2
Proportion of Speech Act Types Used by Teachers and Children During Activity Times

	Connie		*Terri*		*Petra*		*Averages*	
	Con.	*Ch.*	*Ter.*	*Ch.*	*Pet.*	*Ch.*	*Tea.*	*Ch.*
	(n = *161*)	(n = *106*)	(n = *118*)	(n = *57*)	(n = *97*)	(n = *61*)	(n = *3*)	(n = *3*)
Periods When Teachers Were Stationary								
Control focus								
Direct	.10	.27	.16	.10	.10	.11	.12	.16
Indirect	.07	.02	.02	.02	.07	.02	.05	.03
Negotiation	.07	.01	.00	.00	.03	.00	.03	.00
Total	.25	.30	.18	.12	.21	.13	.21	.18
Positive engagement								
Warm	.25	.05	.14	.04	.08	.02	.16	.04
Information	.18	.57	.28	.42	.40	.59	.29	.53
Real q.	.25	.04	.14	.25	.18	.13	.19	.14
Test q/R.	.04	.04	.24	.17	.08	.11	.12	.11
Non-present	.02	.00	.02	.00	.04	.02	.03	.01
Total	.75	.70	.82	.88	.79	.87	.79	.82
	(n = *146*)	(n = *67*)	(n = *206*)	(n = *90*)	(n = *21*)	(n = *8*)	(n = *3*)	(n = *3*)
Periods When Teachers Were Circulating								
Control focus								
Direct	.22	.30	.17	.06	.29	.12	.23	.16
Indirect	.12	.03	.14	.00	.13	.00	.13	.01
Negotiation	.03	.03	.01	.03	.00	.00	.01	.02
Total	.37	.36	.32	.09	.43	.12	.37	.19
Positive engagement								
Warm	.17	.10	.13	.11	.05	.00	.12	.07
Information	.23	.46	.29	.67	.24	.62	.25	.58
Real q.	.21	.07	.18	.04	.05	.25	.15	.12
Test q/R.	.01	.00	.04	.07	.00	.00	.06	.02
Non-Present	.01	.00	.01	.02	.24	.00	.09	.01
Total	.63	.64	.68	.91	.57	.88	.63	.81

advantage over teachers in the number of topics initiated and both children and teachers asked both open and closed questions (see Table 7.3). These findings suggest much greater equality of speaking roles than is found in classroom discourse in elementary schools (see Cazden's reviews, 1986, 1988). However, the expected differences in speaking roles did appear in the kinds of questions asked by children and teachers: Teachers were far more likely than children to ask closed questions, especially when extending topics.

Differences between the two portions of activity time again ap-

TABLE 7.3
Strategies Used for Topic Development by Teachers and Children During Activity Times

	Connie		*Terri*		*Petra*		*Averages*	
	Con.	*Ch.*	*Ter.*	*Ch.*	*Pet.*	*Ch.*	*Tea.*	*Ch.*
	(n = *213)*	(n = *127)*	(n = *128)*	(n = *62)*	(n = *131)*	(n = *60)*	(n = *3)*	(n = *3)*
When Teachers Were Stationary								
Initiations								
Open q.	.02	.03	.00	.00	.00	.00	.01	.01
Closed q.	.03	.02	.02	.08	.02	.05	.02	.05
Statements	.03	.06	.03	.06	.02	.12	.03	.08
Extensions								
Closed q.	.17	.06	.21	.05	.10	.05	.16	.05
Open q.	.03	.02	.10	.02	.06	.02	.06	.02
Clarifying	.14	.00	.19	.05	.18	.00	.17	.02
Resp. open q.	.00	.06	.02	.06	.00	.10	.01	.07
Resp. closed q.	.00	.13	.04	.31	.02	.18	.02	.21
Resp. clarifying q.	.00	.07	.05	.10	.00	.17	.02	.11
Statements	.35	.35	.19	.15	.49	.23	.34	.24
Conversational functions								
Maintaining	.05	.03	.14	.12	.05	.06	.08	.07
Nonresponse	.00	.08	.01	.02	.00	.00	.01	.03
Other	.13	.04	.00	.00	.03	.02	.05	.03
	(n = *178)*	(n = *68)*	(n = *251)*	(n = *82)*	(n = *24)*	(n = *8)*	(n = *3)*	(n = *3)*
When Teachers Were Circulating								
Initiations								
Open q.	.02	.03	.00	.00	.00	.00	.01	.01
Closed q.	.04	.04	.02	.00	.00	.00	.02	.01
Statement	.03	.04	.08	.10	.04	.12	.05	.09
Total	.09	.11	.10	.10	.04	.12	.08	.11
Extensions								
Open q.	.03	.01	.04	.01	.00	.00	.02	.01
Closed q.	.15	.06	.19	.02	.08	.12	.14	.07
Clarify'g	.08	.00	.10	.00	.08	.00	.09	.00
Resp. op.q.	.01	.03	.01	.08	.00	.00	.01	.04
Resp. clo.q.	.03	.10	.02	.23	.00	.00	.02	.11
Resp. clar.q.	.01	.03	.01	.12	.00	.12	.01	.09
Resp. state.	.46	.38	.41	.30	.71	.38	.53	.35
Conversational functions								
Maintaining	.12	.15	.13	.12	.08	.12	.11	.13
Nonresponse	.00	.03	.00	.00	.00	.00	.00	.01
Other	.02	.09	.01	.00	.00	.12	.01	.07
Total	.14	.27	.14	.12	.08	.25	.12	.21

peared, reflecting the different organization of these times. One difference appeared in the frequency with which statements were used to extend a previous statement. These were more common in teacher speech during circulating time than during stationary times (Connie: 46% vs. 35%; Terri: 41% vs. 19%; Petra: 71% vs. 49%). In contrast, during circulating times, teachers did relatively less extending of conversations using questions than during stationary times (Connie: 26% vs. 34%; Terri: 33% vs. 50%; Petra: 16% vs. 34%).

Questions were used a little over half the time by all except teachers during circulating time. The use of questions as opposed to statements was associated with a more active effort to elicit information and extend interactions. Thus, the relatively heavier reliance on questions during stationary portions of activity times suggests that teachers expend more effort attempting to elicit and understand children's ideas at these times than when they are circulating during activity period. This conclusion is supported by the fact that, for each teacher, there were roughly twice as many clarificatory questions during stationary portions of activity time than during circulating portions. This increase indicates increased efforts to understand children—a prior condition to helping them extend and elaborate their comments.

Summary

When teachers' talk during activity time is analyzed using the three coding systems, patterns emerge indicating that richer conversations occur when teachers are stationary than when they circulate around the room. In Figure 7.1 results of categories of teacher interactional behaviors from each coding system that are supportive of extended talk are displayed (i.e., nonpresent talk, positive engagement, extending questions). For each teacher it is clear that more of the desired interactional strategies occur during times when teachers are stationary.

Qualitative Examination of Activity Time Talk

The variability in talk during activity time reflects two interacting factors: the nature of the ongoing activity and the teacher's agenda. These factors were not distinct, because a teacher's agenda could serve either to override the current context or to heighten its effect.

Stationary Activity Times: The Responsive Stance. During portions of activity times when teachers were stationary, a teacher could adopt a stance of responding to the ideas of children. This responsive approach tended to result in divergent topics, some of which took the

FIGURE 7.1a
Conversational Topic Coding.

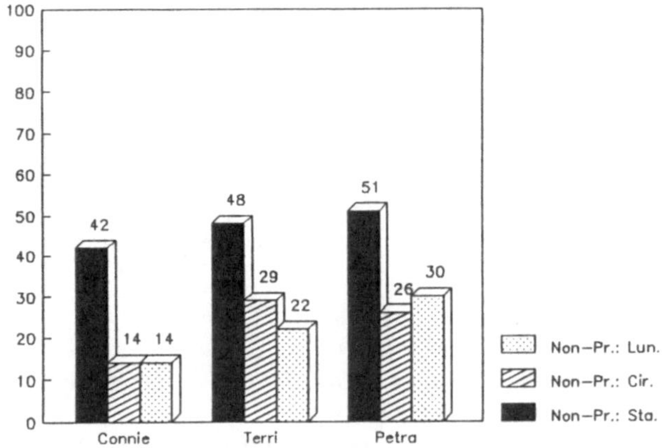

FIGURE 7.1b
Speech Act Coding

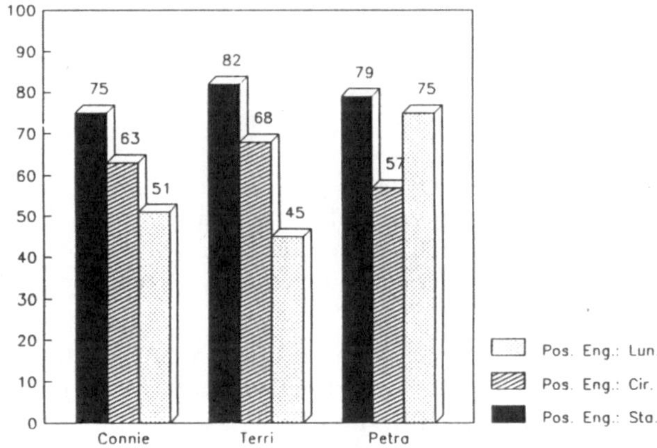

FIGURE 7.1c
Topic Development Coding

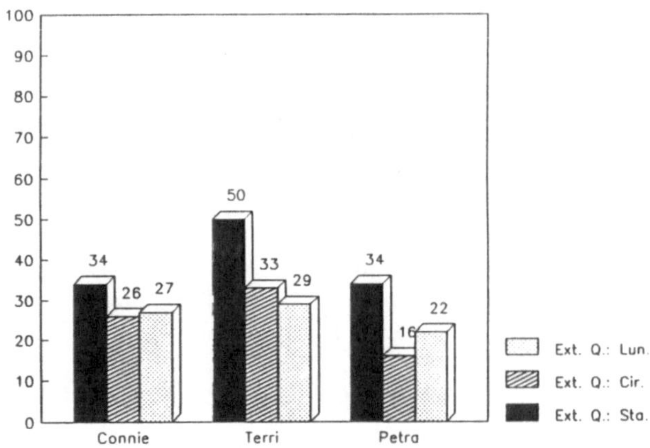

FIGURE 7.1. Proportion of utterances coded reflecting conversations conducive to use of decontextualized language.

conversation well beyond the immediate present. For example, during one such period, children were drawing and using peg boards near where Connie was seated. During the following conversation, which lasted for nearly 10 minutes, Connie was given a picture by a boy, leading to a description of the picture.

> Connie: See my rainbow?
> Mark: Yeah.
> Connie: Isn't that nice? And here's an airplane . . . And what's that?
> Mark: Train!
> (Soon, the conversation moved beyond the present)
> Mark: Yeah, and then you have to put them on your wall, your wall.
> Connie: Should I bring them home and put them on my wall?
> Mark: Yeah.
> Connie: Okay. Which wall should I put them on? What room?
> Mark: In your bedroom.
> Connie: In my bedroom. Okay. Those are very nice pictures to have on my wall. Thank you.
> Mark: Look at them . . . You can look at them if you want and your dogs can look at them too.
> Connie: Well I don't have a dog so I guess I'll be the only one that looks at them. But I'll think of you when I look at them!

Here we see the topic shift to Connie's home and from the present into the hypothetical future. Mark does such a good job of envisioning Connie's life at home that he even populates it with an imaginary dog! This interchange is immediately followed by Mark telling about his dog and cat, a topic that Connie supports and other children subsequently extend.

A feature of several conversations during this portion of the activity time was their duration. In the foregoing as well as the following conversation, we see Connie working to keep the topic on the floor. One way she does this is by displaying enthusiasm and extending the child's meaning:

> Wilma: My grammy said she's gonna take me and Erin there tomorrow.
> Connie: Tomorrow? You're gonna go?
> Wilma: With Erin and grammy.
> Connie: Wow!
> Connie: After school you're gonna go? Oh that will be nice.

Here we see Connie exhibiting appropriate enthusiasm, emphasizing the future nature of the activity. She then extends Wilma's comment, by adding the information about when this activity will happen.

During the same stationary portion of this activity period, Connie continued to talk with Mark about pets he has at home (more talk about nonpresent objects and activities), listened as a child told about her cold, participated in a pretend birthday party that arose from imaginative use of a peg-studded board, discussed rainbows being drawn by children, and enforced a rule governing where toys should be used. Four of these six topics grew from ongoing activities (discussion of the drawings given to Connie, the birthday party, discussion of rainbow drawings, rule enforcement), revealing the importance of setting on topic choice. Two of these topics moved beyond the present (the child's drawing given to the teacher and the birthday party), and one of the other two topics dealt with a future activity. During these exchanges three strategies helped children to construct extended discourse: (a) enthusiastic and playful entrance into the child's frame of reference, (b) asking questions that require elaboration or encourage children to make implicit information more explicit, and (c) elaborating and extending children's contributions.

Stationary Activity Times: Instructional Agenda.. During times when teachers were able to remain stationary, they might adopt a more active conversational stance, pursuing goals of their own, instead of primarily responding to children's interests. This orientation is exemplified by Terri's interactions with children at a table set up with magazines, scissors, markers, paper, and paste. During her first extended stay at this table, Terri engaged in an extended sequence of exchanges about a picture of a clock:

Terri: Is that a toy you found in the magazine that you like?
Lea: Yeah.
Terri: What does it look like? . . . What do you think happens with this toy? . . . I can see things on it. . . . What do you think? . . . What is on that xxx?
Lea: It tells numbers.
Terri: It tells numbers. . . . How many?
Jake: No!
Lea: Un huh.
Terri: I see a number. It tells numbers? . . . What do you think? . . . If it tells numbers what does it tell you? Does it look like . . .
Lea: Tells you if it's warm out.
Terri: If it's what?
Lea? Warm out.
Terri: Do you think it might be like that thing on our wall? . . . Look. . . . Do you think it might be like that clock? . . . Do you think it's a clock that tells time? . . . Let's look.

Terri later returns to this table and finds children beginning to write using letters on the papers that they were putting pictures on. In this case she builds on a comment a child makes about knowing how to spell "cat." Initially she responds to the child's excitement and extends the discussion, allowing him to demonstrate additional knowledge about letters. After several exchanges the conversation turns to the question of whether a letter is a *p* or a *b*. This leads to the following sequence:

> Leana: It's a *p*.
> Terri: It's a *p*? Do you know what starts with *p*?
> Leana: What?
> Terri: Oh and there's a what?
> Leana: A *d*!
> Terri: A *d*! I didn't know you knew so many letters!
> Leana: (unintelligible)
> Terri: Do you know what starts with a *p*?
> Leana: No.
> Terri: Can you think of something that starts with a *p*? . . . Eliza? Does Eliza start with a *p*?

As the children at the table begin to pick up the lesson format that Terri is establishing, energy grows, resulting in an activity that continues for about another 5 minutes.

In both these sequences we see Terri striving to derive the type of educational benefits she hoped would flow from the planned activity. In contrast to the receptive, responsive stance assumed by Connie, Terri guides children's attention, building on interest sparked by the activity. Topics again move away from the immediate present, but instead of exploring a diverse range of personal topics, conversation is channeled to topics that build world knowledge, vocabulary, and encourage reflection on language. As a result of this task-oriented, didactic interactional style, neither narrative nor expository language is elicited or modeled.

Circulating Activity Time. When teachers were circulating they were generally concerned with maintaining order and keeping children involved. For example, after the stationary phase of Connie's activity time discussed earlier, Connie began circulating and immediately dealt with a variety of organizational matters including overseeing proper storage of pegs, asking a child to stop teasing another child and supervising use of spoons being employed for pretend cooking. In each area that she subsequently entered, peg boards, house area, painting, and blocks, she initially dealt with some organizational matter. Additionally, while she was circulating she attracted children who had problems (e.g., complaints about being teased) and she moved to intervene to stop rowdy behavior throughout the room.

In addition to working to maintain order, Connie spent time getting children started on constructive activity. For example, in the painting area she oversaw the donning of a smock and initial painting attempts; in the block area she got children started reconstructing a building that had fallen. On those occasions when she found children successfully engaged, Connie sought to encourage continued engagement or responded to children's efforts to validate the importance of their work. For example, the following exchange occurred when she entered the painting area:

Nicki: See!
Connie: Oh, that's beautiful! You know what I noticed about this?
Nicki: What?
Connie: You made them all going across this way, and they're all going straight across instead of up and down. That's interesting. Where should I put your name?
Nicki: (nonverbal response)
Connie: Right here? Okay. I love this picture. You filled up the whole paper! Would you like to do another one?
Nicki: Yeah.
Connie: Okay. Here' some more paper.

Here we see that Nicki anticipates a teacher response, reflecting the routine nature of the following exchange. In her comments Connie specifies what she likes about the painting, thereby teaching the child what she values in paintings and encouraging continued effort. Connie's final move, asking Nicki if she wants to continue, reveals the importance of keeping children engaged.

The effect of teacher efforts to organize and maintain activities is to shift the interactional focus to the present. Topics discussed become the child's current or immediately impending behavior or the materials being used. Thus, increased concern for control goes hand in hand with a restriction of attention to the present.

Within-setting Agenda Shifting. Of course, teacher-child talk is not totally determined by contextual factors. Even during the circulating portion of activity time, a context that encouraged all teachers to adopt a controlling stance, a shift could occur if the teacher was flexible enough to shift into a more playful mode:

Connie: Joey! I think you're teasing Aaron and I'd like you to stop.
Aaron: Erin!
Connie: What honey?
Aaron: You said Erin. Errrin.
Connie: I thought I said Aaron. Did it sound like Erin?
Aaron: Yup.
Connie: Did it? Well next time I'll be more careful.
Aaron: Be more careful.
Connie: Oh I sure will!
Aaron: If you don't be more careful then you'll fall.
Connie: I will fall on my words? If I'm not careful with my words?
Aaron: Yup.
Connie: But I'm sitting down!
Aaron: Well if you stand up you'll—
Connie: If I stand up and if I'm not careful I will fall?
Aaron: unintelligible
Connie: How about when I'm talking if I'm not careful?
Aaron: If you're talking, if you're . . .

This conversation ended abruptly as Connie intervened to solve another problem, reflecting her ongoing monitoring of the room. Nevertheless, she had managed to sustain development of complex and whimsical verbal play with language that had led Aaron into use of the hypothetical "if-then" structure that he was struggling with at the point when Connie had to leave.

Lunchtime: Topic Analyses

Comparison of teachers during lunchtime reveals greater variability between teachers than was evident during activity times (see Table 7.4). Talk during Connie's and Terri's lunches was heavily concentrated on present topics (87% and 79% respectively), whereas Petra's talk was somewhat less present-oriented (62%). The present orientation of Connie's and Terri's lunches can almost be completely accounted for by their greater emphasis on enforcement of rules (23% and 22%; 8% for Petra). Time not spent dealing with present-oriented topics tended to be used to talk about future events, absent actions and objects and, less often, to analyze physical events or human motivations.

Lunchtime: Speech Act Analyses

The speech act analysis revealed sharp divergence between teachers and children in the distribution of speech acts during lunch (see Table 7.5). Teachers used nearly twice as many controlling acts as children,

TABLE 7.4
Proportion of Children's and Teacher's Talk Addressing Different Topics During Lunch

	Connie		*Terri*		*Petra*		*Averages*	
	Con.	*Ch.*	*Ter.*	*Ch.*	*Pet.*	*Ch.*	*Tea.*	*Ch.*
	(n = *142*)	(n = *102*)	(n = *80*)	(n = *62*)	(n = *158*)	(n = *143*)	(n = *3*)	(n = *3*)
Present focus								
Actions/obj.	.36	.45	.44	.49	.40	.31	.40	.42
Feelings/own	.27	.33	.12	.51	.13	.25	.17	.42
Rules	.23	.04	.22	.00	.08	.02	.18	.02
Total prop.	.87	.82	.79	.71	.62	.59	.76	.71
Analytical								
World/human	.03	.02	.05	.04	.08	.09	.05	.04
Cognition	.00	.01	.02	.00	.04	.01	.02	.01
Language	.04	.01	.00	.00	.00	.00	.01	.00
Total	.08	.04	.08	.04	.12	.10	.20	.05
Past, future, & absent								
Actions/obj.	.01	.02	.05	.04	.16	.15	.07	.07
Future	.04	.09	.09	.22	.07	.08	.07	.13
Narrative	.00	.03	.00	.00	02	.08	.01	.04
Total	.06	.14	.14	.26	.25	.31	.15	.24
Didactic								
Preschool k.	.00	.00	.00	.00	.00	.00	.00	.00
Symbols/books	.00	.00	.00	.00	.00	.00	.00	.00
Total	.00.	.00	.00	.00	.00	.00	.00	.00
Total non-p.	.14	.18	.22	.30	.37	.41	.24	.30
Total pres.	.87	.82	.79	.71	.62	.59	.76	.71

reflecting a shift toward much greater emphasis on behavior management. For both Connie and Terri, about half their speech acts were controlling, a figure roughly one and a half times that observed during the circulating portion of their activity periods. Also, during lunch, for all three teachers, direct control statements were about twice as common as indirect statements, an increase relative to the ratio observed during activity time, possibly indicating a greater sense of urgency in the directives made during lunch.

Distribution of positively engaged speech acts was similar to that observed during activity times. Children and teachers again showed divergent patterns, with children most often providing information while teachers more evenly distributed their talk over several categories (information giving, real questions, warm, supportive comments). It is noteworthy that, during lunch as well as during activity periods, test questions were nearly absent.

TABLE 7.5
Proportion of Speech Act Types Used by Teachers and Children During Lunch Conversations

	Connie		*Terri*		*Petra*		*Averages*	
	Con.	*Ch.*	*Ter.*	*Ch.*	*Pet.*	*Ch.*	*Tea.*	*Ch.*
	(n = *148)*	(n = *124)*	(n = *96)*	(n = *51)*	(n = *184)*	(n = *216)*	(n = *3)*	(n = *3)*
Control focus								
Direct	.33	.21	.32	.10	.17	.13	.27	.15
Indir.	.14	.07	.17	.02	.08	.00	.13	.03
Negoti.	.02	.01	.06	.12	.00	.01	.03	.05
Total	.49	.28	.55	.23	.25	.15	.43	.23
Positive engagement								
Warm	.14	.04	.04	.00	.10	.07	.09	.04
Infor.	.14	.59	.13	.65	.27	.69	.18	.64
Real q.	.15	.07	.18	.08	.27	.04	.20	.06
Test q/r.	.06	.02	.04	.00	.02	.00	.04	.01
Non-pr.	.03	.00	.05	.04	.10	.06	.06	.03
Total	.51	.72	.45	.76	.75	.85	.57	.78

Lunchtime: Topic Development Analyses

Lunch talk, when viewed through the lens of the topic development analysis, did not show major contrasts with activity times (Table 7.6). However, where consistent differences did appear among settings, the similarities were again greatest between lunch and the circulating portion of the activity time. Interesting patterns appeared in those categories that had differentiated the two portions of activity time—use of statements instead of questions to extend topics. In each case the lunch pattern was close to that seen during the circulating portion of activity time.

Qualitative Examination of Lunchtime

The role of context and teacher agenda as forces shaping interaction again emerged during the lunch interactions. Two results of greatest interest appeared in the quantitative measures: (a) control concerns were dominant, resulting in a cluster of patterns suggesting similarity between lunchtime talk and circulating portions of activity time, and (b) there were marked differences between Petra and the other two teachers in the extent of the dominance of control issues during lunch.

Qualitative examination of lunchtimes reveals even more striking differences among teachers than are captured by the three coding systems. These differences can be sensed by examining what topics

TABLE 7.6
Proportion of Topics Developed by Teachers and Children During Lunch Using Different Strategies

	Connie		*Terri*		*Petra*		*Averages*	
	Con.	*Ch.*	*Ter.*	*Ch.*	*Pet.*	*Ch.*	*Tea.*	*Ch.*
	(n = *104)*	(n = *57)*	(n = *128)*	(n = *62)*	(n = *177)*	(n = *129)*	(n = *3)*	(n = *3)*
Initiations								
Open q.	.00	.00	.02	.00	.01	.00	.01	.00
Closed q.	.04	.04	.03	.00	.03	.08	.03	.04
Statement	.05	.05	.06	.16	.06	.11	.06	.11
Total	.09	.09	.11	.17	.10	.19	.10	.15
Extensions								
Questions								
Closed	.13	.07	.12	.03	.12	.01	.12	.04
Open	.01	.02	.04	.01	.02	.00	.02	.01
Clarifying	.13	.07	.13	.01	.08	.02	.11	.03
Total	.27	.16	.29	.05	.22	.03	.26	.08
Statements								
Resp.op.q	.01	.00	.01	.06	.00	.02	.01	.03
Resp. clo.q.	.02	.21	.01	.10	.04	.15	.02	.15
Resp. clar.q	.00	.04	.00	.03	.00	.03	.00	.03
Statements	.40	.33	.38	.37	.47	.33	.42	.34
Total	.43	.58	.41	.56	.51	.53	.45	.56
Conversations								
Maintaining	.17	.16	.16	.14	.16	.16	.16	.15
Nonresponse	.00	.00	.00	.02	.01	.02	.00	.01
Other	.00	.02	.03	.07	.00	.08	.02	.04
Total	.20	.18	.19	.23	.17	.26	.19	.22

were given extended attention during the two most contrasting lunches—Terri's and Petra's. Topics that extended across four or more speaker turns were identified and are briefly described in Table 7.7. Examination of Terri's topics reveals a consistent and overriding concern with appropriate behavior, quantity and quality of food eaten, and efficiency. The only topic not associated with such matters was Terri's query about children's plans to attend the school's potluck. Children apparently sensed her agenda, because they initiated no home-related topics.

Petra's lunch conversations stand in striking contrast to those seen at Terri's table. Although Petra shared Terri's concerns with diet and organization, very little time was spend on such matters. Even when they were dealt with, it was often in a playful context. For example, Petra bridged into urging a child to eat more by building from the child's comment that her pants kept falling off, by suggesting that her pants would not fall off if she would eat more. The engaged, playful

TABLE 7.7
Lunch Topics Extending for Four or More Speaking Turns

Initiated By teacher	*Initiated By Children*
Conversations at Terri's table	
	Request to return salad.
Who likes salad?	
Did John eat his salad and how did he dispose of it?	
	Request to move to nearby table where children are pretending. (Request denied)
Stay facing your own table; talk with friends at other table later.	
Say name of person from whom you are requesting items.	
Is anybody coming to the potluck dinner?	
	Request for a hamburger.
Manners: how to make a request, don't grab and don't spill	
Behaviors required for finishing lunch	
Conversations at Petra's table	
Children ever meet Betsy's Dad?	
	Doughnut preferences; friends and relatives also discussed
	Pillow fight experience
	Use of fork to comb hair; Petra suggests is bad idea
	Pizza vs. tunafish preference
Problem solving related to milk	
What are you going to do this weekend?	
	Watches: new, old
	Request for milk
	Dumbo (topic emerged from long watch discussion)
Compliment on how much eating done; encouragement to slow eaters	
How was your morning? (after child repeated :"Oh good morning three times)	
	My friends and my brother woke me; leads into home life
What were you talking to the teacher about?	
	Play fighting with friends
	My pants keep falling down; (Petra extends into urging to eat more lunch)
Mad Max (book, movie, or T.V. show)	
Eat some salad (playfully requested)	
	I'm gonna kick you (T.) out of school (playful manner)
Why are you being mean?	
	Requests for a cherry
Discussion about completing salad	
Cleaning up	

tone at Petra's table encouraged children to initiate a wide range of topics, several of which dealt with home experiences. When narratives emerged, Petra encouraged them.

Jesse: You know what? With me and my cousin David we—
David: Hey! Two Davids!
Jesse: We got pillows—
Petra: That's right. Your name's David.
Jesse: Yeah—and I got pillows and my cousin they got pillows (unintelligible) punching each other and we had a pillow fight.
Petra: You had a pillow fight!
Jesse: Yeah.
Petra: Were you angry?
Jesse: No. No I was just playing the pillow fight.
Petra: Oh, it was a playing pillow fight.
David: Well we had a fight like—
Jesse: Yeah. And first I got a pillow then David got a pillow and we were punching each other.
Petra: Did anybody get hurt?
Jesse: No
Petra: No? It was just fun?
Jesse: Yeah.
Petra: That sounds like fun.

Here we see Petra balancing the needs of two children, acknowledging David's presence, but protecting the continued development of Jesse's narrative by ignoring David's attempt to break in with his pillow fight experience. She supports elaboration by revealing continued interest and by asking questions indicating information that could be added. At the conclusion of the first version of his narrative, Petra echoes the final words, "You had a pillow fight," indicating comprehension and interest. She then asked a question that pushed Jesse to include information about her emotional response. This ploy succeeded in eliciting the desired information and more detail about the sequence of events. Following this elaboration Petra once again encouraged extension by probing for an evaluative response.

In the following lunchtime conversation we see the same strategies—echoing to reflect interest and request more, and probes requesting evaluation of the event:

Petra: What were you talking with Terri about?
Jake: We were talking about bad things.
Petra: Bad things? What bad things?
Jake: Like kids pushing me and hitting me and punching me.

Petra: Kids were pushing you and hitting you and
(gap in tape)
Jake: . . . sometimes but not always.
Petra: How did that make you feel
Jake: Mad and angry bad.

The differences between Terri's and Petra's lunch table conversation can be summarized as being one of tone. Terri's management concerns dominated the entire situation, resulting in a serious and rather oppressive tone. Petra dealt with similar management issues, but they were not the focus of her attention. She maintained a playful tone, handled management issues quickly, and remained receptive to what children offered. Children seemed to sense each teacher's lunchtime agenda. Children at Terri's table wanted to move to another table where more interesting talk was going on; children at Petra's table initiated diverse topics, engaged in elaborated talk of a personal nature, and listened to and extended each other's talk.

Discussion

Having examined three teachers as they talk with children in three different settings using three coding systems, several general conclusions can be drawn. The result of special importance to consideration of narrative development is the finding that, in this child-centered developmentally oriented classroom, personal narratives are rare during lunch and activity times. This finding is made more significant by the added finding that not only narratives were rare. We also found little extended expository discourse (e.g., expanding world knowledge, speculating about causation) and only limited talk about other nonpresent topics (e.g., future events).

The relative scarcity of extended discourse suggests that structural factors at least partly account for the discourse patterns observed. This supposition is supported by the finding that there was considerable consistency in the interactional patterns of the three teachers across setting. Within activity time, occasions when the teacher circulated tended to be grounded in the here-and-now. Relative to stationary portions of activity time, circulating times had higher frequencies of controlling speech acts, more present-focused talk, and more reliance on statements instead of questions to extend topics. For Connie and Terri, the cluster of results associated with the circulating portion of activity time also characterized lunchtime conversations. These results all point to the dominating influence of control-related concerns: If management concerns are dominant, they restrict talk to the present and limit opportunities for development of extended discourse.

Moreover, context is not simply a matter of the activity setting; rather, it results from an interaction between ongoing activities and the goals of the participants, especially the teacher's. This conclusion is primarily based on the finding of differences between how different teachers responded to the constraints imposed by the same settings. During lunchtime a teacher could focus on management issues or could deal with these quickly and concentrate instead on conversing with the children. Similarly, during stationary portions of activity time, teachers could pursue a focused academic agenda or could respond to the interests expressed by the children.

Across all settings, the virtue of flexibility and the importance of general affective tone became apparent. Even in the midst of situations requiring attention to control issues (e.g., lunch, circulating activity time), teachers could elicit personal information or could engage in sophisticated verbal play if they could momentarily put control issues aside. Children responded to the relaxed, playful tone present when teachers were able to make this shift, resulting in more elaborated and more personal conversations.

The finding of differences in how teachers respond to similar situational demands suggests that teachers might adopt consistent and different interactional styles. I have far too little information about any one teacher to make claims regarding stylistic variation, but interesting patterns did appear. As we noted, Terri was highly control-oriented during lunchtime and self-consciously pursued an academic agenda during activity time. Additionally, an analysis of her book-reading style (Dickinson & Keebler, 1989), revealed that she emphasized reconstruction of literal sequences of events of stories and was conscious of using cognitively oriented questioning strategies that she learned in her teacher education program. In contrast, as we noted, Petra placed much less emphasis on control during lunch. During stationary portions of activity times she engaged in no didactic instructional sequences such as observed during Terri's activity time. The analysis of book-reading styles revealed that, although her book readings were done in a highly controlling manner, her follow-up discussions tended to be relaxed, informal, and conversational, and lacked the instructional focus seen in Terri's discussions.

In the present study Connie fell roughly between Terri and Petra in the frequency of behaviors deemed to be supportive of decontextualized language growth (e.g., topic-extending, nonpresent talk, positive engagement). Similarly, in the book-reading study Connie was like Terri in that she strove to extend children's understanding of the story with discussions while the book was being read. The tone of her discussion, however, was less didactic than that seen in Terri's talk and more like Petra's relaxed follow-up discussion.

This quick description of three teacher interactional strategies across settings suggests that there appear to be some consistencies across settings, but that variability associated with shifts in activity settings reduces the degree to which such consistency is observed.

Another important question raised by this study is whether it is generally the case that, in preschools teachers and children spend relatively little time engaged in sustained discourse that moves beyond the here-and-now? We address this question briefly in the following study by reporting data from additional classrooms.

STUDY TWO

Currently Catherine Snow and I are in the early stages of a longitudinal study of language and literacy development of low-income children. In this study we are observing children in their home and preschool settings. Preschool observations include recording the conversations of children and teachers throughout an entire morning by asking target children and teachers to wear small backpacks containing the tape recorders while observers take context notes. The tapes of classroom talk are being analyzed using a coding scheme that is less fine-grained than the scheme used for study one, but codes topics in a comparable manner. It focuses on conversational topic because it was thought that topic best marks stretches of talk where extended, decontextualized discourse occurs. Given the volume of data being collected, we are coding these tapes directly, without transcription. We catalogue the tapes by noting the ongoing activities and key phrases, coding the gist of teacher-child exchanges, and timing the duration of each type of interaction. Coders work closely with each other and with me to ensure consistency in approaches to coding.

Results and Discussion

The results of the coding of the teacher's talk in eight centers has now been completed. In Table 7.8 I report data from the classrooms where we recorded small group teacher-led activities, general free activity times, and mealtimes—times comparable to those examined in study one. These results once again indicate that nonpresent topics often are rare, accounting for more than 10% of a teacher's talk during a

TABLE 7.8
Study Two: Teacher Conversational Topics (In Minutes: Seconds) During Free and Small Group Activity Times and During Meal Times

	Time	*Control*	*Lit/Lang*	*Non-Prst*	*Other*
		Private Centers			
Center #1					
Free activity	0	—	—	—	—
Small group activity	45:49	768	9	—	13
% of small group activity		30	1	—	1
Center #2					
Free activity	27:27	181	108	67	53
% of free activity		11	18	4	3
		Headstart Centers			
Center #1					
Free activity	42:39	326	55	329	0
% of Free activity		13	2	12	0
Small Grp activity	8:03	0	24	29	24
% of Small Grp activity		0	10	12	10
Center #2					
Free activity	36:50	933	20	56	0
% Free activity		42	2	2	0
Breakfast	19:37	163	37	150	0
% Breakfast		14	3	13	0
Center #3					
Free activity	20:06	178	26	159	51
% Free activity		15	2	13	5
Breakfast	11:16	48	0	33	0
% Breakfast		7	0	5	0
Center #4					
Free activity	44:18	177	180	16	14
% Free activity		7	5	1	1
Breakfast	24:55	88	0	109	98
% Breakfast		6	0	7	7
Center #5					
Free activity	41:42	0	37	10	36
% Free activity		0	1	1	1
Breakfast	8:13	0	0	0	0
% Breakfast		0	0	0	0
Center #6					
Free activity	14:23	335	75	0	0
% Free activity		39	9	0	0
Small Grp activity	7:16	129	45	17	24
% Small Grp activity		30	10	4	6
Snack	3:11	0	0	0	0
% Snack		0	0	0	0

Note. Data displayed does not reflect an exhaustive coding; rather, only selected categories of special interest.

given time only three times, twice during free time, and once during lunch. In addition, it is important to note that there was considerable variation among centers in the amount of such interaction, with a low of less than 1% of the total time coded to a high of 24%. Talk dealing with language, literacy, or numbers also was variable and could be infrequent, ranging from a low of 2% of coded time to a high of 26%.

Unlike in study one, there were many factors that varied between classrooms making it hard to identify consistent patterns of effects of activity on teacher-child talk. Nevertheless, looking across classrooms our mealtime data provides some information regarding the effect of context on teacher-child talk. We found several centers where teachers were not present during mealtimes except in a supervisory role, suggesting that this is often viewed as a break time for teachers (for similar findings see Dickinson, 1989; Innocenti et al., 1986). On the other hand, during those mealtimes when there was some teacher-child talk, there could be a relatively large amount of time spent in nonpresent talk (Head Start #2: 13%), although relatively minimal amounts of such talk were also found (Head Start Center #3: 5%; Head Start #4: 5%). The amount of time spent in control-oriented talk again varied dramatically, with the teacher in one classroom spending 42% of her time during activity time engaged in control-oriented talk. Amount of time spent in such conversations varied greatly by center and, in some cases, by setting, making generalizations impossible.

Unfortunately, structured activity periods—times when teachers were most likely to remain with the children—occurred only twice during the time we visited these centers, making it impossible to draw general conclusions regarding the effect of teacher mobility during activity time on classroom talk. Nonetheless, even our small sample of structured activity times indicates the enormous effect that teacher agenda can have. In private center #1 the teachers were almost exclusively concerned with keeping children quiet while they completed worksheets. We can say with considerable certainty that teachers with such an orientation will have minimally stimulating language climates regardless of the nature of more subtle variables such as teacher location.

SUMMARY

The first study revealed that activity and mealtimes in preschools provide relatively few opportunities to discuss topics that are likely to encourage children to produce or understand narratives or other types of decontextualized language. The second study broadened the lens through which classrooms were viewed, including additional classrooms and covering a larger slice of time. This work supported the general conclusion that it is not common for informal conversations between preschool teachers and children to include narratives or to deal with other nonpresent topics.

Study one also concluded that the nature of the activity affects teacher-child interaction by shaping the content of topics discussed and altering power relationships. Study two allowed a much less precise examination of context effects because of the uncontrolled variation of factors other than activity setting across classrooms (e.g., children, number of teachers present, physical layout, etc.). Nevertheless, it is significant that mealtimes were found to be occasions when narratives could appear with some frequency, supporting the conclusion of study one that such talk could emerge during mealtime if the teacher's agenda was conducive to it.

Finally, both studies indicate that teacher agenda may have a major impact on teacher-child interaction. In study one, despite the evidence that setting had a strong impact on all teachers, during the lunch conversations there was variability among teachers, indicating an effect of different agendas during this time of day. In study two, the great variability found across classrooms in the amount of nonpresent talk within the same type of activity (e.g., lunch) and throughout the day, underscores the importance of teacher variables. Organizational matters must be dealt with in all settings and certain minimal levels of control must be maintained, but teachers find many ways to handle these matters. Some solutions to these problems result in interactions allowing teachers and children to engage in extended, personal conversations that naturally move away from the present into the past and future of children and teachers.

Central to the Vygotskian approach to understanding development is the belief that children acquire new cognitive structures as a result of social exchanges. Consistent with this perspective on development is the claim that certain types of teacher-child interaction may foster development of discourse skills that may facilitate later literacy. The most typical way Vygotskian analyses proceed is to identify settings where intense interpersonal engagement may occur and analyze in detail the movement from inter- to intrapsychic functioning (e.g., Damon & Phelps, in press; Forman & Cazden, 1985; Michaels, 1985; Pratt, Kerig, Cowan, & Cowan, 1988). The current studies operate at a different level, analyzing the social scene to determine when and if children have opportunities to engage in the type of sustained, elaborated discussions hypothesized to support narrative and literacy development. Our finding that, in many preschools, children have relatively few opportunities to engage teachers in extended dialogues, is consistent with Tizard and Hughes's (1984) findings from England. Whereas structural constraints (i.e., adult-child ratio, breadth of knowledge about the child's home life, depth of emotional involvement) necessarily limit teachers' opportunities to engage children, we also found that teacher agenda—teacher's sense of what matters—can powerfully influence the tone and content of her conversations with children. In light of this finding, it is important to note that awareness of the significance of supporting discourse growth apparently seems not to be widespread among preschool teachers. Support for this claim comes from teacher responses to interviews included in our ongoing longitudinal study of language and literacy development. When we asked teachers their views regarding approaches to supporting language development, most interpreted our question as referring to acquisition of English as a second language (a logical interpretation given the prevalence of multilingual classrooms). However, after we made clear our interest in support for first language acquisition, most teachers had few ideas that they could articulate. In a similar vein, we had one teacher who resisted requesting a child to tell about some home experience (a routine part of our data collection) because "she didn't know the child well enough yet." Such responses suggest that some preschool teachers are unaware of the importance of providing opportunities for use of rich, extended discourse. If this is the case, it is not surprising that they do not intentionally structure opportunities for children to acquire literacy-related discourse skills.

Implications

Even if our hypotheses regarding language-literacy linkages are correct, we can only make informed guesses regarding which experiences support development of narrative and other decontextualized language skills, and we have almost no idea how frequent such experiences need to be to have a positive effect. Thus, for now we must work with the global assumption that "more is better," and strive to find settings and strategies that might facilitate teacher-child interactions supportive of decontextualized language skill.

If teachers become aware of the value of fostering growth of decontextualized language skills through informal conversations, changes in how the classroom is structured might greatly increase opportunities to encourage such interactions. Possible beneficial strategies include devising staffing patterns that allow one teacher to remain with a group of children for an extended period of time. Such a change could be made during traditional times such as activity time and during times when the children eat. It might also occur at times specially constructed for this purpose. For example, efforts might be made to engage children when they first arrive from home because this might be a time when narratives and sharing of personal information could occur naturally. Additionally, during at least one group time, teachers could divide the class into small groups instead of meeting with full-class groupings and use this time for language-related activities.

A number of changes might be made during activity times to enhance opportunities for supporting decontextualized language. In addition to attempting to allow a teacher to remain with a group for an extended time, unnecessary circulating might be avoided, thereby reducing teacher availability for minor matters that could be settled without her. Also, activities could be planned that naturally encourage children to talk about past or future experiences and teachers could make self-conscious efforts to maximize the opportunities inherent in the activity (e.g., cutting out pictures about when you were a baby, drawing pictures about home and family, etc.).

Aside from receiving sufficient funding to support hiring additional teachers, the most important single improvement would be to increase teacher's awareness of the value of encouraging elaborated narratives. All of the ideas previously suggested are being implemented in many classrooms, but in most cases teachers are not fully aware of the potential value of their activities; hence these activities may not be fully exploited. Skilled teachers undoubtedly can find many ways to foster decontextualized language if they view this as a priority item on the shifting agenda that they carry with them throughout the day.

ACKNOWLEDGMENTS

This research was supported, in part, by a grant from the Ford Foundation. I thank Stephanie Ross for her tireless efforts at data collection and analysis.

APPENDIX

Topic Coding

Actions/Objects: Comments, questions, attention-directing utterances referring to objects, pictures or people immediately present or descriptions of actions as they are taking place or immediately after completion.

Feelings & Ownership: Talk about ownership of objects, discussion of bodily sensations or health, or talk about emotions or personal preferences.

Rules: Justifications, explanations or comments about actions or words that include consideration of rules or norms of behavior.

World/motivation: Analysis of objects and events in a manner that considers issues of physical or motivational causation, or discussion linking objects to broader taxonomic categories.

Cognition: Talk about how one came to know something or degree of certainty of knowing.

Language: Discussion of the meanings or words, talk about language as a system (e.g., "I speak English"), talk about special features of language (e.g., rhymes, puns).

Non-present actions or objects: Comments or questions referring to objects, pictures, people not present or talk about pretend actions, habitual actions and past actions not in narrative form; (note: narrative codes take priority over this code).

Future: Discussion of events that are about to happen (e.g., upcoming activity) and more distant future actions.

Narrative: Personal narratives (i.e., description of action occurring prior to the school day being coded that involves the speaker) and second-hand narratives (i.e., sequences of action observed or read about but in which the speaker did not participate directly).

Preschool knowledge: Reference to concepts common to preschool curricula such as color, locative adjectives (e.g., over, under) and size relationship.

Symbols/books: Reference to books or their content, print and numbers, or engaging in routines involving letters or numbers (e.g., counting).

Other: Talk used to manage the interaction, responses filling required slots in turn-taking exchanges but which lack specific semantic content (e.g., echoing the prior speaker, exclamations), and unintelligible utterances.

Speech Act Coding

Direct Control: Explicit statement of disapproval of actions, command hearer to do something or use specified words, warn or threaten hearer, or direct hearer's attention to an object or person.

Indirect control: Suggest actions, use indirect devices such as rhetorical questions, irony, sarcasm or teasing to get hearer to comply with wishes.

Negotiation of control: Agree or promise to do something, ask or grant permission, or resist efforts of other to get speaker to do some action.

Warm Engagement: Show attention to hearers without any particular semantic contribution, indicate approval of hearer or demonstrate affection, offer help, use humor, or use politeness formula (e.g., thank you).

Informative engagement: Explain or justify actions, teach hearer how to carry out act, inform hearer of some fact about the physical or social world.

Real question: Request information thought to be known by the person being questioned.

Test question or response: Determine whether the hearer knows information that is known to the speaker, or a response to a test question.
Non-present: Statements uttered while pretending, requests to join in pretending, speculative statements, or planning future actions.

Topic Development Coding

Statements and questions all coded as initiating or extending topics, as responses to questions, as maintaining interaction, or as failure to response to the prior response.
Open-ended question/response: Questions with many possible responses asked in an effort to gain information, or responses to such questions.
Close-ended question/response: Questions with only one or two possible answers (yes/no questions, choice questions with limited possible responses), or responses to such questions.
Clarifying Question: Question contingent on previous utterance that seeks clarification of some part of it.
Maintaining: Repetition or echoing of prior utterance or showing attentiveness without developing the topic.
Other: Unintelligible, gaining the hearer's attention, or no identifiable function.

REFERENCES

Allen, J., & Mason, J. (1989). *Risk makers, risk takers, risk breakers.* Portsmouth, NH: Heinemann.
Anderson, A. B., & Stokes, S. J. (1984). Social and institutional influences on the development and practice of literacy. In H. Goleman & A. Oberg (Eds.), *Awakening to literacy* (pp. 24–37). Portsmouth, NH: Heinemann.
Anderson, R. C., Wilson, P. T., & Fielding, L. G. (1988). Growth in reading and how children spend their time outside of school. *Reading Research Quarterly, 23,* 285–303.
Bissex, G. L. (1980). *GNYS at WRK.* Cambridge, MA: Harvard University Press.
Brown, M. H., Cromer, P. S., & Weinberg, S. H. (1986). Shared book experiences in kindergarten: Helping children come to literacy. *Early Childhood Research Quarterly, 1,* 397–405.
Cazden, C. B. (1986). Classroom discourse. In M. C. Wittrock (Ed.), *Handbook of research on teaching* (3rd ed.) (pp. 432–463). New York: MacMillan.
Cazden, C. B. (1988). *Classroom discourse: The language of teaching and learning.* Portsmouth, NH: Heinemann.

Cazden, C. B. (1989, March). Vygotsky and Bakhtin: From word to utterance and voice. In E. Forman (Chair), *Extending Vygoskian theory*. Symposium conducted at the annual meeting of the American Education Research Association, San Francisco, CA.

Chafe, W. L. (1982). Integration and involvement in speaking, writing, and oral literature. In D. Tannen (Ed.), *Spoken and written language: Exploring orality and literacy* (pp. 35–53). Norwood, NJ: Ablex.

Chall, J. S. (1983). *Stages of reading development*. New York: McGraw-Hill.

Cochran-Smith, M. (1984). *The making of a reader*. Norwood, NJ: Ablex.

Cummins, J. (1983). Language proficiency and academic achievement. In J. Oller (Ed.), *Current issues in language testing research* (pp. 230–283). Rowley, MA: Newburg House.

Damon, W., & Phelps, E. (in press). Peer collaboration as a context for cognitive growth. In S. Strauss & L. Lands (Eds.), *Culture, cognition, and schooling*. Hillsdale, NJ: Lawrence Erlbaum Associates.

Davidson, R., Kline, S., & Snow, C. (1986). Definitions and definite noun phrases: Indicators of children's decontextualized language skills. *Journal of Research in Childhood Education, 1*, 37–48.

De Hirsch, K., Jansky, J. J., & Langford, W. S. (1966). *Predicting reading failure*. New York: Harper & Row.

Denny, P. (in press). Rational thought in oral culture and literate decontextualization. In D. R. Olson & N. Torrance (Eds.), *Literacy orality & mentality*. New York: Cambridge University Press.

Dickinson, D. K. (in press). An environmental approach to informal evaluation in preschool. *Linguistics in Education*.

Dickinson, D. K. (1987). Oral language, literacy skills and response to literature. In J. Squire (Ed.), *The dynamics of language learning: Research in the language arts* (pp. 147–183). Urbana, IL: National Council of Teachers of English.

Dickinson, D. K. (1989). Effects of a shared reading program on a Head Start language and literacy environment. In J. Allen & J. Mason (Eds.), *Risk makers, risk takers, risk breakers* (pp. 125–153). Portsmouth, NH: Heinemann.

Dickinson, D. K., & Keebler, R. (1989). Variation in preschool teacher's style of reading books. *Discourse Processes, 12*(3), 353–376.

Dickinson, D. K. (1990a). Implications for organizing an appropriate language program. In E. Tittnich, L. A. Bloom, R. Schomburg & S. F. Szekeres (Eds.), *Facilitating children's language: Handbook for child-related professionals* (pp. 59–66). Binghamton, NY: Haworth.

Dickinson, D. K. (1990b). Review of relevant research: Long-term effects of facilitating oral language development. In E. Tittnich, L. A. Bloom, R. Schomburg, & S. F. Szekeres (Eds.), *Facilitating children's language: Handbook for child-related professionals* (pp. 35–54). NY: Haworth.

Dyson, A. H. (1984). Emerging alphabetic literacy in school contexts: Toward defining the gap between school curriculum and child mind. *Written Communication, 1*, 5–55.

Dyson, A. H. (in press). Learning to write/learning to do school: Emergent writers' interpretation of school literacy tasks. *Reading Research Quarterly.*

Ehri, L. C. (1985). Effects of printed language acquisition on speech. In D. R. Olson, N. Torrance, & A. Hildyard (Eds.), *Literacy, language, and Learning* (pp. 333–367). New York: Cambridge University Press.

Elley, W. B., & Mangubhai, F. (1983). The impact of reading on second language learning. *Reading Research Quarterly, 29,* 53–67.

Emerson, C. (1983). Bakhtin and Vygotsky on internalization of language. *Quarterly Newsletter of the Laboratory of Comparative Human Cognition, 5,* 9–13.

Erickson, F. (1984). School literacy, reasoning and civility: An anthropologist's perspective. *Review of Educational Research, 54,* 525–546.

Feagans, L., & Short, E. J. (1984). Developmental differences in the comprehension and production of narratives by reading disabled and normally achieving children. *Child Development, 55,* 1727–1736.

Feagans, L., & Short, E. J. (1986). Referential communication and reading performance in learning disabled children over a three year period. *Developmental Psychology, 22,* 177–183.

Feitelson, D., Kita, B., & Goldstein, Z. (1986). Effects of listening to series stories on first graders' comprehension and use of language. *Research in the Teaching of English, 20,* 339–356.

Feldman, C. F. (in press). Oral metalanguage. In D. R. Olson & N. Torrance (Eds.), *Literacy, orality and mentality.* New York: Cambridge University Press.

Ferreiro, E., & Teberosky, A. (1982). *Literacy before schooling.* Portsmouth, NH: Heinemann.

Forman, E. A., & Cazden, C. B. (1985). Exploring Vygotskian perspectives in education: The cognitive value of peer interaction. In J. V. Wertsch (Ed.), *Culture, communication and cognition: Vygotskian perspectives* (pp. 323–347). New York: Cambridge University Press.

Gee, J. P. (1987, March). *What is literacy?* Paper presented at Mailman Family Foundation Conference on Families and Literacy, Harvard Graduate School of Education.

Gee, J. P. (1985). The narrativization of experience. *Journal of Education, 167,* 9–35.

Goldfield, B. A., & Snow, C. E. (1984). Reading books with children: The mechanics of parental influence on children's reading achievement. In J. Flood (Ed.), *Understanding reading comprehension* (pp. 204–218). Newark, DE: International Reading Association.

Goody, J., & Watt, I. P. (1962/3). The consequences of literacy. *Comparative Studies in Society and History, 5,* 304–345.

Goody, J. (1977). *The domestication of the savage mind.* New York: Cambridge University Press.

Graybeal, C. M. (1981). Memory for stories in language-impaired children. *Applied Psycholinguistics, 2,* 269–283.

Groff, P. (1978). Children's oral language and their written composition. *Elementary School Journal, 78,* 181–191.

Hammill, D. D., & McNutt, G. (1980). Language abilities and reading: A review of the literature on their relationship. *Elementary School Journal, 80,* 269–277.

Harste, J. C., Woodward, V. A., & Burke, C. L. (1984). *Language stories and literacy lessons.* Portsmouth, NH: Heineman.

Heath, S. B. (1983). *Ways with words: Language, life, and work in communities and classrooms.* New York: Cambridge University Press.

Heath, S. B. (1986). Separating "things of the imagination" from life: Learning to read and write. In W. H. Teale & E. Sulzby (Eds.), *Emergent literacy: Writing and reading* (pp. 156–172). Norwood, NJ: Ablex.

Holdaway, D. (1979). *The foundations of literacy.* Portsmouth, NH: Heinemann.

Holquist, M. (1983). The politics of representation. *The Quarterly Newsletter of the Laboratory of Comparative Human Cognition, 5,* 2–9.

Innocenti, M. S., Stowitschek, J. J., Rule, S., Killoran, J., Striefel, S., & Boswell, C. (1986). A naturalistic study of the relation between pre-school setting events and peer interaction in four activity contexts. *Early Childhood Research Quarterly, 1,* 141–154.

Lartz, M. N., & Mason, J. (1988). Jamie: One child's journey from oral to written language. *Early Childhood Research Quarterly, 3,* 193–208.

Levy, A. K., Schaefer, L., & Phelps, P. C. (1986). Increasing pre-school effectiveness: Enhancing the language abilities of 3- and 4-year old children through planned sociodramatic play. *Early Childhood Research Quarterly, 1,* 133–140.

Loughlin, C. E., & Martin, M. D. (1987). *Supporting literacy: Developing effective learning environments.* New York: Teachers College Press.

Mason, J. M. (1980). When do children begin to read: An exploration of four-year-old children's letter and word reading competencies. *Reading Research Quarterly, 15,* 203–226.

Mason, J. M., & Allen, J. (1986). A review of emergent literacy with implications for research and practice in reading. In C. Z. Rothkopf (Ed.), *Review of research in education* (Vol. 13, pp. 3–48). Washington, DC: American Educational Research Association.

Mason, J. M. (in press). Reading stories to preliterate children: A Proposed connection to reading. In P. Gough (Ed.), *Reading Acquisition.* Hillsdale, NJ: Lawrence Erlbaum Associates.

McCartney, K. (1984). Effect of quality of day care environment on children's language development. *Developmental Psychology, 20,* 244–260.

McCormick, C. E., & Mason, J. M. (1989). Fostering reading for Head Start children with Little Books. In J. Allen & J. M. Mason (Eds.), *Risk makers, risk takers, risk breakers* (pp. 154–157). Portsmouth, NH: Heinemann.

MacWhinney, B., & Snow, C. E. (1985). The child language data exchange system. *Journal of Child Language, 12,* 271–295.

Michaels, S. (1985). Hearing connections in children's oral and written discourse. *Journal of Education, 167,* 36–56.

Morrow, L. M. (1989). *Literacy development in the early years.* Englewood Cliffs, NJ: Prentice-Hall.

Ogbu, J. U. (1988). Cultural diversity and human development. In D. T. Slaughter (Ed.), *Black children and poverty: A developmental perspective* (pp. 11–28). San Francisco: Jossey-Bass.

Olson, D. (1977). From utterance to text: The bias of language in speech and writing. *Harvard Educational Review, 47*, 257–281.

Olson, D. R. (1984). "See! Jumping!" Some oral antecedents of literacy. In H. Goelman, A. Oberg, & F. Smith (Eds.), *Awakening to literacy* (pp. 185–192). Portsmouth, NH: Heinemann.

Olson, D. R. (1986). The cognitive consequences of literacy. *Canadian Psychology, 27*, 109–121.

Pappas, C., & Brown, E. (1987a). Learning to read by reading: Learning how to extend the functional potential of language. *Research in the Teaching of English, 21*, 160–184.

Pappas, C. C., & Brown, E. (1987b). Young Children learning story discourse: Three case studies. *Elementary School Journal, 4*, 455–466.

Pattison, R. (1982). *On Literacy: The politics of the word from Homer to the Age of Rock.* New York: Oxford University Press.

Pratt, M. W., Kerig, P., Cowan, P. A. & Cowan, C. P. (1988). Mothers and fathers teaching 3-year-olds: Authoritative parenting and adult scaffolding of young children's learning. *Developmental Psychology, 24*, 832–839.

Pellegrini, A. D. (1980). The relationship between kindergartners' play and achievement in prereading, language, and writing. *Psychology in the Schools, 17*, 530–535.

Pellegrini, A. D. (1984). The effects of dramatic play on children's generation of cohesive text. *Discourse Processes, 1*, 57–67.

Purcell-Gates, V. (1988). Lexical and syntactic knowledge of written narrative held by well-read-to kindergarteners and second graders. *Research in the Teaching of English, 22*, 128–160.

Roth, F., & Spekman, N. (1986). Narrative discourse: Spontaneously generated stories of learning-disabled and normally achieving students. *Journal of Speech and Hearing Disorders, 51*, 8–23.

Scollon, R., & Scollon, S. (1981) *Narrative, literacy and face in interethnic communication.* Norwood, NJ: Ablex.

Scribner, S., & Cole, M. (1981). *The psychology of literacy.* Cambridge, MA: Harvard University Press.

Snow, C. E. (1983). Literacy and language: Relationships during the preschool years. *Harvard Educational Review, 53*, 165–189.

Snow, C. E. (1987). Beyond conversation: Second language learners' acquisition of description and explanation. In J. Lantolf & A. Labarca (Eds.), *Research in second language learning: Focus on the classroom* (pp. 1–20). Hillsdale, NJ: Lawrence Erlbaum Associates.

Snow, C. E., Barnes, W., Chandler, J., Goodman, I., & Hemphill, L. (in press). *Unfulfilled expectations: Home and school influences on literacy.* Cambridge, MA: Harvard University Press.

Snow, C. E. & Dickinson, D. K. (in press a). Skills that aren't basic in a new conception of literacy. In A. Purves & E. Jennings (Eds.), *Literate systems and individual lives: Perspectives on literacy and schooling.* Albany, NY: SUNY Press.

Snow, C. E. & Dickinson, D. K. (in press b). Social sources of narrative skills at home and at school. *First Language.*

Snow, C., & Goldfield, B. (1982). Building stories: The emergence of information structures from conversation. In D. Tannen (Ed.), *Analyzing discourse: Talk and text* (pp. 31–74). Washington, DC: Georgetown University Press.

Snow, C. E., & Ninio, A. (1986). The contracts of literacy: What children learn from learning to read books. In W. H. Teale & E. Sulzby (Eds.), *Emergent literacy: Writing and reading* (pp. 116–138). Norwood, NJ: Ablex.

Street, B. V. (1984). *Literacy in theory and practice.* New York: Cambridge University Press.

Sulzby, E. (1985). Children's emergent reading of favorite storybooks: A developmental study. *Reading Research Quarterly. 20,* 458–481.

Sulzby, E. (1986). Writing and reading: Signs of oral and written language organization in the young child. In W. H. Teale & E. Sulzby (Eds.), *Emergent literacy: Writing and reading* (pp. 50–89). Norwood, NJ: Ablex.

Sulzby, E. (in press). Children's development of prosodic distinctions in telling and dictation modes. In A. Matsuhashi (Ed.), *Writing in real time: Modelling production processes.* New York: Longman.

Tannen, D. (1982). Oral and literate strategies in spoken and written narrative. *Language, 58,* 1–21.

Tannen, D. (1984). *Conversational style: Analyzing talk among friends.* Norwood, NJ: Ablex.

Taylor, D. (1983). *Family literacy: Young children learning to read and write.* Portsmouth, NH: Heinemann.

Teale, W. H. (1984). Reading to young children: Its significance for literacy development. In H. Goelman, A. Oberg, & F. Smith (Eds.), *Awakening to literacy* (pp. 110–121). Portsmouth, NH: Heinemann.

Teale, W. H. (1986). Home background and young children's literacy development. In W. H. Teale & E. Sulzby (Eds.), *Emergent literacy: Writing and reading* (pp. 173–206). Norwood, NJ: Ablex.

Teale, W. H., & Martinez, M. (1986). Teachers' storybook reading styles: Evidence and implications. *Reading Education in Texas, 2,* 7–16.

Teale, W. H., & Sulzby, E. (1986). Introduction: Emergent literacy as a perspective for examining how young children become writers and readers. In W. Teale & E. Sulzby (Eds.), *Emergent literacy: Writing and reading* (pp. VII–XXV). Norwood, NJ: Ablex.

Tizard, B., & Hughes, M. (1984). *Young children learning.* Cambridge, MA: Harvard University Press.

Torrance, N., & Olson, D. R. (1984). Oral Language competence and the acquisition of literacy. In A. Pellegrini & T. Yawkey (Eds.), *The development of oral and written language in social contexts* (pp. 167–181). Norwood, NJ: Ablex.

Torrance, N., & Olson, D. R. (1985). Oral and literate competencies in the early school years. In D. R. Olson, N. Torrance, & A. Hildyard (Eds.),

Literacy and language learning (pp. 256–284). New York: Cambridge University Press.

Vygotsky, L. S. (1962). *Thought and language.* Cambridge, MA: MIT Press.

Vygotsky, L. S. (1978). *Mind in society: The development of higher psychological processes.* Cambridge, MA: Harvard University Press.

Wadsworth, M. E. J. (1986). Effects of parenting style and pre-school experience on children's later verbal attainment: Results of a British longitudinal study. *Early Childhood Research Quarterly, 1,* 237–248.

Weaver, P. A. & Dickinson, D. K. (1982). Scratching below the surface structure: Exploring the usefulness of story grammars. *Discourse Processes, 5,* 225–243.

Wells, G. (1985). *Language development in the pre-school years.* New York: Cambridge University Press.

Wertsch, J., & Stone, C. A. (1985). The concept of internalization in Vygotsky's account of the genesis of higher mental functions. In J. V. Wertsch (Ed.), *Culture, communication and cognition: Vygotskian perspectives* (pp. 162–182). New York: Cambridge University Press.

Whitehurst, G. J., Falco, F. L., Lonigan, C. J, Fischel, J. E., DeBaryshe, B. D., Valdez-Menchaca, M. C., & Caulfield, M. (1988). Accelerating language development through picture book reading. *Developmental Psychology, 24,* 552–559.

CHAPTER 8

The Dismantling of Narrative

Sarah Michaels
The Literacies Institute

In some form or another, each of the other chapters in this book deals with the *development* of narrative structures. In this chapter, I want to suggest that much of what goes on in urban, public school settings promotes the *dismantling*[1] or breaking down of narrative performance and artistry—in favor of alternative forms of meaning making deemed more scientific, rigorous, reliable, intelligent, or important.

Elaborated narrative (both oral story telling and personal story writing) is a restricted genre in most U.S. classrooms, decreasing inversely with grade level. And from the early grades on, the narrative discourse that *is* tolerated is often shaped by teachers and instructional activities into a simplified, homogenized form (Michaels, 1985).

The process of dismantling narrative development is, in my view, a central part of what it means to become literate in school, to acquire the forms of discourse—description, explanation, and justification—that get accorded a privileged status in school and other institutions of power in this society. If this is so, there is a pressing need for more systematic studies of narrative abilities and opportunities in school settings. In this chapter, I want to explore the processes by which

[1] By *dismantling*, I mean not an analytic separating and taking apart of individual skills or strategies. Rather I use the word to suggest the destruction or suppression of a particular narrative style in toto, because it is deemed inappropriate or incoherent, and hence is not tolerated by teachers in official school speaking or writing activities. In the second part of the chapter, I look specifically at what kind of narrative *is* tolerated and shaped by teachers.

narrative discourse tends to get homogenized or suppressed in grade school, and to explore the relationships among narrative discourse, school activities, and literacy.

I am not the first to notice the relationship between narrative dismantling (or suppression) and schooling. In a paper called "Narrative Thinking and Storytelling Rights: A Folklorist's Clue to a Critique of Education," Hymes & Cazden (1980) engage in something of a dialogue (grounded in a series of narratives) on the topic of narrative rights and the privileging of nonnarrative discourse in school. Hymes suggests that "one form of inequality of opportunity in our society has to do with rights to use narrative, with whose narratives are admitted to have a cognitive function" (p. 126). In her piece of the dialogue, Cazden gives several examples of the use and perception of narrative versus nonnarrative alternatives among Harvard graduate and undergraduate students; Hymes comments:

> Certainly the students at Harvard that Cazden discusses are being encouraged to repress or abandon personal narrative in certain settings and roles. Very likely something similar happens in many schools at many levels of education. The student or child is told in effect that his or her own experiences do not have weight (except perhaps as diversion). Not that there is not an essential purpose to going beyond individual experiences. But if . . . narrative of individual experience is a complementary mode of solution of cognitive questions, then a pattern of discouraging it is a pattern of systematically discouraging what is at least a valid starting point, and may be an essential means of thought. (pp. 131–132)

Hymes goes on to make strong conjectures about the privileging of nonnarrative forms of meaning making at the expense of home or peer-group-based narrative forms, suggesting:

> Perhaps some of the decline in education in the country is connected with this suppression of the narrative function. . . . Students may come from homes in which narrative is an important way of communicating knowledge. They may take part in peer groups in which experience and insight is shared through exchange of narrative. A classroom that excludes narratives may be attempting to teach them both new subject matter and a new mode of learning, perhaps without fully realizing it. (p. 132)

Finally, Hymes indirectly links the acquisition of new forms of discourse with ways of valuing and acting, suggesting that the devaluing, suppression, or what I call the dismantling of narrative in school has both cognitive and political repercussions, pointing to "a major dilemma in our society." He notes:

> Success in technical, professional fields is defined in such a way that someone cannot both stay at home, or return there, to serve, and feel successful. This is a major problem for persons with strong ties to their communities of origin. . . . One needs advanced training in order to be competent, to be able to cope with problems faced by the community of origin, but the advanced training embodies a message of on, upward, and away. Perhaps the fundamental failing of higher education in the United States is to educate for status and not for service. Or to define service without regard to considerations of locality, so that local is inevitably seen as lesser. Perhaps the treatment of personal narrative in educational settings plays a part in all this. (p. 133)

METHODOLOGICAL CONSIDERATIONS

One hears a great deal about the ideological nature of schooling, but we rarely see actual analyses of how political or ideological factors play themselves out in learning to produce oral and written texts in classrooms. To a large extent, this is because there are few good methodologies for linking up broad-based social-structural issues with narrowly linguistic phenomena in a developmental framework. In thinking about literate oral or written language in school, we tend to break apart the phenomenon and focus our attention on isolated aspects, such as (a) the textual component—the texts students produce (analyzing errors or linguistic complexity); (b) individual, cognitive mechanisms—such as a student's composing process (reviewing and planning strategies); or (c) the social and institutional setting—as in ethnographic studies of general patterns and practices, norms, and values attached to writing or speaking in classrooms—often ignoring the linguistic properties of the texts that get produced. Breaking apart the phenomenon makes it simpler to study and there is much of value that has come out of work in each of these areas. However, I would argue that ignoring the complex interrelations between the individual, social, and textual, creates fundamental obstacles to understanding the development and deployment of oral and written discourse in school.

This chapter is an attempt to lay out a more general theoretical and methodological approach to the study of literacy development in school settings by focusing on the use, shaping, and evaluation of narrative in young students' oral and written discourse. The goal is to study the relationship between the public, standard discourse of the classroom and the personal, individual voice of the learner. In particular, I am concerned with how learning to merge public signs (or forms of discourse) with private meanings is accomplished in the production of oral and written texts in schools.

Narrative discourse in the texts of children can be seen as a kind of tracer—a readily identifiable form of discourse (Labov, 1972) that can be spotted and studied as it gets transformed. But the focus on narrative is more than methodologically driven. As the piece by Hymes & Cazden (1980) suggests, "Narrative forms of thinking are inescapably fundamental in human life." (p. 131) Moreover, they are well developed in even very young school-age children and reflect the traditions of meaning making through talk that one develops in the family and community (Smitherman, 1977). In charting occurrences of narrative discourse and its transformation in school, we can see the ways that home and school worlds connect, mingle, or conflict. We can also see, over time, how certain forms of discourse, certain ways of making and displaying meaning, often nonnarrative in nature, come to be privileged, promoted, and "taken" into children's talk and writing. How this privileging and concurrent narrative dismantling occurs and how students come to or fail to control new forms of discourse is examined through actual studies of classroom interaction.

To magnify the complexity of an already complex problem, it is undeniable that schools differ widely with respect to institutionalized discourse norms and practices. Classrooms, moreover, even within the same school, differ widely as learning environments and discourse communities. So at one and the same time we need to be able to talk generally about the discourse of schooling but always bear in mind the importance of sociocultural and sociolinguistic variability across settings. Public discourse is inevitably community, context, and activity specific.

Nonetheless, inherent in school speaking or writing activities is an often implicit contradiction—that language is an expression of an individual student's voice, but a voice that is significantly constrained by the narrowly defined community and school-based standards of what counts as literate discourse. That is, if students are to be evaluated as competent speakers, thinkers, or writers, they must come to control, or "take," the school-based norms and discourse forms into their own texts.

I explore the issues of narrative display and transformation in the context of both oral and written discourse activities in classrooms. Harvey Sacks suggested that stories are "sequenced objects articulating with the context in which they were told" (Jefferson, 1978, citing Sack's lectures on stories), that is, significantly influenced by the larger speech event in which they were embedded. I focus on contrastive analyses of "Sharing Time" in first- and second-grade classrooms and composition writing activities in sixth-grade classrooms. The sharing time turns were recorded as part of year-long studies of sharing time activities in Berkeley, California and in Boston-area first- and second-grade urban classrooms—in which I looked at sharing time as a kind of "oral preparation for literacy." (See Michaels, 1981 and Michaels & Cazden, 1986, for detailed descriptions of these studies.) The writing and conferencing activities were recorded as part of a three-year study of computers used for writing in urban sixth-grade classrooms in the Boston area (see Michaels & Bruce, 1989 and Watson-Gegeo, Cohen, Strucker, & Craig, 1987 for detailed descriptions of this work.)

I view these contrasting oral and written activities as analogues of each other. In the case of sharing time, the goal is for the child to produce an oral narrative or descriptive account in front of the class, describing an object brought from home or a recent past experience. The teacher plays an active role as primary listener, asking questions and probing for elaboration or clarification. In the case of composition writing, the goal is for the child to produce a written text through a series of drafts. Through group discussions or conferences with the teacher, the student is expected to edit and revise the text. In both cases, the student is called on to create a monologue of a sort—a turn, or a first draft—followed by a dialogic exchange between teacher and child. Through questions, comments, suggestions, and so forth, the teacher seeks to expand, clarify, or alter the text—in accordance with the teacher's own, often implicit, expectations about what counts as an appropriate or successful text. In both kinds of activities, across a range of classrooms and grade levels, I have found that teachers tend to interpret and evaluate student discourse against a narrowly defined literate standard. And in both cases, the teacher's comments, questions, or alterations on the student's text serve as a public ratification or privileging of certain forms of discourse, certain text structures, which, like stories, articulate with the larger, recurring classroom speech events. I am concerned here with the process and results of these activities in which students' narrative and nonnarrative discourse is elicited, shaped, and evaluated. In each domain, I examine the discourse activities generally, and then follow a single student's discourse productions over time.

In thinking about what it means to "take" from the social, public realm of discourse in the production of text, I have adopted a Vygotskian theoretical framework, suggesting that development moves from the social to the individual plane—or, as it is often said, from the interpsychological to the intrapsychological. Interestingly, writing development, in Vygotsky's view, stands as the parallel/opposite extreme of inner speech—one being maximally reduced and internal, the other being maximally external. And yet, just as inner speech has a social genesis, so too does writing. Learning to write is a process whereby public signs or forms of discourse are appropriated or internalized by the individual. The difference is their endpoint and function—one inwardly directed, the other public and typically outwardly directed. In this sense, both sharing time accounts and written compositions are public texts and public performances.

In studying the development of thinking, Vygotsky (1986) argued that it was critical to find a unit of analysis that was an irreducible intersection of the social and the individual—for him it was the word. Moreover, in studying the development of concepts (words), he argued that we must look at the process rather than the product of development. I suggest that this framework is well suited to the study of discourse development as well. In this case, the appropriate unit of analysis is the text (at one and the same time embodying both public and personal meanings). And to study development, we need ways of analyzing text—not as a static product, but as a dynamic, evolving process. To this end, I propose to carry out a kind of Vygotskian genetic analysis of oral and written text development as a way of studying the process of the dismantling of narrative in school.

My overarching questions in this chapter are: How do students take from the social world (in this case, the public discourse of the classroom) in constructing text? How does this differ in oral discourse activities such as sharing time versus composition writing activities? And, what relationship does this "taking of text" bear to narrative development and the acquisition of literacy?

SHARING TIME

Sharing time (sometimes called "Show & Tell" or "Newstime") is a common oral language activity in early elementary school classrooms throughout the country. It is typically thought of by teachers as a noninstructional activity where children are encouraged to talk freely in front of their classmates about an object brought from home or to give a narrative account about some recent personal experience. However, my research on sharing time (in collaboration with Courtney Cazden) in a range of classroom settings has documented that a great deal of implicit literacy-related instruction actually occurs (Michaels & Cazden, 1986). Teachers typically play an active role at sharing time, interjecting questions and comments that attempt to clarify and extend the child's original contributions. Teachers will frequently prompt children to be lexically explicit, saying, "What's that called?", even when it is obvious to everyone in the audience what the object is. They often ask students not to assume shared background knowledge on the part of the audience, and to put all the meaning into words. For example, a first-grade child had brought in two candles she had made at day camp. After describing them, the teacher said:

Example 1:

Teacher:	That's neat-o. Tell the kids how you did it from the very start. Pretend we don't know a thing about candles.
Child:	[No response]
Teacher:	OK, what did you do first? What did you use? Flour?

The child was then able to build on the teacher's base and give a detailed account of the materials and procedure involved in candle making. In another case, a child had brought in a Tom and Jerry board game to show the class. The teacher asked him to explain to everyone how you played it. The child immediately began to open up the game saying, "Well, see . . . ," whereupon the teacher said, "Don't show us. TELL us how to play. Pretend we're all blind and can't see the game."

These and other recurring comments suggest that teachers are looking for a certain kind of narrative account, with literate-like characteristics, closer to simple descriptive prose. For this reason, I have come to view sharing time as a kind of "oral preparation for literacy." But this oral preparation turns out to be far more successful with some children than with others. Children from different backgrounds come to school with very different ways of telling narratives that reflect divergent ethnically based narrative traditions. At sharing time, some of these "ways of sharing" (giving narrative and descriptive accounts) match teachers' implicit expectations better than others. That is, some narratives are easier for teachers to deal with than others.

For example, there are striking differences between the sharing time narrative styles of middle-class white children and Black working-class children—findings that have been replicated in urban classrooms in different regions of the country. Middle-class white children tend to tell short, concise accounts about a single time and place with a marked beginning, middle, and end, a kind of sharing time style that has been called *topic-centered.* These children often use a noticeable, exaggerated rising intonation contour in setting the scene and marking continuity in the setting and action, which gives the discourse a distinctive sing-song quality. Teachers typically know just what the child is getting at and have no trouble asking questions at the appropriate time and level—even when the child's discourse is somewhat imprecise and inexplicit to begin with. The following is an example of a topic-centered turn, full of fuzzy references, and yet "hearable" by the teacher as a simple story with a focus and a point. The rising arrows indicate sharing time intonation.

Example 2:

Carl: Well / last night / my father / was at work /
he / every Thursday night they have this thing /
that everybody has this dollar /
and it makes up to a hundred dollars /
and my / and you've gotta pick this name out /
and my father's name got picked /
so he won a thousand dollars // a hundred dollars //

Teacher: Tell us what he's gonna do with it // . . .[2]

In contrast, working-class Black children (and particularly Black girls) tend to use a very different narrative style, which typically results in the juxtaposition of several concrete anecdotes all thematically linked

[2] The notations I have used in transcribing speech were developed by John Gumperz (1976) and his collaborators, based on the work of John Trim. In some of the transcripts in this chapter, to make for greater readability, I have used a considerably simplified version of the notation. In all cases, speech is chunked into tone group units (i.e., segments with a continuous intonational contour). These units are then designated as minor tone groups (signalling "more to come," akin to a comma—indicated as "/") or major tone groups (ending with some indication of utterance closure, akin to a period in writing—indicated as "//"). Sharing intonation is indicated with rising arrows or extended rising and falling lines over an entire word or phrase. In later examples of Deena's narratives, more prosodic details are included in the transcript as follows. Within a tone group, several features are indicated: (1) location of the nuclei (i.e., the syllable or syllables marked by change in pitch): " " low fall, " " high fall, " " low rise, " " high rise; (2) other accented syllables in the tone group, " " high, " " low, " " level; (3) paralinguistic features such as (a) shift to a high pitch register " " or shift to low pitch register " " (both applying to the entire tone group), (b) pausing: ".." indicating a break in timing and ". . ." indicating a measurable pause, (c) speech rate: "acc." indicating accelerating tempo and "ret." indicating slowing down, (d) loudness over an entire tone group is indicated by "p" (soft) or "f" (loud). Doubling of one of the symbols indicates extra emphasis.In later transcripts where a teacher is conferencing with a student over a written text, the teacher's utterances are capitalized when she is reading (outloud) from the student's draft.

to make an implicit point. This *episodic* or *topic-associating* discourse tends to be longer and always includes shifts in time, place, and key characters.

For teachers expecting topic-centered discourse, this style is often hard to understand. When asked to comment on these narratives, teachers frequently describe them as "rambling," "unplanned," "skipping from one thing to the next," and as "having no beginning, middle, and end," that is, no point. The children who talk this way are often evaluated as not taking the time to think in advance about what they want to say, and hence are often judged as simply talking "on and on just to hear their own voice." Careful analysis has shown that these turns do indeed have a point, and the stories are often highly sophisticated in their display of devices, which in literary texts would be admired, such as syntactic parallelism, repetition, word play, and structural symmetry. Shifts in episodes are invariably marked by rhythm, temporal markers, and intonation, but the listener must infer the point from understanding the unstated thematic links. These children also use exaggerated sharing intonation, but it serves a different rhetorical function. Typically it is used not to mark continuity, but to highlight discontinuity, marking the separation of narrative segments and a shift in temporal orientation, location, or focus. To illustrate, I have selected a story told by a second-grade girl. It is shorter than most episodic narratives, but does display the characteristic features. (In the transcript, I have skipped a line between narrative segments. Colons indicate vowel elongation; dots indicate pausing; slashes indicate intonational phrases or breath groups.)

Example 3:

1. Leona: On George Washington's birthday /
2. I'm goin' / ice: / my gra:ndmother /
3. we never / haven't seen her since a long ti:me /
4. and / . . . and she lives right (n) nea:r u:s /
5. and / . . . she: / and she's gonna /
6. I'm gonna spend the night over her house //

7. and / . . every weekend / she comes to take me /
8. like on Saturdays and Sundays / awa:y /from ho:me/
9. and I spend the night over her house /

10. and one day I spoi:led her di:nner /
11. . . um and we was having um / we was / um
12. she paid ten dollars /

13. and I got eggs / . . . and stuff /
14. and I didn't even eat anything //

The structure and thematic development may not be obvious from simply reading the transcript, so it is worth saying a bit about how Leona makes meaning in her sharing time story. She begins with a time marker ("On George Washington's birthday") and a future-tense orientation, using sharing intonation tempo and contours. She marks the end of this segment with increased tempo in line 6, "I'm gonna spend the night over her house." The second segment begins with a shift in time from the future, to the iterative "and every weekend," with a resumption of sharing intonation, tempo, and contours. This segment too ends with increased tempo in line 9, a lexical and prosodic repetition of line 6. Played side by side, these two phrases are indistinguishable, an implicit signal of the association across these segments. What they have in common is the fact that on both the holiday and the weekend, Leona spends the night at her grandmother's—the implicit point being that her grandmother is an important figure in her life. The third segment shifts to a particular occasion, "one day," and shifts focus to dinner, rounding the story out to a close with a twist of humor, again highlighting the relationship with her grandmother. The closing is marked by staccato rhythm and falling tones.

In an experimental study of adult responses to children's sharing time turns, a mimicked version of Leona's grandmother story was played to Black and white adults, all graduate students at Harvard. The mimicked version maintained Leona's rhythm and intonation but changed Black dialect grammatical and phonological features to standard English. Twelve adults (five Black, seven White, all graduate students at Harvard) were asked to comment on the well-formedness of the story, and to make evaluative statements as to the probable academic success of the child telling the story. As it turned out, Black and White informants responded very differently. White adults' responses were uniformly negative: "Terrible story; incoherent," "Hard to follow," "Mixed up," "Not a story at all, in the sense of describing something that happened," "This kid hops from one thing to the next." When asked to make a judgment about her probable academic standing, they uniformly rated her below children who told topic-centered accounts, saying, for example, "This child might have trouble reading if she doesn't understand what constitutes a story." Some referred to "language problems" affecting school achievement and others suggested that "family problems" or "emotional problems" might hold this child back.

Black informants reacted very differently, finding the story well-formed, easy to understand, and interesting, "with lots of detail and description" and "real emotion." Three selected it as the best story of the five they had heard. All five commented on "shifts" or "associations" but none were thrown by them. In addition, all but one of the Black informants rated the child as highly verbal, very bright, or successful in school. One commented on her "good language skills," which should provide "good language experience for writing." Interestingly, the Black informants appreciated both the topic-centered and episodic stories, seeing differences in them, but finding both well-formed.

The results of this experiment confirm what we see repeatedly in classrooms. Where students' narrative strategies do not match the teachers' expectations for good sharing time talk, teachers' have consistent difficulties appreciating and building on the child's talk. Their questions and comments may interrupt the student or miss altogether the point the student is trying to develop. Interruptive probes as to "what happened when" often serve to cut short rather than build on the child's narrative intentions, or to help the child be lexically explicit.

I now turn to a careful look at one student's experiences at sharing time, during the course of her first-grade year. The guiding question is what the child comes to take from the oral discourse activity over time, and how it influences her narrative development.

Deena Morris (a pseudonym) was a very bright, highly verbal 6-year-old Black girl in a first-grade, Berkeley classroom, taught by a very experienced, dedicated, white middle-class teacher, Mrs. Jones (also a pseudonym). Deena lived with her mother and two sisters (one 3 years older, one 4 years younger) in a lower-working-class Black neighborhood in the Berkeley "flatlands." Her older sister had taught her to read "for fun" when she was still in kindergarten. She was as a first grader the very best reader in her class and the only Black child (in a class that was half white and half Black) who was in the high ability group for reading and math. Deena's ability group cohorts were all middle- and upper-middle-class white children, who lived in the Berkeley hills. And although these children accepted Deena, her friendship allegiances were clearly with the other Black children in the class (all low or middle ability group members). It was these children whom she ate lunch with, and played with at recess or free time. And whereas she performed similarly to her white peers in small group lessons and seat work assignments, her discourse patterns matched those of the other Black children. She consistently used topic-associating strategies at sharing time, and had consistent problems establishing conversational engagement and cooperation with Mrs. Jones during sharing time exchanges.

Sharing time in this classroom was a daily activity that took place during "Rugtime," the first large group activity of the day. Mrs. Jones sat in a chair in front of the children who sat close together on the rug. The "sharer" came up next to Mrs. Jones, who put her arm around the child. Sharing time—as in all the classrooms I have studied—was marked by the children as a ritual speech event. Children used a consistent, exaggerated intonational pattern when they talked (most pronounced at the beginning of their turns), which I have come to call "sharing intonation." In this class, the Black and white children used a slightly different contour:

White children	Black children
Y e s t e r d a y	Y e s t e r d a y

Deena was an avid, willing participant at sharing time. In fact, during the 48 recordings of sharing time made during the year, Deena shared in over 70% of them, the highest percentage of any student. There is thus a large corpus of Deena's sharing time turns to look at over time. In what follows I chart some of the influences on Deena as a sharer by looking at key sharing time turns at the beginning, middle, and end of the year.

Early in the Year

On September 20, during the second week of school, Deena shares the following account about a trip to the doctor:

Example 4:

Deena:	When I went to the—when I went to the doctors and I thought I was gonna get a shot but I didn't and / I had to uh put this thing in mouth for a long / long time //
Teacher:	What was it?
Deena:	It was a . . .
Teacher:	Did it start like this: th— What was it?
Deena:	Yeah It was a thermometer //
Teacher:	Right // What's that for Deena?
Deena:	Huh?

Teacher:	What was that for?
Peter:	Take your temp–
Teacher:	Why do you have a thermometer put in your mouth?
Child:	To take your temperature //
Teacher:	Right // What's that tell a doctor?
Child:	(. . .)
Teacher:	It tells the doctor if you're OK / if you're not too . . warm or too cool // (. . .)
Deena:	Arnd I went to / another and I went into another
Child:	or too hot //
Deena:	room / at the doctors . . and / I had to take my clothes off and put on this go:wn //
Teacher:	Uh huh // OK Deena // Thank you //

Deena here begins her turn with temporal orientation, initiating a narrative account about her experience at the doctors. Mrs. Jones's contributions, beginning just after Deena mentions having to put "this thing in my mouth," serve not to extend or develop this narrative, but rather to clarify the name, function, and purpose of thermometers. It becomes a vocabulary lesson, eliciting information for a descriptive account with no complicating action whatsoever. In this respect, it is closer to object-description show-and-tell-type discourse than to the event-oriented narrative accounting that Deena began with. Furthermore, Mrs. Jones's questions seem to throw Deena off balance so that the descriptive information that is part of this limited account ends up being supplied, not by Deena, but by other children or Mrs. Jones herself. After a series of questions from Mrs. Jones, Deena regains the floor, saying "a:nd" with a level tone and vowel elongation (overlapping the teacher and another child), and continues on with her account as if nothing had intervened, shifting settings to a different room at the doctor's office and shifting focus from the thermometer to disrobing and putting on a hospital gown. The teacher's "OK // Thank you" serves to end the turn rather abruptly. In this case, unlike the first example, Mrs. Jones does provide slots for the kind of descriptive information she is looking for, but not in a way that provides actual practice for Deena. (In contrast, Michaels, 1979 and 1981 provide contrasting cases of Mrs. Jones asking questions of white children that do provide for this kind of practice.)

One week later, Deena gives a narrative account in which she moves fluidly from topic to topic without making explicit the thematic ties connecting (or separating) the various topics.

Example 5:

MacDonalds

1.	Deena:	Um . . . I went to the beach / . . Sunday /
2.		and / to MacDonalds /
3.		and to the park /
4.		. . . and / . . I got this for my / . . birthday //
5.		. . . My mother bought it for me /
6.		. . and um / . . . I had / . . um / . . two dollars for my birthday
7.		and I put it in here /
8.		. . and I went to where my frie-nd /
9.		. . named Gi Gi /
10.		. . . I went over to my grandmother's house with her /
11.		. . . and um / . . . . . she was on my back /
12.		and I / . . and we was walkin around /
13.		. . . by my house /
14.		. . and um / . . . she was hea— —vy /
15.		She was in sixth or seventh grade //
16.	Teacher:	OK I'm going to stop you. I want you to talk
17.		about things that are really really very important.
18.		That's important to you but tell us things that are
19.		sort of different. Can you do that? And tell us what
20.		beach you went to over the weekend.
21.	Deena:	I went to um . . . um . . . ..
22.	Teacher:	Alameda Beach?
23.	Deena:	Yeah.
24.	Teacher:	That's nice there huh?
25.	Deena:	I went there two times
26.	Teacher:	That's very nice. I like it there. Thank you Deena.

Unable to appreciate that Deena was producing discourse with connections, albeit implicit ones, the teacher simply stops Deena's narrative flow altogether in order to request a specific geographical label, and abruptly and forcefully ends Deena's turn after she supplies that label—even though Deena indicates a willingness to continue (line 25). In a sense, what the teacher is glossing with the word *important* is her own implicit schema for stories. Deena is working with another quite different notion of what is important to a story.

Middle of Year

By midyear, Mrs. Jones began to use more explicit strategies to help children like Deena focus their turns better. On one occasion she modeled for all the children what kind of sharing time turn she did not want to hear, illustrating the notion of importance in a highly implicit manner. It makes sense only if one already has a topic-centered schema and uses lexicalized markers to signal why the topic is important.

Example 6:

Teacher: Anybody else have anything to share that's important? . . . I think I need to remind you / . . . just to talk about important things / . . . or show important things // Please don't tell me / um / yesterday / when I went home / I had to wipe my feet on the rug before I went in the front door //

Deena: Why? //

Heshimu: [black boy]: Mu:d! //

Teacher: I'm going to say this again // Just tell me important things // Dont tell me / yesterday / I went home // yesterday / I went home and I had to wipe my feet on the . . . mat / before I went in the front door // . . . because that is not: ——

Several children: IMPORTANT!

Teacher: Important // Is it? Is it?

Deena: I have something that / I have something to share //

Teacher: I think it should really be quite important // . . . Is it really really important Deena? //

Deena: [nods]

Mrs. Jones talked a bit more about having the kids help her decide "whether or not things are important" and not wanting kids' feelings to be hurt. Deena then enthusiastically stood up beside Mrs. Jones to share. As she began, I quite vividly recall feeling both surprised and extremely uncomfortable, because Deena appeared to be saying precisely what Mrs. Jones had said she did not want to hear.

Example 7:

Deena: After I came home / . . . from school / . . . um my mother wasn't at home and then she came . . . back / and / and / I went / I went outside / . . . and . . . um I almost fell backward 'cause / . . . 'cause this dog was chasing me . . . and this cat . . . around . . . and . . . and they almost made me fall backwards //

Peter [white boy sitting in front]: That wasn't important!

In this case, Deena's problem is not one of topic choice—dog stories were always considered an appropriate topic. As in example 4, the issue is one of discourse strategies for highlighting the "point." Deena begins with details about her mother not being home, then returning home, and Deena going outside and almost falling backward—before the dog is introduced. When the dog is introduced, it is embedded in a because clause and referred to as "this dog." In order to make this sound important to the teacher (and to children such as Peter), Deena instead would have had to begin, after setting the time and place, with a fully lexicalized introduction and description of the dog. Then the chase, the "falling backwards," and no doubt the terror that all of this inspired (but was left to be inferred by the audience) would have been heard as important. It is worth noting that this turn is an example of single-topic discourse, and as such, is evidence that Deena could indeed stick to a particular topic. However, the talk is organized in such a way (with the introduction of her mother) that it appears to deal with more than one character and topic.

Late In the Year

Late in the year, beginning in May, Mrs. Jones had begun to emphasize to the children that they should talk only about "one thing." She stressed this new "rule" especially with Deena and a few of the other Black girls. In the following example, Deena shows some signs of having "taken" from Mrs. Jones's implicit and explicit attempts to stick to descriptive accounts of simple events or objects. At the same time, the turn is evidence of misunderstanding and working at cross purposes. Deena still attempts to break into elaborated narrative and is cut short (much as she was in the very first example).

Example 8:

Coat

1. Teacher: Deena / I want you to share some- one-thing / that's very important //.
2. one / thing // from where you are // . . . is that where you are // . . .
3. is that where you were //
4. Deena: no //
5. Teacher: OK //
6. Deena: um // . . . in the su:mme:r / . . . I mean / . . . w-when um / I go back to
7. school / I come back to school / in Septe:mber / . . . I'm a ha:ve a new
8. coat / and I already got it // . . . and / . . . it's / . . . u:m / . . .(. . .)
9. got a lot of broo:wn in it // . . . a:nd / . . . when- / um / and I got it
10. ye:sterday / . . . and when . . . I saw it / my um . . my mother was . . was
11. going some . . where / when my . . when I saw it / . . . on the cou:ch / and
12. I showed my si:ster / and I was readin somethin out on . . on the ba:g
13. and my bi:g sister said(. . .)
14. Child: um close the door
15. Deena: my big sister said / Do you have to keep that away / from Keisha /
16. cause that's my baby sister / and I said no // . . . and I said the
17. plastic ba:g / . . . because / . . . um / . . . when / . . . u:m / . . sh-when the
18. um . . she was u:m (with me) / wait a minute / . . . my / cou:sin and her
19. (. . .)
20. Teacher: wait a minute // you stick with your coat now // I s-said you could tell
21. one thing // . . . that's fair //

22. Deena: this was about myc-
23. Teacher: OK all right / go on
24. Deena: this was-
25. and today / and yesterday when I . . got my coat / my cou:sin ran outsi:de /
26. and he (..) ran to tried to get him / and he / he he start- / . . . an when
27. he get in- when he got in my house / . . . he layed on the floor / and I
28. told him to ge:t up because he was cry:in //
29. Teacher: mm-what's that have to do with your coat //
30. Deena: h-he . . . becau- he wanted to go outside / but we . . couldn't // (exasperated)
31. Teacher: why //
32. Deena: cause my mo:ther s-wanted us to stay in the house //
33. Teacher: what does that have to do with your coat //
34. Deena: bec- um uh
35. Child: (whispers)
36. Deena: because / . . . . I don't know //
37. Teacher: OK // thank you very much Deena //
38. Child's: (talking)
39. Teacher: OK / do you under stand what I was trying to do // Deena / I was trying to
40. get her to stick with one / . . . thing // and she was talking about her/
41. Child's: coat //
42. Teacher: new /
43. Child's: coat //
44. Teacher: coat // it sounds nice Deena //

I discuss this example in great detail elsewhere (Michaels 1981, 1985) and comment more briefly on it here. In understanding what goes wrong between Deena and Mrs. Jones in this turn, it is important to notice several things. First of all, Deena begins her turn in line 6, with an account and description of her new coat that she will be wearing when she comes back to school in the fall. The structure of her talk here is nonnarrative, as evidenced both in her choice of tense and in her prosody (rhythmic chunking with high sustained pitches). In line 10, she shifts into a narrative account, marked by the use of "yesterday," a shift to past-tense verbs and more typical narrative prosody. In this segment, she adds the information that her "mother was goin' somewhere," and introduces her two sisters. It appears that Mrs. Jones hears the talk about the plastic bag and her sisters as related to the topic of her new coat. But in line 18, when Deena introduces her cousin, Mrs. Jones interrupts her and tells her to stick with her original topic. This begins a dialogue between Deena and Mrs. Jones, with Mrs. Jones asking several times, "What does that have to do with your coat?" and finally, in line 36, with a sigh of frustration, Deena says, "I don't know" and sits down.

Mrs. Jones, it appears, was unable to follow Deena's prosodic cues signaling a shift from preamble to narrative, and could hear no overarching connection between the coat and the anecdotal accounts of her sisters and her cousin. In an interview, Mrs. Jones indicated that she interpreted Deena's "shifts" as free associations from one topic to another, thought up on the spur of the moment so that Deena could continue talking. This impression was reinforced by Deena's inability to explain the connection between her cousin and her coat when asked explicitly to do so.

Several months later, with Deena now a second grader, I interviewed her (with both of her sisters, ages 10 and 4, present) about what she had thought of sharing time in first grade.

In the interview, Deena expressed a keen sense of frustration about being interrupted during sharing time. She saw this as an indication that the teacher was simply not interested in what she had to say, explaining:

> Deena: Sharing time got on my nerves. She was always interruptin' me sayin', "That's not important enough," and I hadn't hardly started talkin'! . . . I felt like slappin' her upside the head, . . . sayin' 'Well it's important to *me*, so you just listen when I'm talkin' to you woman!

Her older sister recalled similar frustrations from her sharing experience 5 years earlier, in both kindergarten and first grade.

In addition, during the course of the interview, I played the tape of the "coat" turn, asked her what she had meant and what she thought

Mrs. Jones's point had been in interrupting her. Deena was able to clarify and articulate many of the unstated connections in her discourse. First, when asked about the link between her baby sister and the plastic bag, her older sister chimed in saying "My mama say keep plastic out of Keisha's reach, 'cuz she might put it over her head," with which Deena quickly agreed. In addition, she explained the link between her cousin and her new coat, saying that her cousin was "a *ba:d* little boy, and when he came back in the house, he started to put his hands on my coat, . . . and his hands was *DIRTY*!!" Thus it appears that for Deena, there *was* an intended semantic link between the coat and the two subtopics in the narrative, her cousin and baby sister. In one case she was protecting a young child from the coat and in the other case, she was protecting the coat from a young, messy child. The key line in the narrative, to understand the significance of the theme highlighted by the coat, is "and my mama was goin' somewhere." The theme thus is taking care of others and oneself on one's own, which is refracted through the object of the "new coat."

Whether these links or the underlying theme would have been verbalized during the course of the original telling had Mrs. Jones not interrupted or questioned Deena is a moot point. It is important to note, however, that the teacher and child were unable to collaborate on elaborating the topic and making these connections fully explicit. At the heart of this failure to collaborate, I believe, is a lack of shared goals and an appreciation of the other's goals.[3] Deena's goal was to tell a good story about something that was important to her, using the coat as a vehicle. But the goal of the teacher was not to listen for the story behind the coat. Mrs. Jones was not attempting to promote more explicit, elaborated narrative meaning making—to help Deena develop as a storyteller to inform others about life through examples from her own valiant struggles and achievements. Mrs. Jones's goal—a valid one in the context of schools as we know them—was to help Deena give a short, organized, explicit account of her coat, so that the others could imagine it in their minds on the basis of her words alone. Unfortunately, neither Deena nor the teacher understood that each had a valid (albeit different and conflicting) goal.

Moreover, Deena had interpreted Mrs. Jones's question, "What

[3] It is important to note that another significant factor in Mrs. Jones's inability to appreciate Deena's story was her lack of awareness of the existence and validity of alternative structures or schemata for telling a narrative. Had she been more aware of the nature of the story-telling tradition that Deena was drawing on, or primed to be on the lookout for the logic in this story, she might have been better able to acknowledge the detail and organization in Deena's story, even while trying to get her to tell a different (and simpler) kind of narrative.

does that have to do with your coat" (lines 29 and 33), quite literally. She thought Mrs. Jones wanted to know *more* about her cousin, saying in the interview, "she probably wanted to know, like, did he *do* something to it, or *what*?" Mrs. Jones, however, was not asking Deena to talk more about her cousin, but rather, was indirectly trying to get her to leave him out of her account altogether and stick to a topic-centered description of her coat. This is evident in Mrs. Jones's final comments to the class (lines 39–44), "I was trying to get her to stick with *one thing*, and she was talking about her new . . . coat." Deena, however, had interpreted these questions within the framework of her own topic-associating narrative schema.

Interestingly, Deena's descriptive preamble about her coat may well have been an accommodation to the teacher's repeated attempts to elicit topic-centered description. This kind of narrative preamble does not occur either in her early sharing time turns or in her informal narrative accounts that I recorded with her sisters. However, Mrs. Jones was unable to follow the transition from preamble to narrative, as it was not marked prosodically or lexically in a way that she could interpret. Moreover, full-blown narrative was not what Mrs. Jones was looking for at all, so that even if she had been aware of the shift, she might still have cut Deena off. As a result of both factors, Deena's efforts to produce topic-centered description were not fully appreciated or reinforced.

Additionally, when I asked Deena during the interview what she thought Mrs. Jones meant by "tell about one thing," Deena said, "she meant tell about one thing, not 35,000 other things. Like, don't say, 'Yesterday, I had a fight (pause) I saw some roses.' " I take this as a further indication that Deena did indeed have a sense that some topics were related and others were not, and that she was not simply moving from topic to topic in an arbitrary, unmotivated manner.

When asked what she thought Mrs. Jones wanted the children to do at sharing time, Deena offered the following example of "good" sharing talk.

Deena: She just wanted us to say like / well /
well yesterday /
blah blah blah /
blah blah blah /
blah blah blah blah /
blah blah blah blah /
blah blah blah blah //

Deena begins with a sharing time formula (used by all the children in beginning a narrative account) "yesterday," using pronounced sharing intonation. She then provides an account without words, which is segmented prosodically into what sounds like a beginning (orientation), middle (elaboration), and end (resolution). Interestingly enough, this captures precisely the intonational contours of topic-centered discourse (Michaels 1981, 1983). This indicates that Deena had "taken" from Mrs. Jones and other sharers the prosodic flow of topic-centered discourse, and knew this was what Mrs. Jones wanted, but was unable (or perhaps unwilling) to impose this prosodic framework on her own narrative style and expectations.

Sharing time might have provided Deena with the extended practice she needed to internalize a new descriptive account schema and a new set of strategies, enabling her to replace her blah, blah, blah's with words. But sharing time did not provide Deena with this kind of practice. Instead, during sharing time, she and Mrs. Jones seemed to be working at cross purposes: Mrs. Jones was looking for simple, descriptive discourse (similar to that in the preamble—which she glossed as "telling about important things" or "telling about one thing only"), while Deena was building up a personal narrative whereby the overall point had to be inferred from a series of concrete anecdotes, without any explicit statement of the topic. Misinterpretations of each other's intent may explain in part why topic-associating strategies persisted over time, despite the fact that children like Deena got frequent opportunities to share and were generally able learners, as shown by their improvement over the course of the year in other literacy-related skills, such as handwriting or spelling.

Moreover, Mrs. Jones's perception of topic-associating children as having difficulty planning their discourse in advance, *selecting* an appropriate topic, and sticking with it accounts for her emphasis on "importance" and "telling about only one thing." The fact that these children *did* have an "important" theme in mind and systematic set of strategies for thematic development explains in part why these sharing time "maxims" were not particularly informative or effective with children like Deena. Differing expectations and values with respect to narrative, lack of a shared sense of topic, and strategies for narrative development, and apparent misreading of prosodic cues resulted in asynchronous pacing of teacher/child exchanges, less rather than more coherent talk, and misevaluation of intent on both teacher's and child's part.

I do not mean to imply that the difficulty Mrs. Jones experienced with children like Deena was due either to prejudice or incompetence. To the contrary, she was a highly qualified, dedicated teacher, held in high regard by the principal, fellow teachers, and myself as well. Rather the problem appeared to relate more generally to differences in ethnic and communicative background, and different values attached to the role of narrative discourse in school. Hymes (1980) noted:

> If the narrative function is excluded in an institutional setting, such as a college or school, the implication is that the students are defined as NOT co-members of a group with those who teach them. . . . Certainly it is more and more the case that teachers come from districts outside the district in which they teach, even from outside the city. Possibly schools worked better in the past when staff and students shared more of the same world of experience, and narrative use of language was more acceptable between them. (p. 132)

It is worth noting that on one occasion, when the teacher arrived late to school, I led sharing time. In spite of my heightened analytic awareness of topic-associating strategies, I found myself unable, on the spot, to follow this kind of discourse thematically and ask appropriately focused questions. I simply let the children talk until they were finished and at one point I found myself saying to one topic-associating girl, "Just *one more thing* because we're running out of time" (emphasis added here).

There was also a Black instructional aide in this classroom who on one occasion led sharing time. Although in general the aide was a less-skilled teacher than Mrs. Jones, during this particular sharing time session, she was better able to pick up on the narrative intentions of the topic associaters, ask them thematically appropriate questions, and help them round out and organize their narrative accounts. In addition, interspersed with the children's narratives, she told her own, prompted by a previous child's turn; for example, telling a long narrative about fishing for catfish over the weekend, in response to a stuffed animal fish a child had brought in. This is something Mrs. Jones never did as leader.

The consistent problems that Mrs. Jones had with Deena had to do, not with attitudes, but with automatic, unconscious processes at the level of discourse interpretation—in part a result of Mrs. Jones's own home-based narrative experiences (that differed from Deena's) and her socialization as a teacher in a public school—oriented to helping children produce simple, comprehensible proselike texts. Mismatches in narrative style and expectations also resulted in misevaluation of children like Deena, as less capable of producing organized, well-planned texts. These negative evaluations, over time, may in turn have influenced the teacher's expectations and treatment of and attitudes toward these children as learners.

The effect of conversational mismatches is especially striking when seen from a longitudinal perspective. In the beginning of the year, topic-centered turns were characteristically short and concise (as in example 2). Topic-associating turns, in contrast, seemed long-winded and "rambling," as in Deena's MacDonald's turn (example 5). By the end of the year, many of the topic-centered turns were long and involved, evidencing a high degree of collaboration with Mrs. Jones. In contrast, topic-associating children were frequently cut short, owing in large part to the teacher's well-ingrained expectation that their discourse would be hard to follow and her interpretation of this talk as unplanned. Deena, for example was cut short or interrupted during 4 of her last 5 sharing turns (one of which was the "coat" turn, example 8). Thus in terms of sheer amount of talk per turn generated, the pattern had become reversed. Moreover, the white children (who tended overwhelmingly to give topic-centered accounts) were sharing more frequently than the Black children by the end of the year. In the first 10 recorded sharing time sessions, the Black and white children shared equally (approximately 4 Black and 4 white children per session). In the last 10 sessions recorded, white children shared proportionally more often (approximately 5.2 white children and 4.0 Black children per session). Those children who already had literate-like features in their oral discourse got extended practice using them more effectively. Those children whose oral style and narrative schemata were at variance with the teacher's were not able to establish the kind of engagement and cooperation with the teacher that seemed to be a prerequisite for successful collaboration and practice at sharing time. These results suggest a kind of Catch 22 for these children. You have got to start out having elements of a topic-centered narrative schema if you are going to get practice developing it. If not, the narrative schema you have will be devalued, and you are unlikely to receive help in producing narratives of any sort—topic-centered or otherwise. It is for this reason that I see the process as one of *dismantling* narrative abilities.

COMPOSITION WRITING IN A SIXTH-GRADE CLASSROOM

I turn now to composition writing activities in an urban, multiethnic sixth-grade classroom. In this classroom, compositions were written over several days during a variety of oral and written discourse activities. There was thus not a single speech event such as in the case of sharing time, but several. Over the course of any particular assignment, a series of drafts were produced and the teacher, whom I call Mrs. Stone (a pseudonym) conferenced with each student over each draft. Narrative elements were present in nearly every piece of text produced, thus it is possible to study the deployment of narrative strategies in written text and the teacher's response to them—across different drafts and over time. It is the fact that there was so much interaction around writing in this classroom and so many drafts produced, that makes this a particularly good place to carry out a genetic analysis of narrative text production.[4]

Taken together, writing and conferencing in this classroom present an interesting analogue to the sharing time activities previously described. It is possible to look at what text the student produced independently (akin to the sharing time monologue) and how the discourse was interpreted, shaped, and evaluated by the teacher. Moreover, it is possible to contrast this process early and late in the school year.

Because of the institutionalized power differential between teachers and students, I have paid particular attention to teacher led discussions and teacher-student conferences.[5] In these encounters, the teacher's

[4] I want to emphasize that I do not use this example of one teacher's approach to the teaching of composition as an example to be emulated or criticized, nor to be considered as typical. I emphasize this because whenever you look closely at anyone's performance, you can always pick it apart and magnify flaws. There may be much in what this teacher did that people would say is not "real" process writing. That is not my point here. I use this as a real example of text production and instruction in a real classroom with a teacher who was juggling many agendas, curricular goals, pressures from outside and inside, and working with kids who were considered by her and most other school personnel to have weak writing skills. My goal here is not a critique of this teacher's teaching, but a far more general, methodological goal of laying out a research framework and set of analytic tools that can be used—by researchers and perhaps by teachers as well—to deepen our understanding of writing development in schools. Only then does it make sense to evaluate, or suggest improvements, and only in light of clearly and carefully articulated notions of whose interest the evaluation serves.

[5] Because of the methodological complexity given the number and diversity of speech events over the course of composition writing in this classroom, I would like to say a bit about how the data came to be collected. This study was carried out in collaboration with Chip Bruce, Courtney Cazden, Karen Watson-Gegeo, and a team of research assistants, Cindy Cohen, Janie Simmons de Garcia, John Strucker, Polly Ulichny, and others. The project looked at classroom writing where computers were used in two urban, predominantly working-class classrooms. In the course of the study, it became clear that we needed to develop conceptual and methodological tools that would allow us to link more systematically broad scale classroom patterns, rules, and practices with students' written products. To this end, we developed and refined the notion of classroom *writing system* and used it as an analytic construct to mean *the activities, norms, rights and obligations for speaking and acting, including uses of technology*, which influence and constrain student writing in the classroom. As we use the term, the writing system is the

goals and interpretations significantly constrain the meanings, evaluations, and outcomes of the interactions. A study of these exchanges thus reflects both macro- and micro-level forces. It provides a window on some of the institutional constraints on writing in the form of teachers' goals and ideology about what counts as good writing—what can become ratified as public discourse. At the same time, we can chart the impact of these exchanges on student texts from draft to draft, providing evidence of the ways that teachers' goals, expections, and discourse are taken by students into their texts.

In what follows, I analyze the compositions that were written over

---

day-to-day practices of a *curriculum*, shaped largely by the teacher, but partly by the students, and partly by outside forces that impinge on the classroom. By forces outside of the classroom, I have in mind influences from the school department—in this case a particular approach to writing that all the fourth- to sixth-grade teachers in the district were taught, which was a modified Gravesian process approach. This approach entailed a fixed series of steps in completing a piece of writing, brainstorming, first draft (written on yellow paper, double-spaced), editing and revising, and final drafting (on white paper, single-spaced), and some kind of publishing or sharing. Other outside forces had to do with social organization at the school building level—with respect to policies about class size, pull-out programs, and so forth. Finally there are influences from the family, community, and societal cultures of the students, the home languages of the students and values and norms for speaking and socializing, as well as the wider urban American cultural norms that influenced what students brought to classroom writing tasks. Out-of-school knowledge, skills, and interests influenced what students chose to write about, patterns of language use, attitudes toward writing, and values about school and education in general.

The construct of a writing system critically influenced our data collection, which in turn has influenced the kind of analysis we can carry out. By this definition of the writing system, the writing produced by students is not a part of the system, but rather a material product of the system. The texts can be taken out of the classroom; the writing system exists only within the classroom, embedded in social interaction and classroom activities and meanings. Taken out of the classroom, as objects of analysis, they are potentially stripped of their context and the real time interactional information that helped shaped them. And while a great deal of linguistic analysis can be done on an isolated text, we cannot fully interpret the text and the intentions of the author without some understanding of the social forces (both general and specific to that occasion) surrounding its production. For this reason, when we collected written texts that were to become objects of linguistic analysis, we attempted to have systematic observations and tape recordings of the social context and the key interactions that influenced their form and content. In our two classrooms these key interactions included: (a) whole group brainstorming sessions in which the writing task is laid out by the teacher, along with vocabulary and suggestions for how to organize the composition; (b) teacher-student conferences; and (c) peer-peer interaction during writing and at the computer.

In attempting to relate the notion of a writing system to actual written texts, we selected for detailed analysis typical assignments at the beginning and end of the school year, and followed them from start to finish, collecting on audiotape and through field notes as much as we could of these key interactions.

the course of two separate writing assignments, one at the beginning of the school year and one at the end. The data from these two assignments include tape recordings of all whole group discussions, all teacher-student conferences, and nearly all student drafts (although for a few students, their end-of-the-year drafts were lost and had to be reconstructed from the conferences).

In analyzing the data, I summarize some general findings based on data from all the students but illustrate the process of "taking" text through a detailed case study—what might be thought of as the life history of two compositions—one written at the beginning of the year, one at the end of the year, by a sixth-grade girl named Lewana. In tracing the development of Lewana's texts from initial to final draft, I provide a comparative (intertextual) analysis of talk (group discussion, writing conferences) and text. That is, through a detailed analysis of the social interactions around the writing, it is possible to chart quite literally what is "taken" from the social context into Lewana's texts.

Ethnographic Background

Mrs. Stone was a Black woman in her 30s, with 10 years of teaching experience and an excellent reputation in the school and district. She taught sixth grade in the largest elementary school in the city, located in a working-class neighborhood in the heart of the city's Portuguese immigrant community. There were 16 students in this class, all except one from working-class backgrounds—predominantly Portuguese but also including some American and Jamaican blacks, Hispanic students, and a few students of Italian and Irish descent.

The student I focus on, whom I call Lewana, was a street-wise, highly verbal Black girl who had recently moved to this school from a much larger neighboring city. Lewana was perceived by Mrs. Stone as a smart, capable girl with something of an attitude problem.

Writing, like nearly all academic work in this classroom, was largely individually paced. Writing assignments were given by Mrs. Stone, in large group brainstorming sessions. Students were then expected to complete a first draft (on yellow paper) without much interaction with their peers and have an individual writing conference with Mrs. Stone. Students were then expected to incorporate changes into a next draft, have another conference—recursively—until the teacher deemed the text ready to be a final draft "on white" and then typed into the computer. Toward the end of the year, the white draft was skipped and students typed their final drafts directly into the computer. As a result of both the teacher's desire for a polished product and the relaxed schedule and pacing of the day, students wrote several drafts (sometimes as many as five or six) before completing a final draft, and occasionally wrote more than one final draft as well.

Let me turn now to the first writing assignment. It occurred after the entire class took a field trip to the Barnum and Bailey Circus. Several students had never been to the circus before. The next school day, the students were told that they would be writing about this experience. In the prewriting brainstorming session with the whole class, the teacher summarized the task as follows: "Whatever your favorite part of the circus would be / a particular act / think of some name that would be an appropriate title for your composition //." Later, as the students were beginning to write, she reiterated the task: "to write about just one thing / to stick to that one particular act //."

It is worth mentioning that through the brainstorming discussions, as well as through comments made to individual students, there is converging evidence that—although never fully and explicitly articulated at any one point—the teacher had, in addition to expectations about good writing at the level of word choice, spelling, and punctuation, a clear set of expectations, or what I call a *schema*, about how the circus composition should be structured. This schema called for a composition structured into three distinct segments with particular linguistic, thematic characteristics. She was looking for a beginning section that was narrativelike in syntax, specifying date, place, and the name of the circus (which might be thought of as an introduction). This was to be followed by a middle section describing and evaluating the particular "act," which might be thought of as a shift to specific, analytic detail. Finally, there was to be a final section that entailed a return to the general, the circus as a whole, which might be thought of as a summary and conclusion section. Michaels (1987) contained a detailed analysis of the student compositions in light of this tripartite schema. I found that out of 14 students who finished the assignment, 10 of them did not conform to the teacher's schema in their first drafts but through a series of conferences ranging from 4-8, and a series of drafts ranging from 4-9, all the mismatches were shaped into matches. (See Michaels 1987 for the full analysis.) In addition to looking at how students took the teacher's schema, however, I want to show how they took text from the public discourse of the classroom. For this, I turn to Lewana's story.

After the circus brainstorming discussion, Lewana wrote a first draft on yellow paper, skipping lines. I display her text with an independent clause per line, but without changing any of the spelling or punctuation.

Lewana's first draft—circus composition

Lewana Allen Oct. 22, 1984

Antolek Chimps

1.–I went to the circus on friday October 19, 1984
2.–And I loved the Chimpanzees Act.
3.–I thaught they were so cute with those cloths on.
4.–And I thaught their act was "incredible".
5.–I could not believe they were in the circus.
6.–And I wish I could go back to the circus just to see the Chimpanzees Act.
7.–And when my aunt went Saturday October 20, 1984
8.–I was mad because I couldn't go.

In asking what in this text specifically originated from the public discourse of the classroom, the following points are worth noting. The brainstorming discussion began with the teacher saying:

Teacher: Alright / on Friday the entire class along with all the other sixth grade students went to the circus //

The teacher then elicited from the students the different kinds of acts they remembered. Lewana volunteered the word *monkeys*. All the words the students suggested got written on the board. The teacher then elicited a variety of descriptive words, saying,

Teacher: OK / most of the things that are on the board now would all be considered nouns like the type of animals and the type of acts / a lot of times when you're gonna write a story / to make it more interesting / you need a lot of / . . . words that are descriptive words / to make your writing a lot more colorful and exciting //

In the context of this discussion, the words *fantastic* and *incredible* were elicited and written down. Following this discussion, the teacher says,

Teacher: OK / now besides fantastic and incredible what other words could you / think of /

A student says "great."

Teacher: OK / great // Let's pick a particular noun and see if we can do something with that / if I say we're gonna talk about the clothes that the people wore / the costumes / OK / If we're gonna talk about the costumes / think of adjectives that might only apply to costumes //

The teacher then goes on to elicit more descriptive adjectives followed by a lengthy discussion of "practice, training, and experience." Finally, toward the end of the discussion, she returns to the task, saying:

Teacher: alright / without talking / without saying anything else / just take about a minute and think about what was your favorite act or favorite part of the circus / don't confer with anybody sitting beside you / don't tell me / I don't wanna know outloud / just take a minute to think what was your favorite what was your favorite part of the circus //

She then suggests that the kids find out the proper name of the act they have chosen, getting the circus book and saying,

Teacher: . . . you can look in the book and you can refer to them by their particular name / OK so instead of just saying the dogs / maybe we can look in the book and see that they were the Albert Act

During this discussion of act names, she says,

Teacher: alright / and the monkeys / anybody want the monkeys / alright / I'll have to write it here you'll have to remember where it was it's called the Antalek Chimpanzees / you just call them the chimps //

As a very gross index of what was taken from this discussion, at a quite narrow, textual level—counting words in isolation, such as "incredible" (it even appears in quotes in Lewana's draft) and phrases or paraphrases, (such as "our class went to the circus"), it turns out that 18% (14 of 76 words) of the text mirrored the talk directly or, in metaphorical terms, was "taken" from the public discourse of the social setting. Conversely, it is important to note that the topic itself and nearly 82% (62 of 76 words) of the text—(such as the narrative tag at the end) came, again metaphorically, from what Lewana, herself, brought to the writing task. As another index of Lewana's personal voice, it is worth noting that "I" appears nine times in the short text.

The following is the transcript of Lewana's second writing conference. The first was less than 30 seconds and involved no substantive response from the teacher other than a directive to go back and look for capitalization and punctuation errors (noting that Friday was not capitalized). In the transcript, capitalization indicates that text is being read.

Teacher:	OK / why don't you make this two different sentences / I WENT TO THE CIRCUS / ok / with who / and then we can say: / THE ACT I LOVED THE BEST WAS / or make this a different sentence / the act I enjoyed the most was . . the / Antalek Chimpanzees // give 'em their name / the Antalek (writing) / Chimpanzees // OK?//
Lewana:	(. . .) right way to spell it //
Teacher:	Uh huh // I THOUGHT / you spelled thought wrong // I THOUGHT THEY WERE SO CUTE WITH THOSE / what kind of clothes did they have / cowboy clothes (. . .) // what'd they have on (Lewana) cowboy clothes on? //
Lewana:	They had on / a white hat and a white sweater //
Teacher:	Uh huh / AND I THOUGHT THEIR ACT WAS INCREDIBLE // why? //
Lewana:	'Cause / I . . . liked it //
Teacher:	'Cause I liked them doesn't tell me why it was incredible // 'cause I liked them / you liked them / but why was it incredible? // . . . don't say 'cause if you don't do it // 'cause / 'cause (chuckles) . . . 'cause what? // (long pause) And why couldn't you believe they were in the circus? //
Lewana:	'Cause I didn't think they could walk //
Teacher:	OK / but you should explain all those things // and before you get down here about why you want to go back and all like this / explain why you thought it was incredible / explain somethin' about the clothes that they had on / not a whole lot of detail / and explain what it was they did // you didn't tell me anything they did // you didn't tell us about what they did when they were out in the ring // you have to tell what they did // want me to write it down on the top so you don't forget all the things you have to try? //

During this conference, the teacher solicited more information about the monkey's clothes (writing *EXPLAIN* above the word clothes), why the act was incredible (writing *WHY*? after incredible) as well as asking her to say more about what they did (without making any written comment). In responding to the first two questions, Lewana described the monkeys' clothes ("They had on a white hat and sweater") and explained that she had not known that monkeys could walk. She never said anything about what the monkeys did in the ring.

The following is Lewana's second draft. It was written on yellow paper, double spaced, marking it as a draft in progress.

Lewana A______________ October 23, 1984

Antalek Chimps

1. On Friday October 19, 1984 all of the six grades went to see Ringling Brothers and Barnum and Bailey Circus at the Bostan garden along with Mr. Strucker and Miss Craig.
2. I thoght the antalek Chimps we the cutest animals
3. they had on a white hat, sweater, and pants
4. they were so cute
5. and It was "incredible"
6. because I didn't know that they could walk.
7. They must of had lots of practice and talent
8. because they were good.
9. And I wish I could go again just to see them.
10. My aunt went Saturday 20, 1984
11. and I was mad
12. because I couldn't go
13. and my sister could.
14. I just wanted to go to see the Antalek Chimps
15. and when my sister came home
16. I asked her what did she like the best
17. she said the monkeys.

In Lewana's second draft, both bits of information that were verbalized by Lewana, and solicited in writing by the teacher got incorporated—and as I see it, this must be considered a case of a joint construction—the teacher suggesting the kind of information needed but the student providing the actual content. No new text about what the monkeys did in the ring was added. However, the narrative kernel at the end was expanded. Interestingly, during the writing conference, the narrative kernel at the end had been bracketed off in red ink on the first draft by the teacher but not specifically commented on, other than to say "before you get down here about why you want to go back and all like this" do this other stuff. In the second draft, the narrative is extended, or perhaps simply completed; it is possible that it had not been finished in the first draft.

In making sense out of other additions in this second draft, it is worth noting that directly following the first writing session and initial conferences, there were several other whole group discussions. During one discussion, the teacher explicitly commented on what would be a good beginning:

Teacher: I noticed some people started / their cos-us their compositions / explaining what we: / went to see / now I didn't tell you to do that / and that was smart for the person who picked up on that / they explained that it took place on Friday / the 19th 1984 / and worked in someway that it was a class trip / that we went to the Boston Gardens / see Ringling Brothers and Barnum and Bailey circus // Kay? // give credit where the credit is due // I mean we could've gone to Wilmington to see the Shriners' circus // so explain wheth—what circus we went to see / and where we went to see it //

At a later point, during a sentence-generating discussion, the sentence "On Friday October 19th, our class went to the circus" was written on the board. The names of the chaperones (actually the classroom ethnographers) had also been written on the board, and had perhaps been prompted by the teacher's comment reading Lewana's initial draft "I WENT TO THE CIRCUS // . . . ok with who?" At some point, new vocabulary words were elicited, along with practice, training, and experience." Words like "flexible" and "sparkle" were added to the board. Lewana raised her hand and said "talent." Talent, then, came from Lewana.

Given my characterization of the teacher's tripartite schema for how the circus composition should be structured (orientation, analytic detail, general evaluation), the narrative account at the end of her composition does not conform to the teacher's expectations for a good ending—it does not return to the circus at a general level and evaluate it. Rather it shifts time and key participants in talking about another trip to the circus, highlighting, through the eyes of her sister, her own positive evaluation of the monkeys' act. It is, I might add, in tone and in content, the clearest example of Lewana's individual voice. It deals with personal knowledge, of real meaning and significance to her, and uses a strategy of indirectly associated, concrete anecdote to make a general evaluative point, a culturally valued and highly developed discourse strategy among urban Blacks. I would then say, again metaphorically, that this narrative stands out as Lewana's personal or out of school "voice" incorporated into a text that, otherwise, has taken much from the public discourse of the classroom.

Characterizing this second draft then with respect to the question of personal versus public voice, by number of words, we arrive at the following very gross characterization of the text:

personal, 56% (77 of 138);	public, 34% (47 of 138);	joint, 10% (14 of 138).

It is also interesting to note that in this second draft, which is nearly twice as long as the first one, there are now only seven, as opposed to nine, occurrences of "I."

The following is the transcript of the third conference with Lewana:

Teacher: Kay / when I read this—this was a lot clearer than what you had yesterday / so you did work on it // sit down // . . . alright / ON FRIDAY 19 / 1984 ALL THE SIX GRADES / sixth grades / cause now that makes it look like six grades went instead of sixth / T H / ALL THE SIXTH GRADES WENT TO SEE RINGLING BROTHERS AND BARNUM AND BAILEY CIRCUS AT BOSTON GARDEN // ALONG WITH THE TEACHERS / MR. STRUCKER / MISS CRAIG / AND MISS COHEN / HELPED CHAPERONE //

.

.

Teacher: alright / and here you have cutest / and down here you have cute // so instead of using cute twice / what's a word you're gonna substitute for cute //

Lewana: (inaudible)

Teacher: beautiful's not the same / . . . type of wo:rd as cute // they're not really synonymous // they're not synonyms for each other // beautiful and pretty / cute and maybe funny // but not beautiful and cute / they're not the same thing // . . . I rather somebody told me I was beautiful or pretty / but not cute // it's not the same / level of / description // so cute might go with funny / and beautiful might go with pretty / but / they're not really synonyms for each other / cute and beautiful / . . . you rather have somebody tell you you're cute or beautiful? //. . . . or pretty or funny? // which—which two go together out a those four? // pretty and beautiful / maybe cute and funny // so if you're gonna call 'em the cutest animals up here / you don't wanna call 'em cute down here // that's like bein' / repetitious / you're sayin' the same thing *again* / just two sentences later // so what else can you say they were? // can they be . . . um: . . .

Lewana: I thought they were so / f-funny //

Teacher:	Okay! / then instead of cute / now you're gonna say you thought they were also / . . . funny / so we'll change this cute to: / . . . funny / okay / a:nd / . . . you thought it was / you didn't know monkeys could walk? /
	.
	.
Teacher:	[continues, reading] IT WAS INCREDIBLE BECAUSE I DIDN'T / KNOW THAT THEY COULD WALK / THEY MUST OF HAD / LOTS OF / PRACTICE / AND TRAINING // now you put talent /
Lewana:	yeah
Teacher:	and I changed your talent to . . . training / 'kay? / [reading] THEY MUST HAVE LOTS OF PRACTICE AND TRAINING 'CAUSE THEY WERE GOOD // . . . take out this *A:ND* // I'm gonna outlow a:nds beginning my sentences // I WISH I COULD GO AGAIN JUST TO SEE THE CHIMPS // and I ended it there // you started telling about your aunt went on Saturday and you were upset you couldn't go / and your sister said / that's not important / okay? // go back and rewrite this for me // with those corrections in it //
Lewana:	I'm go:in' ba:ck Sa:tunday anyway //
Teacher:	'kay? // I know well you can write me a different composition but it doesn't fit on this one // how's that? // go back and recopy that for me //
Lewana:	on white? //
Teacher:	on yellow // no // yellow // . . . that's still a yellow //
Lewana:	skip li:nes? //
Teacher:	yep // it's still a yellow //

Before this conference, Mrs. Stone had read Lewana's second draft and had made several editorial changes and suggestions in red ink. She had circled words that needed to be capitalized, corrected Lewana's spelling above the misspelled words, altered and expanded one sentence, and had drawn arrows to highlight two cases of repeated words. She circled and crossed out one case of sentence initial *and* and *crossed off the entire ending narrative about Lewana's sister.* Next to the crossed off section, Mrs. Stone had written *end.* During the writing conference, Mrs. Stone talked Lewana through these written comments, explaining, justifying, and elaborating as she did so. She engaged Lewana in a lengthy exchange on synonymy where Lewana had used the word *cute* twice, only two sentences apart. When Lewana selected as a substitute *beautiful* Mrs. Stone suggested that cute and beautiful were not really "the same thing" and suggested that a more appropriate synonym might be funny. Lewana then opted for funny, which Mrs. Stone wrote on her paper next to the second occurrence of cute. In this exchange, we get a glimpse of the kind of folk theories of composition (in this case of synonymy) that teachers often implicitly invoke in guiding student revision. We also get a glimpse of the way that Lewana follows the teacher's lead.

Finally, Mrs. Stone explains to Lewana that she ended her composition with the sentence, "I wish I could go again . . . ," taking out all the text about her aunt, sister, going back on Saturday, and so forth. She explains, simply, "that's not important / okay? //" and then tells her to rewrite her draft incorporating these corrections. Lewana responds by saying "I'm go:in' ba:ck Sa:turday anyway" (with a slightly irreverent tone, as if to say, "Don't make no difference to me, 'cause I'm goin' back Saturday anyway"). This exchange over the deleted text is evidence of a clear difference in the teacher's and student's perspective on why the narrative is not appropriate. For the teacher, the issue is one of formal structure ("it doesn't fit on this one"), which determines what kind of circus information is relevant to the topic at hand, glossed by Mrs. Stone as important. For Lewana, the issue is one of meaning; it is no longer important because in fact, she *is* going back to the circus.

The resulting text, in Lewana's third draft on yellow paper, conforms well to the teacher's schema, and, not surprisingly, contains proportionally less of Lewana's out-of-school experiences and personal voice. In this draft, there are only four occurrences of "I." The resulting percentages along the personal/public dimension are:

personal,	public,	joint,
29%	57%	14%
(28 of 95);	(54 of 95);	(13 of 95).

There is perhaps something apt then about the teacher's comment, "I'm gonna outlaw ands at the beginning of *MY* sentences." However, rather than seeing this as a text the teacher appropriated from Lewana, I want to suggest that we should think of it as a text that Lewana progressively took, with some assistance, from the teacher, or rather from the classroom writing system. In this classroom, the teacher's voice is institutionally privileged, both in terms of access to the public arena and in terms of interpretive clout. A word the teacher suggests is automatically a good word. Of course it does not have to be that way, but often is.

But what got appropriated in the sense of "learned," not just taken into the text, is not clear. What Lewana learned about writing, its purpose or value, about synonymy or good endings in line with the teacher's schema for a circus composition is simply impossible to determine from this example. There is some evidence that Lewana failed to understand fully what made her remaining ending a better ending than her original narrative account. For one thing, when she went to copy her double-spaced yellow draft onto white paper, she forgot to turn over her page and copy the text from the second side of the page. She simply ended her composition with "It was incredible because I didn't know that they could walk," thus deleting her final two evaluative sentences. She also commented in an interview with me that she thought her original ending made the composition "*much* more interesting," but then added, "but you got to do what the teacher says."

During the interview, Lewana also clarified some of her original intentions. When I asked her what she would have done if her sister had liked the horse act the best, rather than the monkeys, she said, "Then I wouldn't have written it!" (in a "how dumb can you get" tone of voice). "All that stuff about my sister / well the thing was / she thought the chimps was the best too //." It may well be that Lewana was working with a competing topic-associating schema calling for a focus on one act from a variety of perspectives: the performance she saw (lines 1–8), the circus in general (she mentions in line 9 wanting to "go again" to the circus "just to see [the monkeys]"), and concrete detail highlighting someone else's corroborating opinion of the act (lines 10–17). This kind of structure is precisely what Deena was attempting in her sharing time accounts, examined earlier. In light of this alternative schema, the anecdote about her sister would serve as a fully appropriate ending. Through concrete detail, it illustrates Lewana's statement of her own desire to go back to see the monkey act and demonstrates the generalizability of her positive evaluation. Interestingly, both Lewana's and Mrs. Stone's schema can be seen equally to call for specifics and general evaluation, but they call for a different set of rhetorical strategies in accomplishing them. In the teacher's schema, personal narrative was inappropriate as a generalizing tool. *The issue is thus not simply one of whether narrative is tolerated, but where and for what rhetorical ends.* The early narrative clauses (part of the public discourse) remain in Lewana's final text, but the developed personal narrative is taken out.

Lewana's case is typical of many of her classmates in writing the circus compositions. In every case, they had taken text from the public discourse of the classroom (in increasing proportion with each successive draft) and incorporated it into their own text. And in the cases of other students who had inserted personal knowledge in narrative form in the service of description or general evaluation, it was deleted in the course of conferencing (see the case of Mario in Michaels, 1987).

But this is only one half of the story. It is important to ask what changed, in both the students' texts and in the students' "ways of taking," over time.

I now turn to the last assignment of the school year, comparable in the sense that it too was based on a class trip, but in this case, a trip to a nearby island—which entailed a bus ride and then a boat ride—to a recreational, educational center out in the city's harbor. As with the circus compositions, the day following the trip, there was a lengthy brainstorming discussion in which the teacher elicited vocabulary and a recounting of the day's events—from getting on the busses outside of the school building, to the boatride over to the island, to the activities on the island, and the return trip. She emphasized the importance of sequence in writing but ultimately left the task open-ended:

Teacher: Think for a minute about something you could say // maybe you want to tell about the whole day for me // maybe you want to tell about a particular part of the day //

I look first at the development of Lewana's island composition and then summarize how it reflects aspects of the overall pattern for the class as a whole.

Unfortunately, Lewana was one of the students whose drafts were lost in the shuffle of the last days of the school year. However, there is a fair amount of evidence to go on in the conferences (when Mrs. Stone read her text aloud). I feel fairly confident about my reconstruction of the words of her first draft, but less confident about her spelling and punctuation. Following her first draft is her final draft (which was collected), with all changes from the reconstructed first draft underlined.

Lewana's First Draft
Harbor Island

1. I had a wonderful time on May 21, 1985
2. All of the six and seventh graders went to Harbor Island.
3. We went outside the school to get on the bus to go to Hearst Wharf.
4. I really enjoyed the ride,
5. I had never been on a boat before.
6. I was scared but when the boat started to move I wasn't scared anymore.

7. When the boat went to the Island, it was sunny and hot.
8. Mr. Z. came over too talk to us.
9. We played three new games.
10. I could only remember two of them,
11. they were called Vampire and flamingo tag.
12. Mr. Z. was a nice man.
13. He took us down to the river, where our class caught a crab and five jelly fish, but Lorette slapped it out of my hand and it got dirty.
14. I wanted another one, but I couldn't get one because we were too far from the river.
15. After we returned from the river, we ate.
16. After we finished we talked about the Island and the animals.
17. Then it was time to leave,
18. we went back to the boat.
19. I really had a nice time there.

Lewana's Final Draft
Harbor Island

1. I had a wonderful time on May 21, 1985.
2. All the six*th* and seventh graders went to Harbor Island.
3. We went outside the school to get on the bus to go to Hearst Wharf.
4. *When we got on the boat,* I really enjoyed the ride,
5. I had never been on a boat before.
6. I was scared *for a while when the boat was tied to the dock, because it was shaking.*
7. When the boat came to the Island, it was sunny and hot.
8. *A man that showed us around named* Mr. Z. came over too talk to us.
9. *He taught us how to* play three new games.
10. I could only remember two of them,
11. they were called Vampire and *F*lamingo *T*ag.
12. Mr. Z was a very nice *cooperative* man.
13. He took us down to the river, where our class caught a crab and five jellyfish, but Lorette slapped it out of my hand and it got dirty.
14. I wanted another one, but I couldn't get one because we were too far from the *shore.*
15. After we returned from the river, we ate *our lunches.*
16. After we finished we talked about the Island and the animals.
17. Then it was time to leave,
18. we went back to the boat.
19. I really had a nice time there.

For Lewana's first draft the rough estimates of personal or public voice as evidenced in the text are: personal, 41% (79 of 193); public,

59% (114 of 193). The estimates for the final draft are: personal, 33% (72 of 218); public, 56% (123 of 218); joint, 11% (23 of 218).

Is there evidence of development from the circus composition assignment to this one? Notice the parallel constructions in the early and late compositions: "All of the six grades went to" (circus) and "All of the six and seventh graders went to" (island). On the face of it, the use of the same construction suggests no development, compounded by the repeated mistake with "six grade[r]s" which had been corrected by the teacher in the first case. But it is important to note that in the circus composition, the introductory line, "All of the six grades went to . . ." was not present in her initial draft. It appeared in her second draft, only after class discussion. Thus what got "taken" from the talk of others into the later version of her circus compositions was spontaneously incorporated into her first draft of the island composition. It seems to have been appropriated by Lewana as an appropriate way of introducing the topic of the trip.[6]

There are other notable differences in both product and process of the circus and island compositions. As texts, the final drafts differ in length, syntactic complexity (use of subordination, and connectives other than "but"), all suggesting that Lewana, indeed, developed as a writer over the course of the year. But even more striking and suggestive of development are the relative proportions of personal and public discourse from first to final draft in the two assignments. In the circus composition assignment, Lewana begins by taking only 18% of her text from the public discourse of the classroom, and does not use the tripartite structural schema expected by Mrs. Stone. In the island composition assignment, Lewana takes 50% of her first draft from the public discourse of the classroom, and takes as well the expected structural schema. Notice also that in the island composition, there is no dramatic reduction of the personal text as there was in the case of the circus composition (which went from 82% personal to 29% personal). At the same time the breakdown of personal, public, and joint voices on the final draft of both the circus and island compositions is remarkably close. In the circus composition, the final draft is 29% personal, 57% public, and 14% joint. The island final draft is 33% personal, 56% public, and 11% joint.

Another indicator of development is Lewana's deployment from first to final draft of first-person, singular pronouns (I or me) and personal names, which I suggested were indices of personal voice in the compositions. In the island composition, the number of first-person pronouns gets reduced by only one occurrence from first to final draft, going from nine to eight. In the circus composition, the occurrences

[6] I owe this point to Vicki Morse.

are reduced by over half, from nine to four. Thus it appears that Lewana is better able to control and maintain her personal voice by the end of the year.

In the island composition, just as in the first draft of the circus composition, Lewana crafts a segment of charged, personalized narrative. In the island text, the segment begins in line 13 with a shift from first-person plural pronouns (He took *us* down to the river, *our* class . . .) to the use of a classmate's name and first-person self-reference, shifting perspective from the class as a group to a minidrama between her friend and herself (Lorette slapped it out of my hand . . . I wanted another one, but . . .). The difference between this text and the circus composition is that the personal, somewhat emotional narrative "fits" on this one. It fits into the already narrative syntax of the middle section, maintaining temporal sequence, and participants, but nonetheless bringing in her own story, her own voice. Thus, Lewana has managed to merge more successfully the public and the personal discourse.

Shifting now to the entire group of students, the following findings are worth mentioning. Along many different indices, one might be inclined to say the students as a group had developed as writers. They, on average, wrote over three times as much text in their first drafts of the end-of-the-year composition. (In Lewana's case, her initial island composition was two and half times longer than her initial circus draft). The students had only one-third the number of conferences before their compositions were ready to become final drafts (in this case to be typed into the computer—bypassing the white draft step). They wrote fewer yellow drafts overall, in most cases only two, whereas the average was three in the circus compositions.

There was one other striking index of development in this end-of-year assignment. Every single student, in their first draft, told a narrative of the entire trip—again using a tripartite structure, but different in the middle section from the circus compositions. The schema the students adopted for the island composition was:

1. an introduction that gave date, place, and participants;
2. a lengthy middle section that recounted the events of the trip—in almost every case, mentioning the same events in the same order—bus ride, boat ride, tour leader, games played on the island, beach, lunch, lecture about the island, and return trip;
3. a conclusion that ended with the kids going home (or arriving back at school) and optionally saying something summative like, "I had a great time."

As every single student began with all the elements of the schema in the proper order, *there were thus no "mismatches" to be turned into matches*. In no cases were large sections of text added or deleted on the basis of something the teacher said during a conference. The texts were all different, but they bore a striking similarity to one another (in structure and in content), and all mirrored the brainstorming discussion. This is most noticeable in the case of the two students who missed school the day of the trip but who wrote compositions anyway: In spite of not being there, they recounted the *same events in the same order*. This is not to say that the students did not add personal voice to the texts. In nearly every case, including Lewana, they did—most often marked by use of the pronoun "I" or by naming a classmate. But from first to final draft, there was no dramatic reduction in personal voice that we saw in Lewana's circus story. Overall I found that there was striking convergence in form across all the students' compositions and this convergence was evident in what got "taken" from the very start into their first drafts. Personal voice was incorporated and maintained through to the final draft. It appears that the students had learned to "take" fluently from the public discourse of this classroom community. The teacher's role in shaping their compositions was far more indirect. The students had internalized (I would suggest somewhat tentatively) an effective way of taking from the public discourse and the teacher gave them much to take from.

An alternative explanation of these findings might be that the experience of the island trip itself led students to write a blow-by-blow narrative, reinforced of course by the blow-by-blow brainstorming session. The circus trip, on the other hand by its nature, lent itself to divergence in the selection of acts; the brainstorming discussions could not cover a "talking through" of each act. Although there is perhaps something to this, it is worth noting that the other sixth-grade classroom we studied also went on the field trip to the island, and also wrote island compositions after a blow-by-blow brainstorming session. In this room, while most of the compositions evidenced the same tripartite structure, fully one quarter of them did not. One example of a "divergent" composition was called "The Boat Ride."

The Boat Ride

In the boat that was going to Harbor Island, kids were doing things that they shouldn't have done. For example, they were boozing, smoking, and swearing. They got their drinks at the bar when the grownups weren't watching. They got to smoke at the bathroom. They swore freely in the boat. The teachers didn't know this was going on the boat. You could tell who was drinking by smelling them. Some of them looked drunk. They looked like they enjoyed themselves.

Nobody would catch me smoking because smoking makes me cough like crazy and it's also bad for the lungs. I never drink because I hate the taste of liquor. It makes you feel strange if drink a lot of it.

The moral of the story is grownups should keep their eyes open for unexpected things. [sic]

CONCLUSION

The moral of this story is that different classrooms, and different oral and written discourse activities within classrooms, orient students to different ways of taking text from the public discourse of the classroom, and different ways of deploying narrative discourse. And as Bakhtin and many others after him suggested, in taking discourse,[7] we acquire not just words or constructions, but ways of making sense, ways of valuing, ways of drawing inferences, as well as perspectives on purposes and audiences for communication (Bakhtin, 1986; Cazden 1988; Gee 1989b; Hymes 1980; Lemke 1986).

In the two contrasting cases presented, we have seen recurring examples in which certain forms of narrative discourse were excluded, disallowed, and devalued when they occurred in student texts. At the same time, these cases give evidence of particular forms of narrative being encouraged or at least tolerated in the oral and written performances of students, through teacher-guided dialogic exchanges. We have seen examples of recurrent activities, at different times during the school year, and can ask how these activities interact with the discourse practices of the students to promote or hinder the development of narrative performance.

In the cases of sharing time and writing instruction, a teacher has very different opportunities and obligations for shaping discourse. Both with respect to medium (oral vs. written text) and opportunities for revision, these two kinds of discourse activities create different occasions for prompting, modeling, and evaluating discourse.

In the case of sharing time, the teacher must respond to a fleeting text, on the spot. The teacher can ask questions or make comments, but the opportunities for expansion or revision are highly constrained. Moreover, unless the teacher immediately hears the logic in the student's text, questions and comments are likely to interrupt the child's thinking rather than to build on and extend it. Given the typically fast-paced oral performances of students at sharing time, and the constraint that a teacher must attend both to the speaker and to the

---

[7] Here, I mean taking discourse into a text but also "learning new forms of discourse" as well.

audience of other students, it may be unrealistic to expect teachers to hear the logic and structure in discourse that is organized differently from what they are expecting. When structured as it was in Mrs. Jones's classroom, sharing time may not be an ideal activity for promoting the development of new forms of discourse. On the other hand, it may well serve to communicate *powerful* messages about what kind of language, or by extension to the speaker, what kind of student is valued.

In the case of writing and conferencing activities, at first glance the nature and pacing of the activities appears to create a more promising social arena for constructing, juxtaposing, and shaping discourse, and hence developing new discourse forms. Conferences are typically one-on-one or small group conversations, and hence interactively simpler than whole group activities. They are mediated by a fixed text that can be reread, pointed to, or written on. There is a chance for multiple revisions and hence multiple readings. The result of the conference is another text; something of value can be salvaged from draft to draft and the student is left with a "finished" well-formed product at the end.

And yet, these possibilities for more focused reading, reflecting, and mindful response often go unrealized in the real time press of interaction in classrooms. Though conferences allow a teacher time to focus on a single text and student, there is an entire classroom full of students to be conferenced. Teachers rarely study and reread texts carefully before or during a conference. And in spite of the availability of multiple drafts, the drafts tend not to be juxtaposed, compared, and used as evidence of development. One thing I have never seen in all of the self-proclaimed "process writing" classrooms I have observed is a teacher who looks at two drafts, early and late, at the same time.

Writing conferences are interactively achieved interpretive events, and the expectations of the teacher and the teacher's "reading" of the text tend to guide and channel the ultimate interpretation and status of the student draft (Ulichny & Watson-Gegeo, 1988). Moreover, teacher's criteria for "good" text are often highly implicit, and hard to articulate explicitly. (Recall that both Mrs. Stone and Mrs. Jones used the word *important* to characterize what it was they were looking for in a good composition ending or an appropriate sharing time turn.) So although there are better opportunities for students to "take" text and text schemata from the teacher in a writing conference, teachers are highly constrained as readers by their own discourse history, the pace of school activities, and by their perceived institutional responsibility to shape the text into an appropriate piece of school-writing.

In this case study of writing and conferencing activities, Mrs. Stone's attempts with Lewana were in many respects more successful than Mrs. Jones's with Deena. In the circus composition, Lewana ended up with an acceptable, finished composition, albeit one with a watered-down ending. By the end of the year, she was able to maintain her narrative voice in her composition, seamlessly woven into the public forms so that it was not edited out.[8]

In both Deena's and Lewana's cases, however, it is clear that the complex narrative strategies that these students evidenced in their early texts were not appreciated or developed further in school. For both, progress required the suppression of their full repertoire of narrative abilities. At the end of the year, Deena was perceived as having made no real progress in giving appropriate sharing time accounts. Lewana, in the island composition, included a brief segment of personalized narrative, but it was embedded within the larger blow-by-blow narrative of the middle section of the composition. It was not deployed strategically to evaluate or extend the meaning of the piece as the narrative segment (about her sister) had been used in her initial circus draft. Lewana, it seems, had learned that school compositions are not the appropriate place to use her full repertoire of narrative strategies in the service of description, analysis, or evaluation.

It makes sense to reflect on each of these discourse activities to think about what teachers can learn from the particulars of these case studies. Research of this type, looking genetically at text production in particular classrooms, does not lend itself to programmatic recommendations, that is, to specific guidelines about good methods of teaching writing, organizing group activities, or integrating technological tools. To the contrary, it suggests that teacher and student expectations, coupled with the real-time interactive nature of classroom activities, will determine what students take into their texts and what values or perspectives on discourse, knowledge, and voice they take along with that text.

On the other hand, this research can lead to effective change. *Teachers can use this information to help them listen or read text differently.* Analyses of Deena's and Lewana's texts highlight the fact that there is indeed structure in texts that appear at first hearing or first glance to be unstructured. This should lead teachers to *expect* that their students' texts will be structured and to prod them to look, self-consciously, for the inherent logic and the students' use of structuring devices. One first-grade teacher, several weeks after learning about sharing time research, commented that now she reads students' writing differently, and notices many episodic characteristics in their texts. Often she

[8] It is also worth reiterating that the students as a group in Lewana's class were writing more similar, homogenized compositions by the end of the year, both with respect to the language of the text and text schemata.

cannot see the connections in their texts, but finds that if she probes for implicit connections, the children can explain them to her. She said that "simply assuming the connections are there gives us a common ground to work from." Teachers can also reorganize sharing time or writing activities. One teacher stopped participating in sharing time herself and turned it over to the kids; another created two different kinds of sharing time: One was for oral storytelling in which she let children tell narratives any way they liked, and the other was for generating written text, in which she talked explicitly about different kinds of stories, and had children practice a variety of genres, thus helping them develop a metalinguistic sensitivity to differences in style.

But more important than suggesting new methods for running sharing time or teaching writing, I suggest that we need to look further at how different classrooms support or promote ways of taking public discourse into student texts, and how students' learn to take and yet integrate the public with their personal knowledge and discourse. And we need to think hard about how teachers themselves might think about their own classrooms as environments for taking discourse—to become more aware of what they expect students to take, and how they control what gets taken.

To this end, teachers need tools for thinking deeply about the type of speakers and writers they want their students to become, the types of literacy (literacies) required in different social settings, and the type of language appropriate for different communicative demands. Given particular goals, teachers need skills to analyze their own classroom writing and speaking activities, to judge whether or not these activities support their goals, and how they are perceived differently by different students. This calls for teachers to assess broad-scale patterns of social organization, the language patterns and interpretive strategies that their students bring with them from home, and the "ways of taking" fostered in their setting.

A growing number of teachers interested in oral and written discourse and the complexity of teaching and learning are becoming practitioner/researchers in their own classrooms (Duckworth, 1986; Goswami & Stillman, 1987). These teachers have become theory builders in their own right, able to critically evaluate their own goals, and the practices carried out in their own classrooms. They treat new curricula, methods, and technological tools as hypotheses to be tested out and evaluated in light of their own pedagogical goals, strengths as a teacher, and classroom constraints.[9]

---

[9] Such a course of study is currently the goal of the Literacies Institute, a newly funded school-university consortium in the Boston area devoted to an interdisciplinary

Becoming teacher researchers interested in the discourse of schooling sounds good on paper. In reality it is a long and complicated process of enculturation, for both teachers and researchers. It requires long-term collaboration and contact between teachers and interdisciplinary academic researchers, and requires that institutional changes in schools and schools of education be made to support and nurture this process. It requires the creation of a new, hybrid discourse that draws on the worlds and tools of typically quite separated communities.

Teacher/researchers and researchers together need to better understand what research techniques are most effective and manageable in the classroom. How can training in ethnographic methods and discourse analysis be used in daily practice by already overextended classroom teachers to help them assess and critique the ways of talking and ways of taking text that occur in their settings? We need to work together to garner support at the building, district, state, and national levels to nurture teachers who are "reclaiming the classroom," who view "teacher research as an agency for change" (Goswami & Stillman, 1987). This entails a commitment to social change at the level of the classroom, school, community, and university—ultimately a political commitment to teacher researcher partnership and activism. But the dismantling of student narratives, and the concomitant dismantling of those students' powers as speakers and writers, is too great a price to pay for business as usual.

ACKNOWLEDGMENTS

This chapter is a much expanded version of a paper presented at the Boston University Conference on Language Development in October 1987. I want to thank Jim Gee, Allyssa McCabe, Vicki Morse, and Cathy O'Connor for their comments and suggestions on an early draft. I also thank the teachers and children—Deena and Lewana in particular—who made this work possible.

---

approach to literacy. The institute integrates concerns for written language, spoken language, and critical thinking, and the social, cultural, and institutional complexities of teaching and learning. Stressing the inherent plurality of literacy across social groups, social settings, and across the curriculum in schools, the institute provides training in theories of literacy development relevant to school practice, discourse studies, the study of home and school cultures, and social influences on cognitive development. The goal of the institute is to increase the autonomy and professionalization of teachers as teachers of literate thinking, reading, writing, and speaking in a cross-cultural and curriculum-wide approach to literacy.

REFERENCES

Bakhtin, M. M. (1986). *Speech genres and other late essays.* Austin: University of Texas Press.

Cazden, C. (1988). *Classroom discourse: The language of teaching and learning.* Portsmouth, NH: Heinemann.

Duckworth, E. (1986). Teaching as research. *Harvard Educational Review, 56*(4), 481–495.

Goswami, D., & Stillman, P. (Eds.) (1987). *Reclaiming the classroom: Teacher research as an agency for change.* Portsmouth, NH: Heinemann.

Gee. J. (1989a). What is literacy? *The Literacies Institute Technical Report #2.* Newton, MA: Education Development Center.

Gee, J. (1989b). Literacy, discourse, and linguistics. Journal of Education, *171*(1), 1–176.

Gumperz, J. (1976). Language, communication and public negotiation. In P. Sanday (Ed.), *Anthropology and the public interest,* (pp. 273–292). NY: Academic Press.

Hymes, D. (1980). *Language in education: Ethnolinguistic essays.* Washington, DC: Center for Applied Linguistics.

Hymes, D., & Cazden, C. (1980). Narrative thinking and story-telling rights: A folklorist's clue to a critique of education. In D. Hymes (Ed.), *Language in education: Ethnolinguistic essays* (pp. 126–138). Washington, DC: Center for Applied Linguistics.

Jefferson, G. (1978). Sequential aspects of storytelling in conversation. In J. Schenkein (Ed.), *Studies in the organization of conversational interaction.* New York: Academic Press.

Labov, W. (1972). The transformation of experience in narrative discourse. In *Language in the inner city: Studies in the Black English vernacular* (pp. 354–396). Philadelphia: University of Pennsylvania Press.

Lemke, J. (1986). *Using language in classrooms.* Victoria, Australia: Deakin University Press.

Michaels, S. (1981). "Sharing Time:" children's narrative styles and differential access to literacy. *Language in Society* 10(3):423–442.

Michaels, S. (1983). Influences on children's narratives. Quarterly newsletter of the Laboratory of Comparative Human Cognition, *5(2),* 30–34. San Diego: University of California Center for Human Information Processing.

Michaels, S. (1985). Hearing the connections in children's oral and written discourse. *Journal of Education, 167*(1), 36–56.

Michaels, S. (1987). Text and context: A new approach to the study of classroom writing. *Discourse Processes, 10,* 321–346.

Michaels, S., & Bruce, B. (1989). *Classroom contexts and literacy development: How writing systems shape the teaching and learning of composition.* Technical Report. Urbana-Champaign: Center for the Study of Reading.

Michaels, S., & Cazden, C. B. (1986). Teacher/child collaboration as oral preparation for literacy. In E. B. Schieffelin & P. Gilmore (Eds.), *The acquisition of literacy: Ethnographic perspectives* (pp. 132–154). Norwood, NJ: Ablex.

Smitherman, G. (1977). *Talkin and testifyin: The language of Black America.* Boston: Houghton Mifflin.

Ulichny, P., & Watson-Gegeo, K. (1989). Interactions and authority: The dominant interpretive framework in writing conferences. *Discourse Processes, 12,* 309–328.

Vygtosky, L. (1986). *Thought and language.* Cambridge, MA: MIT Press.

Watson-Gegeo, K. A., Cohen, C., Strucker, J., & Craig, B. (1987) *Microcomputers and literacy project: Part II* (Grant No. G-83-0051). Washington, DC: Office of Educational Research and Improvement.

Author Index

K

L

M

T

U

V

Subject Index

D

For Product Safety Concerns and Information please contact our
EU representative GPSR@taylorandfrancis.com Taylor & Francis
Verlag GmbH, Kaufingerstraße 24, 80331 München, Germany